WILD HORSES OF THE GREAT BASIN

Social Competition and Population Size

Joel Berger

THE UNIVERSITY OF CHICAGO PRESS
Chicago and London

JOEL BERGER is an associate professor of wildlife ecology at
the University of Nevada in Reno and a research associate
of the Smithsonian Institution's Conservation and Research
Center.

The University of Chicago Press, Chicago 60637
The University of Chicago Press, Ltd., London
© 1986 by The University of Chicago
All rights reserved. Published 1986
Printed in the United States of America

95 94 93 92 91 90 89 88 87 86   5 4 3 2 1

Library of Congress Cataloging in Publication Data

Berger, Joel.
  Wild horses of the Great Basin.

  (Wildlife behavior and ecology)
  Bibliography; p.
  Includes index.
  1. Wild horses—Great Basin—Ecology.   2. Wild
horses—Great Basin—Behavior.   3. Competition (Biology)
—Great Basin.   4. Mammal populations—Great Basin.
5. Mammals—Great Basin—Ecology.   6. Mammals—
Great Basin—Behavior.   I. Title.   II. Series.
SF360.3.U6B47   1986   599.72'5   85-8604
ISBN 0-226-04367-3

*In 1904 a Russian-born immigrant, Harry
Ordin, entered this country. He died in 1982—
an educator, a dentist, and a gentle man.*
To my grandfather

Contents

Preface

Nowadays we live in a very explosive world, and while we may not know when the next outbreak will be, we might hope to find ways of stopping it or at any rate dampening down its force. It is not just nuclear bombs and wars that threaten us, though these rank very high on the list at the moment; there are other sorts of explosions.

Charles S. Elton (1957)

In his 1946 book *Animal Farm,* George Orwell wrote, "All animals are equal, but some are more equal than others." Few people would disagree. Giraffes[1] and horses are more popular than rats and snakes. But how does one decide which species are more important? Or how does one resolve conflicts that arise over maintaining both introduced and native species while still using land wisely? These problems are difficult and simple answers are not available.

It is often suggested that, because introduced species have profound effects on ecosystems, they should be removed. Yet numerous mammals of Asiatic origin—bison, bighorn sheep, elk, moose, and even man—successfully colonized North America during periods of the Pleistocene. Most scientists view movements by immigrant species as natural historical events. But here we face a dilemma. Should the permanent recolonization of the New World by Europeans in the fifteenth century and the consequent dissemination of prickly pear cacti, fruit flies, house sparrows, and feral animals also be considered inevitable historical events? What could have prevented the havoc caused by these intrusions? Indeed, should these intrusions have been prevented?

Introductions of non-native species spark lively controversy over both the definition of *native* and the reputed economic, educational, and aesthetic impact of the colonizing species. Many argue

1. Scientific names are found in Appendix 1.

xv

that, because wild[2] horses are rooted deeply in the folklore of American and other societies, the sight of them running free and the sound of their thundering hooves should be forever exalted. Others suggest that horses are the "modern day mongrels of the range" (Woodbury 1981) and should be removed. Unfortunately, these issues are fraught with emotion and fall far short of the realm of empirical science.

Sentiment aside, this book is about individuals and forces that operate on them to shape populations. The phrase, *struggle for existence*, known for centuries (Zirkle 1941), was used by Darwin (1859) to refer to two processes: the immediate survival of individuals and the competition of individuals that "struggle" to leave behind as many offspring as possible. I have concentrated on each process, although my emphasis is on the latter. Whereas many studies examine interactions between a species' behavior and its demography by focusing on populations, I have approached the subject by focusing on the biology of individuals. In doing so, I explored three interwoven themes.

First, by understanding the ecological settings of individuals, factors influencing population densities and reproduction can come to light. The relation between behavioral ecology and population biology is complex, but if viewed from different perspectives, it can offer insight into how behavior influences population processes and how population processes influence behavior.

Second, males and females in polygamous societies confront differing sets of problems concerning their genetic survival. Adult male behavior is strongly dependent on age, and most males are successful breeders for only a few years. Virtually all facets of male development—growth, feeding, play fighting, etc.—contribute toward their later abilities to secure females. In contrast, females often breed until death. They may form bonds with other females, aid one another at times of duress, and maximize food intake to convert food reserves into milk and offspring. Males and females differ not only in behavior but in their reproductive lifespans.

The third theme is the horse—a large mammal that evolved mostly in North America. Many people study horses because they enjoy them, in itself a powerful reason. However, horses have rarely been studied as mammals whose behavior is inexorably tied to their ecology or evolution. Horses and other members of the Equidae (zebras, kulans, asses) form a unique family in many re-

2. Feral is the more appropriate term—see chapter 2.

spects. In most group-living ungulates, males are larger than females, are adorned with horns, antlers, or tusks, and defend harems only seasonally, if at all. Equids are exceptional in almost all of these characteristics: male and female equids are similar in body size; neither possesses conspicuous weapons; and harems are defended year-round in three species in addition to wild horses.

Originally, my goal was to study social behavior and reproduction of a mammal that lived in open habitats, had small home ranges, was diurnal, and whose individuals were recognized easily. Horses in the Great Basin Desert met these criteria. As with almost all people who study animals, unforeseen logistical problems occurred. The splendor of fieldwork was challenged by piercing cold and snow. Tents failed in brutal winds, and choices over which data were really the most important to collect made for pressing decisions. Politics often turned wishful dreams into nightmares of reality. I soon discovered it was impossible to study horses or even their environments without paying attention to controversies. Whether one discusses horses in the courts, in academic circles, or in the kitchens of angry ranchers, questions about populations, controlling mechanisms, or evolution arise. My purpose in writing this book is to address these issues and to extend them to other species of mammals.

This book is primarily about the biology of horses, not their management. I cannot do justice to the pungent smells of the Great Basin, the echoes of pounding feet nor the beauty of horses running against panoramic mountain sunsets. However, I urge those interested in conservation to contribute to efforts that preserve the greatest possible diversity of species and to experience the sights, sounds, and smells of wild places, for they are vanishing all too rapidly.

Acknowledgments

Many people deserve credit for helping me through my studies, and I regret that not all can be mentioned. I remember when, in 1974, I promised George Fisler that I would never again study horses. I could not have been more mistaken. He and Andrew Starrett introduced me to field ecology and guided me through some early years. In the interim, Marc Bekoff focused my interests on behavioral ontogeny and evolution and taught me the value of being one's self.

Chris Wemmer provided a remarkable environment for research at the Conservation and Research Center of the Smithsonian Institution. He aided me in ways not easy to forget and too numerous to elaborate upon. Ingrid Porton was instrumental in developing my plans for a study of Great Basin wild horses, while Jon Rood and Mel and Fiona Sunquist suggested sources that would later defray research expenses. Ben Beck offered valuable ideas about social systems, and together he and George Rabb made facilities available at the Chicago Zoological Society. The work of John Eisenberg and Tim Clutton-Brock influenced my thinking.

William J. Hamilton III provided office space, solidified some of my thoughts, and orchestrated my initial meetings with his colleagues at the University of California at Davis. Matthew Rowe listened to my chatter for sixteen months and provided a sounding board for many of my notions, while Barbara and Stan Kus helped in other ways. Mark and Delia Owens introduced me to home computers and then suffered along as I accidentally erased important script. Mark also adapted his skills as a bush pilot of Kalahari savannas to the mountains of the Great Basin.

Problems in the field were made less significant by the Bureau of Land Management in Winnemucca, Nevada. The efforts and contributions of their biologists and staff, most notably Roger Bryant, Glen Stickley, Frank Shields, Les Boni, and Dave Boyles, made life in the Great Basin less wild and more enjoyable. In particular, Paul

Jancar visited the study site, arranged transportation, helped with transects, and identified animals when I was away. Nevada Division of Wildlife biologists George Tsukumoto, Willie Mollini, Mike Hess, Jim Jeffers, Mike Wickershim, and Gary Heron shared data, knowledge, and equipment. Gary Vinyard and Stephen Jenkins were most gracious in arranging office space at the University of Nevada at Reno. I also profited from the experience of Gary Bateman, Carol Cunningham, Dennis Daneke, Nancy Dodson, Mike Kock, Murray Fowler, Mark and Delia Owens, and Matthew Rowe, who assisted in immobilizing horses.

My co-workers in the field—Bart and Neal Berger, Martin Berbach, Carol Cunningham, Debbie Dole, Dennis Daneke, Alison Harris, Lynn Roberts, Becky Rudman, and Craig Stockwell—played seminal roles in making observations and gathering data. Neal, especially, gave his time altruistically, surveying outlying areas and trudging through deep snow in the dead of winter. Gary Bateman, Tim Clutton-Brock, Dennis Daneke, Mark and Delia Owens, Matt Rowe, John Wehausen, and Chris Wemmer fueled campfire discussions with their insights of wildlife and ecology. Ranchers Joe Selmi and Bub and Vicki Williams and members of the Bogard clan of Planet X Ranch also offered valuable assistance and information about Granite horses.

To those who suffered through my initial drafts or provided help in other ways I am deeply appreciative. They include Cheryl Asa, Steve Berwick, Lee Boyd, Brian Bertram, Tag Demment, Charles Douglas, Patrick Duncan, Valerius Geist, Robert Gibson, W. J. Hamilton III, Hendrick Hoeck, Katherine Houpt, Tim Kittel, Ron Keiper, Devra Kleiman, Hans Klingel, David Manski, John Menke, Patti Moehlman, Y. Nishikawa, Delia and Mark Owens, Sharon Pfeifer, Kent Redford, Peter Rodman, Peter Rossdale, Oliver Ryder, Ulysses Seal, John Seidensticker, Michael J. Simpson, Peter Stacey, Ronald Tilson, and Tom Whitham. I am very grateful to Matthew Rowe, John Wehausen, Stephen Jenkins, and Dennis Daneke for their thorough scourings of many chapters or their critical insights.

The Harry Frank Guggenheim Foundation, National Geographic Society, Bureau of Land Management, and Smithsonian Institution's Conservation and Research Center contributed to the support of this project.

To my parents I can only say thanks from the bottom of my heart. Words alone cannot do justice. Finally, I offer my warmest appreciation to Carol Cunningham. Not only did she remain with the project for more than three years, but she delayed personal opportunities for the study. At times she ran the operation in complete isolation, taught students, performed analyses, and labored through my drafts of the manuscript—the list is long. This book is as much hers as it is mine.

1 The Struggle for Existence

Certain aspects of the ecological environment, such as climate, predators, parasites, food resources, etc., are well understood as evolutionary factors. Their treatment receives a large share of attention in the literature of adaptive evolution. . . . I will concentrate here on certain problems of ecological adaptation that seem to have had less than a fair share of attention. One such problem is the role of the . . . social environment

G. C. Williams (1966)

1.1 INTRODUCTION

Why live with group members in a home area? What are the consequences of moving? Has domestication changed behavior that was produced over millions of years? Can answers to questions such as these help in understanding populations? This myriad of quandaries reflects diverse biological interests; I focus on these quandaries as they relate to equids.

Since Thomas Malthus's *Essay on Population* (1798), various factors that govern animal populations have been examined and debated. Even Charles Darwin had hoped "to discuss it at considerable length, more especially in regard to the feral animals" (Darwin 1859,80). Of course, populations result from the varied genetic input of individuals. Because individuals vary in their propensity to reproduce and natural selection operates on individuals, knowledge about processes that affect populations can be gained only by understanding at the very least some properties of individuals and their evolution.

My central theme is simple: *if individuals that are likely to reproduce do not do so because of the behavior of others, then social limitations are imposed on the size of the population.* However, unraveling the complex network of factors that governs interactions between individuals and their environments is not so simple. Because our knowledge of the role that behavior plays in population regulation

1

is limited, additional study will benefit our understanding of the relationships among individuals and their effects on populations. In this chapter I introduce some contemporary thoughts on these topics.

1.2   ADAPTATION AND NATURAL SELECTION

All individuals are confronted with common and basic problems. They must meet the demands of the physical environment, avoid predators, locate shelter, and acquire food if they are to reproduce. Although different environments require specific solutions, individuals that not only survive but leave behind more offspring will be represented to a greater extent in later generations than those that do not. Natural selection is simply the process by which genes are propagated at different rates in subsequent generations. Properties (e.g., structural, physiological, behavioral, etc.) that contribute to an organism's survival and reproduction are adaptations (Williams 1966; Wilson 1975).

It is generally agreed that natural selection operates on individuals, and individuals act selfishly to improve their own genetic representation (Dawkins 1976, 1982). Many examples argue against the idea that individuals act for the benefit of the group or species as once believed (see Krebs and Davies 1982; Wittenberger 1981). If individuals behaved to improve the fitness of the group or species at the expense of their own fitness, we would not expect infant killing (Hrdy 1979), cannibalism (Goodall 1977), maiming and combat mortalities (Hamilton 1979), or countless other examples (Brown 1975; Wilson 1975) of behaviors that benefit participants but not the group as a whole. It should not be surprising, therefore, that individuals vary in their behavior and that most differences arise as a result of natural selection; feeding, investing in progeny by parents, and fighting are but a few of the many areas on which selection has acted. In addition to behaving selfishly, individuals act to improve their own genetic representation by kin selection—the process of aiding relatives—thereby increasing frequencies of genes shared by common descent in subsequent generations (Hamilton 1964).

1.3   THE SEXES

Two facts about the sexes are generally understood: males and females contribute differently to population size, and females have profound effects on rates of population increase. In mammals, females make greater reproductive investments than males (Fisher

1930; Trivers 1972). Because males can inseminate more than one female, sexually mature females are the class of individuals over which the greatest intensity of competition occurs. Females are more valuable resources than males in terms of the population because females determine many properties of a species' demography, including its rate of growth.

Darwin ([1871] 1888) was the first to consider formally the selection pressures on the sexes and the influence of gender on a species' social organization. He also used sexual selection to explain differences in body size and ornamentation between males and females. Recently, much renewed attention has been focused on these processes (Brown 1975; Wilson 1975; Wittenberger 1981; Thornhill and Alcock 1983). When females are in short supply and male competition is intense, males tend to be sexually dimorphic and ornamented (i.e., dewlaps, enlarged inflatable proboscises, antlers, etc.). This is because (1) as males compete with one another for mating opportunities with females, not all are successful breeders; and (2) relative to males, a greater proportion of females mate. The result is that male mating success varies more than that of females, and traits favoring male competitive abilities are promoted.

According to theory, species characterized by relatively large ratios of variance in reproductive success should exhibit sexually dimorphic features (Emlen and Oring 1977; Wade 1979). The predicted relationship is generally stronger in primates, pinnipeds, and ungulates than it is in other taxa (Clutton-Brock and Harvey 1977; Alexander et al. 1979). However, horses and other equids are among the exceptions, a problem discussed in section 9.7.

Male and female mammals also invest differentially in offspring, with females making greater investments (Trivers 1972). For example, elephant seal females sacrifice eating for up to thirty-four days after birth while nurturing their pups. During this time they lose up to 270 kg but still convert enough fat stores into milk to enable their pups to gain almost 100 kg (Riedman and Ortiz 1979; Reiter, Pankin, and LeBoeuf 1981). Although seals are an extreme example, female mammals incur costs associated with gestation and lactation, expenses not shared by males. While male parental care may occur in monogamous mammals, it is rare in polygynous ones (Kleiman 1977; Kleiman and Malcolm 1981).

Darwin's original concept of sexual selection is now seen as natural selection acting on each of the sexes. Its operation has recently been explained most elegantly for virtually all aspects of male and female behavior (Clutton-Brock, Guinness, and Albon 1982). When viewed in this light, body size (Ralls 1976), reproductive physiology (Schwagmeyer 1979), pair-bonding (Wrangham 1980), habitat selection (Shank 1982; Wehausen 1980), and social behavior influence female reproductive potential and, hence, the demography of a given species.

1.4 ECOLOGY, SOCIAL ORGANIZATION, AND LEVELS OF EXPLANATION

Over one hundred years ago, Francis Galton realized that evolutionary forces influenced the correlation between a species' behavior and its ecological background. Galton (1871) described how South African cows, when separated from the herd, tended to return to the safety of the group in response to the unforeseen threat of lion predation. The "selfish herd concept" has since explained with surprising accuracy why diverse species form groups (Hamilton 1971; Caraco 1979); rarely is there good evidence that animals are spaced randomly (Waser and Wiley 1979).

A rekindled interest in explaining the diversity of spacing and social systems has focused on the relationships among behavior, ecology, and life-history variables. Multidisciplinary approaches have incorporated historical, sociobiological, demographic, bioenergetic, and ecological factors (Clutton-Brock and Harvey 1977; Eisenberg 1981). The best correlations among body size, ecology, and social organization have been found in ungulates and primates. Simply put, the argument has been that species exploiting open environments tend to be larger in size and more gregarious than those exploiting more thickly vegetated habitats. And because body size affects metabolic rate, constraints are placed on food demands, foraging locations, antipredatory behavior, and spacing systems (Eisenberg 1981; Jarman 1974; Geist 1978a).

In all generalizations there are problems. Among the above relationships each variable may be related to another. Consequently, a clear picture of cause and effect is often not possible. Correlations simply indicate that relationships occur, however, they are valuable for the insight they offer into the complexity of systems. And with experimental (or natural) manipulations, cause and effect can be inferred.

When considering explanations in behavioral ecology, it is useful to distinguish between underlying causes of phenomena. Ultimate explanations underscore questions about why a given response evolved and require evolutionary explanations (Wilson

1975). In contrast, proximate explanations deal with how a process is achieved. For example, male-biased mortality in a polygynous species could be explained by proximate factors such as increased susceptibility to disease, poor nutrition, or fight wounds. An ultimate explanation would be that males experience greater mortality as a result of male-male competition for females. Each would be correct in this hypothetical case; only the level of explanation differs.

1.5 SOCIAL LIMITATIONS AND POPULATION SIZE

Designing hypotheses to examine the ultimate bases for individual or species differences in behavior is challenging, but no less so than discovering the proximate responses of individuals, populations, or species to their ecology. Evolutionary theory provides a paradigm for understanding why individuals behave in certain ways, but it does not always explain how processes work. Phenomena such as group size, feeding patterns, movements, and mating systems are responses to ecological conditions but still are influenced by natural selection. By understanding how these processes work, knowledge about the dynamics of populations can be gained.

Populations never increase indefinitely. They are products of immigration, emigration, birth, and death rates. In mammals, extrinsic factors like predation (Schaller 1972; Kruuk 1972; Messier and Crête 1984, 1985), disease (Berry 1981), minerals (Botkin, Mellino, and Wu 1981), and weather (Klein 1968) have played roles in affecting population sizes. Food, however, is the most frequently cited cause of limitations (Watson 1970; Sinclair 1977; Fowler and Smith 1981). When food is "limiting," populations experience density-dependent effects, and intraspecific competition can be expected to intensify.

Considerable past attention has focused on parameters that depress populations: social behavior (Dittus 1977, 1979; Ebling and Stoddart 1978), shade and water (Newsome 1965), hibernacula (Anderson, Armitage, and Hoffman 1976), and food (Klein 1968; Leader-Williams 1980) are some; the list is lengthy and could be extended (Caughley and Krebs 1983). Most likely, more than one single factor is involved (Watson and Moss 1970).

For my purposes it is important to differentiate between regulation and limitation. The dictionary (Morris 1981) defines *regulation* as "to control or direct according to a rule" or "to adjust in conformity to a specification or requirement," whereas *limit* is the "point, edge, or line beyond which something cannot proceed." I adopt the terminology of Sinclair and Norton-Griffiths (1982) who used *limitation* to refer to a "depressive effect on population numbers" and *regulation* for "limitations specifically by density-dependent mortality."

In subsequent chapters I develope the hypothesis that competition among males for mates acts in association with female-female competition to alter female reproductive rates and, hence, population size. This is critically evaluated in chapter 10.

1.6 SUMMARY

1. Natural selection is the differential propagation of genotypes. It is principally through competition among individuals that more successful genotypes are found in successive generations. Properties of individuals that render them more likely to reproduce are favored over those that do not. Thus, individuals with acquired traits that enhance their reproductive success tend to pass along such qualities to their offspring. These properties are known as adaptations.

2. An association occurs between a species type of mating system and its degree of sexual dimorphism. In many ungulates where male competition for females intensifies, sexual dimorphism predominates. The Equidae are exceptions to this general pattern.

3. Explanations in behavioral ecology distinguish between the causes of phenomena. Proximate explanations seek to understand the underlying bases (e.g., immediate mechanisms) of how particular events are achieved, whereas ultimate explanations are concerned more with evolutionary causation.

4. Population size is influenced by birth, death, immigration, and emigration rates. Although food is the most important factor that affects these processes in large mammals, direct competition over mates also occurs. Social limitations may be imposed on population sizes, but to discover if they are clearly operative, a variety of other factors must be ruled out.

2 Horses and Native Equids: History, Habitats, and Habits

Buffon says, that Herodotus speaks of wild horses . . . being found on the banks of Hyparis in Scythia; that Leo Africanus places wild horses in Africa and Arabia, and saw a white colt brought forth amongst the wild horses of Numidia; . . . that Marco Polo mentions a herd of ten thousand . . . in Persia . . . our author alludes . . . to the American wild horses.

Don Felix de Azara (1838)

2.1 INTRODUCTION

The biology of any species is complex. The biology of horses is particularly complicated because their gene pool has been altered not only by natural selection but by what Darwin (1868) called artificial selection—the way in which "man may select and preserve each successive variation, with the distinct intention of improving or altering a breed." This chapter reviews various aspects of the history and biology of extant and extinct forms, including their ancestry, associations with humans, distributions, and "niches." It also considers the popular images of horses and sets the stage for understanding horses as mammals by examining the relationships between their primary weapons (canine teeth) and social systems.

2.2 EXISTENCE AND DISTRIBUTION OF WILD HORSES
Native Horses

Przewalski's horses (fig. 2.1) are the only native species of horses that exist in the world today. They are presumed to be extinct in their native ranges of China, Russia, and Mongolia (Klimov and Orlov 1982), but as of late 1983 between 480 to 500 individuals have survived in zoos. These horses are the descendants of 11 wild-caught animals taken around the turn of the century and a wild mare captured in 1947 (Ryder and Wedemeyer 1982). The zoological community has concentrated on finding ways to avoid the

FIG. 2.1   Przewalski's horse herd at Askania Nova in the Soviet Union. Photo courtesy of Oliver A. Ryder.

damaging effects of inbreeding in this species (IUCN–Survival Service Commision 1982; Foose and Foose 1983).

Virtually no information exists about the behavior of Przewalski's horses in their native habitats or in their natural social groupings. Both Mohr (1971) and Bokonyi (1974) described the mountainous and steppe environments where Przewalski's horses were once found and also provided historical accounts taken from the European literature. Based on early reports from the wild and more recent observations in zoos, it is known that Przewalski's horses are organized into distinct breeding groups called bands. Each band contains a stallion and his harem (mares, juveniles, and young). In zoos, nonbreeding males are usually placed into separate enclosures (Bouman, Bouman, and Groeneveld 1982).

Much of the basic biology of noninbred Przewalski's horses remains unknown, and, although many zoologists are now concerned with the horses' behavior and morphology, it will never be known whether the patterns observed today are similar to ones that were exhibited by their wild ancestors. And generalizing about the behavior of Przewalski's horses by relying on comparisons with domestic horses may be dangerous; there is no independent way of knowing (1) what effect inbreeding has had upon Przewalski's horse behavior (since noninbred populations are not available for comparison), and (2) whether behavioral characteristics found in domestic and feral horses, but not in Przewalski's horses, arose as a result of genetic drift, adaptation, or domestication per se.

Understanding the components of behavior that were derived by phylogenetic inheritance and those that resulted from other pressures in native and domestic horses is complicated by yet another possibility. It is sometimes difficult to tell whether differences exist at all. Perhaps behaviors not now observed in Przewalski's horses would have occurred if these equids were not inbred or, more likely, if they were not maintained solely in captivity. These intertwining variables make it easy to see why problems occur in attributing behavior to various influences such as phylogeny, domestication, etc. However, I argue in chapter 9 that natural selection operates in feral horses and that many observable behavioral phenomena are adaptive.

Horses and Nomenclature

Horses were the last of the common livestock to be domesticated— about 2,500 to 5,000 years ago (Clutton-Brock 1981). Today they are ubiquitous. In addition to domestic horses, free-ranging populations of horses can be found in both North America and Australia where more than 40,000 individuals occur (U.S. Dept. of Interior, Bureau of Land Management 1982a; McKnight 1976). Historically, romantic names such as mustang and cayuse in North America, brumby in Australia, and cimarron, begual, or monstreco in South America were applied to free-ranging horses. Today's horses, regardless of nomenclature, are feral animals whose ancestors were once domesticated. (*Feral* refers to a wild state of existence for domesticated animals.) The process of feralization is straightforward; it merely involves an animal's fending for itself. Given sufficient time, individuals that fared well, that encountered other similarly fated animals, *and* that reproduced, founded the genes for a population.

Throughout this book I refer to feral horses as wild horses and vice versa. Although *feral* is the more common term in scientific circles, I prefer *wild* as a matter of convenience since it is already accepted terminology in most cultures and because ranchers, "outback" dwellers, and most others know what it means. Nevertheless, the only true extant native horses are Przewalski's horses.

Geographical Considerations

Large, free-ranging mammals, whether native or feral, remain so not because of millions of years of adaptation and evolutionary refinement, but primarily by the grace of humans. The mammals survive for at least one of four principal reasons: (1) their habitats

remain intact; (2) they live in remote regions; (3) they are protected; and (4) their behavior is flexible enough to enable reproduction under a broad spectrum of ecological conditions.
Horses have persisted in a wild state due to all of these factors.

The most characteristic feature of horse habitat is its savanna-
like expansiveness. Horses are relatively large-bodied consumers of
grasses found in shrub/steppe, plains, island, and desert environments (National Research Council 1980). Within these habitats
horses are widely distributed around the world. They occur in wild
populations on islands of the Atlantic Coast of North America
(Welsh 1975; Keiper 1976; Rubenstein 1981), on subhumid and
arid plains of continental Australia (McKnight 1976), and in remote deserts and mountains of western North America (Salter and
Hudson 1982; Miller and Denniston 1979; Berger 1977). Free-
roaming but managed populations occur in England's New Forest
(Tyler 1972; Pollock 1980) and Exmoor's Preserves (Gates 1979)
and in the Camargue Delta of France (Duncan 1980).

Wild horses once lived in South America where they were abundant on the Falkland Islands (Darwin 1845) as well as in Argentina,
Brazil, Chile, Peru, and Venezuela (Nichols 1939; Wyman 1945).
In 1838 Don Felix de Azara commented on the problem of Para-
guayan horses:

> these wild horses congregate together everywhere in such immense
> herds, that it is no exaggeration to say, they sometimes amount to
> twelve thousand individuals. They are most troublesome and preju-
> dicial; for, besides consuming vast quantities of pasture, they gallop up
> to the domesticated horses whenever they see them; and, passing
> amongst or close to them, call and caress them with low affectionate
> neighings . . . and easily induce them to incorporate within their troops.
> (P. 5)

Three years later Lieutenant Colonel Charles Hamilton Smith
wrote of their resiliency:

> The time is not perhaps far distant, when they will be gradually again
> absorbed by domestication, excepting those which will retreat toward
> the two poles; as the species is not restricted by the rigor of the climate,
> but solely by the extent of available food, the wilds of Patagonia and the
> latitudes of the northern deserts will continue to maintain them in free-
> dom. (Smith 1841, 474–75)

Wild horses have indeed flourished under extreme climatic conditions. Since 1738 they have existed on Sable Island, a fragmented
chain of sand dunes situated in the North Atlantic Ocean (Welsh

1975). Horses also persist in British Columbia, Alberta (Salter and Hudson 1982), Wyoming (Boyd 1979), and the northern Great Basin Desert (fig. 2.2) where snow may cover the ground for six months a year and temperatures as low as −40°C may occur. At the opposite extreme, horses in Australia and Death Valley, California, rely on sparsely distributed water and food and may be exposed to ambient temperatures in excess of 42°C.

Introduction of Horses into North America

The evolution of the horse family was centered in North America (Simpson 1951), but horses became extinct there at least 8,000

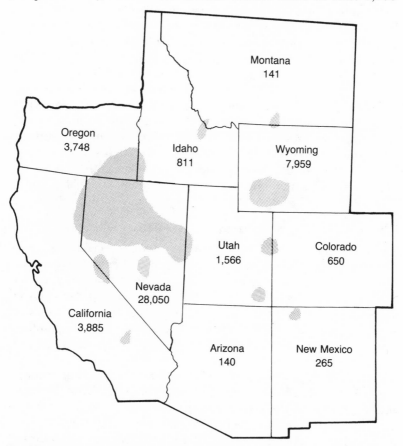

Fig. 2.2 Estimated population sizes and major areas (darkened) of wild horses in the western United States as of late 1983. Estimates for Nevada and Colorado are from 1982. Data courtesy of Bureau of Land Management, U. S. Department of Interior.

years ago (Martin and Guilday 1967). All the feral equids (horses and asses) that now inhabit North America are probably derived from stock that escaped from ranchers, miners, or American Indians. Few, if any, of these horses show affinities to the Spanish horses that escaped from Hernando Cortés's 1519 landing near Vera Cruz, Mexico, or Hernando de Soto's 1543 travels on the Mississippi River (Wyman 1945).

In the early eighteenth century a gradual northward movement of horses from Mexico to the central Rocky Mountain states began, progressing to the Snake River Plains in Idaho (ca. 1700), the Dakotas (ca. 1750), the northern Central Valley of California (ca. 1775), and Canada (mid to late eighteenth century) (Dobie 1952; Haines 1938). Within these areas most American Indians had acquired horses prior to the spread of wild populations (Wyman 1945). Roe (1955) and Ewers ([1955] 1980) provide the most thorough accounts of relationships between horses and Indian cultures.

Size estimates of the early populations vary widely, and most reports are regional only (see fig. 2.2). Ryden (1970) estimated that a hundred years ago there were perhaps 2 million wild horses in the United States. Current U. S. Department of Interior estimates give a minimum of 44,930 horses and 11,870 burros (U. S. Dept. of Interior, Bureau of Land Management 1982a), although the accuracy of census methods has been questioned (National Research Council 1982).

2.3   HORSES AS COMPANIONS AND ENEMIES OF HUMANS

Over 45,000 books have been written about horses (Barclay 1980), a number that testifies to the animal's overwhelming popularity. Horses and humans have long been associated throughout history. Early relationships between these two mammalian species involved Przewalski's horses as the prey, as suggested by bones found in caves. Przewalski's horses were also the subjects of cave paintings such as those created about 12,000 years ago in the vicinity of present-day Lascaux, France (Baskett 1980).

Domestic horses have had profound influence on human beings and can be found in art forms and in mythology. Throughout history they played roles in exploration, war, sports, leisure, and agriculture. Some of the best early documentations of horses are found among the Greek and Roman cultures where horses were revered as beasts of beauty, strength, and valor. Some species acquired divine status, becoming symbols of ancient gods. Pegasus, the winged steed, became the name for a later constellation, while Centaur, half-man and half-horse, was the focus of much lore. William

Shakespeare (in *Henry V*) wrote about Pegasus, "It is a beast for Perseus: he is pure air and fire; and the dull elements of earth and water never appear in him: he is indeed a horse: and all other jades you may call beasts."

Even today horses are considered majestic animals unparalleled by others: "Since man began to take control of this planet, he has been concerned with two things: first to survive; second, to enjoy himself while doing it. And, in looking about for another animal to help him, he discovered a lithe, spirited and independent creature with which he could strike up a profitable and agreeable alliance. This was the horse" (Vernon 1939, vii).

Although domestic horses receive much acclaim in the popular literature and from the media, reactions to feral horses are mixed. Frank Dobie, in his 1952 classic *The Mustangs*, closed with,

So sometimes yet, in the realities of silence and solitude,
for a few people unhampered a while by things,
the mustang walks out with dawn, stands high, then
sweeps away, wild with sheer life, and free, free, free—
free of all confines of time and flesh.

However, not all people hold such a positive opinion of wild horses. In many areas they are viewed as pests or nuisances, and I know of specific instances where wild horses have been shot or illegally trapped. Thomas (1979) summarized numerous controversial issues concerning wild horses from the perspective of a rancher and documented numerous killings of wild horses.

2.4   ECOLOGY AND NICHES OF NATIVE EQUIDS

Przewalski's and feral horses are not the only members of the Equidae. Six native equids now exist—three species of zebras (Common, Mountain, and Grevy's), an Asiatic hemione or half-ass (kulan), an African ass, and the Przewalski's horse. A seventh species, the quagga, a splendid animal from southern Africa that was partially striped, became extinct when its last member died in captivity in 1883. All of the native equids occur in Africa or Asia (fig. 2.3), but their taxonomy is not uniformly agreed upon (Groves and Mazak 1967; Groves and Willoughby 1981). Sources of confusion tend to center on subspecies status. Asiatic hemiones are a good example of such disagreement, and several regional names (kulans, onagers, or kiangs; Groves 1974) are applied to this single species.

Morphology and Ecology

A species' ecology is tied to its morphology and influenced by its habitat and by sympatric species. Given knowledge of a group's

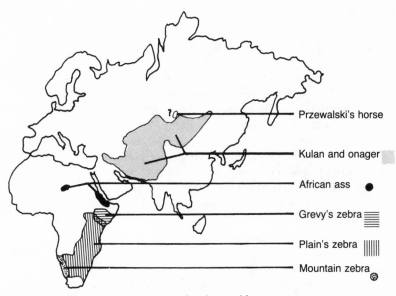

Przewalski's horse

Kulan and onager

African ass

Grevy's zebra

Plain's zebra

Mountain zebra

Fig. 2.3   Geographical distribution of native equids.

morphology, broad inferences about its role in a community may be made. Consider, for example, what may be extrapolated about niche exploitation if handed the bills of two hypothetical species of birds. The bill of the first type is large and strongly recurved. The second is small, short, and broad. We might conclude that the first species is a predator that kills for food whereas the second is a seed eater. Of course, these deductions are general and could be unsatisfactory since some predators scavenge and some seed eaters eat insects and there is more to niche exploitation than food consumption (Hutchinson 1957; Eisenberg 1981). Although this section is about the ecology of modern equids, ecology must be set within a broad context. An improved understanding of equid niches can only arise from knowledge of the functions of internal and external morphological features and the influence of other community members.

Food Acquisition and Processing

Equids are grazers, generally weighing between 250 and 450 kg (Kingdon 1979; Grubb 1981; Smuts 1975a). Although they differ most from one another in their chromosomes and external appearance (Ryder, Epel, and Benirske 1978), all species are remarkably similar in reproductive physiology, feeding patterns, antipredatory behavior, fighting styles, stomach anatomy, and general behavior (table 2.1). Some popular accounts have called horses "food processing machines." Equid teeth include 12 incisors that are well honed for cropping grasses and 24 large, hypsodont molariform (3 premolars and 3 molars in each row) cheek teeth that triturate and grind up food. All species exploit habitats containing coarse, fibrous vegetation, high in cellulose (Janis 1976).

Almost all ungulates use microbial symbionts to break down food in the digestive tract, but sites of fermentation differ among groups. The consequences of these stomach differences and body size (Demment and Van Soest 1985) dramatically affect the ecology and niches of ungulates. Unlike most ruminants which possess four-chambered stomachs, equids and all other perissodactyls (tapirs and rhinos) have monosacculated stomachs with the cecum rather than the stomach being the primary site of fermentation. The digestive tracts of equids comprise a little less than one-third the proportion of total body weight compared to those of rumi-

TABLE 2.1 Summary of Grouping Patterns and Recent Literature on Native Equids

Equids	Social Groupings	Distribution & Ecology	Evolution & Genetics	General Behavior
Przewalski's horses (*Equus przewalski*)	year-round bands and bachelor groups	2, 4, 10, 23, 32	5, 6, 28	23
African asses (*Equus africanus*)	no stable associations, mixed sexes	33	6	22
Onagers and kulans (*Equus hemionus*)	no stable associations, mixed sexes	1, 8, 31	27	3, 22
Mountain zebras (*Equus zebra*)	year-round bands and bachelor groups	13	6	11–13, 17, 25, 26
Common zebras (*Equus burchelli*)	year-round bands and bachelor groups	9, 18, 29, 30	6, 29	3, 9, 16–20, 24, 29, 30
Grevy's zebra (*Equus grevyi*)	no stable associations, mixed sexes	14	6	18

General review papers: 7, 15, 20–22

Sources: (1) Andrews 1933; (2) Antonious 1937; (3) Berger 1981; (4) Bokonyi 1974; (5) Bouman and Bos 1979; (6) Churcher and Richardson 1978; (7) Groves 1974; (8) Groves and Mazak 1967; (9) Grubb 1981; (10) Hopwood 1936; (11–13) Joubert 1972, 1974a, 1974b; (14) Keast 1965; (15) Kingdon 1979; (16–22) Klingel 1967, 1968, 1969a, 1969b, 1972, 1975, 1977; (23) Mohr 1971; (24) Monfort and Monfort 1978; (25–26) Penzhorn 1979, 1982; (27) Ryder 1978; (28) Ryder, Epel, and Benirshke 1978; (29–30) Smuts 1975b, 1976a; (31) Solomtim 1973; (32) Tsevegmid and Dashdorj 1974; (33) Zicardi 1970.

nants (see Janis 1976). Being fairly nonselective (roughage) feeders on grasses that are low in protein/fiber ratios, nonruminants sustain faster rates of food passage and higher intakes than ruminants. Economically, ruminants of equivalent sizes that feed on the same low-quality diets would be at a disadvantage compared with cecal digestors since lignified food requires energy for ruminating and time for processing (Van Soest 1980).

Interpretations of Niches

As a result of these basic differences in stomach anatomy and feeding patterns, equids are able to exist on Asiatic steppes and deserts and in xeric areas of Africa where few ruminants live (Groves 1974); they probably attain the largest single species biomass in such places (Allen 1940; Solomatin 1973; Zicardi 1970). In contrast, most savanna ungulate faunas in Africa are dominated by a greater diversity and biomass of ruminants (Foster and Coe 1968; Mentis 1970). Food resources are partitioned by selection of different habitats, by consumption of different food items and plant parts (Bell 1970, 1971), through migrations (Sinclair and Norton-Griffiths 1982), and by external morphology (Jarman 1974).

Due to this complexity, it is neither practical nor wise to speak simply of the "niche of equids" or even of "the" zebra, or horse, or kulan. Descriptions of niches are dependent upon the resources available and the presence, distribution, and abundance of other species. In cold deserts or steppes with their coincident diminished large-mammal faunas, it is probably easier to study processes of food exploitation and community dynamics than in other more complex ecosystems. Still, many questions about equid feeding ecology remain. Are some species facultative browsers? How much do food habits change seasonally, altitudinally, and geographically? What are the limits of our deductions about a species' ecology since equids now live in mere remnants of former habitats? Clearly, additional work in natural environments is needed if more precise views of equid niches are to surface. Unfortunately, all species of native equids except Common zebras are now endangered, and it is unlikely that answers will be forthcoming unless effective conservation measures are adopted immediately.

2.5 Predation on Horses and Native Equids
Predator Avoidance

The processing of food represents only part of a species' niche, for if a species is to survive, its members must also avoid predators, locate shelter, and reproduce. Equids use olfactory, visual, and auditory senses to detect predators (Schaller 1972). Although adult male zebras occasionally attack small-bodied predators (Klingel 1967; Kruuk 1972; Malcolm and van Lawick 1975), equids must often rely on speed to thwart predation.

In 1922 Roy Chapman Andrews of the American Museum's Asiatic Expedition witnessed a kulan's use of speed and endurance in the Gobi Desert:

> [It] was very clever in its attempts to reach the sandy gravel of the lower plane . . . the highest speed that it could reach was forty miles an hour; however, this could be maintained for only a short dash. . . . Subsequently, we found that only a few of the fleetest individuals could reach that speed, but that all could do 36 miles an hour. . . . To me the most amazing exhibit was the endurance. . . . The stallion which we followed travelled 29 miles before it gave up. The first sixteen were covered at an average speed of thirty miles an hour, as well as could be estimated. During this time there was never a breathing space . . . this is considerably better than a wolf can do, for after several turns, we were convinced that thirty-six miles an hour is the Mongolian wolf's fastest pace. The wolf is the only natural enemy of the wild ass. (Andrews 1933, 6–7)

Little is known about the long distance running abilities of other equids, but in Plain's zebras, acidemia and myopathy occur during long pursuit by vehicles (Hartthorn and Young 1974, 1976). The most thorough accounts of zebra predator avoidance are found in Schaller (1972) and Kruuk (1972).

Horses

Extant wild horses have few effective predators, although scattered, mostly anecdotal reports of predation by wolves, lions, and bears exist. Remarkably, the head of a horse even turned up in a shark's stomach in Australia (Wexler 1982). Wyman (1945, 61) suggested the possibility that de Soto's fifty lost horses may have been "destroyed by the puma and wolf and natives in the thick cover of the region." Cases of wolf depredation on foals have been verified (Fritts 1982; Zimen 1980), and at least one instance of predation on a donkey has been relayed (Schaller 1980).

A former United States president, while ranching in North Dakota, described interactions among horses and predators:

> They [wolves] are fond of trying to catch young foals, but do not often succeed . . . the foal is easily able to run at good speed for a short distance. . . . Full grown horses are rarely molested, while a stallion himself becomes the assailant. . . . The cougar is hardly ever seen round

my ranch; but toward the mountains it is very destructable . . . to horses. . . . the grizzly works a good deal of havoc among the herds . . . towards the evening [the stallion] came galloping in with three or four gashes in his haunch, that looked as if they had been cut with a dull ax. . . . The horse had been feeding when the bear leaped out at him but failed to kill at the first stroke; then the horse lashed out behind, and not only freed himself, but also severely damaged his opponent. (Roosevelt 1885, 23, 25, 385)

Numerous anecdotes have been told of mountain lion predation in California, Arizona, Colorado, and New Mexico (Young 1946), and few foals are raised under free-ranging conditions on Arizona rangeland, an area where mountain lions (also called pumas) regularly prey on cattle (Shaw 1981). In the Great Basin, horses may be under the heaviest predation pressure, although it is far from common. Their remains have been found in puma feces (Robinette, Gashwiler, and Morris 1959), and twenty-one cases of puma predation on wild horses (between 1954 and 1975) were confirmed in Nevada (Ashman 1976). These occurred in areas where deer densities were presumed to be low, so pumas may have taken horses since they were relatively more abundant than deer (Ashman 1976).

Native Species

African lions and hyenas are the most common predators of zebras (Schaller 1972; Kruuk 1972), although other predators have been documented (Malcolm and van Lawick 1975). Predation may control the size of some zebra populations (Sinclair and Norton-Griffiths 1982) and alter adult sex ratios in others (Berger 1983a).

2.6 PALEOECOLOGY AND LATE TERTIARY HORSES OF NORTH AMERICA
Early Ancestral Horses

The early Tertiary period of North America was characterized by thick, broad-leaved tropical forests with few grazers (Webb 1977). The first members of the horse family appeared in the Eocene (55 to 60 million years ago) of both North America and Europe, although their evolutionary history subsequently centered in North America (Simpson 1951; Woodburne 1982). *Hyracotherium*, the first genus, consisted of small, tetradactyl animals about the size of domestic cats. Some species were sexually dimorphic (Gingerich 1981) and all were frugivores or foliovores, as indicated by their bunodont (low-crowned) molars and comparative analogy with similar-sized mouse deer (Janis 1982). *Mesohippus* and *Miohippus* were the next successful steps in equid evolution (Stirton 1940). Each genus was larger than its ancestor, tridactyl, and each had teeth that remained low crowned. These animals "were essentially browsing forms living on soft vegetation in forests" (Romer 1966). One species, *Miohippus acutidens,* from the John Day Formation of Oregon (Sinclair 1905), had enormous canines (fig. 2.4) and was probably sexually dimorphic (Osborne 1918). They are of interest because equids are rarely thought to possess dangerous weapons.

Spread of Savannas and Equid Evolution

Although grasslike plants occurred in late Oligocene sediments, expansive grasslands developed in the Miocene; with sufficient canopy cover they were known as savannas (Van Couvering 1980).

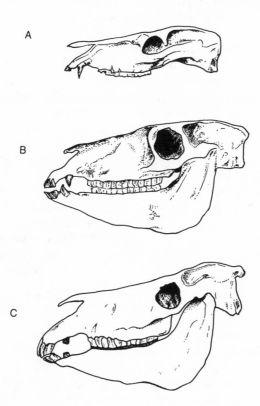

Fɪɢ. 2.4   Skulls of equids from three time periods: (A) Oligocene, (B) Miocene, (C) Holocene (Recent). Note changes in canine size in these males: (A) *Miohippus acutidens* from Oregon, (B) *Merychippus* spp., a grassland dweller from Nevada; (C) a modern Plain's zebra from Africa.

At this time ungulate evolution in North America experienced its
greatest radiations and morphological adaptations for open habitats—high-crowned (hypsodont) molariform teeth, elongated
metapodials, and digitigrade, padded feet became widespread in
many taxonomic groups (Webb 1977). In horses, *Merychippus* became the first grazer, and others (*Hipparion, Ancitherium*) crossed
the Bering Land Bridge to Asia and Europe (Kurten 1968;
Churcher and Richardson 1978). Still, not all Miocene horses were
grazers, and browsers such as *Parahippus* and *Archaeohippus* could
be found in among savanna mosaics (Webb 1977).

Fossil Horses of the Great Basin

By the Pliocene, the interaction of the Madro-Tertiary geoflora of
the southwestern United States and the Arcto-Tertiary geoflora to
the north slowly combined to produce complex vegetation changes
that alternated among cool, mesic, and more xeric types (Axelrod
1958, 1976). These changes affected all faunas. During the late
Tertiary at least seven genera of horses inhabited the mountainous
basins between the Rocky Mountain and Cascade/Sierra cordilleras
(the Great Basin region), along with camels, chalicotheres, rhi-
noceratids, and mastodons (Downs 1956; Gazin 1932; Wallace
1946). The Great Basin horses "vary in morphology from one-toed
to three-toed forms, and from delicate, almost antelope-like forms
to heavy-limbed types comparable to a dray horse. They all have
high-crowned teeth and their appendicular skeletons indicate
many adaptations for speed in running. . . . single-toed grazers appear much later than three-toed grazers" (Shotwell 1961, 203). The
groups to which Shotwell referred constitute the vast equid material found throughout northern and western Nevada, eastern
Oregon, and southern Idaho; the latter where *Plessipus* spp., a
Grevy's zebra–like equid that had been regionally abundant (Gazin
1936).

The Pleistocene and Equid Extinctions

In the Pleistocene, the modern genus *Equus* arose and successfully
colonized North America, Asia, Europe, and Africa. On the central
plains of Mexico's upland plateaus perhaps eight species of *Equus*
developed; some were onager-, zebra-, and horselike and sympatric with ancestral pronghorns and deer (Mooser and Dalquest
1975)—a situation perhaps not unlike that found in areas of the
Great Basin today where horse, deer, and pronghorn distributions
overlap.

Equids were remarkably abundant Miocene and Pliocene North American mammals, where in some fossil beds they obtained the greatest biomasses (Vorhies 1969). Nevertheless, during the Pleistocene and Holocene all North American equids, camels, llamas, mastodons, mammoths, saiga antelope, and yaks became extinct for reasons that are not yet well understood. Various theories regarding climate, disease, and predation (Martin and Wright 1967) have been proposed for the different periods of mammalian and avian extinctions in the New World. A formerly popular idea, the "overkill" hypothesis (Martin 1967; Moismann and Martin 1975), has fallen out of favor after the introduction of a climatic change hypothesis (Martin and Neuner 1978). The controversy is far from resolved (Grayson 1977).

2.7   CANINE TEETH AND SOCIAL SYSTEMS

Among mammals, secondary sexual characteristics and social systems are most clearly related in primates and ungulates where canines, tusks, antlers, and horns show positive relationships with the degree of variation in polygyny (Clutton-Brock, Guinness, and Albon 1982; Clutton-Brock and Harvey 1977; Leutenegger and Kelley 1977). These structures are more pronounced in males than females and are used by males primarily in intraspecific combat (Geist 1966; Harvey, Kavanah, and Clutton-Brock 1978).

The extant equids are enigmatic. Sexual dimorphism in body size and weaponry would be expected since Przewalski's horses and Plain's and Mountain zebras live in polygynous societies. Males sequester females and defend harems year-round (Klingel 1975), yet, except for small canine teeth in males, the equids are virtually monomorphic in skull dimensions (Allen 1940; Willoughby 1974).

Darwin ([1871] 1888) first realized the peculiarity:

> When the males are provided with weapons which in the females are absent, there can be no doubt that they serve for fighting with other males. . . . stallions have small canine teeth, . . . but they do not appear to be used for fighting, for stallions bite with their incisors, and do not open their mouths wide like camels and guanacos. . . . The reduction of those teeth in males seems to have followed from some change in their manner of fighting, often (but not in the horse) caused by the development of new weapons. (Pp. 764, 785)

William Clarke in his classic but overlooked 1879 treatise, *Horses' Teeth: . . . The Teeth of Many Other Land and Marine Animals Both, Living and Extinct*, stated:

Fig. 2.5   Combat and attempted foreleg bite by male onagers at the Conservation
and Research Center of the National Zoological Park.

Fig. 2.6   Play fighting by young male zebras at the Conservation and Research
Center. Note attempted foreleg bite and the "tucking in" of the leg to avoid bite.

Fig. 2.7   Fighting by young male bachelors in the Great Basin Desert.

The canine teeth comparatively speaking are of little practical use . . . to the modern horse. They have been much reduced in size during the evolution of the horse, and, if Mr. C. R. Darwin's theory is correct, are probably "in the course of ultimate extinction." . . . the horse sometimes uses them in tearing bark from trees . . . the sharp points of the tushes penetrate the bark more readily than the incisors, and apparently the horse wishes to save his incisors, thus showing his horse sense. (Clarke 1886, 75)

If the teeth of equids were unimportant as weapons, one would not expect to see the development of specialized fighting techniques to achieve and thwart bites (figs. 2.5–2.7), especially to vulnerable areas such as legs, where bite wounds might limit abilities to escape predators or obtain mates. Nevertheless, all species of zebras and both species of Asiatic equids (Przewalski's horses and kulans) drop on their legs to protect them from bites while attempting to bite the opponent's legs (see Berger 1981; Klingel 1972). It now appears that earlier reports that equids possess harmless "weapons" and rarely receive combat-related injuries were premature. This does not imply that equids (including feral horses and burros) do not use their forelegs or rear up to block bites (Berger 1981) or that hind-leg kicks are not damaging or unimportant in

the behavioral arsenals of aggressive individuals, only that escalated combat necessitates the use of more dangerous fighting techniques (Geist 1974, 1978b; Maynard Smith and Price 1973). By
employing canines, males may lacerate digital flexor muscles and
tendons of the lower leg, which has occurred during combat in
Great Basin Desert wild horses (chap. 7).

2.8 SUMMARY

1. Biological information on the Equidae is presented to place
   horses within a contemporary evolutionary and ecological
   framework.
2. Six native species of equids exist. Domestic horses arose from
   Przewalski's or Przewalski's-like horses. Feral (or more popu-
   larly, wild) horses were derived from domestic horses. Feral
   horses are now widely distributed in North America and Australia, where population sizes are at least 40,000 individuals but
   probably many more.
3. Domestic horses and humans have associations spanning 2,500
   to 5,000 years. Throughout most of the time, horses have been
   held in high esteem, and, although such perceptions have probably changed little, feelings about feral horses are often mixed.
4. Detailed knowledge about the ecology and habitat use of native
   equids is limited. All equids are grazers and have monosacculated stomachs. Equids had been a successful evolutionary group
   partly due to their ability to process rapidly fibrous foods of low
   quality. Reasons for the extinction of North American equids as
   well as other species of large mammals are still poorly
   understood.
5. Three species of native equids are polygynous, and males of
   these species defend year-round harems from rival males. Unlike many polygynous species of ungulates where the males are
   armed with conspicuous weapons, equid males have only small
   canine teeth, a feature noted first by Darwin.

3   The Study and the Great Basin Ecosystem

When the traveller from California has crossed the Sierra and gone a little way down the eastern flank, the woods come to an end. . . . mountains are seen beyond rising in bewildering abundance, range beyond range.

John Muir (1878)

3.1   INTRODUCTION

One of the best areas in which to study wild horses is the Great Basin Desert of North America. This chapter explains why this is true, describes features of the ecosystem, and provides methods of data collection, an ethogram, and other pertinent material.

3.2   THE STUDY

Although wild horses exist in remote areas of ten western states, they occur in few expansive shrub/steppe habitats with native ungulates and without the confusing influences of cattle grazing or human disturbances. The Bureau of Land Management (BLM) is responsible for the management of free-ranging equids in most areas of the United States. Because populations are "rounded up" at unpredictable intervals, it seemed fruitless for me to begin a project only to have the study animals disappear by unnatural causes, as has happened to other biologists studying feral equids. Therefore, in 1979 I spent almost three months in New Mexico, Colorado, Arizona, Nevada, California, Oregon, and Utah looking for a roadless study area that had (1) horses, (2) native ungulates, (3) little human disturbance, and (4) sanctions against cattle grazing. This latter condition was essential because I believed I could only begin to understand horse ecology if the effects of cattle could be removed. The area that met the above conditions was the Granite Range of northwestern Nevada.

My study has dealt with some animals from birth to death, but the lifespans of most animals are considerably longer than the

25

study period. Long-term studies are needed if generalizations about population phenomena are to be considered valid. In fact, field studies must be repeated to incorporate potential temporal and spatial differences in a population's response to its environment. For instance, for many years it was considered that the ecological segregation of Serengeti herbivores was achieved by selecting different plant parts during feeding (Bell 1970, 1971; Gywnne and Bell 1968). Recently, it has been pointed out (Sinclair 1979) that this work was conducted at a time when wildebeest and buffalo population levels were reduced due to disease. Therefore, the low levels of interspecific competition observed in the 1960s might result in different patterns today (Sinclair and Norton-Griffiths 1982). The message is clear; it will take long and broad-based comparative study to demonstrate the effects of temporal differences in ecological conditions on individuals, populations, and ecosystems.

The generalizations based on Granite Range horses are made with the realization that they are but a glimpse in time of a population under a given set of conditions. Some of my sample sizes are small, but I thought it best to have detailed information on several individuals rather than very general data on many animals.

3.3   THE GREAT BASIN ECOSYSTEM
Location and Topography

In 1844 the last unexplored and unnamed physiographic province of the continental United States was reported by John C. Frémont to be one of "interior basins with their own systems of lakes and rivers." Today, the Great Basin remains the least-inhabited area of the United States. The region contains Death Valley, the lowest point in the Western Hemisphere (-87 m), while its tallest mountain, White Mountain Peak, falls a mere 70 m shy of equaling Mount Whitney (4,418 m), the highest point in the continuous United States. Some regions have still been barely explored. Less than thirty years ago a glacially carved lake was discovered in the Pine Forest Range, a little to the northeast of the Granite Range (fig. 3.1). Overall, the Great Basin ecosystem covers about a half-million km^2. It is broadly bounded by the Snake River of Idaho to the north, the Sierra/Cascade cordillera to the west, the Rocky Mountain Plateau to the east, and the Mojave Desert to the south (fig. 3.1). More than three hundred parallel north-to-south insular mountain chains occur within these borders, some in excess of 150 km in length and 4,000 m in elevation, as well as almost one hundred broad valley basins and an undetermined number of volcanic plateaus. Virtually the entire region is characterized by interior water drainage.

Vast playas, the remnants of pluvial lakes, are common; the more notable include the Bonneville Salt Flats and the Black Rock Desert. These mud-surfaced areas are often flooded by melting snows from nearby ranges in the spring. Mountains of the Great Basin achieved their modern character sometime in the Miocene when volcanic activity was prominent in the north and uplifting and tilting was pervasive along major vertical faults throughout the area (see Mifflin and Wheat 1979).

Glacial Phenomena and Quaternary Environments

"The monuments of the Ice Age in the Great Basin have been greatly obscured and broken. . . . the last of the basin glaciers have

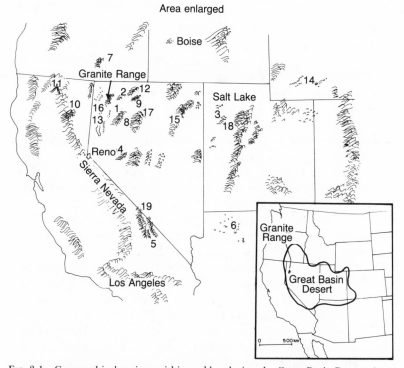

FIG. 3.1 Geographical regions within and bordering the Great Basin Desert. Areas mentioned in the text are designated as follows: (1) Black Rock Desert; (2) Black Rock Range; (3) Bonneville Salt Flats; (4) Clan Alpine Range; (5) Death Valley; (6) Grand Canyon; (7) Hart Mountain; (8) Humboldt Range; (9) Jackson Range; (10) Mount Lassen; (11) Mount Shasta; (12) Pine Forest Range; (13) Pyramid Lake; (14) Red Desert; (15) Ruby Mountains; (16) Smoke Creek Desert; (17) Sonoma Range; (18) Wasatch Range; (19) White Mountains. Major mountains are indicated on map.

but recenlty vanished and the almost innumerable ranges . . . were loaded with glaciers that descend to the adjacent valleys" (Muir 1878, 184, 190). John Muir was indeed correct. Glaciers vanished 11,000 to 25,000 years ago (Wells 1979), but atop some mountains today snowfields still remain year-round. During the Wisconsin period, pluvial lakes were common, cold-adapted shrub/steppe communities widespread, and forests of white fir (*Abies concolor*), Douglas fir (*Pseudotsuga mienziessi*), and Ponderosa pine (*Pinus ponderosa*) found in mosaics throughout the central Great Basin (Wells 1983). In the last 8,000 to 10,000 years these communities have retreated to higher latitudes and altitudes, and lakes have dried in response to increasing temperatures and decreasing precipitation regimes. Not surprisingly, these changes have resulted in a reduced mammalian fauna (Grayson 1982; Thompson and Mead 1982).

Vegetation

Numerous investigators have documented plant communities in the Great Basin (Billings 1950; Cronquist et al. 1972; Crichfield and Allenbaugh 1969). General features of plant associations are as follows: salt-desert scrub, dominated by shad scale (*Atriplex* spp.), greasewood (*Sarcobatus* spp.), and winter fat (*Certoides* spp.); northern desert scrub, including big sagebrush (*Artemisia tridentata*) and stands of rabbitbrush (*Chrysothamnus* spp.); grasslands, lacking shrub overstory but including bunchgrasses (*Poa* spp.), rice grasses (*Hilaria jamesii, Oryzopsis hyemenoides*), and salt grasses (*Sporobolus* spp.) or exotic grasses (see below); woodlands (intermediate elevations), full of juniper (*Juniperus osteosperma*), pinyon pine (*P. monophylla*), sagebrush, bitterbrush (*Purshia* spp.), serviceberry (*Amelanchier* spp.), and mahogany (*Cercocarpus* spp.); mountain brush (usually above treeline), including big sagebrush (see Tueller 1975), snowberry (*Symphiocarpus* spp.), mountain mahogany (*C. ledifolius*), currant (*Ribes* spp.), fescue (*Festuca* spp.), and bunchgrasses; subalpine and alpine (highest elevations), including limber pine (*P. flexilus*), whitebark pine (*P. albicaulus*), white fir, bristlecone pine (*P. aristata*), and spruce (*Picea* spp.). Aspens (*Populus tremuloides*) and willows (*Salix* spp.) are found at many altitudes and in riparian zones. Overall, Great Basin mountains and ranges are islandlike areas surrounded by seas of desert.

The constituents of pristine vegetation prior to the advent of European exploration is unknown. Reconstructions of accounts of early travelers (Robertson and Kennedy 1954; Vale 1975a) and field investigation (Brotherson and Brotherson 1978; Young, Evans, and Tueller 1976) produce conflicting views about shrublands and grasslands and combinations thereof. Succession has been rampant in the last century due in part to the absence of nature preserves in the Great Basin and the lack of enforcement of grazing laws (see chap. 11). It would be surprising if any areas had a reprieve from the onslaught of domestic species. Seral stages, disclimax, and other consequences of overexploitation are discussed in Cottam and Evans (1945), Tueller (1973), Wagner (1978), and Young and Evans (1973), who concluded that grazing, primarily by cattle, has seriously depleted most natural grassland communities.

3.4 MAMMALS
Insular Biogeography

Hall (1946) and Durrant (1952) provided classical accounts of Utah's and Nevada's mammals. These authors recognized the insularity posed by Great Basin mountains and the modern distributional patterns that resulted from past glacial events. Mountaintops in deserts have been viewed as islands of varying sizes and distances from major mountain masses (e.g. Rockies, Sierras). Predictions about the diversity of their inhabitants have been generated based on assumptions about extinction-immigration equilibria (see MacArthur and Wilson 1967). Why mammalian species on Great Basin mountaintops were more numerous than predicted by theory was explained by Brown's (1971, 1978) pioneering work. Marmots, pikas, ground squirrels, chipmunks, wood rats, jumping mice, shrews, and weasels were among the species studied, and each occurred widely throughout the Great Basin. Brown found that boreal zones contained greater species diversity than expected from their size and distance from the major mountain masses, and he attributed this finding to the temporal differences required for the stabilization of extinction rates. Since Pleistocene avenues of boreal habitats had only recently been severed from one another, remaining species had not yet achieved equilibrium within available habitat. Historical events had only slightly modified small mammal distributions.

Ungulates and Carnivores

The distribution of large mammals has been affected to a much greater extent by contemporary human activity than has that of small mammals. Bison occurred within modern times in shrub/steppe areas of the western and northern Great Basin (Merriam 1925; Butler 1978). Mule deer and pronghorn are the most widely distributed ungulates in the northern or central areas. Bighorn sheep are regionally abundant in remote locations, and mountain goats and elk have been introduced into one or more mountain ranges. Remarkably, as recently as 1961 a two-year-old moose wandered into northern Nevada where it was shot illegally by a person who "thought it was a buffalo" (Nevada Division of Wildlife, unpub. files). Information on the behavior and ecology of Great Basin ungulates can be found in Beale and Smith (1970, 1973), Berger, Daneke, Johnson, and Berwick (1983), McCullough (1969), McQuivey (1978), Papez (1976), Robinette, Hancock, and Jones (1977), Wehausen (1980, 1983), and Welles and Welles (1961).

The carnivore community consists of various mustelids (weasels, skunks, badgers), canids (coyotes, kit and gray foxes), procyonids (raccoons, ring-tailed cats), and felids (bobcats, pumas) (Hall 1946). Black bears are occasionally found along the eastern Sierra crest and western Wasatch front. Wolves once occurred in the northern Great Basin where they were heard in the Black Rock Desert (Delano 1849, as cited in Wheeler 1979), and one was killed north of the Granite Range (Hall 1946). Information on Great Basin pumas, bobcats (Ashman 1976; Golden 1982), and kit foxes (Egoscue 1975) is also available.

3.5 THE GRANITE RANGE
Setting

The Granite Range attains the highest elevation (2,762 m) in Nevada's remote northwestern corner. The range towers almost 1.5 km above waterless Pleistocene lake beds and is surrounded by basalt flows and granitic mountains. The shrub/steppe of this area has been referred to as a "Forgotten Ecological Province" (Young, Evans, and Major 1977). Broadly defined, the Granite Range area encompasses 13,000 km^2 (Retterer 1977). Vehicle entry to the range itself is prevented by escarpments at all but its northern borders, and the only road access to higher elevations is problematic at best due to rock slides and snow cover. Only five times in five years did I encounter people who wandered into the mountains; no one lives in the Granite Range. Except for the primitive base camps established for the study, the presence of native American artifacts, some old fence posts and troughs, and a forty- to fifty-year-old dilapidated stone cabin, no signs of prior habitation occur.

The Granite Range is surrounded on three sides by impressive playas (fig. 3.2), the Black Rock Desert (about 1,600 km²) to the east, and the Smoke Creek Desert (about 800 km²) to the south and southwest. The southern part of the range is rugged and bisected by several deep canyons that rise progressively to higher but less steep plateaus to the north. At the southern end of the range is Granite Basin, an enclosed 20 km² area at about 1,475 m to 1,600 m (fig. 3.3). It comprises spring, winter, and fall habitats for wild horses. Below Granite Basin, escarpments give way to bajadas (fig. 3.4) which eventually meet flat mud playas. Above Granite Basin a series of sharp and exposed ridges lead to a complex series of sheltered meadows at about 2,000 m. These and adjacent areas above Granite Basin (but below the next series of plateaus) will be referred to as "Ten Meadows," although it is an area of more than ten meadows and it also consists of rocky and sagebrush regions. The locations above this exceed the tree line (2,350 m), and, because there are numerous high-altitude meadows, they are known colloquially as "subalpine" areas. Numerous regions of talus and granite, including two peaks above 2,750 m, also exist.

From either peak unadulterated vistas abound. The southern Cascades with Mount Shasta more than halfway to the Pacific Ocean, Mount Lassen to the west, and the Sierra Nevadas to the

FIG. 3.2 Granite Range looking south. To the left below snowline is Granite Basin and to its left is the Black Rock Desert Playa. The Ten Meadows area is in the center (in snow). Photo by Emory Kristof, © National Geographic Society.

south can all be viewed. Snowy ranges and austere playas sprawl eastward while formidable lava fields pervade views northward. The forces of time are also evident immediately north of the peaks. Deeply cut water drainages and precipices form barriers to the volcanic tablelands of the Granite Range. Horses are found in all areas

FIG. 3.3   Views of Granite Basin. Upper: steep escarpments that enclose it (January 1983); lower: partial view looking eastward, exposing lightened surfaces that were burned by fire (April 1980).

south and east of the peaks, but movements to the north and west are generally blocked by the steep terrain. At varying seasons horses use the four tiers described: (1) bajadas, (2) Granite Basin, (3) Ten Meadows, and (4) subalpine areas. Figure 3.5 is a schematic overview of the study area.

Natural fires occur in the Great Basin and the Granite Range, but their frequency is unknown. A lightning fire erupted in the Granite Basin in 1974 (BLM, unpub.) and the entire area was closed to cattle grazing by the federal government. This fortuitous closure provided a rare opportunity to observe demographic responses of horses without cattle grazing.

Water is relatively abundant in the Granite Range. Several permanent streams occur in precipituous canyons where horses cannot reach them. In Granite Basin three springs yield water year-round, and an emphemeral stream has flowed during the spring and summer in four of the five study years. At high elevations, seeps and springs are common but may often be frozen.

Weather and Annual Cycle

The Granite Range has short, hot summers, and its winters are dominated by maritime polar air masses that deposit most precipitation as snow (Houghton, Sakamoto, and Gifford 1975). In the

Fig. 3.4   Bajadas below Granite Basin and along the eastern front of the Granite Range. Note riparian zones and small band of running horses. Photo by Emory Kristof, © National Geographic Society.

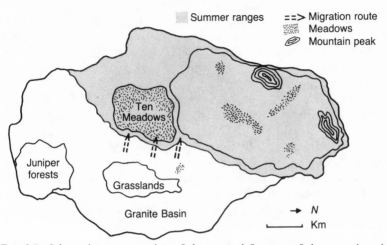

FIG. 3.5 Schematic representation of the general features of the central study areas within the southern Granite Range. Summer (high-altitude) ranges are not drawn to scale.

Black Rock Desert at the base of the range, the "growing season" (4°C+) is generally less than three months (Sakamoto and Gifford 1970), and temperature extremes have ranged from −38°C to +40°C. Annual precipitation at Gerlach, the only settlement with records in the Black Rock Desert, averaged 134 mm. At high elevations it probably exceeds 550 mm.

Freezing temperatures have occurred during every month in the mountains. Generally, the first snows dust the peaks in September or October and make their way to the desert floor by November or December. In Granite Basin snow is unpredictable. I have seen horses almost belly deep in drifts in November and little snow in January. Below Granite Basin snow rarely remains for more than a few days. At high altitudes heavy snowfalls regularly deposit up to 700 mm of snow during single storms, and it is not unusual for spring snowpacks to exceed 3 m. June snowfall occurred at least once in each year of study, and, except for one year, winter snow patches remained at higher elevations into July.

As snow accumulates at higher elevations during the fall, some of the Granite Range's more than three hundred pronghorn leave northern plateaus, and a portion of the mountain's more than fifteen hundred mule deer use areas in or next to Granite Basin. At these times, porcupines are often found scurrying about in forays that have turned diurnal. By winter, water is frozen throughout the day, wind pierces the valleys, and ground fog envelops the lower altitudes. Deer form huge daytime feeding aggregations; the largest I observed numbered at least 230. The first green buds usually appear around February on southfacing slopes, yet much snow still remains at upper elevations. By March, streams flow at lower altitudes, but in Granite Basin grasses are still matted and dormant. Coyote choruses are heard, kit foxes are denning, and pronghorn and rabbits may become increasingly visible.

The winds begin in late winter or early spring and persist undamped for a couple of months. They howl up and down canyons and chill the land. Ranges are blown dry, pup tents are uprooted, and equipment is caked with dust. Soil is lifted from the Black Rock and Smoke Creek playas and sent billowing hundreds of meters into adjacent mountains and valleys. These dust storms reduce visibility from well over a hundred kilometers to several hundred meters and sometimes less. Animals disappeared and could not be found at this time; it seemed as if they were literally blown out of Granite Basin. Because the anemometers that recorded wind velocity only measured up to 115 km/h, I never knew how much greater wind speeds really were. The strongest gusts must have regularly exceeded 170 km/h. Since air masses hit the Granite Range from the west with such force, the basin was engulfed with both northern and southern winds only a few minutes apart. In other ranges of the Great Basin some biologists no longer carry tents because the winds are too strong.

Sage sparrows, meadowlarks, shrikes, and blackbirds signal the arrival of spring. Snakes and lizards bask in the sun. Magpies, ravens, and an occasional turkey vulture scavenge about. The grasses are finally green and the flowers diverse. The range's few bighorn sheep graze on precipitous cliffs and bear their young. The grunting and fighting vocalizations of horses signify the peak of the mating season. By summer, desiccated grasses on alluvial fans and hardened dusty playas contribute to the seemingly lifeless desert floor while meadows, creeks, and cool air dampen the mountains above. This is a representative annual cycle.

3.6 WILD HORSES OF THE GREAT BASIN AND GRANITE RANGE

Origins of wild horses in the Great Basin are obscure. Free-ranging horses occurred as early as 1841, according to the report of an emigrant settler, John Bidwell (Amaral 1977). In 1843 the horse of Kit Carson, a member of Frémont's expedition, was stolen by American Indians about 125 km north of the Granite Range (Frémont 1849, 601). Upon entering the Black Rock Desert, Frémont

FIG. 3.6 Distinct facial and body markings in a representative band. Stallion is to far right.

wrote, "A fog, so dense that we could not see a hundred yards, covered the country, and the men that were sent out after the horses were bewildered. . . . and [later] the appearance of the country was so forbidding, that I was afraid to enter it." Horse tracks were later found along the shore of Pyramid Lake, about 100 km to the south of the Granite Range, but the Indians encountered there by Frémont were horseless. Since no previous explorers were reported to have seen Pyramid Lake, it is possible that wild horses may have existed in this or other areas of northwestern Nevada prior to Frémont's visit.

No further inferences about the origin of horses can be drawn from Frémont's journals. By 1911 horses were widely distributed in the Great Basin: "There are perhaps seventy-thousand live, four-legged reasons for believing that the popular obituary of the wild horse is premature. There are more wild horses in Nevada than there are citizens" (Steele 1911, 757). This is also the earliest date that older residents of the Black Rock Desert can confirm the existence of Granite Range horses. As in the times of Rufus Steele, "There are bays, albinos, chestnuts, red and blue roans, pintos, sorrels, buckskins, and milkwhites" (Steele 1909–10, 198).

3.7 METHODS
Recognition of Individuals

I identified individual animals by distinctive color characteristics (fig. 3.6). Even seemingly uniformly colored animals had, upon closer inspection, distinguishable body conformations, carriages, sizes, markings, tails, or manes. Although some BLM "wild horse specialists" claim that horses cannot be recognized individually, horses are far easier to identify than are baboons, chimpanzees, langurs, lions, jackals, Bewick's swans, red deer, and zebras. All of these species are more uniformly colored than horses, and they have been studied in natural environments as individuals.

Study Period and Observations

In 1979 all animals in the southern Granite Range and portions of populations to the north and west (fig. 3.5) were identified. In the five-year study period (1979–83) none of the southern Granite horses were observed in other areas; since they were found exclusively within the Granite Range, they will be referred to as the Granite population. Unfavorable habitat, steep canyons, and barren playas preclude movements far from the Granite Range. Throughout the study no new, previously unidentified horses entered the population, although a few study animals occasionally formed temporary associations with a rancher's domestic horses along the eastern front of the range. These groupings never lasted longer than a few days.

Two field camps were established in 1979. The first was located on a kopje in Granite Basin (Base Camp I) from which more than half the basin could be viewed (fig. 3.7). The second base camp

FIG. 3.7 Granite Basin as viewed from a kopje to illustrate the visibility from base camp. The most distant point (middle left) exceeds 4 km.

(Base Camp II) was in a small valley with restricted visibility just below the subalpine areas. Except in 1979, data were collected most intensively from March through July while a team of field assistants and I were at the study site. Fieldwork was also done from October 1980 into January 1981, in November 1981, and during every month (except February) of 1982 and 1983 until October. The last data were collected in late December 1983. The field crew, some of whom spent two or three years with the project, correctly identified the horses, and all used standardized systems of data collection. The data we collected was based on more than 8,000 hours of actual observation time. In addition, I took part in aerial censusing at least once annually: by helicopter three times and fixed-winged aircraft six times. For 1973 to 1978 I relied on data from the Nevada Division of Wildlife aerial surveys.

Observations of behaviors included focal-animal (continuous) and instantaneous (point) techniques and scan samples. These first two techniques offer systematic ways of concentrating on individuals (or specific events) for predetermined time periods, and they provide unbiased estimates of activity budgets and rates of interactions (Altmann 1974, 1980). Scan samples of animal location, behaviors, and associations were conducted daily at prescribed times.

Typically, more than one observer worked a shift from 0600 to 1000 hrs and from 1600 until dark, while at least one other person sampled from 1000 to 1600 hrs. These schedules were switched every other day. Data collection was concentrated on prearranged groups or individuals that were located 95.5% of the time. However, when events necessitated further observation, additional data were gathered. Distributions of all animals encountered were recorded at first and last light in Granite Basin each day. Because visibility was exceptional (figs. 3.3, 3.7), some data were recorded from Base Camp I even when observations were unscheduled. Events such as courtship, interband aggression, copulations, or births were always noted, but such opportunistic observations were excluded from analyses of rates of behavioral events.

Once foals were born, data collection focused on their bands for a minimum of one shift daily, when possible, since parous females normally experience postpartum estrous (Ginther 1979; Rossdale 1975). After copulations were observed, these bands were still monitored at least every third day in the event that females were not impregnated (or suffered postzygotic mortality) and resumed cycling.

Reproductive Classifications

Bands refer to permanent or semipermanent associations of individuals. They are composed of one or more males (stallions), females, and their young (collectively, the latter two are harems). Males that do not form consortships with females are bachelors, and when these males band together, they are called bachelor groups. One-year-old animals are yearlings. Animals between two and four years were considered young adults. This definition was necessary only when information on their sexual status was unavailable and the young animals could not be designated as either sexually immature or mature. Immature animals older than a year were juveniles.

Fieldworkers often infer puberty in females after first successful copulation and in males at first intromission or at attainment of established body size. In such cases these animals should rightfully be classified as mature. However, some males of adultlike body size die without ever leaving behind offspring, and copulations may go unseen in females that in successive years produce no young. Although in appearance these animals may be adult, without accompanying physiological data one cannot be sure they are capable of producing offspring. Likewise, copulations in such animals might go undetected, and these individuals could erroneously be designated as immature. Rather than attempting to estimate without corroborative evidence which animals were capable of reproduction, it seemed more appropriate to use age broadly and label these two-to-four-year-olds as adults. Although most animals remain sexually immature at one year, the two-to-four-year-old category corresponds to the physiological transition between juvenile status and adulthood. Where appropriate, reference will be made to either animals' ages or reproductive status. Additional details are given where necessary. Nulliparous females are those that have not given birth; primiparous females are those that have produced only one offspring; and multiparous females are those that have had two or more young.

Band Nomenclature

Bands were designated by capital letters (e.g., A, B), and individuals within them by names that began with those letters. The first three initials of the mother were given to her offspring. For example, in band A, Alvin was the stallion and Alice a mare in the harem. Alice gave birth to Ali (1979), Aliman (1980), Alimo (1981),

Alisam (1982), and Alien (1983). Nomenclature became more complex as young individuals aged, changed bands, and gave birth. Bands that accommodated individuals from other bands received new designations that included the first initials of the new members. Thus, if two T females and a B female joined A, the new band might be A+T+T+B. If a bachelor took over a harem the band was also renamed.

It is easy to visualize how difficult it would be to convey meaningful band relationships if the detailed records of all changes were presented. To maintain band nomenclature at a tangible level, letter designations will simply refer to bands of different individuals. Specific animals, genealogies, and vagaries of the system will be given when pertinent.

Band stability denotes the condition of constancy of membership. Stable bands are those whose stallions and females consorted for eleven months or more. Unstable bands are those where resident stallions were deposed by another male or where individuals joined new bands.

Chemical Restraint

It was necessary to immobilize horses so that age and body characteristics (fig. 3.8) could be related to an individual's ecology. In wild horses the social environment influences an individual's ability to reproduce, as it does in several group-living carnivores and pri-

FIG. 3.8 Measuring an immobilized stallion at the end of winter. Photo by Emory Kristof, © National Geographic Society.

mates (Packer and Pusey 1983; Hrdy 1977). Since fecundity of female horses is related, in part, to band stability (Berger 1983b), a major dilemma concerned restraining individuals without disrupting the social structure.

Succinylcholine chloride, a potent paralyzer of voluntary muscle, was selected because of its rapid action (about two minutes) and quick recovery time (about thirteen minutes) (Berger, Kock, Cunningham, and Dodson 1983). Most animals ($N=28$) that were immobilized were returned to original bands in less than ten minutes, although in a few cases multiple-hour periods were needed to assure maintenance of original band compositions. No females aborted due to the immobilization effort, which spanned sixteen months. In one case, a bachelor male removed the tranquilizer dart from the rump of a younger bachelor by pulling it out with his mouth; similar behavior has occurred in Kalahari lions (M. and D. Owens, personal communication).

Body Weight and Age

To estimate body weight, a priori visual assessments were compared with those determined subsequently on twenty-eight immobilized wild horses and three domestic horses of known weight by: $W=G^2L/k$, where $W=$body weight, $G=$chest girth, $L=$length (point of shoulder to hip), and $k=$a constant (Milner and Hewitt 1969). When tested on captive horses of known weight, this formula predicted weights with over 94% accuracy (Milner and Hewitt 1969). When I compared my visual estimations of body weight of wild horses with those determined by the above formula of the same horses (when immobilized), my accuracy in predicting weight averaged 94.7% ($SD \pm 5.7$). Thus, I estimated body weights of horses that were not immobilized, although those judged not to differ by the standard deviation were recorded as equivalent weight. Undoubtedly I made errors in visual estimations of nonimmobilized horses, but my intent was to evaluate body weight relative to others in the population. After years of studying the same individuals I gained a good idea of individual sizes and seasonal variation compared to others whose weights were known from actual measurements.

Ages were known by birth dates and estimated by tooth wear. Because tooth-wear criteria were developed for domestic horses (National Research Council 1982), the measures are not directly comparable to those for wild horses. Wear in the latter is accentuated by the ingestion of grit and silaceous material. For domestic

FIG. 3.9 Body-size profiles of a pregnant female (left), a nonpregnant young female (center), and a four-year-old male (right).

horses, standard incisor wear patterns give reasonable one- to two-year gradations up to about fifteen years of age (American Association of Equine Practitioners 1971). Additional details and precautions about the ways teeth were used to determine age are found in Appendix 3.

Births and Deaths

Signs of impending birth could be detected because females in their last trimester of pregnancy had enlarged or distended abdomens (fig. 3.9), and near parturition they usually had swollen mammary tissue. Only three nulliparous females were judged incorrectly to be nonpregnant. Because 96% of all females were accurately assessed as pregnant and copulation dates for many of these were known, birth dates were determined by locating and then checking suspected females for foals around projected birth dates.

No experienced mothers departed from their bands at parturition. However, primiparous mothers occasionally left at this time, returning one or two days later with a new foal. I assumed neonatal deaths occurred when nulliparous females in late stages of pregnancy left their bands at projected birth dates and returned without a foal. Birth locations were found by observing (1) amniotic and chorionic membranes, (2) unusual attractions of coyotes to bands, and (3) lack of band movements in conjunction with newly born animals.

Deaths were noted when bodies or skulls and skeletons were

found. In sixteen cases it was possible to assign identities to the dead horses by matching hair fragments (tails, manes, pelage) with prior descriptions of missing animals. Six deaths were assumed because animals were missing for longer than a year. Since the distinction between dispersal and death has important consequences for understanding a species' demography, it is necessary to consider the reasons for treating these incidents as mortalities. First, there is no evidence that animals migrate across playas or away from the Granite Range. Ranchers who have lived their entire lives near the Granite Range have never observed horses (who were not first harassed) on playas. Also, members of my study group and I never found horses, feces, or tracks away from the study areas, although we had checked at all seasons and in aerial surveys. Second, animals disappeared during situations that were suggestive of mortality. Four horses were last observed alive at high altitudes in autumns of different years. These are areas where horses are susceptible to death due to entrapment by winter snowstorms, as pointed out in section 5.4.

The other two deaths occurred under different conditions. One involved a multiparous, lactating female that vanished from Granite Basin in early summer. Based on body fat, lack of rib prominence, and estimated milk production, she was in good condition at the time of disappearance (chap. 5). Her three-month-old foal was alive and well in a juniper-covered area dominated with large boulders, about 3 km to 4 km from the remainder of the band. I suspect a puma may have preyed on the mare since she was small (ca. 365 kg; pumas are sympatric with horses), and at no other time in the study was a mare ever found to desert a foal. It is virtually impossible that this mare was removed by humans since any intruders would have been detected. Still, it is perplexing that the body could not be located.

The final case involved a five-year-old harem-holding male in poor body condition. He disappeared after losing his harem in two escalated fights with older bachelors. Because he was already in debilitated condition and males have died as a result of combat-related wounds (chap. 7), death was presumed.

Statistics

Because the information base was voluminous, not all data nor combinations of analyses could be presented. Where appropriate, both parametric and nonparametric statistics were used (Conover 1971; Siegel 1956; Sokal and Rohlf 1969).

Some data are presented as percentages to standardize differences in the sampling of rates of events. Analyses of differences between rates involved the Brandt and Snedecor method (Snedecor 1956) and the arcsine transformation for testing the equality of two percentages (Sokal and Rohlf 1969). Briefly, this method generates a test statistic that is compared with the area under the normal deviate. For frequency data other statistical tests were performed, although reference in the text may simply note the percentages. Univariate tests were done when samples were too few to permit more complex testing, as in cases concerning annual reproductive events. The specific tests are numbered in brackets throughout each chapter, and values and analyses are given at the end of respective chapters. Levels of significance were accepted at $p=0.05$, and, unless designated otherwise, all tests were two tailed.

3.8   ETHOGRAM AND SOCIAL GROUPINGS

Horses employ a variety of behavior patterns when interacting (Waring 1983). Those pertinent to this study as well as vocalizations and categories of social groups are listed below. The first six behavior patterns occur during aggressive interactions.

Behavior Patterns

Ears retracted: Ears are laid back or flattened along the posterior (dorsal) portion of the head.

Teeth bared: The lips are pulled upward and the incisor teeth are exposed.

Rear-leg lift: A rear leg is partially lifted off the ground to deter the approach of another horse.

Rear-leg kick: A single rear leg is used to strike at another animal. When both legs are used it is a double rear-leg kick.

Front-leg kick: A front leg is used to strike outward at another animal.

Bite: Teeth are used to grasp or seize an opponent.

Arched neck: Head is held up and the neck is strongly curved. This behavior occurs in aggressive encounters between males and when males approach females during courtship.

Vigilance: The ears are erect and forward as an animal focuses its attention in a specific direction.

Play: A variety of social and solitary activities that occur when the ears are not retracted. These include running while kicking outward the front or rear legs, running with sudden starts and stops, chasing, jumping, bucking, head tossing, nonserious biting, and pushing.

Herding posture: This behavior has been observed only in adult males. It involves lowering the neck and head with the ears retracted while pushing or driving females in a given direction. Cowboys have often described it as "snaking behavior," since a stallion sinuously moves his head from side to side while he moves toward females.

Leg drop: Males use this motor pattern primarily as a defensive action during fights. An individual tucks or "drops" his front or rear legs rapidly under his body in response to bites directed at his legs. In escalated encounters, each individual may shield his legs by resting on them.

Vocalizations

Snort: A forceful expulsion of air through the nostrils that usually lasts less than one second.

Squeal: A short (less than 1 sec) high-pitched vocalization that occurs most often during male-male aggression or male-female consortships.

Nicker: A broad-banded, low-pitched call of about the same duration as squeals.

Whinny (neigh): A relatively long (ca. 1.5 sec), initially high-pitched vocalization that drops in frequency. Most often they are heard when a foal or other group member becomes separated from the band.

Social Groupings

Bachelor male: A male not in association with a harem.

Band: A group consisting of one adult male and one or more females.

Harem: Sexually mature females, with or without young, which are affiliated with one or more adult males.

Multimale band: A band with more than one adult male.

Stallion: An adult male member of a band.

Patterns of Interaction and Cooperation

Naso-naso: A pattern in which the nostrils of two individuals are in close proximity.

Aggression: A hostile act directed toward a conspecific.

Aggressive contest: A fight between two males in which both animals arch their necks, attempt bites or kicks, and either knock an opponent to the ground or chase him 40 m or more.

Escalated contests: An aggressive contest in which bites are directed at opponent's legs or rear-leg kicks are directed at opponent's heads.

Alliance: A relationship between males of a multimale band in which each rebuffs approaches of males from other bands. These actions need not occur simultaneously. A stallion from band A might drive away a group of bachelors trying to steal females from his band, while a few days later another stallion in band A might do the same. Thus, these two males have helped each other protect their females by individually thwarting the approaches of other males.

Defensive alliance: A situation in which both members of an alliance simultaneously aid the other during defense of their harem by cooperating to rebuff males from other bands. This occurs when an alliance member is interacting with one or more rival males and his partner leaves the harem to participate in defensive actions.

Favor: Each time a male defends his harem and the alliance partner benefits by not having to participate. Hence, the latter male received a "favor."

3.9   SUMMARY

1. Wild horses occur in at least ten states in the western United States. Most are found within the Great Basin Desert, an area characterized primarily by shrub/steppe vegetation, broad valleys, and several hundred mountain ranges.
2. The five-year study was situated in the Granite Range, an insular fault-blocked mountain in northwestern Nevada. All of the 149 horses that lived in the study area were known individually. Over 8,000 hours of observational data were collected.
3. Descriptions of study methods, sampling procedures, reproductive, age, and weight classifications, an ethogram, and other material pertinent to later findings are provided.

4 Land-Use Systems and Resources

It is impossible to separate living creatures from their surroundings. To do so in fact is to kill them.

Patrick Geddes and J. Arthur Thompson (1911)

4.1 INTRODUCTION

Wild horses appear to use their environments in similar ways. They feed on grasses, drink at water holes, and try as much as possible to avoid inclement weather. Yet subtle if not striking differences occur both among individuals and bands. These differences can be related to factors that include the location of home ranges and the resources within them, band size, an individual's age and sex, seasonal use of altitudes and habitats, and selection of refuges during winter storms. Most important, however, these patterns of resource exploitation affect how well individuals reproduce. This chapter describes these patterns with regard to home-range ecology.

4.2 VEGETATION DESCRIPTION AND USE OF HABITATS

In the Granite Range, seven cover types were delineated based on aerial photographs and ground mapping; six included plant communities. They are as follows: (1) *shrublands*—the major overstory consisted primarily of sagebrush with native (mostly perennial) grasses and forbs as understory vegetation; (2) *grasslands*—covering areas where fire had removed sagebrush or other woody species (see fig. 3.3) (exotic grasses, principally cheatgrass and forbs such as phlox and lupine formed the bulk of invader species); (3) *juniper forests*—such regions were represented by a preponderance of juniper trees (understory in such places consisted of grasses or shrubs, but junipers were clearly the dominant feature); (4) *rabbitbrush patches*—homogeneous patches dominated by rabbitbrush; (5) *riparian zones*—areas with mesic vegetation along permanent or intermittent water sources; (6) *meadows*—moist areas characterized by sedges, rushes, and bent grasses; (7) *waste*—rocky, talus, or sandy areas that were of little general use to horses. All seven cover types were found below 2,100 m, whereas (1), (5), (6), and (7) were abundant above 2,100 m.

During the fall, winter, and spring, shrubland and grassland habitats received the most use (80.1%), followed next by junipers and then meadows [1] (fig. 4.1). Meadows received the greatest use in proportion to their availability—nearly 61 times. At high-altitude sites, where most horses spend their time, shrublands and meadows received more than 99% of the use.

4.3   FOOD RESOURCES
Assessment of Vegetation Mosaic

To determine the extent to which the above cover types represented underlying patterns of plant diversity and dispersion, 153 32-m transects (88 on low-altitude ranges; 65 at high-altitude sites)

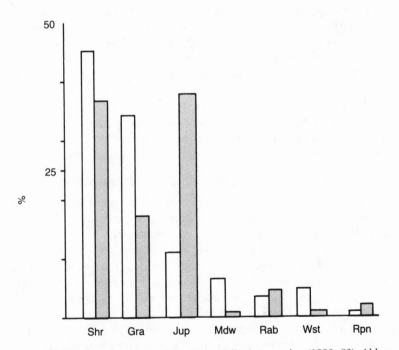

FIG. 4.1   Relative use of communities during fall-winter-spring (1980–83). Abbreviations from left to right represent the following: shrub, grass, juniper, meadows, rabbitbrush, waste, and riparian. Observed (light) and expected (dark) values are shown for habitat use in relation to availability. Based on 14,380 quarter-hour sampling points.

and 1,090 1-m² quadrats (654 and 436, respectively) were run (Appendix 4). Because discriminant function analyses revealed variations in species composition and distribution, all cover types (except waste regions) were poor predictors of underlying plant patterns. Consequently, data from specific areas were used to construct more detailed vegetation maps. The original cover types were subdivided so that underlying patterns of the vegetation mosaic within each cover type could be expressed on final maps. This was done by comparing mean values of characters from different sites by using discriminant function analyses. The extent to which group means (known as *centroids*) varied was determined by the function that accounted for the greatest proportion of total variance within and between groups. Groups were ranked on a gradient, and a stepwise selection procedure was used to choose variables in the discriminating functions (see Klecka 1975; Srivastava and Carter 1983). Multivariate F ratios were used to test for differences among group centroids. As a result, thirty-four different microhabitats were found across the seven cover types. Frequency of microhabitat use was then noted by visual observations of 1 m² quadrats (Appendix 4).

Overview of Food Sites

Feeding site quality was determined for these thirty-four areas by analyses of (1) the size and dispersion of potential food patches, (2) use of key species within each area, and (3) crude nutritional approximations of such species. Areas of relatively concentrated food and potentially better nutritional value were ranked higher than regions where plants were not as concentrated or were of lower potential value. For example, some microhabitats in juniper forests lacked most species of bunchgrasses; instead, species of little food value to horses such as stands of the exotic grass, *Bromus,* as well pussytoes, mature Great Basin wild rye, and yarrow were widely dispersed. Based on the method outlined in Appendix 4, this area received a relatively low rank because the food sources within it were poor. In contrast, shrubland areas dominated by species such as spike bent grass, bluebunch wheatgrass, clustered fieldsedge, and galeta grass, all of which are relatively nutritious food plants, received a high ranking. Thus, the various microhabitats used by horses could be ranked according to their potential food value and then compared to one another.

At low-altitude sites, the poorest feeding locations were waste areas and rabbitbrush patches. These latter areas had small grass patches that were separated more widely than other cover types. Juniper stands were slightly better than grasslands and both were exceeded by shrublands. Variation occurred within each site. Among low-altitude sites, the superior regions for feeding were the burned areas along mountainous slopes and in the shrubland passes found to the north of Granite Basin. Overall, low-altitude areas (late-fall-winter-spring ranges) can be viewed as a mosaic of microenvironments varying in potential food value. The best areas were situated along the western and northern boundaries of Granite Basin, while its southern borders with heavy juniper cover were quite poor (see fig. 3.5). Areas between these boundaries include shrublands, rabbitbrush patches, grasslands, and waste.

At high-altitude (summer) sites, shrublands represented potentially better feeding areas than those found below, presumably due to the better nutrition afforded by less desiccated and more abundant bunchgrasses. However, variation was also considerable within cover types. For instance, some high-altitude shrublands, especially on eastward slopes, had the lowest potential feeding values simply due to high shrub densities.

Distribution and Use of Food Plants

Cheatgrass, a common alien species after fire or heavy grazing, was found in most low-quality areas of Granite Basin. It was rare above 2,250 m. Bunchgrasses and clustered fieldsedge were the most abundant species in areas that received higher quality ratings, and they were found at both high and low altitudes (Appendix 5). Spike bent grass and rushes were common meadow plants at all elevations. Forbs that predominated were dandelion, desert parsley, microsternis, Russian thistle, locoweed, lupine, pussytoes, and false forget-me-not, but only pussytoes and dandelions received moderate foraging pressure (Appendix 5). The flower heads of balsamroot were consumed regularly as well during brief periods in late spring, but these observations were not quantified.

Of grasses, bluebunch wheatgrass, Idaho fescue, Sandberg's bluegrass, needle-and-thread grass, and Thurber's needlegrass were used often. These findings are similar to those conducted on other ranges with broadly similar habitats (Hansen and Clark 1977; Nawa 1978; Olsen and Hansen 1977; Hubbard and Hansen 1976).

4.4   HOME-RANGE CHARACTERISTICS
Definitions and Locations

Home ranges were defined as the areas where animals restricted their activities and sought shelter, food, and/or potential mates

(Burt 1943; Bowen 1982). They were determined by constructing 50%, 75%, and 90% frequency-use polygons (Bekoff, Wieland, and Lavender 1982) of individual or band locations taken at 15-minute intervals. Core areas were designated as regions that enclosed the most clustered 50% of observation points (see Michener 1979). Locations where animals spent less than 10% of their time were considered as forays and excluded from further analyses.

Bands varied in observability due to home-range locations and use. However, home-range estimations should be fairly accurate since (1) bands were almost always found within any given two-day effort of searching, and (2) the number of points on which the data were based was large for over 90% of the bands ($\bar{X}=3,841\pm928$; range 2,246–4,862) each year (1980–82). Areas of use were classified according to season, but since most summer home ranges were above 2,000 m and winter, spring, and fall ranges were below, I refer to these areas as summer and fall-winter-spring ranges collectively.

Low-altitude areas used by horses were smaller in size (ca. 34 km^2) than high-altitude areas (ca. 60 km^2). To shift from one region to the next required a movement of about 8 km and an ascent of (or descent from) steep ridgelines and slopes (figs. 3.2–3.4). The length of time necessary to complete these movements varied from two weeks to two months, but generally took about one to one and a half months.

Seasonal Ranges and Core Areas

The size and shape of core areas varied considerably (fig. 4.2). At low-altitude sites, maximum (90% frequency-use polygons) band ranges averaged 6.73 ($SD\pm1.61$; range 4.44–9.80) km^2, a value significantly smaller than that for bachelors [2] (table 4.1). Among bachelors, older animals (9+ yrs) had the largest home ranges, exceeding by more than 35% the size of ranges used by equivalent-aged males possessing harems. Males younger than nine years without harems were intermediate in home-range size (table 4.1). These same patterns also occurred on summer ranges: old bachelors ranged the widest, then younger bachelors, and finally, bands [2]. In all cases summer ranges were larger than those at other times (table 4.1).

Home ranges differed not only between bands and bachelors, but among bands themselves. Sizes for low-altitude core areas varied among bands from the surprisingly small value of 1.17 km^2 to 4.96 km^2, over a fourfold difference ($\bar{X}=2.21\pm1.06$ km^2). Young bachelors had larger core areas ($\bar{X}=2.70$ km^2) than bands, but

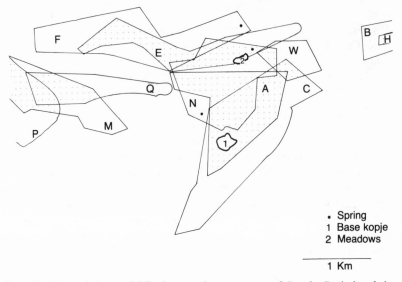

FIG. 4.2 Size and shape of fall-winter-spring core areas of Granite Basin bands in 1982. Bands H, B, P, and M extend beyond limits of figure.

these were exceeded by older males ($\bar{X}=4.81$ km^2) (table 4.1). Such trends in core-area differences were consistent at high altitudes as well [2].

Over the study period a progressive shift away from the central grasslands of Granite Basin toward outlying areas took place. Although I never measured quantitatively the vegetation changes that occurred in this area, I suspected that use of central areas declined because of excessive trampling by horses and a rise in weedy (e.g., non-nutritious) species. Increases both in movements away from this central area and in home-range sizes occurred. Of bands that existed when the study began, all except one used larger home ranges at the end of the project. During the last year of study when population size was greatest, winter home ranges were largest and movements away from Granite Basin the most dramatic (see sec. 5.6).

Annual Fidelity to Core Areas

Horses showed remarkable fidelity in their annual use of home ranges. Fidelity was determined by examining whether individuals returned to and used at least half of their core area from the previous year. Because it was possible for any male to change his home range in a given year, all data were treated as independent annual

TABLE 4.1   Mean Home-Range Size (km^2) for Bands and Bachelors
during Summer (High Altitude) and Fall-Winter-Spring (Low Altitude), 1979–1983

		90%	75%	50%
Low Altitude	Bands	6.73 ± 1.61	3.69 ± 1.46	2.24 ± 1.06
	Bachelors$_y$	$8.06 \pm .94$	$5.02 \pm .49$	$2.70 \pm .39$
	Bachelors$_o$	$8.97 \pm .99$	6.99 ± 1.47	4.81 ± 2.44
High Altitude	Bands	25.12 ± 5.98	17.26 ± 3.79	11.28 ± 3.66
	Bachelors$_y$	30.37 ± 6.85	24.41 ± 1.76	19.83 ± 2.83
	Bachelors$_o$	$35.62^{9.51}$	33.07 ± 8.16	24.96 ± 6.06

Notes: % = frequency-use polygons; bachelors$_y$ = 8 years or less; bachelors$_o$ = 9 years or more; $\pm$ standard deviation.

events. For animals in which data spanned at least four years, stallion fidelity was 81%; 29 of the 36 stallions returned to low-altitude core areas. Five of the 7 animals whose land-use patterns changed were males that lost or regained harems. Thus, of stallions not involved in harem changes, 94% (29 of 31) returned to regions incorporating formerly used areas.

Unlike stallions, bachelors were not faithful to core areas. Only 19% (5 of 26) returned to core areas used in the previous year; some of these individuals showed greater fidelity once they obtained harems [3]. If the exploitation of food resources was the only factor underlying fidelity, there should be no consistent difference between males with harems and those without them. However, males with females were more faithful to home ranges, suggesting that social factors associated with harem maintenance or perhaps band stability are important determinants of home-range use (see chap. 9).

By nature of the association between a stallion and his harem, females in stable bands also showed a high degree of fidelity. However, the fidelity of mares was not calculated, since females that changed bands used different core areas in subsequent years. Calculations of female fidelity would reflect the faithfulness of males, since stallions play a more important role in home-range site selection than females (see sec. 7.7).

Exclusivity of Areas

The defense of core areas or any other geographical region was not observed, and no places were exclusively used. Territoriality in its classical sense (e.g., Burt 1943; but see Brown 1975) was absent in the Granite Range as it is in other populations of horses (Keiper 1976; Feist and McCullough 1976; Miller and Denniston 1979;

Welsh 1975) and harem-dwelling equids (Klingel 1975; Joubert 1972; Penzhorn 1979). The only exception is a dense barrier island population where vegetation is distributed in a fashion that permits territoriality (Rubenstein 1981).

Most areas used by Granite horses overlapped those of other bands. In a representative year (1982), 90% of the bands had maximal frequency-use polygons on low-altitude sites that overlapped; average core-area overlap was about 43% (fig. 4.2). On high-altitude ranges maximal home-range areas overlapped in 87% of the bands, although average core-area overlap decreased to 30% [4]. This reduction stemmed from lowered animal densities at the more expansive high-altitude sites. To summarize, most bands had sympatric home ranges and core areas. The extent of overlap varied among areas and no locations were defended.

4.5   DIURNAL AND NOCTURNAL MOVEMENTS

It was possible to establish minimum daily and nightly movements because bands were readily observable and used relatively small areas. However, viewing conditions varied between high- and low-altitude sites as well as at day and night. As a result, sampling schedules were modified for each area. At low altitudes, movements were calculated only when observations of animals (1) occurred within an hour of both dusk and dawn, and (2) included eight additional hours of which at least one fell between 1100 and 1300 hrs. At high-altitude sites, the fragmented and more rugged habitat precluded sampling in the same manner. Consequently movements were estimated if animals were observed for at least six hours.

Nocturnal distances were obtained at lower sites by comparing locations at dusk and the subsequent dawn. For regions above 2,000 m they were based on points collected within about ninety minutes of sunrise or sunset. This latter sampling scheme undoubtedly biased nocturnal movements, but it was the only possible measure since it took time to traverse ridgelines to locate animals. Thus, data on nightly movements were conservative estimates based on direct-line distances between where animals were last observed at night and then first observed at light. Diurnal distances of travel more accurately reflected actual movements since animal locations were plotted throughout the day. To correct for problems stemming from differential observability at high and low altitudes, data on movements were based on "dawn-to-dusk distance," not per observation period.

Patterns among Bands and Bachelors

Bands traveled three times as far during the day ($\bar{X}=1.32$ km) than they did at night ($\bar{X}=0.45$ km; table 4.2) at all seasons [5]. Although annual differences in daily movements occurred, those at night varied little [6]. For example, nightly movements for all bands during spring were remarkably similar and averaged 0.33($\pm$.09) km in 1980, 0.35($\pm$.06) km in 1981, and 0.39($\pm$.09) km in 1982. At all seasons, nocturnal movements were not too different (table 4.2).

On the other hand, bachelors traveled greater distances than bands throughout each season and year, permitting the following conclusions: (1) Both day and night movements were greater in males lacking females than in those with harems [7]. (2) Among bachelors, those older than nine years traveled further than younger ones [8]. (3) Among bachelors, the least variability in diurnal travel occurred in older animals during the spring (e.g., 2.41 km in 1980, 2.35 km in 1981, 2.58 km in 1982). (4) Overall, daily movements for all horses combined were not only of greater distance than those at night, but also of greater variability [9].

Proximate Causes of Variation

Numerous factors could account for patterns of variation in diurnal travel distances. Of these, the stability of bands, ages of stallions, and social interactions among bands exerted no discernible influences. Factors that did affect movements were female reproductive status, seasonal home-range size, and weather.

TABLE 4.2 Mean Linear Diurnal and Nocturnal Movements (km) at Different Seasons

	Day			
	Spring	Summer	Fall	Winter
Bands	$1.33\pm.30$	$1.12\pm.25$	$1.61\pm.78$	$1.23\pm.49$
Bachelors$_y$	$1.70\pm.27$	$1.98\pm.23$	2.80 ± 1.03	$1.10\pm.44$
Bachelors$_o$	$2.47\pm.68$	$2.92\pm.66$	2.91 ± 1.01	1.42 ± 1.11
	Night			
	Spring	Summer	Fall	Winter
Bands	$.36\pm.08$	$.40\pm.05$	$.55\pm.11$	$.41\pm.05$
Bachelors$_y$	$.66\pm.14$	$.60\pm.16$	—	$.69\pm.06$
Bachelors$_o$	$.76\pm.06$	$.64\pm.16$	$.67\pm.10$	—

Notes: Summer movements are high-altitude sites. $\pm$ standard deviation.

Female Reproductive Status. Since daily travels are restricted on dates
of parturition in at least one other troop-dwelling mammal (e.g.,
yellow baboons; Altmann 1980), bands of horses might also be expected to move less on foal birth dates. The data did not support
this prediction [10]. However, when the reproductive experience
of females is considered, an effect on the movements of its band
members is detectable. Multiparous females and their bands covered over twice the distance (1.59 ± 1.09 km) on days of birth than
did animals from bands containing primiparous females
(0.78 ± 0.33 km) [10].

Home-Range Size. There were no consistent correlations between
the daily movements of bands and their home-range frequency-use
polygons. When data for individual bands are pooled and the
home-range size of bands and bachelors are compared with daily
movements, a strong positive relationship emerges [11]. Although
it was then possible to predict on a given day which classes of animals might move relatively further (or lesser) distances, individual
variability was great. Some bachelors and bands exhibited little
variation in their daily patterns; others were highly unpredictable.

Weather. Extremes of heat and cold in conjunction with wind
yielded the clearest variation in patterns of movement. On cold,
windy (or stormy) days horses moved little (see sec. 4.7).

4.6 VERTICAL MIGRATIONS AND ALTITUDINAL SEGREGATION OF
BANDS

Most, if not all, mountain-dwelling, northern temperate ungulates
migrate altitudinally during some time of the year (Autenrieth and
Fichter 1975; Darling 1937; Geist 1971; McCullough 1964; Oosenberg and Theberge 1980). In the Granite Range, bands moved
from low- to high-altitude sites in late spring/early summer, presumably in accordance with newly emerging vegetation. Factors
such as temperature and insects also coincide with emergent vegetation and may affect movements, as suggested for other species
(see Hoefs and Cowan 1979). Since temperature, precipitation,
snow cover, and other factors vary annually and influence the timing and quality of food (Hebert 1973; Wehausen 1980), it is not
surprising that patterns of migration are correlated with more than
any single variable.

In the Granite Range, dates of migrations fluctuated among

TABLE 4.3   First and Median Dates of Altitudinal Shifts

Area	1979			1980		
	I	II	III	I	II	III
Subalpine 2,300 m	—	July 4	—	June 20	July 7	June* 10
Ten Meadows 2,000 m	—	June 24	—	June 10	June 21	May* 13
Granite Basin 1,600 m	—	—	—	—	Oct 18	—
Area	1981			1982		
	I	II	III	I	II	III
Subalpine 2,300 m	May 27	June 29	May 29	June 9	June 10	June 1
Ten Meadows 2,000 m	May 12	May 26	May* 12	June 1	June 7	May* 19
Granite Basin 1,600 m	Nov 24	—	Nov 24	Oct 1	—	Sep 28

Notes: I = median date for bachelors; II = median date for bands; III = date of first band. * denotes the same band.

years (table 4.3). In every year, forays of bachelors and bands to and up mountainous slopes were indications of impending spring migrations; a clumping of bands at the north end of Granite Basin would follow a few days or weeks later (see fig. 3.5). One band (N) moved to the higher altitude Ten Meadows area first every year, preceding others by at least ten days. Between late May and late June at least 50% of the bands moved above 2,000 m (fig. 4.3; table 4.3).

Although most bands moved to summer ranges at some point in the year, some remained at low altitudes throughout the study (fig. 4.3). These include band M, which remained in Granite Basin the last four years of study, and several bands whose stallions were less than eight years of age (fig. 4.4). One such band (H) remained for three and a half years in the Basin, and another stayed there for a year until its stallion died. As a result bands were stratified at different altitudes. These patterns were most distinctive during summers, but also occurred at other seasons (fig. 4.3). Individuals that failed to exploit newly sprouting high-altitude grasses by migrating in summer were expected to reproduce poorly, and they did (see sec. 4.9).

Several of the factors implicated as cues that trigger movements

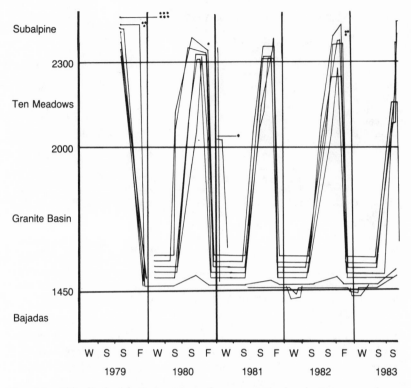

FIG. 4.3   Altitudinal migration patterns of representative bands. Extreme and median bands indicated. Note the two bands that failed to migrate. Numbers refer to elevations (m), and dots represent altitudes of mortalities.

to lower altitudes in ungulates are inclement weather and snow, lack of food, photoperiod, females, and shelter (Geist 1971; McCullough 1964; Staines 1976). In Granite Range horses, three arguments support the idea that lack of food, caused by snowfall, may be the most important, although not necessarily the only factor. First, animals remained on summer ranges until after the first autumn snowstorms. Only 7% of the bands moved to Granite Basin prior to storms. Second, in the fall of each year more than 80% (N=26) of the high-altitude bands moved to lower sites within four days after snowstorms [12]. Third, three bands that had been in Granite Basin in the fall of 1980 returned to southward, high-altitude slopes (2,100 m, 2,470 m, and 2,560 m respectively) in December 1980 and January 1981 after snow had melted from these areas. These data suggest that fall migrations are influenced most by snow cover.

4.7 SELECTION OF REFUGES
Winter Ecology and Snowstorms

Horses normally spent most of their time in exposed areas of grassland and shrub (fig. 4.1). This pattern changed from November until April when it became increasingly difficult to locate bands, particularly during and after wind and snowstorms. Often Granite Basin was searched only to find that three or four bands had departed, apparently for "greener pastures" at lower or more sheltered regions. Areas that offered protection, regardless of season, were designated "refuges."

To determine the extent to which bands sought shelter, locations of horses were recorded for the following indexes of wind-chill: I= 0°C; II= −1°C to −9°C; III= −10°C to −18°C; IV= −19°C to −36°C. Windchill is an index of the transfer of human heat to the environment due to the combined effects of ambient temperature and wind and therefore is not directly applicable to nonhumans. However, it provides a relative scale of animal responses to heat-loss gradients and has been used effectively for

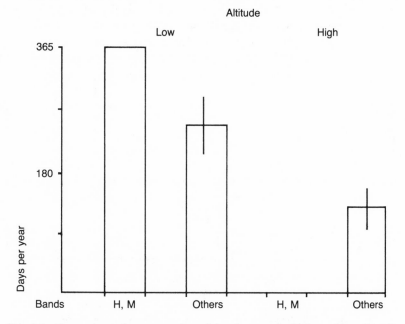

FIG. 4.4 Comparison of mean number of days/yr spent at high- and low-altitude sites over a two-year period. Extending lines show standard deviation.

other ungulates (Hoefs and Cowan 1979; Staines 1976, 1977).
Windchill was measured in an exposed location by taking the average of at least three anemometer readings of wind speed over a
two-minute period. The windchill index was then derived by looking up standard values for the corresponding ambient temperature
in a windchill chart.

Despite interband variations, horses avoided grass- and
shrubland areas as wintry weather intensified (fig. 4.5) [13]. Refuge
was occasionally sought on slopes and in ravines, but most frequently in small, scattered clumps of junipers, especially when
weather was severe (fig. 4.6). Horses browsed on bitterbrush, rabbitbrush, or mahogany when snow cover was more than 10 cm to
12 cm; only four times did I observe an adult horse eating sagebrush. Local ranchers have reported the ingestion of small juniper
branches by horses when snow was about a meter deep.

Winter movements of horses were reduced on days of storms.
Individuals traveled small distances daily, although occasionally a
band or several bachelors moved 3 km to 4 km and then remained
in that area for days or weeks. This occurred most often when
winds exceeded 100 km/hr on successive days or snow cover persisted for weeks in Granite Basin. Unfortunately, reduced winter
travel is not reflected in the data on diurnal movements (table 4.2)
because horses were sampled less often on days of severe storms.

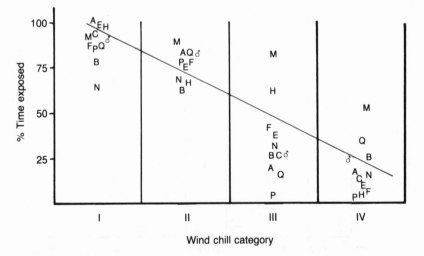

FIG. 4.5   Windchill categories and percentage of time exposed to inclement conditions. Symbols refer to bands or bachelors (as designated). Means per band were
calculated from two temperature rankings per category (N=3,541 points).

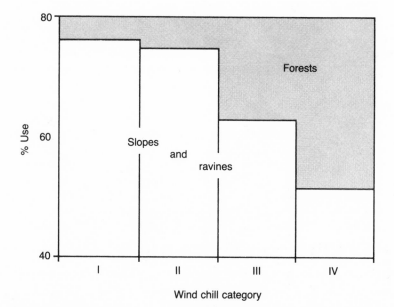

Fɪɢ. 4.6 Windchill categories and percentage of use of different windbreaks (slopes/ravines or forested areas). The percentage of forest use increases with windchill ($N=3,541$ points).

Several patterns in refuge use emerged among bands; these were related to home-range features of bands (table 4.4). Band P lived in a home range that contained mostly juniper forest, and they were the most sheltered band. In contrast, the home range of M had little tree cover and few canyons; this band was the most exposed during storms (fig. 4.5). Radiant energy loss has been minimized by similar shelter-seeking behavior in island horses (Ford and Keiper 1979; Gates 1979; Welsh 1975) and other Holarctic ungulates such as bighorn sheep, moose, and deer (Edwards 1956; Geist 1978a).

Summer Ecology and Insects

If winter represents the most difficult period, late spring and summer are probably the least stressful. Horses, at least in the White, Black Rock, Jackson, Clan Alpine, Sonoma, and Humboldt ranges of the Great Basin consume food along altitudinal gradients. Horses in these areas are not as tightly restricted in their movements by water availability as are horses in Arizona's Grand Canyon (Berger 1977) or Wyoming's Red Desert (Miller and Denniston 1979). At this time of year, Granite horses had new shiny pelage,

TABLE 4.4 Major Resource Features of the Principal Granite Basin Bands, 1979–1983

Band	Duration (yrs)	Core-Area Resources			
		Shelter	Water	Meadows	Grasses
F E B	4 5 5	locally available (except B)	abundant	available (except B)	clumped; mostly native
A N C	5 5 5	abundant	locally available	available (except C)	mixed; alien and native
Q H P	2½ 2½ 4	abundant	available (except P, 3–4 km away)	available (except P, 3–5 km away)	mixed; alien and native
M W	2 1½	1–3 km away	1–3 km away	M: 1–3 km away W: unavailable	alien
Bachelor males		abundant	available	available	mixed

their ribs no longer protruded, and they appeared fit and healthy.

Nevertheless, horses and other large mammals are rich sources of protein and therefore host numerous biting and bloodsucking insects, Diptera primarily. Up to 500 cc of blood may be lost daily from domestic ungulates (Tashiro and Schwardt 1953), and in Nevada a domestic horse death resulted from insect harassment after the animal ran into a fence (Webb and Welles 1924). Insect pests have also caused nursing to be interrupted in wild ungulates (Espmark and Langvatn 1979; Kelsall 1968). Among Great Basin horses I have observed bleeding from sores opened by insects.

In the Granite Range the most damaging biting flies are horseflies (*Tabanus aegrotus* and *T. atratus*) and deerflies (*Chrysops furcata* and *C. fulvaster*). Females of these fly species require blood to develop their eggs which are deposited in wet meadows. The flies emerge in late spring or early summer, and their activity is influenced greatly by vegetation and daily weather patterns (Hughes, Duncan, and Dawson 1981); activity also increases with temperature and humidity but not wind.

Since the days of early naturalists (e.g., Seton 1909) it has been known that animals behave in ways that optimize their resources. For instance, meadows represent important feeding areas for horses, but they are also used by biting flies. If insect harassment is a factor affecting summer habitat use, bands should feed in meadows during cool weather, when insect activity is low (Hughes, Duncan, and Dawson 1981), and then move to other areas for resting. Conversely, if insect activity is unimportant to horses, then times at which horses use various areas should not correspond to insect activity.

The frequency with which flies alight on horses could not be measured directly because being close enough to count flies would have disturbed horses. However, since insect activity and tail swishing are correlated (Hughes and Duncan, as cited in Duncan and Vigne 1979), tail swishing was used as a measure of insect abundance. The horses' response to insects was monitored by examining feeding and resting times in relation to six high-altitude summer areas: meadows, shrublands on level planes, shrublands on the lower third of slopes, shrublands on the upper third of slopes, ridgecrests, and remnant snow patches (after Keiper and Berger 1982). At this time of the year, thermal gradients create strong afternoon winds that are strongest along ridgetops.

Horses differed in their choice of resting and feeding areas throughout the day. Resting began primarily in mid- or late morning and most often occurred adjacent to or in snow, along ridgecrests, and near the tops of slopes [14]. Of sites used, snow patches were preferred, being selected more often than expected based on their limited distribution; these were followed next by ridgecrests [15].

These data suggest that horses minimized alighting insects by feeding early in the day (when most tabanid activity was low) and seeking refuge on ridgelines and near snow patches. These areas are likely to be windy or cool, and thus the horses would have less insect harassment. Similar findings have been reported for Camargue horses (Hughes, Duncan, and Dawson, 1981) and reindeer, which sought sandy patches (Helle and Aspi 1984). In contrast to Granite horses, those on Assateague Island rest in bays (Ford and Keiper 1979; Keiper and Berger 1982). The above data do not rule out the possibility that individuals optimized movements and habitat use to minimize thermoregulatory stresses, as Belovsky (1981) found for moose and as has been intimated for other species (Huey and Slatkin 1976; Moen 1973). Since insect activity and summer daily temperatures are correlated, it seems reasonable that both factors may influence choices for refuge.

4.8   HOME-RANGE QUALITY

Probably the most essential resource in a horse's home range is food supply, although shelter, water, and other factors are also important. Yet determining how various home-range components affect individual breeding performances has not been easy, making it more difficult to define home-range quality. Not only can food sources vary in protein, carbohydrates, and other properties that are influenced by a plant's stage of growth (Klein 1962; Staines and Crisp 1978), but individuals may differ in their assimilation abilities. Thus, a question that has important consequences for understanding relationships between horses and their habitats is: Does the use of dissimilar food resources by individuals produce differing reproductive performances when other factors are equal? If the answer is no, then one cannot rely on statements concerning the importance of differential resource use. Fortunately, the answer is yes. Animal scientists have experimentally verified that variations in diet quality affect growth, metabolic, and breeding performances (Arnold and Birrel 1977; Dyrmundsson 1973; Butterworth and Blore 1969; Gunn 1972, 1977). And, while the influences of confounding variables in the field have been difficult to minimize, careful empirical study has demonstrated that habitat quality affects individual reproductive performances in mammals (Clutton-Brock, Guinness, and Albon 1982), birds (Moss, Watson, and Parr 1975), and insects (Whitham 1980). Thus, differences among the home ranges of horses should influence reproduction if areas differ in quality.

I judged home-range quality by ranking the relative value of food sites found within them, as described in section 4.3 and in detail in Appendix 4. Briefly, the thirty-four microhabitats outlined earlier were scored according to their richness in food plants. I reasoned that home ranges containing a higher proportion of tightly clumped grasses that were high in potential food value should be of superior quality (e.g., more important) than those lacking such characteristics. The top third of these areas were then designated "high quality," the bottom third "low quality," and those in between "medium quality." Other constituents of home ranges, such as proximity to water and amount of shelter, were not included in the formal ratings of quality.

4.9   Intrapopulation Differences in Home-Range Ecology

So far, phenomena concerning home-range sizes, refuges, movements, etc., have been described at the population level. However, horse populations are composed of bands, and bands of individuals. These differ from one another in how they use their microenvironments. Variation occurs in the degree of core-area overlap. Most bands migrate vertically but some do not. What factors cause such differences and how are they related to home-range ecology and breeding success?

Resources and Home-Range Size

The ecological area used by a species is universally related to its metabolism, biomass, and trophic level (Eisenberg 1981). Since food requirements are proportional to biomass (McNab 1963), large bands should occupy greater home ranges than smaller ones, providing that food is of equivalent value and distributed evenly. For Granite horses, this prediction was supported; home-range sizes increased with band sizes on fall-winter-spring ranges (fig. 4.7) [16]. At summer sites this relationship was obscured, possibly because larger bands occupied meadows more often than smaller ones.

Although band size and home-range size were correlated in Granite Basin, such relationships are often more complex because vegetation is neither distributed nor used evenly in many areas. For

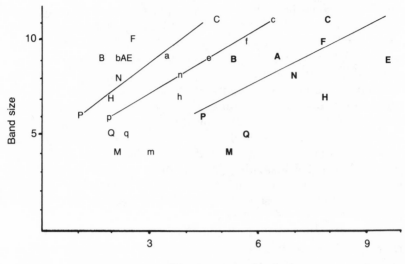

Fig. 4.7 Fall-winter-spring home-range and band sizes (letters). Home ranges calculated for 50% (capital letters), 75% (lower-case letters), and 90% (bold capitals) frequency-use polygons. Only yearlings or older used for band sizes.

example, in Assateague Island horses, Zervanos and Keiper (1979) found that primary plant productivity, rather than size of areas of use, correlated better with band size. It is not uncommon that intraspecific variation in home-range size occurs for species that occupy environments differing widely in ecological conditions (Berger 1979b; Clutton-Brock 1977; Fisler 1965).

Home-Range Locations and Quality

Accessibility to regions containing native grasses, shelter, meadows, and water differed among bands as a consequence of their home-range locations. Almost 33% of the population had no meadows within their respective core areas; that of band P lacked shrub- and grasslands, M had relatively few junipers or sheltered sites, and W fed mainly on alien grasses. Other bands (e.g., B, E, and F) commonly consumed native grasses such as crested and bluebunch wheatgrass, Idaho fescue, Sandberg's bluegrass, or needle-and-thread grass. Such bands also had easy access to meadows and water located within or near their core areas. The availability of shelter, water, meadows, and different species of grasses varied among bands. Bands whose core areas were located principally within the center of Granite Basin traveled relatively shorter distances to feed in meadows than bands (e.g., P, M, or W) that were peripherally located. Table 4.4 summarizes the major differences in core-area resources found among Granite Basin bands.

If food resources differed in value and were used in varying amounts, then differences among individuals should be reflected in parameters associated with energy balance (and, ultimately, reproductive success). These might include body weight, growth rate, suckling rate, age at puberty, or offspring production, since all are influenced directly by nutrition. To determine the degree that resource use varied among bands, the relative frequencies that each band used the microhabitats delineated earlier (sec. 4.3) were examined for individual bands. Meadow usage at low altitudes was evaluated separately since only three meadows existed and absolute use (e.g., total time in hours) could be recorded. Meadows were easily viewed from base camp (they were about 1 km away). Band-specific resource-use values were then plotted against the number of foals produced per female during the *following* year (fig. 4.8). Only data for females that had been sexually mature for at least a year and that had remained in the band for about a year were included. This removed the effect of band instability, which reduces fecundity (Berger 1983b). My concern was to investigate whether there was a relationship between home-range use and breeding success; other factors are also crucial to reproduction and are considered later.

Breeding Success and Home-Range Quality

At summer altitudes, no patterns of resource use were correlated with breeding success, possibly because (1) summer ranges were used for relatively short periods of time and thus had little effect; (2) categories of food resource patches were not measured at the resolution needed to detect differences; or (3) quality differences among areas were small.

However, on fall-winter-spring ranges female breeding success was affected by how long (e.g., the percentage of total time) individuals fed in the four sites that received the highest ranking for potential food value. Mares from bands B, E, and F had better breeding success than did mares from bands that fed for relatively less time in these four sites (fig. 4.8). Overall, female breeding success was correlated with the percentage of food-patch use only when the sites contained (1) the four highest quality rankings (the correlation was positive; $p<0.01$), and (2) the four lowest quality rankings (e.g., a negative correlation; $p<0.02$) [17]. The amount of time spent feeding in intermediately ranked areas was not useful in predicting an animal's subsequent breeding performance.

Besides the above relationships in resource use and foal production, the amount of absolute time spent feeding in meadows was a good predictor of breeding success. This is indicated by the high breeding performances of C and E females that used meadows the most, while M, H, and Q females had relatively poor breeding success and used meadows considerably less (fig. 4.8) [18]. Meadow use was also related to the percentage of time spent feeding in the four highest ranked feeding areas [19].

Meadows were of nutritional value to horses. In Granite Basin they were the result of nearby springs, which provided high year-round soil moisture; thus the vegetation remained greener longer than in other areas. In the nearby Sierra Nevada Range, meadow

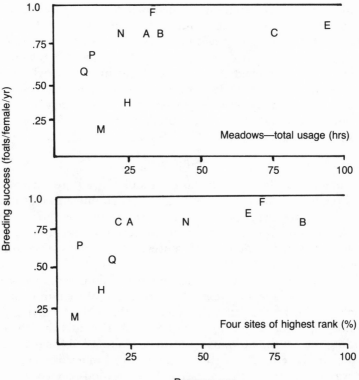

FIG. 4.8   Average adult female breeding success and use of feeding sites (meadows and four sites of highest food ranking) on low-altitude ranges. Letters refer to bands.

species such as bent grass and rushes contain protein longer and maintain higher phosphorous levels than plants found in drier soils (Wehausen 1980); this should also be true for Granite Basin meadows.

While meadow use predicted female foaling success (fig. 4.8), a few individuals did not conform to this pattern. For example, some mares in bands Q and H consistently produced foals but used meadows less than 4% of their total feeding time, while more fecund females (e.g., P) used them less than 0.5% of their total feeding time.

The apparent contradiction between meadow usage and breeding success in a few female exceptions may occur because the exploitation of home ranges depends on numerous factors. There may not be a single "best" solution to the problem of finding the most nutritious diet. The most successful animals in successive years did not maximize use of only one feeding area, but instead they used combinations of resource patches in different regions. Band B (fig. 4.8) had the greatest proportional use of high-quality feeding areas, yet two females experienced abortions in 1982 and its breeding success was not the highest of all bands. Members of B fed in meadows less than those from some bands that had consistently higher offspring production. This finding suggests that the use of varied feeding areas may be the optimal feature. Although breeding success for the population was correlated with feeding in high-quality areas (fig. 4.8), food in itself was not the only factor of importance.

The location of fall-winter-spring home ranges and use of habitats at different altitudes also affected breeding success. Bands such as M, which infrequently used winter shelter during severe storms (fig. 4.5), produced on the average only 0.2 offspring per female per year—the lowest of all bands. Also, females that failed to migrate averaged only 0.28 foals per yr, while those that migrated were more than three times as successful [20].

The above data indicate that numerous features of home ranges influenced breeding success. Bands whose home ranges contained meadows, shelter, water, and relatively better feeding areas produced more offspring per adult female than bands whose home ranges lacked either shelter, or good feeding sites, or some combination thereof. Numerous other factors also modify reproductive success (e.g., age, sociality, etc.). These factors and reasons why individuals live in areas that differ in home-range quality are considered subsequently (chaps. 7 and 9).

4.10   COMPARISONS WITH OTHER EQUIDS

Both feral and native equids occur in diverse areas on several continents. Since environments often differ in resources and population densities, neither populations nor species might be expected to use habitats similarly. Plain's zebras occur at high densities on expansive tropical grasslands (Sinclair and Norton-Griffiths 1982), while they occur at low densities in more xeric areas (Smuts 1975b), as do feral asses (Woodward 1979). Desert-dwelling horses and asses (Moehlman 1974) migrate altitudinally when mountains are available. Most equids are facultative grazers, but asses in Death Valley are browsers (Norment and Douglas 1977). Because mountains, deserts, grasslands, and islands differ climatologically and in numerous ecological properties, the appropriateness of broad comparisons of land use between American feral equids and African equids is questionable. Asiatic equids would make better sources for comparison since they live in a variety of temperate ecosystems, but reliable information is sparse.

Among North American wild horse populations, Granite horses appear typical in most respects based on the few reports of year-round ranging patterns. Like other Great Basin populations, they migrate altitudinally and alter feeding patterns seasonally. Unlike island populations which have smaller areas of use and (generally) higher densities (Rubenstein 1981; Welsh 1975; Keiper, Moss, and Zervanos 1980), Granite horses exploit larger regions, due in part to their expansive summer ranges. Granite animals appear somewhat unique since a majority of bands use a single wintering area, but additional study of other populations during the winter would be needed to determine how unusual this may be. The Granite population has responded predictably to increasing population densities by ranging more widely (chap. 10)—options unavailable to horses at carrying capacity that live on islands.

4.11   SUMMARY

1. The study site was divided into seven cover types with thirty-four microhabitats that differed in underlying vegetation. These were ranked according to the size of possible food patches and the potential nutritional value of each. The top third were designated as high quality, the bottom third as low quality, and intermediately ranked areas as medium. Of the cover types, shrubland and grassland areas were used the most. Microhabitats within the cover types differed in quality and their use varied.

2. Horse home ranges varied in size, and differences were attributed to band size, seasons of use, and the presence or absence of females. Bands had smaller home ranges than bachelors, and among bachelors, older males covered greater areas than younger ones. For all groups, winter ranges were smaller than summer ranges, and daytime movements were about three to four times as great as nocturnal ones.

3. Most horses migrated vertically to higher elevations during the late spring, returning to lower altitudes in the fall after snowfalls. A few bands never shifted to high altitudes, and they experienced relatively lower rates of breeding success.

4. Winter and summer movements reflected patterns of habitat use designed to minimize discomfort. As the intensity of winter storms increased, horses sought shelter in ravines and in juniper forests. During the summer when insect pests increased, horses fed in meadows early in the day when it was cool (and insects were not as active) and rested in or adjacent to snow patches and on windy ridgelines as the day progressed.

5. Bands differed in their home-range ecology. Those that fed in high-quality areas experienced greater breeding success than bands that used them proportionately less. Positive relationships existed among time spent feeding in high-quality sites, meadows, and female foal production.

6. Differences in regional habitat features must be considered if valid patterns of species or population land use are to be deduced. Patterns detected among Granite Range horses appear typical of Great Basin wild horses, while some populations on true islands may be more restricted in their movements.

Statistical Tests

1. Comparison of observed versus expected values of habitat use. Chi square goodness-of-fit test: $X^2 = 42,956$, $df = 6$, $p < 0.001$.

2. Comparison of home-range sizes of (a) 50%, (b) 75%, and (c) 90% frequency-use polygons among different social groupings (bands, and young and old bachelors) at low- and high-altitude ranges.

Low Altitudes
(a) One-way analysis of variance: $F_{2,13} = 4.31$, $p < 0.05$.
(b) One-way analysis of variance: $F_{2,13} = 37.28$, $p < 0.001$.
(c) One-way analysis of variance: $F_{2,13} = 16.02$, $p < 0.001$.

High Altitudes
(a) One-way analysis of variance: $F_{2,10} = 12.90$, $p < 0.005$.
(b) One-way analysis of variance: $F_{2,10} = 4.10$, $p < 0.05$.

(c) One-way analysis of variance: $F_{2,10} = 2.48$, $0.01 < p < 0.001$.
3. Comparison of fidelity in bachelor males ($N=26$) and bachelors that later obtained harems ($N=5$).
Chi square test with Yates correction for small samples:
    $X^2 = 90.07$, $df = 1$, $p < 0.001$.
4. Comparison of percentage of core-area overlap among bands between summer ($N=10$) and fall-winter-spring ranges ($N=8$) (1982 data).
Analysis of percentage differences with arcsine transformation:
    $z = 3.06$, $p < 0.002$.
5. Comparison of day and night band movements. Data for each year treated independently (minimum values indicated).
Wilcoxin matched-pairs test:
    Winter: $T = 6.5$, $N = 17$, $p < 0.001$.
    Spring: $T = 4$, $N = 35$, $p < 0.001$.
    Summer: $T = 6$, $N = 17$, $p < 0.001$.
    Fall: $T = 2.5$, $N = 9$, $p < 0.02$.
6. Comparison of the effects of season and year (1980–82) on day and night movements.
Analysis of variance:
    Day: $F_{3,95} = 7.71$, $p < 0.01$.
    Night: $F_{3,95} = .15$, NS.
7. Comparison of day and night movements between bachelors and bands.
Mann-Whitney U test:
    Day: $z = 2.70$, $N = 57$, $p < 0.01$.
    Night: $z = 3.35$, $N = 52$, $p < 0.001$.
8. Comparison of day and night movements between young and old bachelors.
Mann-Whitney U test:
    Day: $U = 13$, $n_1 = 7$, $n_2 = 6$, $p < 0.02$.
    Night: $U = 4$, $n_1 = 3$, $n_2 = 5$, $0.05 < p < 0.06$.
9. Comparison of variation between day and night movements of all groups.
F-Max test: $F = 4.81$, $df = 52$, $p < 0.001$.
10. Comparison of mean daily band movements (a) on days of birth ($N=35$) and those following it ($N=49$), and (b) those of primiparous ($N=9$) and multiparous ($N=26$) females.
Student's t test:
    (a) $t = 1.39$, $df = 83$, NS.
    (b) $t = 3.02$, $df = 33$, $p < 0.01$.
11. Correlation between mean home-range size and daily move-

ments of bands and bachelors at high- and low-altitude sites (data treated independently for young and old males).
Spearman rank correlation coefficient: $r_s = .94$, $N = 6$, $p < 0.02$.

12. Comparison of the number of bands at high and low altitudes in the fall before and a week after snowstorms (1980–82).
G test: $G = 15.91$, $df = 1$, $p < 0.001$.

13. Correlation between frequency of band movements (means for two temperature ranges within each index for each band were used) in exposed habitats and wind chill categories.
Pearson product-moment correlation coefficient: $r = -.83$, $df = 46$, $p < 0.001$, $Y = -12.37X + 109.37$.

14. Comparison of resting and feeding during 4 hr bouts ($N = 74$) in 6 habitats (see text).
G test: $G = 216.39$, $df = 5$, $p < 0.001$.

15. Comparison between use and availability of snow patches and ridgecrests.
G test: $G = 3944$, $df = 1$, $p < 0.001$.

16. Regression of band size on frequency-use polygons of (a) 50% areas, (b) 75% areas, and (c) 90% areas (1982 data).
Pearson product-moment correlation coefficient:
(a) $r = .69$, $df = 8$, $p < 0.05$, $Y = 4.54X + 1.45$.
(b) $r = .72$, $df = 8$, $p < 0.02$, $Y = 3.76X + 1.09$.
(c) $r = .59$, $df = 8$, $.10 < p < 0.05$.

17. Correlation between foal production in a given year by adult females and percentage frequencies that they used: (a) 4 high FQI areas and (b) 4 low FQI areas in the previous year (1980–83; female reproductive performance analyzed individually for each year, e.g., a foal is either produced or it is not; $N = 70$); (c) foal production averaged for each band and compared with average use per band of 4 highest FQI areas for the study duration.
(a) Point biserial correlation: $r_{pb} = .33$, $df = 68$, $t = 2.91$, $p < 0.01$.
(b) Point biserial correlation: $r_{pb} = -.29$, $df = 68$, $t = 2.50$, $p < 0.02$.
(c) Kendal rank correlation: $tau = .84$, $df = 8$, $z = 3.13$, $p < 0.002$.

18. Correlation between foal production in 1981 and female use of low-altitude meadows in the prior spring, winter, and fall (data used for this year since every month except February was spent at the study site).
Kendall rank correlation: $tau = .69$, $df = 8$, $z = 2.59$, $p < 0.01$.

19. Correlation between 1980 use of meadows and percentage frequency use of high-quality feeding areas.
Kendall rank correlation: $tau = .48$, $df = 8$, $z = 1.89$, $p < 0.059$.

20. Comparison of foals produced between bands that migrated to summer ranges and those that remained at low altitudes (1979–83). $N=70$.
   G test: $G=8.16$, $df=1$, $p<0.01$.

5 Population Features

For everything there is a season. . . . a time to be born, and a time to die.

Ecclesiastes 3:1–3

5.1 INTRODUCTION

Wild horses are similar in their basic biology to domestic horses except for one important difference: reproductive opportunities are limited not by humans but by natural events. Although feral horses live without food provisioning, constructed shelters, or medical attention, they reproduce and survive well. Some populations often have higher reproductive rates than their domestic conspecifics, and the rates of increase in these populations regularly surpass those of many native ungulates. This chapter considers the reasons for these rates by focusing on aspects of horse demography. It also suggests why females outlive males and describes how population size affects reproduction and emigration.

5.2 CHANGES IN GRANITE RANGE POPULATION SIZE
History

Earliest recollections of cowboys who lived in proximity to the Granite Range during the 1920s placed the population size at around forty to sixty animals. I attempted to determine on what basis these figures were claimed, but my success was minimal. And, although I accept the premise that horses have lived for a long time in the Granites, I remain dubious about the accuracy of any early estimates. The first quantitative information available for Granite horses were aerial censuses conducted by Nevada Division of Wildlife (NDOW) personnel during the early and mid-1970s. Aerial censuses offer reasonable estimates of horse population sizes in treeless terrain (National Research Council 1982) but the goal of NDOW flights in our area was to survey native ungulate abundance and distribution. Horses were recorded when observed (M.

Hess, Nevada Division of Wildlife, personal communication). As a result, I include these data (fig. 5.1) only to offer an idea of what the population size may have been like at that time. These data were not used in detailed measures of rates of increase since they were not systematic estimates.

Rates of Increase

During the early and mid-1970s the Granite population appeared relatively stable (fig. 5.1). In 1979 all animals at the study site were identified, and thereafter population size was known rather than estimated. Over the five-year period from 1979 until December 1983, the population increased from 58 to 149 animals, an increase greater than two and a half times (157%) the original absolute population. Early in the fourth year of study the population doubled. The finite rate of increase, which is the ratio of change in population size per unit time, averaged 31% per year over the study period. This figure, although based on absolute numbers, is only an

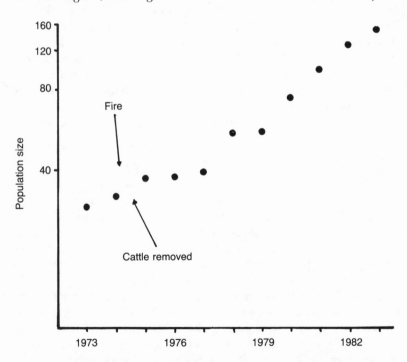

FIG. 5.1 Changes in the size of the Granite Range study population. Numbers refer to the population at the end of the year, while the arrows indicate when the fire occurred and the cattle were removed.

approximation because as the population grows a greater proportion of young animals is recruited. Only when the age structure stabilizes do rates of increase approximate growth over a several-year period (Wilson and Bossert 1971; Caughley 1977). When the Granite Range data are converted to an exponential rate of increase using the differential growth equation, $N=N_0 e^{rt}$, where N is the total population size, N_0 is the initial size, e is the constant for the base of natural logs, r is the exponential rate of increase, and t is time in years, the value for r is 18.8. Due to this rapid growth, the population was composed primarily of young animals. At the study's end 54% (81/149) of the horses were two years or less in age, while only 7% were older than fourteen years.

Causes of Increase

Like many other feral horse populations in the United States, Granite horse numbers have increased. Causes are numerous, but they can be divided into two general categories: human and biological factors.

The major influence of humans upon horses occurred through the passage of the Wild and Free-Roaming Horse and Burro Act in 1971. This law assured federal protection of feral equids and made the control or harvesting of them illegal. It resulted in a (presumed) cessation of culling (e.g., by cowboys or commercial food processors) of herds. With few natural predators and no human control, populations have expanded in the last dozen or so years (National Research Council 1980, 1982).

In the Granite Range, the scenario of population increases is presumed to have occurred as follows. In the early 1970s the population changed little, probably as a result of limited grass due to its being eaten by cattle. According to conversations with ranchers and government officials, cattle were grazed both legally and illegally prior to and during that time. At least one rancher (Cliff Williams, Sr.) recalls when he and others tried to "catch those damn mustangs" before the protection act was passed. Therefore, the possibility exists that some human control was practiced in the Granite Range prior to the inception of my study. In adjacent regions horses shot by poachers have been found, but I discovered none nor was any evidence of shooting found in the skulls or skeletons that I located.

After the imposition of federal protection, biologically related factors were more likely to influence horse demography. In the Granite Range, a lightning fire burned several thousand hectares in 1974. Because sagebrush and other shrubby species were burned, a series of successional communities dominated by grasses began. In 1975 the federal government imposed a moratorium on cattle grazing in the Granite Range, leaving horses free to forage in the absence of large grazing competitors. The population increased rapidly in the late 1970s and early 1980s. However, it will be impossible to determine whether the effects of the lightning fire or the removal of cattle was responsible for the large increase of horses. Beginning in 1983, cattle reintroductions were sanctioned by the Bureau of Land Management. By summer, cattle were finding their way to the top of the Granites. This was unfortunate because it removed a unique and essential opportunity to evaluate how, without the burdensome effects of cattle, intraspecific interactions among horses influence population levels.

Comparisons with Other Feral Horse Populations

Until very recently little empirical data were available on population increases in feral horses. Prior population projections (e.g., Conley 1979; Wolfe 1980, 1982; National Research Council 1980) were controversial and based either on information derived from domestic horses on western ranges or on assumptions concerning age-specific fecundity schedules, sex-ratio parity, age at first breeding, and adult and infant mortality rates. The major source of controversy involved the supposition that feral horses, with only minimal food and exposure to inclement weather, could not possibly experience higher reproductive rates than those normally found in domestic horses. Nevertheless, as indicated below, the proportion of feral mares that produce young often exceeds the proportion found in domestic ones. For instance, of 6,261 Thoroughbred mares in South Africa, 53.9% had young (General Studbook of South Africa 1981), whereas on Assateague and Sable islands 57.1% and 59.6% of the adult females produced foals (Keiper and Houpt 1984; Welsh 1975).

Census work over several years in the northwestern Great Basin (Beatty's Butte and Jackie's Butte areas of eastern Oregon) has supported the notion that reproduction in feral horses in the American West can also exceed that of domestic ones. In populations from each of these two areas, Eberhardt, Majorowicz, and Wilcox (1982) reported rates of increase of approximately 20% annually. The data on rates of increase from eastern Oregon and the Granite Range indicate that some populations experience rapid growth, a condition that occurs only when foaling rates are high and adult mortality is low.

However, not all feral horse populations grow as rapidly. On Sable Island, herds had fluctuated between 133 and 306 animals from 1961 to 1973, and rates of increase have generally been lower there than in the Great Basin (Welsh 1975). Mortality had been greater and juvenile recruitment poorer on this island. Different environments impose varying costs to individuals, and these will govern rates of reproduction. Until additional and more accurate data are available on horses from contrasting environments or even from the same areas but under different demographic conditions, it will remain difficult to understand causes of population change.

5.3   FECUNDITY

Granite Range horses may bear their first foals at two years and continue to do so until at least twenty-two years. Since the gestation period of horses averages more than eleven months, some females became pregnant as yearlings. About 37% of the two-year-olds and 40% of the three-year-olds produced foals, while females four years and older were more successful at producing foals (fig. 5.2). Individual variation occurred on a year-to-year basis, but for the most part, females between five to seventeen years of age enjoyed the greatest success in foal production (fig. 5.2). At least 83% of

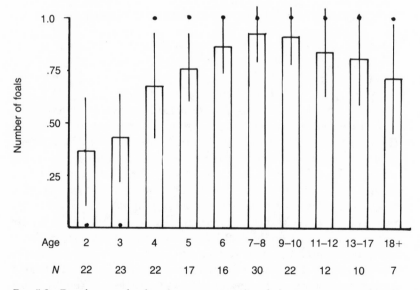

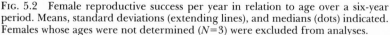

Fig. 5.2   Female reproductive success per year in relation to age over a six-year period. Means, standard deviations (extending lines), and medians (dots) indicated. Females whose ages were not determined ($N=3$) were excluded from analyses.

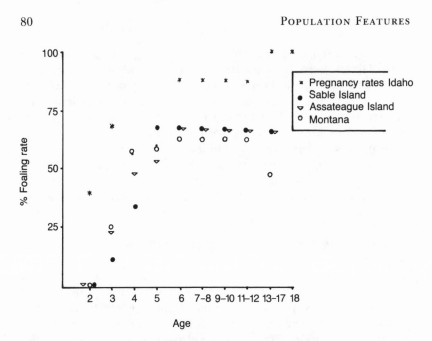

FIG. 5.3   Age-specific variation in foal production (expressed as foals per mare per year) in three horse populations and pregnancy rates in a different (Idaho) sample. Sable and Assateague islands data are from Welsh 1975 and Keiper and Houpt 1984, respectively. The Montana sample was for free-ranging, but not feral, horses (from Speelman, Dawson, and Phillips 1943). Idaho data from Seal and Plotka 1983. Ages of the mares from island populations were known only to six years; I pooled the ages older than this and represented them as a constant.

females within this age cohort gave birth to four foals over a five-year period.

How do these data on foal production in Granite Range horses compare with what is known for other horse populations? In figure 5.3 data on age-specific foal production are summarized from three different areas: 905 free-ranging mares in eastern Montana (from Speelman, Dawson, and Phillips 1943), 240 feral horses from Sable Island (from Welsh 1975), and 164 feral horses from Assateague Island (from Keiper and Houpt 1984). Interpopulation comparisons are not strictly valid since the Montana horses were free ranging but not feral and the ages of mares from the island populations were known only up to five years (on Sable) or six years (on Assateague). Still, at least four patterns emerge concerning relationships between female age and the mean number of foals produced per year: (1) Two-year-olds did not produce foals except in the Granite Range. (2) In all populations three-year-olds produced foals, but the percentages varied from 11% to 25%. (3)

Females five years or older were more fecund than four-year-olds in all populations. Therefore, up until at least five years, reproduction was age graded. (4) Within-cohort rates in each of the three populations were lower than that found in Granite females. Reasons for interpopulation differences could be numerous—exposure to different foods, weather patterns, densities, or a host of other variables—and, due to the lack of controls, the effects of different variables are unknown.

Age-specific pregnancy rates are available from one feral horse population in the American West (the Challis region of Idaho), and these rates have also been indicated in figure 5.3. Of the 137 horses for which information was available (from Seal and Plotka 1983), pregnancy rates were fairly comparable to the data presented for Granite horses (fig. 5.2), but one important distinction must be borne in mind. Pregnancy rates are not the same as foaling rates. The former offers a look at the potential number of offspring that might be produced under optimal conditions. However, many ecological and social factors influence reproductive rates (chaps. 7 and 9), and, because females less than six months pregnant are more susceptible to some of these, not all pregnant females successfully raise offspring.

The Granite population experienced growth rates that exceeded those found in other populations. This appeared due to the lightning fire which, coupled with the removal of cattle, created a situation that maximized opportunities for grass consumption in, the absence of competitors. Additionally, the occupation of a mountainous environment with altitudinal stratification of habitats, reliable water sources, and reasonable shelters seemed to create opportunities that were favorable for reproduction and that might have been lacking in other environments.

5.4 MORTALITY

Mortality rates in horses are as low or lower than those found in other comparably sized native mammals. Of 120 foals born in the Granites, 10 (8%) did not live a year. Mortality among 64 yearlings was even lower, 3% (table 5.1), and for animals two years or older, an average of just over 3 per year (16 in all) perished. Based on the number that died divided by the sum alive each year, the average mortality rate of these older individuals over the study period was only 4.9%. Despite what appeared to me to be arduous winters, survival was high in all age cohorts. Still, various factors influenced mortality in age groups.

TABLE 5.1   Survival Rates (%) of Foals and Yearlings

	1979	1980	1981	1982	1983[a]
Foals	92% (12)	90% (20)	93% (28)	90% (31)	93% (29)
Yearlings	78% (9)	100% (11)	100% (18)	100% (26)	100% (28)

Notes: Percentages derived by dividing the number alive at winter's end by the number alive in the previous year. Sample size in parentheses.
[a]Survival as of late fall 1983.

Foals

As mentioned foal survival was high, averaging about 92% (table 5.1). Among 10 deaths, 70% occurred within a foal's first month of life. Of these 86% (6/7) of the foals were less than two days old. The other 3 foals died between eight to ten months of life. Several factors were attributed to these mortalities. First, maternal inexperience or related parameters (e.g., young age, small body size, light weight) could have been responsible, because 70% of the deaths were attributed to primiparous mothers. However, primiparity in itself was not an entirely satisfactory explanation because more than two-thirds of the primiparous mothers successfully reared their offspring. Also, 2 of the foal deaths attributed to first-time mothers did not occur shortly after birth. Instead, both mothers and their foals died in high-altitude winter snowstorms (see below). Thus, of deaths that occurred within the first month of life, 86% were attributed to first-time mothers, but the majority of primiparous mothers were likely to rear their offspring successfully.

Predation was a possible mortality factor, but its effects appeared insignificant. Though one foal was observed attacked and killed by a coyote, the day-old foal had not stood and its mother had left it. Healthy foals in the Granites were never bothered by predators (Berger and Rudman 1985).

The few data available on foal mortality from other populations indicate similar trends. In Wyoming's Red Desert, 14% and 8% of the foals born in two different years died by their first month of life (Boyd 1979). Over an eight-year period a figure of 14% was recorded on Assateague Island (Keiper and Houpt 1984); 6 out of 7 deaths were during the first three days of life (Keiper 1979). In studies that lasted less than a year, no foal mortality was observed in the Jicarilla area of northern New Mexico (Nelson 1980), and an 11% loss occurred in the Pryor Mountains of Montana (Feist and

McCullough 1975). On Sable Island mortality averaged 25% over a three-year period for foals up to four months of age (Welsh 1975).

Drought is another factor that affects foal survival. During drought conditions, costs of milk production increase (see Berger 1979b) and the availability of milk to foals would be expected to decrease. Not only would foals then be predisposed to indirect mortality risks but, because foals are weaker than larger conspecifics, they would be more susceptible to other drought-related risks. For instance, foals become mired in mud while following their mothers to drink (fig. 5.4). In the Owyhee Desert of north central Nevada, eight foals became stuck in the same quagmire (fig. 5.5), a muddy, drying waterhole, where they perished due to their inability to pull themselves out.

Yearlings

Only two yearlings in the Granite population died. Both deaths occurred in 1979 when the animals, along with their mothers, perished on windswept ridges at high altitudes (see below). Annual survival for yearlings was 78% in that year; thereafter it was 100%.

FIG. 5.4   Horses at a muddy quagmire in the Owyhee Desert (north central Great Basin). Note entrapped foal in the foreground. Photo courtesy Bureau of Land Management.

Fig. 5.5   Dead foals pulled from a quagmire in the Owyhee Desert. Photo courtesy
Bureau of Land Management.

Though survival was high among Granite yearlings, in many ungulates yearlings experience considerable mortality. For instance,
among African buffalo up to 48% may die before their second year
of life (Sinclair 1977). Causes of increased juvenile or subadult
mortality could be due to diminished maternal investment, emigration, predation, or other factors (see Jarman and Jarman 1973;
Ralls, Brownell, and Ballou 1980; Clutton-Brock, Guinness, and
Albon 1982). Younger horses, as in other mammals, would be exposed to greater heat loss during cold than larger conspecifics due
to their smaller size and increased surface/volume ratio. If other
factors were equal, yearling horses should be exposed to greater
mortality risks during severe winters.

Fragmentary evidence suggests that this may be so when conditions are extreme. For example, in the Buffalo Hills—an insular,
broken high plateau of lava flows about 12 km west of the Granite
Range—an estimated 300 horses died in the winter of 1977 (BLM,
unpub. data). In the three days I spent there in 1979, I located 41
skulls. Seven were of foals, 14 of yearlings, and 20 of adults. Because the proportion of different age classes in the population was
unknown before the die-off, it was not possible to determine
whether a disproportionate number of yearlings died. However, it
seems likely that more yearlings perished than would be expected
by chance. Even in rapidly expanding populations such as those in

the Granites, yearlings never comprised 41% (14/34) of the yearling and older population, as in the Buffalo Hills skull sample, and it appeared yearlings were more susceptible to death.

The above evidence only weakly supports the notion that small size was the most important factor; other variables might also render young animals liable to heightened mortality risks. For example, fawns and adult males, but not yearlings, suffered the greatest mortality of an estimated 6,900 pronghorn that died during an intense winter on the northern plains in Canada (Barrett 1982). While fawns succumbed to thermoregulatory stresses almost certainly imposed by their small size, adult males did not die due to size effects. More likely, as a result of debilitated condition due to rutting, adult males were more susceptible to greater winter attrition. Thus, due to factors that were operating on other classes, yearlings were not the most vulnerable group (see Barrett 1982). In many other ungulates, young and yearling males may be more susceptible to death than females because of differences in body reserves (Clutton-Brock, Guinness, and Albon 1982), but this is probably due to a complex of factors. A conclusion that yearling horses were more vulnerable than other groups due to the influence of size alone could be verified only with more refined comparative analyses of factors operating on other age and sex groups.

Adults

Sixteen horses two years or older died during the study. Since the composite population over this time period was 329, the mortality rate was 4.9%. Excluded from the sample were 3 foals who had almost attained yearling status. Two had died at eight to ten months of age on high-altitude ridgelines and next to their mothers. Their inclusion in the sample would have pushed the mortality rate to 5.4%. However, foal survival would then be higher since these individuals obviously could not be included in both categories simultaneously.

Most mortality (83%) was related to winter attrition; horses died from the debilitating combination of hypothermia and nutritional stress. Welsh (1975) arrived at a similar conclusion. The bodies of horses he found during Sable Island winters were emaciated, had little body fat, and lacked pathological signs on their internal body organs. Deaths also occurred during other seasons in the Granite Range. Three males died from fight-related injuries (chap. 7), and a multiparous female's early summer disappearance was unexplained.

High-Altitude Deaths

Deaths may be accentuated in the Granite Range due to entrapment by surprise snowstorms at high altitudes (Berger 1983c). In 1979 an entire band of six horses disappeared, as did three others from another band. Two years later, six skulls and skeletons, representative of the sex and age structure of the missing band, were located in proximity to one another on a high-altitude windswept ridge on the summer range at about 2,600 m (fig. 5.6). Portions of body hair, manes, and tails still remained, and they matched descriptions of some of the missing horses. One year later the three skulls and skeletons from the other band were discovered within 100 m of each other at about 2,500 m. The two disparate finds were separated by a couple of ridges about 250 m apart.

Why did the horses die at high altitudes? To address the question, some natural history background is needed on mountain-dwelling, Great Basin horses. In many populations horses migrate altitudinally each year to obtain richer and less desiccated grasses growing at higher altitudes. In the Granite Range most individuals moved from Granite Basin to high-elevation summer ranges where

FIG. 5.6 Skulls of individuals that were alive in 1979 (shown in fig. 6.7) but that died later in the year. The skulls were discovered in summer 1981. Black Rock Desert is to the east and in the background (top of photo). (From Berger 1983a. With permission of the *Journal of Zoology*, © 1983 by The Zoological Society of London.)

Fig. 5.7 Late summer view of high-altitude ridgelines (approx. 2,500 to 2,700 m) where collections of horse skeletons were found. Note lack of shelter and exposure to prevailing westerly winds. Buffalo Hills and Smoke Creek Desert are to the west in background.

they remained until fall, usually driven down by snows. Similar movements have been described verbally by residents familiar with wild horses in other Great Basin ranges. However, not all bands descend the mountains. I observed bands at 2,100 m, 2,470 m, and 2,560 m during December 1980 and January 1981, and above 2,100 m in January 1983. Since these were not subordinate bands, social factors could not explain why they remained on summer ranges even though it was winter. Although these bands may have had access to relatively rich grasses at higher altitudes in late summer or fall, by remaining at these lofty sites they also were more likely to encounter severe and unpredictable winter storms and cold as the seasons progressed.

Such bands died as the result of heavy snowstorms; similar deaths are likely to occur in other mountainous populations as well. In the winter of 1979–80 (when two Granite bands disappeared), each of several snowstorms deposited over 65 cm of snow at about 1,760 m. At high elevations and ridgelines, where the missing horses were found, cliffs are precipitous and no shelter exists (fig. 5.7), and snow accumulation would be much greater.

It is unlikely that these deaths represented isolated events for two reasons. First, in the winter of 1982–83 when numerous storms dropped over 65 cm of snow at 2,000 m, 4 more Granite horses died; only 1 horse perished at lower altitudes where less snow fell. Second, of 43 skeletons located so far, 31 (72%) were above 2,000 m and 28 (65%) were above 2,300 m. The rest were between 1,400 and 2,005 m. Because most horses spent less time at high altitudes and lower sites were searched longer, the disproportionate number of skeletons found at higher elevations corroborates the idea that unpredictably heavy snow accumulation is a principal mortality agent in the Granites (Berger 1983c). In the White Mountains, a massive fault-blocked range over 4,300 m high, a disproportionate number of horse skeletons have also been found at high altitudes (Merrick 1979).

Winter Deaths in Other Temperate Ungulates

Mortality through winter attrition is common in the life cycle of temperate ungulates, particularly those inhabiting ecosystems that receive heavy snow or extreme cold (Leader-Williams 1980). At irregular intervals, heavy winter snowfalls have accounted for large losses: approximately 80,000 saiga (40% of the Russian steppe population) in 1953–54 (Bannikov 1967); 6,900 pronghorns (48.5% of the population on twelve ranges in Alberta, Canada) in 1977–78 (Barrett 1982); and 5,900 caribou (99% of the St. Mathew Island population in the Bering Sea) in 1963–64 (Klein 1968). Based on records from the early nineteenth century, Robinette, Hancock, and Jones (1977, 12) offered accounts of winter effects on two Utah ungulates.

[*Bison.*] In 1849 . . . many buffalo had been present 15–20 years before. However, one winter an immense snowstorm piled the snow many feet deep in the valleys and almost eliminated the buffalo. Baker claimed that he did not see the sun for 35 days. He went on to say that snow-shoeing over the deep snow, he came onto many breathing holes . . . below which were live buffalo. The buffalo subsequently perished. . . .

[*Elk.*] The late W. O. Nelson of American Fork, Utah told Robinette that his grandfather . . . found so many elk skeletons—literally hundreds—in the canyon bottom that he used antlered skulls to build corrals and short drift fences. He believed that the elk perished during a very severe winter in the late 1820's or early 1830's, apparently the same winter when most of the buffalo died.

Large die-offs are infrequent but not unusual natural events. Most appear causally related to population density. Although adult mortality could not be related in a meaningful way to population density in the Granite Range, presumably due to the small sample,

in other ungulates death through winter attrition is relatively greater when dense populations experience cold winters (Grubb 1974a;
Welsh 1975; Klein 1968). Among tropical savanna ungulates, die-
offs appear more prevalent at high densities during the dry season
when food is in short supply (Sinclair 1977), a situation that seems
analogous to winter die-offs in temperate species.

5.5   ADULT SEX RATIOS IN FERAL AND NATIVE EQUIDS
Causes of Variation

The sex ratio (number of males per female) of adult horses in the
Granite Range was .76:1.0 ($N=81$), a difference that was not quite
significant when compared to the 1.30:1.0 birth sex ratio [1]. Assuming the unevenness in adult sex ratio is not due to chance
alone, what factors might explain this disparity? The use of different aging criteria is inadequate to account for sex differences as
adults because males and females averaged the same age when
judged as adults (sec. 8.2, 8.5). Also male emigration away from the
study area is not a satisfactory explanation because the insularity of
the Granite Range precludes movements to other ranges. It seems
probable that adult males suffered more mortality than adult
females. For example, of 42 skulls found (although 43 skeletons
were found, only 42 skulls were located), 19 were males and 11
were females (12 could not be identified by sex), but differences
were not significant [2], perhaps due to the small sample.

In other feral and native equids (Berger 1983a), artiodactyls
(Geist 1971; Sinclair 1977), and mammals in general (Trivers
1972), adult males are not as prevalent as females. This asymmetry
has been ascribed to several causes, including costs associated with
male reproductive competition, greater nutritional stress in males,
and greater male emigration (Estes 1969; Ralls, Brownell, and Ballou 1980; Clutton-Brock, Guinness, and Albon 1982). What evidence exists to support the hypothesis that male equids are more
likely to die than females, mostly as a result of intermale competition rather than other causes?

Confounding Influences

Predation, food shortages, or other factors, all of which may act
together, could easily obscure the effects of male competition and
render one sex more vulnerable to death than the other. For instance, greater predation on females occurs in Mountain and Common zebras (Tilson, von Blottnitz, and Henschel 1980; Kruuk
1972; Mitchell, Skenton, and Uys 1965); they may be the more

vulnerable sex because, unlike males, they lack predator-directed aggression (Kruuk 1972; Malcolm and van Lawick 1975). Also, depending upon the predator community, females may not be selected as often as males. Lions take either sex (Schaller 1972), whereas wild dogs or hyenas prey more on females.

Wild horses and their congenerics offer unusual opportunities to examine how both predation and intermale competition affect sex differences in mortality. This is possible because horses and other equids live in various ecological settings, some of which contain predators while others do not; also they live in societies where the intensity of competition among males varies. Thus, the relative influences that different variables have upon sex differences in mortality can be derived from populations where good census data are available.

Lack of Predator Effects

Female horses outnumbered males as adults in six of eight locations where observations lasted at least six months; the sexes were equal in one and males outnumbered females in the other (table 5.2). Female-biased sex ratios also occurred in feral burros and in Mountain zebras. Predation and uneven sex ratios at birth are inadequate explanations for these distorted sex ratios as adults because predators capable of influencing adult survival were lacking (human manipulations were not great) and birth sex ratios were at parity (table 8.1). Likewise, emigration can be dismissed as an alternative to mortality for the island (Assateague, Sable) and Granite Range populations (see table 5.2).

To investigate whether competition among males could explain differences in adult sex ratios, the intensity of such competition was compared with the ratios. Because males that are successful breeders may incur greater reproductive costs (Geist 1971; LeBoeuf 1974) and stallions defend harems year-round, an inverse relationship between populations with more intensive male-male competition and disparate adult sex ratios should occur. The only available and admittedly crude index of the intensity of intermale reproductive competition within a population was mean band size. Ideally, the socionomic sex ratio ("the number of adult females per adult male per breeding group," Clutton-Brock and Harvey 1977) should be used. Most authors did not specify socionomic sex ratios from their respective areas, so I assumed that their mean band sizes reflected the sum of adult females and a single stallion.

The correlation ($r = -.73$) between mean harem size (e.g., average band size minus one) and adult sex ratio was significant (fig. 5.8) [3]. When the five noninsular populations in which the inseparable effects of emigration and mortality were excluded, the correlation was even greater (r=−.95) [3]. This finding is indicative that either a greater monopolization of females results in a more disparate sex ratio or vice versa. Cause and effect will be inferred (below) from populations with no known emigration.

Effects of Predators

Because the variation of sex ratios in areas lacking predators was known (table 5.2), it was possible to infer how predation modified the preponderance of each sex in areas where there were predators. If predation had no effects or if its effects on each sex were similar, then adult males and females would occur in the same proportions as they did in areas lacking predators. But if one sex was more susceptible to predators than the other, sex ratios would be biased to a greater extent than those found in areas lacking predators. To determine the magnitude that predation and intermale competition affect equid sex ratios, data on Common zebras were

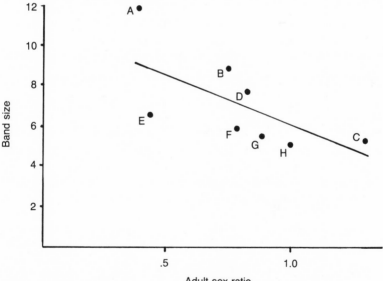

Fig. 5.8   Adult sex ratios (males per female) and mean band sizes for eight populations of North American wild horses: (A) Assateague Island; (B) Granite Range; (C) Sable Island; (D) Sundre (Canada); (E) Jicarilla; (F) Grand Canyon; (G) Stone Cabin Valley; (H) Pryor Mountains.

TABLE 5.2 Adult Native and Feral Equid Sex Ratios Expressed as Males per Female

Species and Location	Sex Ratio	Remarks	Predation Greater On	Source
	Predators Lacking			
Horses				
Grand Canyon	.79 (68)	5		Berger 1977 & unpublished
Assateague Is.	.37 (116)	3,5		Keiper 1979
Pryor Mts.	.54 (35)	4		Feist and McCullough 1975, 1976
Jicarilla	.45 (55)	2,4		Nelson 1980
Sable Is.	1.32 (211)[a,b,c]	1,5		Welsh 1975
Stone Cabin, Nevada	.89 (238)	4		Green and Green 1977
Sundre, Canada	.84 (107)	1,3		Salter and Hudson 1982
Asses				
Western Arizona	.75 (58)	4		Seegmiller 1977
Ossabau Is.	.89 (86)	3		McCort 1979
Mountain zebras				
Mountain Zebra National Park	.89 (103)[d]	4		Penzhorn 1975
	Predators Present			
			Hyenas	
Plain's zebras				
Serengeti (Tanzania)	—	1,5	females	Kruuk 1972
Ngorongoro (Tanzania)	—	1,5	females	Kruuk 1972
Mountain zebras (Namibia)	—	1,5	females	Tilson, von Blottnitz, and Henschel 1980

		Wild Dogs		
Plain's zebras				
Serengeti	—	1,5	females	Malcolm and van Lawick 1975
			Lions	
Plain's zebras				
Kruger National Park (So. Africa)				
Northern area	.66 (597)	1,5	males[e]	Smuts 1976[a]
Central, 1971	.76 (3327)	1,5	males[e]	Smuts 1976[a]
Central, 1976	.67 (919)	1,5	males[e]	Smuts 1976[a]
Pretoriuskop et al.	.74 (297)	1,5	males[e]	Smuts 1976[a]
Crocodile Bridge	.84 (370)	1,5	neither	Smuts 1976[a]
Kafue (Zambia)	—	1,4	females	Mitchell, Skenton and Uys 1965
Nairobi (Kenya)	.37/(?)	1,5	males	Rudnai 1974
Serengeti	—	1,5	neither	Schaller 1972

Notes: Symbol designations are as follows: (1) explicit statement concerning sex differences; (2) greater male emigration suggested; (3) past exploitation by humans; (4) extent of exploitation unknown; (5) little or no known exploitation. Numbers in the table in parentheses indicate sample sizes. Adapted from Berger 1983a.

[a] $\bar{X}$ life span of males = 5.85 yrs.
[b] $\bar{X}$ life span of females = 4.56 yrs.
[c] Based on last year of study.
[d] Population introduced with 11 animals.
[e] Based on fewer live males in the population and collection of skulls.
[f] Because males in the population are underrepresented in the population but preyed on as often as females, they are taken at a greater rate.

examined. I assumed that effects of male-male competition would operate similarly in both Common zebras and horses, since males of each species incur expenses associated with year-round mate defense (see sec. 7.5).

In South Africa's Kruger National Park (KNP), zebra mean band sizes and predation by lions vary both among populations and years (Smuts 1976a). Some of the differences found by Smuts are summarized in table 5.3; they permit an evaluation of some of the factors that modify adult sex ratios. Two lines of evidence support the idea that lions caused greater mortality among male zebras than would have occurred in their absence. First, in the Central area of KNP, mean band size decreased between 1971 and 1976 (table 5.3). This information suggests relatively less intense male-male competition because fewer adult males monopolized adult females. An increase toward a 1:1 sex ratio would be expected if predation affected each sex similarly. However, predation intensity increased, and the sex ratio changed from .76 adult males per adult female to .67:1.0 (table 5.3). Second, in subpopulations from the Southern area similar band sizes existed, yet there was a fivefold difference in predation intensity between areas. In this situation, the adult sex ratio was closer to parity in the area with lightest predation pressure (table 5.3) when compared to the subpopulation with greater predation pressure.

These data suggest that lions killed more adult male zebras when stallion-stallion competition was greater than would have been expected had each sex been preyed upon evenly. They do not, however, reveal whether lions preyed on males that competed for mates (e.g., stallions) or bachelors, or the extent to which they preyed on both.

TABLE 5.3 Zebra Sex Ratios, Mean Band Size, and Predation Intensity by Lions in Kruger National Park

Population Designation	Mean Band Size	Predation Intensity	Adult Sex Ratio
Central area, 1971	4.35 (332)	4.1	.76:1.00 (3327)
Central area, 1976	4.12 (106)	4.1[a]	.67:1.00 (919)
Southern area			
Pretoriuskop et al.	3.52 (123)	13.1	.74:1.00 (197)
Crocodile Bay	3.42 (172)	3.6	.84:1.00 (370)

Sources: Berger 1983a, with permission of the *Journal of Zoology,* © 1983 by The Zoological Society of London; Smuts 1976a.

Notes: Sample sizes in parentheses. Predation intensity is equivalent to #zebras killed by lions/#live zebras × 100.

[a]True value unknown, but estimated by Smuts to be greater.

Intermale Reproductive Competition

Where male costs outweigh those of females, the former should experience greater mortality (see Estes 1969; Ralls, Brownell, and Ballou 1980). The inverse correlation between mean band size and disparate adult sex ratios in wild horses (fig. 5.8) implies that male mortality increases with intermale competition but that cause and effect cannot be separated. It seems that greater male monopolization of females would be a cause of biased sex ratios, not an effect resulting from initial male mortality. This is because males incur wounds when competing for females, some die when trying to obtain females, and others emigrate into unfamiliar areas as a presumed result of searching for females. Reproductive effort in male equids includes the establishment and maintenance of territories in species (burros, Grevy's zebras) that live in arid environments or the year-round harem defense in horses and zebras of wetter regions (Klingel 1975). It appears that equid males fit the theoretical prediction that greater mortality among males is brought about by costs associated with intrasexual competition.

Female-Biased Mortality

Conditions occur where costs of female reproduction should outweigh those of males. In such situations, females rather than males should be more susceptible to mortality. Females might be exposed to greater mortality risks than males during extreme ambient temperatures or drought, since female gestation, and especially lactation, requires substantial energy expenditures under such conditions.

General support for the above idea in regard to ungulates stems from three studies. First, adult male horses lived longer and were more numerous on Sable Island, an area where winter weather influences mortality (Welsh 1975). Second, more gemsbok females died than males during a severe drought in the Namib Desert (Hamilton, Buskirk, and Buskirk 1977). In this case though, the relative abundance of the sexes prior to the drought was unknown, and female deaths may have been accelerated by social factors since males dominated them at waterholes. Third, more wildebeest females died than males during drought in East Africa, but the evidence was somewhat confusing because during the same drought more male than female hartebeest died (Hillman and Hillman 1977). It thus appears that under specified environmental conditions females may be more likely than males to die, but quan-

tifying in advance what these conditions may be has not proved
easy.

Predation and Intermale Competition:
Proximate and Ultimate Factors

In areas with predators it has already been shown that adult sex
ratios may not vary in accordance with the generally supposed pattern of greater male mortality. In zebras, this resulted from their
social system in which males and females responded differently to
predators; stallions attack hyenas and wild dogs and, consequently,
experience less predation than females (Kruuk 1972; Malcolm and
van Lawick 1975). However, to evaluate whether predation influences adult sex ratios requires additional data. It may be that where
predation on one sex is greater, such as in African buffalo (Schaller
1972), its effects upon adult sex ratios is not obvious (Sinclair
1977).

A bias against adult female zebras is equivocal when lion predation occurs, since it varies among areas (Rudnai 1974; Pienaar
1969). Schaller (1972) suspected that more zebra females in the
Serengeti died from disease or malnutrition than males and, therefore, that males were simply more available to lions due to their
greater numbers.

It could also follow that adult male zebras were more susceptible
to predation, not because they were more numerous per se but
because of effects stemming from intermale competition. If this
was true, adult males experiencing more intensive reproductive
pressures (e.g., those with larger harems) should be more vulnerable to lion predation. Greater sex ratio disparities in such populations would support this hypothesis, assuming that equal predation
intensity exists and that mean band size effects operate in zebras as
they do in feral horses.

Data (table 5.3) revealed that the proportion of adult male
zebras was lower than that based on expectations without predation. These findings agree well with those of Smuts (1976a) who
found that lion predation accentuated mortality among zebra
males. Predation was the proximate avenue through which more
male than female zebras met their death.

In this case the distinction between proximate and ultimate reasons for adult mortality creates a problem. Proximate events such
as increased parasite loads or food-related weaknesses might render animals more susceptible to death through predation or other
factors. Proximate causes of death can be confirmed by examina-

tion, but ultimate causes rely on inference. Consequently, death through disease, food shortage, or a combination of other factors could be detectable by examination; ultimate ones, such as male-male competition, could not. For instance, it could be argued that the correlation of mean harem sizes with adult sex ratios is an inevitable consequence of higher age-specific mortality in males rather than a result of direct intermale competition. This possibility is not testable from existing data, although it could be examined under carefully controlled conditions by comparing mortality rates in castrated (i.e., gelding) and intact (i.e., breeding) males. Data for two other mammals—humans and domestic cats (Hamilton and Mestler 1969; Hamilton, Hamilton, and Mestler 1969)—implicate catabolic androgens as factors contributing to mortality, since in both species castrated males outlived intact ones. Hence, proximate factors (e.g., hormones) may mediate increased mortality, but such products also arise as a result of natural selection operating on males.

5.6   EFFECTS OF POPULATION SIZE
Recruitment of Foals

In the Granite Range the proportion of potential mothers (e.g., those who had achieved puberty in the preceding year or were capable of bearing offspring) that produced foals varied from 54% to 66% among years. When this proportion is plotted against the number of yearlings and adults alive at the end of each year (fig. 5.9), it becomes evident that the relationship is not straightforward. Foal recruitment increased in the first two years of study, but it diminished thereafter with increasing population size. The trend over the last three years is suggestive of density-dependent effects on foaling rates in mares. When such effects tend to stabilize a population and proceed through a feedback system, regulation occurs (Krebs and Perrins 1978; Sinclair and Norton-Griffiths 1982).

The Granite data, however, are complicated by the effects of weather. In situations in which weather was constant for a period of years, density-dependent effects could be shown most strongly, but in the advent of erratic fluctuations, any relationship would be difficult to demonstrate. For instance, during 1980–81 relatively little snow remained on the ground in Granite Basin. Streams that were perennial in other years flowed only intermittently or not at all, and most of the high-altitude snowpack was melted before June. Even in January some bands were found above 2,000 m. Evidently, during the mild winter cold-related stress was minimal, and

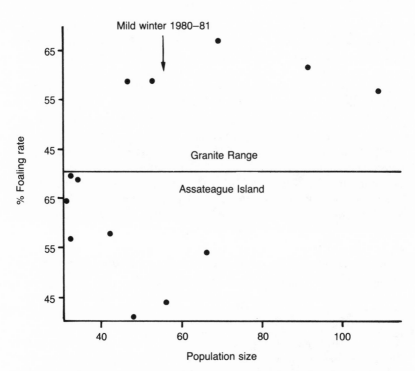

FIG. 5.9   Population size (yearlings and older) and the proportion of potentially breeding females (Granite Range) and adult females (Assateague Island) that produced foals. Data on Granite horses based on winter residents living within 4 km of Granite Basin. Assateague data calculated from Keiper and Houpt 1984. Arrow indicates the mild winter conditions that occurred from fall 1980 to spring 1981.

it resulted in a relatively high number of mares that produced foals in 1981, as indicated in fig. 5.9. During subsequent years winters were more severe. As mentioned in chapter 3, streams ran (almost year-round in the last two years), snow remained at higher altitudes into July (or August of 1983), and precipitation exceeded annual means by 50% to 80%. During these times more individuals were in poor condition and foal/mare ratios declined. The condition of individuals appeared to be affected by the interaction of the food supply with weather, as has been found in both tropical (Sinclair 1977) and temperate (Klein 1968; McCullough 1969; Grubb and Jewell 1974) ungulates. Although I suspect that changes in foal production were related to population density, the effects of weather in itself cannot be excluded (see Clutton-Brock and Albon 1982a).

At least two major reasons account for the lack of clear concordance expected between population density and recruitment. First, although the study spanned five years, the time period is short in terms of large, long-lived mammals. In species like elephants (Laws and Parker 1968) or horses, lag times in density-dependent effects may often be large. Recent data by Keiper and Houpt (1984) indicate that, over an eight-year period, productivity of Assateague Island mares declined with increasing population size (fig. 5.9). Still, the trend detected for Assateague horses may be a bit misleading because, unlike the data on Granite females, Keiper and Houpt counted females as adults only after they foaled or aborted at least once. Excluded from their analyses were young females that had obtained sexual maturity but had not yet foaled. Nevertheless, the inverse correlation between population size and offspring production [4] strongly suggests a density-dependent effect. A second reason why Granite data may have failed to show such a relationship could be related to the high-altitude, density-independent die-offs. In these cases subtle effects of density dependence could be masked by reductions of just a few individuals, since the overall sample was small.

Emigration Distances

Both males and females leave their natal bands within their first few years of life, and although they do not differ in the mean age at which this occurs (sec. 8.5), sex differences in emigration distances occur. Within the first year after leaving natal bands, male emigration distances exceeded those of females by more than six times (fig. 5.10). Whether males grow increasingly independent and enlarge their emigration distances even more during their next few years of life remains to be seen. In both 1981 and 1983 males that had departed natal bands two years earlier had not moved farther from Granite Basin than those males that had left their natal groups only a year earlier (see fig. 5.10).

Not only were there sex differences in emigration distances, but, with increasing population size, the distance moved by males from Granite Basin increased dramatically. Although some bachelors stayed in the Basin and others remained on the periphery, throughout the study period a total of thirteen males moved northward by distances that increased annually (fig. 5.10). Since different individuals were used in these annual measures, the increasing distances moved cannot be explained by supposing the same individuals simply increased their movements. Probably low stallion turnover rates and poor prospects for acquiring harems, coupled with the greater density of horses using Granite Basin, were responsible for these annual increases in emigration distances among males. Still, density alone could not be the sole cause for the observed movements. For although bachelor males ranged widely in their daily and seasonal movements, at least three bachelors were successful at securing domestic mares from a nearby ranch; similar situations in which wild stallions procured domestic mares were reported over 145 years ago on the pampas of South America (Azara 1838) and 215 years ago in Asia (Gmelin 1769 quoted in Zeuner 1963).

It appears that male emigration distances are related to the avoidance of what may be suboptimal conditions. These could be related either to the food supply itself or to opportunities for mate

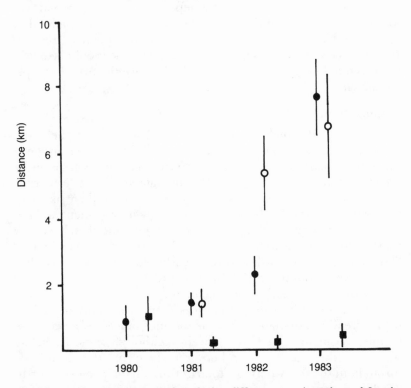

FIG. 5.10 Emigration distances (km) during different years in males and females within two years of dispersal from natal bands. Solid circles, males at one year past natal dispersal; open circles, males at two years past dispersal; squares, combined data for females at both one and two years dispersal. Means and standard errors of means indicated. Emigration distances measured as distances from northern edge of Granite Basin (1981, late summer; fall in other years).

acquisition. In either case it was evident that male movements were more affected by population size than were those of females (fig. 5.10). Clearly, as the population increases, new areas within the Granite Range will continue to be colonized. And, as explained earlier (chap. 4), it is through familiarity with formerly unused areas that males may later return to use such places with females.

Potential Density-Dependent Effects

Among the most obvious factors associated with changes in the size of the Granite population were foal recruitment and male emigration distances. Some of the most common effects of density dependence in other species are (1) increased juvenile mortality, (2) increased ages at sexual maturity, (3) decreased fecundity, and (4) increased adult mortality rates (Hanks 1981). Only the third effect was demonstrated in the Granite Range since fewer foals were recruited with increasing population size. This effect and others are imposed through the interactions of nutrition with population density; supporting evidence comes from deer (McCullough 1979), bighorn sheep (Geist 1971), Soay sheep (Grubb 1974a), caribou (Klein 1968; Leader-Williams 1980), warthogs (Cumming 1975), African elephants (Laws, Parker, and Johnstone 1975), and African buffalo (Sinclair 1977). Some of the most subtle effects of density yet discovered include changes in conception dates, suckling durations, and the timing of winter coats (Clutton-Brock, Guinness, and Albon 1982). Changes in social behavior have also been related to density. For instance, bighorn lambs raised in small groups tend not to develop the degree of complexity in behavioral repertoires found among lambs raised in larger groups (Berger 1979a, 1979b, 1980).

5.7 SUMMARY

1. The Granite Range population increased in size by more than two and a half times during the study period. This change was attributed to increased grass availability—the result of fire and the subsequent removal of cattle for a ten-year period. The exponential rate of increase (18.8) was similar to that reported in two other feral horse populations, both of which occur in the Great Basin. High rates of population growth occur only when adult mortality is low and foaling rates are high—conditions that were met by Granite Horses. Foal production among females began at two years of age and extended until at least twenty-two years.

2. Entrapment by mud and high-altitude winter snowstorms are mortality agents in Great Basin horses. About 83% of the Granite Range deaths were attributed to winter attrition, and more than 70% of the skeletons discovered were at high altitudes.

3. In horses and other equids, females usually outnumber males as adults. The hypothesis that such differences arise as a result of intermale competition for females (and not sex differential predation) was examined by comparing populations of horses, asses, and zebras in predator-free, predator-filled, and insular ecosystems. Most asymmetries in sex ratios were explained by the idea that competition among males leads to greater male mortality. Exceptions occurred and complications arose due to numerous variables.

4. Patterns of foal recruitment during the last three years of study, when population size was greatest, suggest density-dependent effects. Possible factors that obscured such effects over the entire study period included density-independent high-altitude deaths, annual fluctuations in weather, and perhaps an initially small population size.

5. Sex differences occurred in emigration distances. Males moved further from their natal ranges than females; for males a positive relationship between emigration distance and population size existed, but it was absent for females. Poor prospects for obtaining females seemed to be responsible for the greater emigration movements of males.

Statistical Tests

1. Comparison between birth sex ratios and adult sex ratios.
   Chi square test: $X^2=3.40$, $df=1$, $0.05<p<0.10$, $N=194$.

2. Comparison of sex ratios of skulls found.
   Chi square test: $X^2=2.13$, $df=1$, NS, $n=30$.

3. Correlation between mean harem size and adult sex ratios in (a) 8 populations of feral horses, and (b) only insular populations.
   Pearson product-moment correlation coefficient:
   (a) $r=-.73$, $df=6$, $p<0.05$, $y=-5.43X + 11.37$.
   (b) $r=-.95$, $df=1$, NS.

4. Correlation between population size and percentage of mares foaling in (a) Granite Range and (b) Assateague Island horses (from Keiper and Houpt 1984).
   Spearman rank correlation coefficient:
   (a) $r_s=.50$, $N=5$, NS.
   (b) $r_s=-.74$, $N=8$, $p<0.05$ (one-tailed test).

6 Reproduction and Ecology

In order to spend on one side, nature is forced to economise on the other.

Johann von Goethe

6.1 INTRODUCTION

Successful reproduction is based on trade-offs. For example, females that remain in poor habitats may have to feed longer than those in better areas to satisfy the requirements needed for gestation and, finally, for offspring production. An adequate food supply is usually the most essential ingredient for successful reproduction, but social behavior also plays an important role. Both food and behavior figure prominently in the lives of Granite horses. The ways in which these and other factors affect reproduction are the subject of this chapter. Specifically, I describe the time of year when foals are born and factors that modify these dates. Other aspects of seasonality and breeding are considered, including body condition, gestation lengths and estrous cycles, home ranges and puberty, and influences of reproduction upon foraging budgets.

6.2 SEASONS OF BIRTHS
Ungulate Parturition

The timing of births results from the costs and benefits associated with offspring production at varying periods of the year. In temperate ungulates, parturition is finely tuned to periods when mothers can convert food into milk for the least cost (see Berger 1979b) and the probability of inclement weather is low (Bunnell 1982). Consequently, where ungulates have broad geographical ranges and confront diverse ecological and climatic conditions, a temporal birth progression occurs from low-latitude deserts to mountains or higher latitudes (Geist 1971; Bunnell 1982). Intra- or interspecific variability in birth season results from numerous factors, including nutrition and vegetation phenology (Anderson 1979; Rutberg 1984; Sadleir 1969), predation pressure (Estes 1976), individual reproductive histories (Guinness, Gibson, and Clutton-Brock 1978), and photoperiod (Spinage 1973; Sadleir 1969).

The Granite Population

Under confined conditions and with accessibility to mates, domestic horses may give birth throughout the year. In the Granite Range births occurred year-round (fig. 6.1), although 75% of the foals were born in April and May and 85% from April through June. However, foals survived even when they were not born in the spring. A three-day-old female withstood a winter storm with winds in excess of 115 km/hr and ambient temperatures below −23°C. Births that deviated from the March–June (inclusive) period were attributable to both primiparous ($N=2$) and multiparous ($N=4$) females, two of which occurred following band changes late in the previous fall. The timing of births was more variable in new mothers, perhaps because at sexual maturity they fluctuate more in their estrous periods than multiparous females, as has been noted in domestic sheep (Dyrmundsson 1973).

In other wild horse populations variation in the timing of par-

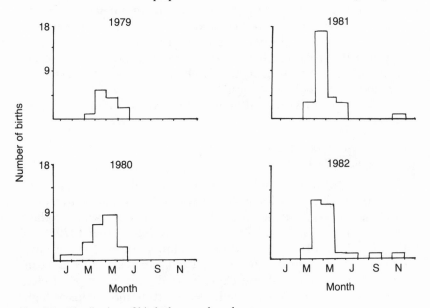

FIG. 6.1   Distribution of births by month and year.

turition has also been reported. On Sable Island, horses foal year-round, although a spring seasonal peak occurs (Welsh 1975). Work in Wyoming, New Mexico, and on Assateague Island also suggests seasonality (Boyd 1979; Nelson 1980; Keiper 1979), but without year-round detailed study, nonspring births would be difficult to detect, especially if some of the foals perished.

6.3   FACTORS INFLUENCING PARTURITION DATES

Parturition depends on ovulation and conception; the former is influenced by reaching a minimum plane of nutrition (Belonje and van Niekerk 1975). Birth and mating dates might be expected to be aligned closely each year since gestation in horses is about eleven and a half months and estrus normally follows in less than twelve days (Ginther 1979; Houpt and Wolski 1982). But what factors affect dates of mating? In addition to the obvious availability of mates, seasonal effects, female receptivity, and male takeovers are important.

Postpartum Estrous Cycles

Domestic mares usually experience estrus a short time after birth, a phenomenon referred to as postpartum estrous. Estrus can be identified when mares lift their tails regularly, urinate frequently, and evert their clitorises (Ginther 1979), although behavioral estrus may not always reflect ovarian cycling (Kirkpatrick and Turner 1983). Generally speaking, mares are seasonally polyestrous, experiencing 4 to 6 days of receptivity followed by about 15 days of nonreceptivity before returning to estrus (Waring 1983). In Granite Range horses, seasonal influences affected postpartum estrous periods. Females bearing young prior to 1 April averaged 24 days until estrus [1], and they were more variable than were mothers that gave birth later in the year [2]. These latter mares experienced postpartum estrous almost two weeks earlier, averaging 10.9 days postbirth. Neither infant sex, maternal age, nor maternal body size affected postpartum estrous.

Conception

Based on the visual method described in Appendix 6, I estimated that conception occurred in 79.5% of the mares during their first estrus and in 20.5% during their second. Tyler (1972) suggested that most free-ranging New Forest ponies were impregnated by their second estrus.

Male Takeovers

If the time at which males took over harems affected parturition
dates, females should have given birth at least a gestation period
(about eleven and a half months) later. Alternatively, if male takeovers had no influence on birth dates, no association between takeovers and birth dates should result.

These conflicting predictions were examined since birth and
takeover dates were known in twelve cases for pregnant females
(Appendix 6) or estimated to be outside the peak breeding season
in six other cases. New stallions were defined as those not previously associated with females, while resident stallions were those
that remained with familiar females. To be conservative in this
analysis, I used only females that gave birth. Had females that
failed to produce foals been included, it would not have been possible to determine how accurately birthdates could be predicted.
Knowing the accuracy of such predictions was essential in understanding whether stallions or sampling biases might account for
changes in birthdates.

The general association between the time of band takeovers and
subsequent birthdates was not good. Ten of the 18 (56%) births
occurred within six months of takeovers rather than a gestation
length or more after the takeovers. This indicates that at least some
of the pregnant females had their foals without having dates of
birth altered. However, 8 of 18 females gave birth about a year
after takeovers. In other words, 44% of the births in bands that
experienced takeovers appeared to be a direct consequence of the
takeover itself.

Might differences among these females arise because, at the
time of takeovers, females at various stages of pregnancy differed
in their ability to carry their fetus to full term? It is logical to expect
that females vary in their susceptibility to prenatal loss because
stage of pregnancy and embryonic mortality are related. Mares
early in their pregnancy are more likely to suffer prenatal deaths
than are those that have carried their fetuses longer (Moberg
1975). Two predictions follow: (1) females in early stages of pregnancy should experience births about a year after takeovers since
such females would be likely to suffer prenatal deaths; (2) females
in later stages of pregnancy would not be likely to have birth dates
altered in association with takeovers.

These predictions were examined by dividing females into two
groups based on their stages of pregnancy when takeovers oc-

curred: (1) six or more months pregnant; and (2) less than six months pregnant. I assumed females in category 1 would give birth on dates predicted (on the basis of their estimated conception plus a standard gestation length) regardless of takeover dates; those in category 2 would fail to bear offspring at dates originally anticipated. For females in category 2, revised dates of predicted parturition were made based on a minimum of gestation length plus two to three weeks beyond takeover dates. This period allowed time for such females to become sexually active and for impregnation by the new stallion to occur.

Females in the two categories of pregnancy differed significantly in their birth intervals after encountering new stallions. Nine of the 10 females that were six or more months pregnant produced young within five and a half months of takeovers, while birth was delayed almost a year in 7 of the 8 mares that were less than six months pregnant when takeovers occurred [3].

Based on the above analysis, I tentatively concluded that the success of pregnancies was determined by the length of time that gestation had been underway when takeovers occurred. However, to show that this is so requires a demonstration—one in which birth dates can be forecast as reliably in bands that experienced takeovers as they can in bands in which no takeovers occurred (e.g., stable bands). Of 78 females from stable bands, 73 birth dates occurred within a standard gestation length. The lack of resultant difference in accuracy in birth forecasting between mares in stable bands and those with takeovers [4] indicates that births could be predicted reasonably well by taking stage of pregnancy into account.

The above information indicates that takeovers (or a combination of factors associated with band instability) influenced parturition dates by affecting pregnancy rates in mares. Not only may parturition be related to season due to photoperiod or food, but also due to social factors. These factors operate in subtle ways. Effects of male takeovers, if not the males themselves, alter the success and timing of pregnancies.

6.4 BIRTH TIMES AND SITES

Most births for which precise data were available ($N=36$) occurred at night or around dawn (86%), a figure that agrees remarkably well with literature on domestic horses (85%, Campitelli, Carenzi, and Verga 1982; 86%, Rossdale and Short 1967). Only once did females from the same band give birth on the same night. Daytime births (N=5) occurred from 0900 to 1600 hrs; 80% were by primiparous females.

Birth locations varied but inluded the following broad categories: mountainous slopes, ravines, flat vegetation-dominated (e.g., shrub/steppe) areas, and flat open (e.g., grassland) areas. Females selected slopes and ravines significantly more often than would be expected based on the availability of these sites (fig. 6.2) [5], but a problem in sampling occurred. Since sheltered sites and those in juniper regions were not as visible, foals born in those areas would be less likely to be detected—at least at their immediate birth sites. However, when habitats could be separated by rock cover, rocky areas were preferred at all types of sites (fig. 6.2) [6]. Despite the use of numerous birth sites, qualitative observations of the first day of life suggest that foals experienced more difficulty on slopes and in ravines than in other areas. On three occasions newly born foals tumbled on steep slopes; once an animal rolled side over side three times down a hill for about 15 m to 20 m until it was caught in a thornbush. There were no differences in survival due to birth areas.

Only one birth was observed (see Waring 1983; Rossdale 1975). On the three occasions when I saw placental membranes, they were consumed twice by coyotes and once (partially) by the neonate's two-year-old brother. A typical birth location on a rocky slope is illustrated in figure 6.3.

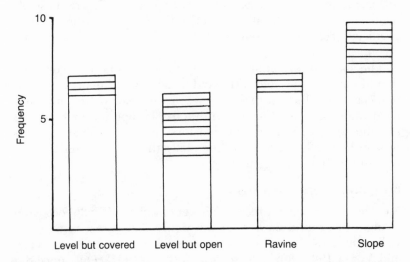

FIG. 6.2   Frequency of birth locations. Shading shows percentage of births in areas dominated by rocks, while unshaded areas were rock free. Level regions were either covered (mostly shrubs) or open (mostly grassland).

Fig. 6.3   A typical birth site on a rocky slope.

6.5   BODY CONDITION AND WEIGHT

Assessments of body condition in wild horses pose special problems because animals cannot easily be handled. In New Forest ponies this dilemma was overcome by Pollock (1980). He adopted a visual method that ranked (into five categories: high, medium, etc.) fat deposition in muscles along the midline of lumbar vertebrae and in the pelvic region. Since Pollock's system predicted well which animals were likely to survive and reproduce, I used it for Granite horses. Individuals were designated as good, average, or poor (see Pollock 1980 for precise details), or intermediate among these categories when judgments were more difficult.

Body weights were determined for twenty-eight immobilized animals as described in the methods section. Since body weights had to be estimated *before* horses were immobilized (in order to decide amounts of drugs needed) and levels of accuracy of weight estimation could then be verified, it was possible to gain an idea of the accuracy of the visual assessments. Levels of accuracy approached 95% (sec. 3.7); thus I estimated adult body weights of nonimmobilized animals visually. For body weights of pregnant mares, I subtracted 10% from total weight if they were in their last trimester of pregnancy. Body weights for immobilized males ($\bar{X}=444\pm40$ kg) and females ($\bar{X}=413\pm54$ kg) did not differ significantly [7]. Of the fourteen females that were immobilized, I estimated that they weighed about 20 kg less than the mean for nonimmobilized females that were five years of age or older. Generally, full body weight in horses and zebras is attained by four to five years (fig. 6.4), although variations occur due to local ecological conditions.

Males and Females

Comparisons of estimated weight and body condition between bachelors and stallions that were five years or older revealed the following relationships: (1) Stallions were slightly ($\bar{X}=453$ kg) but not significantly ($\bar{X}=435$ kg) heavier [8]. (2) No differences existed in body condition, except old bachelors were the most emaciated following winter [9]. (3) A greater percentage of seven-to-fourteen-year-old males held harems than did the other age groups [10]. Neither body condition nor weight was significantly correlated with age.

In females, numerous relationships were confounded by age, since foals may be produced at two years and offspring production may continue until twenty-two years. For females five years or

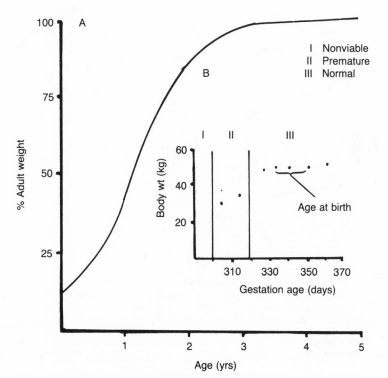

FIG. 6.4   Pre- and postnatal growth rates in equids. (A) generalized growth curve for horses (based on National Research Council 1978; Willoughby 1974) and Common zebras (after Smuts 1975a); (B) birth weight and gestation age in 158 Thoroughbred horses (after Rossdale 1976).

older, weight and body condition were the only parameters related to each other (fig. 6.5); age effects were minimal [11]. Individuals younger than five were often smaller and lighter (see fig. 6.4), and those that lactated emerged from the winter in the poorest condition. Their ribs often were obvious (fig. 6.6).

Seasonal Variations

The body condition of temperate and tropical ungulates changes seasonally with mating activities, weather, and food availability (Mitchell, McCowan, and Nicholson 1976; Murray 1982; Sinclair and Duncan 1972; Sadleir 1969). In the Great Basin, winter is the most stressful period. Horses in all sex and age categories were in the worst condition at the end of winter and in the best during summer (see fig. 6.7) [12]. Females with foals suffered obvious lactational costs in the winter as illustrated by their poor body condi-

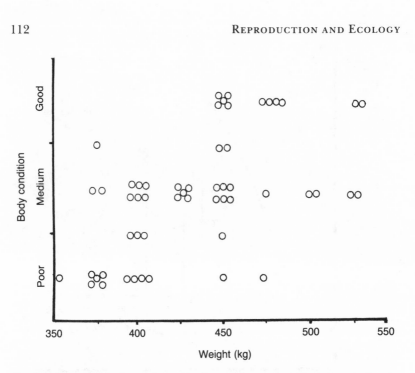

FIG. 6.5   Estimated body weight and body condition at the end of winter in females five years and older.

FIG. 6.6   Poor body condition in a four-year-old female and her daughter at the end of winter.

FIG. 6.7   Good body condition in females on their high-altitude summer ranges. All of these animals died in a winter snow storm.

tions when compared to better conditioned, nonlactating females [13].

These findings agree with those presented for New Forest ponies (Pollock 1980) or for domestic horses that lost winter weight when raised on Montana rangeland (Dawson, Phillips, and Speelman 1945). In addition to seasonal and nutritional stresses, poor body condition was presumably accentuated by dental anomalies. Four Granite horses (two of each sex) had damaged or broken incisors; in the winter those horses were always in poor condition. These animals probably had difficulty masticating their food properly. The females each aborted once, although neither was involved in band changes nor found in the lowest-quality home ranges.

6.6   ECOLOGICAL FACTORS AND OFFSPRING PHYSICAL DEVELOPMENT

In broad taxonomic comparisons neonatal growth follows allometric rules (Eisenberg 1981; Robbins and Robbins 1979), but within species growth rates are easily altered by local conditions (Skogland 1983). Animals in the Granite population provided opportunities to investigate effects of food use on various aspects of offspring development, since ecological differences existed in home ranges. Individuals that used home ranges with similar quality rankings were pooled so that sample sizes for each home-range category could be equalized. Effects that resource use had upon gestation, lactation, and weaning were then examined.

Gestation

The duration of pregnancy is more variable than generally believed. In humans coefficients of variation may be as high as 6.3% (Awan 1967), and horses are considered to be the most variable domesticated mammals (Hafez 1980). In native mammals, intraspecific variation in gestation length has been related to body size and other factors (Kiltie 1982).

For Granite horses, date of conception, maternal body weight, and band stability influenced gestation length; sex of the foal did not. Male and female foals averaged 348.1 ($SD\pm9.3$) and 345.1 ($SD\pm8.5$) days respectively, a difference that was not significant [14]. However, similar trends for sex differences in horse gestation have been reported, and sometimes the differences are statistically significant (see Campitelli, Carenzi, and Verga 1982; Howell and Rollins 1951; Rophia et al. 1969).

Both female body weight and band stability influenced gestation length; mares smaller than the average for the population or in unstable bands had shorter gestations ($\bar{X}=338.1\pm12.4$ days) than those larger ($\bar{X}=347.2\pm11.2$ days) or in stable bands [15]. Since small body size was associated with age in animals less than five years old and younger females change bands more than older ones (Berger 1983b; chap. 7), each of these factors was related. Together body size, band stability, and foal sex accounted for 43% of the variation in gestation length for foals born between 1 April and 30 June.

Why these variables reflect gestation length can be explained by considering the relationships among female physiological condition, pregnancy duration, and infant birth weight. Data for domestic horses indicate that foal birth weight (and survival) is related to a threshold point, very late in gestation, above which fetal weight is no longer positively related to gestation length (Rossdale 1976; see fig. 6.4). Also, gestation is prolonged by poor maternal condition (Howell and Rollins 1951). This suggests that animals with low body reserves should extend gestation since additional time is required for the fetal attainment of birth weight, as has been found in bats (Racey 1973) and suggested for reindeer (Rognmo et al. 1982).

The Granite data do not agree with this prediction. Small and poorly conditioned mares had shorter gestation lengths and lower foal production (sec. 9.5) than larger and better conditioned animals. This counterintuitive result can be explained as follows.

Since a threshold level of body reserves is necessary to support the costs of gestation (Sadleir 1969), a trade-off is made by mares differing in physiological conditions. For those near but not above this threshold point, abortion or foal prematurity will occur, as reported in domestic horses (Rossdale 1976; see fig. 6.4). Although Granite horses had high reproductive rates, they were not always in good condition. Small or lighter animals emerged from winters in the poorest condition (above), and they likely lacked the body stores needed to prolong successful gestation. These females had relatively shorter pregnancy durations than larger mares. Despite the influence of band stability, analysis of variance indicated that body size significantly influenced gestation length [15], with smaller mothers having shorter pregnancies. It was unlikely that shorter gestation lengths in such females resulted from better maternal nutrition instead of a depletion of reserves, since weight and condition were positively correlated in fifty-four females (fig. 6.5). In other words, heavier females came through the winter in better condition and had more body fat along pelvic and lumbar regions than smaller (hence lighter) females. The evidence suggests that large body size and stable bands foster the environment necessary to develop reserves for gestational maintenance.

Lactation and Weaning

Since maternal nutrition affects milk production (Munro 1962; Thomson and Thomson 1953) and animals in better environments suckle longer (Geist 1971; Berger 1979b), parous mares from good home ranges should be characterized by foals with relatively long suckling times. To test this prediction, 1,833 suckling bouts that exceeded three seconds in duration were examined in relation to foal age and sex and maternal home range. Almost 1,200 additional suckling bouts were excluded from analyses because of the following conditions: (1) animals were not consistently observed for at least two successive hours; (2) complete suckle bout durations were not observed (then the entire observation period was omitted since we could not know how much time foals suckled per unit observation period); and (3) foals in question did not live to one month (two foals died before thirty days of age, and their suckling times were two and three times below average).

Home ranges affected foal suckling rates through at least the first two months of life (table 6.1), as has also been found in horses under seminatural conditions (Duncan, Harvey, and Wells 1984). Differences in suckling bout durations were greatest between Granite foals from high- and low-quality areas during their first two weeks of life. Foals from the best-ranked areas averaged more than a minute per hour longer in suckle duration than those from the worst areas (fig. 6.8). Not only did home range affect suckling times, but so did infant age and sex [16]. Suckling rates declined with age for each of the sexes (table 6.1); males suckled longer than females [17]. Similar results have been reported for Camargue horses (Duncan, Harvey, and Wells 1984).

The ages at which foals were weaned varied considerably. Thirty-four of 40 (85%) were weaned prior to their first birthday, and the majority (27, or 79%) of these were not observed suckling after nine months of age. Many of the mothers that had had spring births were facing the middle or end of winter, with food in short supply. About 90% of the lactating females were pregnant, some in their last trimester. Because of winter-related stresses and because the last trimester of pregnancy demands the most nutritionally (National Research Council 1978), mothers weaned their offspring during winters.

I detected no relationships between weaning age and foal sex, home-range ranking, maternal condition, or band stability. Duncan, Harvey, and Wells (1984) also found that the sexes were not weaned at different ages. Among Granite Range horses, only the prior reproductive status of mothers influenced the ages at which young were weaned. Females without foals from the preceding year (e.g., barren females) weaned their offspring at an average of 16 months of age, whereas mothers with yearlings as well as new-

TABLE 6.1 Suckling Times (min/2 hr) until the Third Month of Life

Age (Weeks)	Home-Range Quality					
	Low		Medium		High	
	Males	Females	Males	Females	Males	Females
1–2	$3.46^{\pm.16}$	$2.94^{\pm.18}$	$5.28^{\pm.30}$	$4.42^{\pm.58}$	$5.88^{\pm.45}$	$5.30^{\pm.48}$
3–4	$2.21^{\pm.23}$	—	$2.76^{\pm.48}$	$2.24^{\pm.31}$	$2.72^{\pm.25}$	$2.46^{\pm.29}$
5–6	$1.68^{\pm.09}$	—	$2.08^{\pm.23}$	$1.94^{\pm.20}$	$2.52^{\pm.20}$	$1.96^{\pm.21}$
7–8	$1.88^{\pm.23}$	—	$1.66^{\pm.11}$	$1.46^{\pm.14}$	$2.02^{\pm.12}$	$1.68^{\pm.13}$
N	190	14	455	429	413	332

Notes: Sample based on 43 different foals.

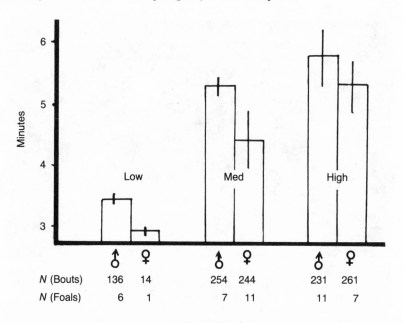

FIG. 6.8 Suckling rate (min/2 hr) and foal sex during first two weeks of life in different home ranges. Means based on total number of suckling bouts (extending lines=SD).

born foals weaned their young at an average of 8.5 months [18]. The longest interval between birth and weaning was 19 months, while 2 months was the shortest. In this latter instance, the mother died but the stunted foal persisted through an arduous winter.

Generally, weaning was not aggressive or abrupt; rather, it was a gradual process that took several months (see Tyler 1972; Waring 1983). However, when yearlings displaced newborn foals to suckle (fig. 6.9), they were aggressively and soundly rebuffed by bites from their mothers.

Puberty and Home-Range Quality

Numerous proximate and ultimate factors are linked to puberty (Stearns 1976; Mitchell and Brown 1974; Berger 1982). The attainment of a critical body mass and not age per se seems to be one of the most crucial factors, although the two variables are usually correlated and others are essential as well (Foxcroft 1980; Gunn 1977; Reimers 1983; but see Wiltbank, Kasson, and Ingalls 1969). Because milk consumption affects physical development (Blaxter

FIG. 6.9 Example of conflict between siblings for milk in Assateague Island ponies. Yearling usurping milk from younger sib. Note foal also attempting to suckle. Maternal rejection of the yearling soon followed. Photo courtesy of Ronald R. Keiper.

1961; Robbins and Moen 1975), differences in foal growth should be reflected by their suckling performances; foals that suckle more should grow and attain puberty faster, providing that other factors are broadly equivalent. To examine this idea I relied on evidence concerning ages at puberty since estimates of yearling or weaning weights were not reliable. My rationale was that animals that grew faster should reach puberty earlier than those that did not, a premise substantiated often for domestic ungulates (Short and Bellows 1971; Milagres, Dillard, and Robison 1979; Dyrmundsson 1973).

Females were considered pubescent when they voluntarily departed their natal bands, turned their rumps toward and raised their tails to approaching stallions, or copulated. These first two categories signify estrus. During a female's first few estrus periods she is likely to wander and advertise to males. This behavior is similar to what Klingel (1967, 1969b) described for Common zebras at puberty. Males were more difficult to judge; I had to assume puberty once they left natal bands. This assessment may have biased some data because social factors influence male emigration as well (chap. 8). Nevertheless, it was the only field measure available.

The evidence (fig. 6.10) supported the idea that home range affected puberty ages. Regardless of sex, individuals from better ranges matured earlier. All 3 females from high-quality areas produced foals at two years whereas only 1 of the 6 females from medium-quality areas had foals at two years; none of the females from the relatively poor ranges had foals before three years (fig. 6.10). A positive relationship between home-range ranking and age of females' first foals existed [19]. This suggests that the home areas in which foals grow up affects their rates of growth and maturation. The amount of milk received early in life may be a major cause of such growth, since preweaning weight gain seems to influence puberty more than postweaning weight gain (Milagres, Dillard, and Robison 1979; Foxcroft 1980). Evidence for the importance of milk versus highly nutritious food for early growth rates is still sparse, but animal scientists have found that orphaned foals experience stunted development despite provisioning with high planes of nutrition (Hintz 1977). This idea is supported by the Granite foal that remained the size of a yearling even when he was three years of age. His mother died when he was two months old, and, even though he fed in home ranges of medium and high quality, his growth was stunted.

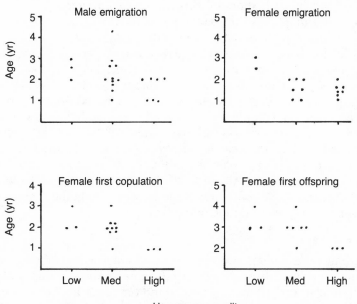

Fig. 6.10 Influence of home-range quality on dispersal ages and female puberty (1979–82).

6.7   EFFECTS OF REPRODUCTION AND HOME RANGES ON FEEDING

Free-ranging horses may spend between 90% to 98% of their time feeding and resting (Keiper, Moss, and Zervanos 1980; Duncan 1980; Kaseda 1983a), each activity being important for the acquisition and processing of food. In dimorphic species the larger sex requires greater absolute amounts of food for maintenance than the smaller, but in horses sex differences might not be expected since body weights are similar [7]. This prediction is, of course, complicated because females commit additional nutrients to gestation and lactation. Females should therefore spend more time grazing than males.

At least three additional factors need to be mentioned before considering this prediction. First, unlike other Holarctic ungulates, male horses defend harems year-round. As a consequence, stallions expend energy in defense throughout the year, and the resultant energy losses should be offset by increased food intake. If male investment in harem defense crudely approximated maternal investment, parity in feeding times should be expected between the sexes. Second, home ranges differ among bands. Individuals on poorer quality diets should compensate by feeding longer or more frequently than those on better diets, providing that low-quality items are not poor enough to impede passage rates. It is known that in domestic horses green grass is usually passed through the digestive system faster than hay, an indication that food quality can alter passage rates. Third, seasonal influences alter food availability and quality. In cervids, winter weight loss is accentuated by reduced nutritional requirements due to lower metabolic rates (Moen 1978) and diminished food sources (Moen 1973). Such deficits are balanced later in the year by increasing fat stores—the result of feeding on improved spring and summer nutrition (Clutton-Brock, Guinness, and Albon 1982). In wild horses, what evidence exists for the above speculations and how do sex, home range, and season modify feeding time budgets?

Seasonal Influences

Feeding time budgets were examined by collecting data at one-minute intervals throughout daylight hours. Animals that walked with their heads oriented to the ground (i.e., searched) or ingested food were recorded as feeding. Individuals of similar status, sex, and equivalent home-range rankings were matched for analyses. Hence, barren females were compared to barren females from good, medium, or poor home ranges, stallions to stallions from the various home ranges, and so forth. The data consisted of a minimum of 1,400 hours for barren females, the least-represented group (fig. 6.11), and spanned a twelve-month period—fall (October–November), winter (January–March), spring (primarily May), and summer (July). If females were lactating, data were standardized by focusing on them at two months after giving birth.

For barren and lactating females and stallions, feeding times were greatest in winter and least in summer. Fall and spring were intermediate and equivalent (fig. 6.11). All seasonal differences among categories were significant except between fall and spring [20]. These results are consistent with those previously reported by Duncan (1980) for Camargue and by Keiper, Moss, and Zervanos (1980) for Assateague horses.

Overall, the feeding budgets of horses were similar to those of other free-ranging ungulates. In the summer, thermoregulatory demands (Belovsky 1981) and insects (sec. 4.7) caused animals to forage more at night. Keiper, Moss, and Zervanos (1980) recorded virtually identical feeding times for day and night periods in As-

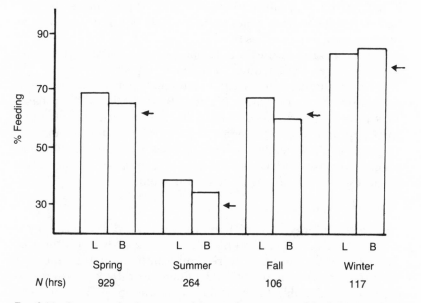

FIG. 6.11   Sex, reproductive status, season, and percentage of daylight spent feeding. (L) lactating females ($N=21$); (B) barren females ($N=5$); arrows=stallions ($N=8$). All individuals are from medium-quality home ranges. N (hrs) refers to minimum hours on which the data are based per group.

sateague horses as I found for Granite horses. In the winter, daytime feeding increased with cold-related stress and diminishing food availability. At these times, both deer and Japanese Misaki horses experience reduced metabolic rates (Moen 1978; Kaseda 1983b).

Lactating and Barren Females

The production of milk during a mare's first three months of lactation make these the most costly months in terms of energy. Increases of 71% in digestible energy, 186% in digestible protein, 120% in calcium, 143% in phosphorous, and 120% in vitamin A are required for maintenance of domestic horses that average the size of Granite animals. These values (National Research Council 1978) are without the additional burden of environmental extremes (e.g., cold, heat, social factors) found in feral populations. Because of these demands, lactating females should feed more than barren females. The data indicate that lactating females feed more (fig. 6.11), but the difference was not close to the expected proportion given the magnitude of change in lactational costs. Differences between these two categories of females in time spent feeding were not significant in winter [21]. At this time of the year barren and lactating females appear to offset impending weight loss by foraging as often as possible.

This observation raises the question of why barren females do not feed more at other times of the year, especially since they do not have lactational demands and additional energy reserves might be built for use during winter (Clutton-Brock et al. 1982). Probably body reserves are stored by barren females because their feeding times appeared relatively higher than those expected for maintenance alone. Presumably, the feeding times of barren females were not extended further because an asymptote exists after which additional reserves can no longer be accumulated.

Sex Differences

Despite the energy costs of harem maintenance (see sec. 7.5 for measurements), stallion feeding values were usually below those of mares (fig. 6.11), and they were significantly lower than those of lactating females at all seasons [22]. These sex differences in foraging were attributable to the stallions' allocation of time to social activities, as has been reported for horses in the Camargue (Duncan 1980). On the average, stallions spent more than 300% as much time as females in aggressive or vigilant behavior.

Home Ranges

Individuals from home ranges of poor quality spent more time feeding than those from higher quality areas (table 6.2). The most striking differences were between lactating females in band P (e.g., poor home-range areas) that fed on the average almost three and a half hours longer per fourteen-hour daylight period than those in B, which occupied better areas. These data on the effects of home-range differences in food are in general agreement with those of domestic herbivores, who also spend more time foraging in areas of less abundant or less nutritious food (Arnold and Dudsinski 1978).

TABLE 6.2   Mean Time Spent Feeding in Different Home Ranges, May 1981

	Home-Range Quality		
	Low	Medium	High
Stallions	70.5 (3)	62.1 (5)	57.9 (3)
Barren females	68.3 (3)	55.6 (3)	58.4 (2)
Parous females	78.1 (6)	66.7 (12)	65.8 (9)

Notes: Mean time given as percentage of 14-hr daylight period. Sample indicated parenthetically; all individuals at least four years old. Data for parous females focused on the second month of lactation.

6.8   SUMMARY

1. Foals were born throughout the year in the Granite Range, although a birth peak extended from April through June.
2. Numerous factors affected the distribution of births. Postpartum estrous cycles occurred about eleven days after foals were born in the spring, but they averaged about twenty-four days later if foals were born in the winter. Pregnancy rates were altered to a greater extent in individuals whose bands were taken over by new males than they were in females that lived in stable bands. Mares less than six months pregnant at the time of takeovers experienced greater prenatal losses and returned to estrus sooner than females that were six or more months pregnant. These latter mares produced foals within five and a half months of takeovers whereas most mares less than halfway through their pregnancies did not give birth until at least eleven and a half months later. Pregnancy rates were modified by the effects of

takeovers, if not directly by the new males. Both ecological and social factors affected birth dates.

3. About 86% of the births occurred at night or near dawn. Mares selected slopes and ravines as birth sites most often, but no relation between foal survival and birth sites existed.

4. Body condition was estimated by visual rankings of fat deposits in lumbar and pelvic regions. Males in the seven-to-fourteen-year age category were in better condition after winters than males in other age groups. Old bachelors emerged from winters in the worst shape. Among females five years or older, body weight was positively correlated with condition at the end of winter. Younger females were usually smaller and had less fat reserves. Mares that lactated emerged from winter in worse condition than barren females.

5. Gestation periods were longer for male foals than for female foals. Social, physical, and ecological influences on gestation lengths included band stability, maternal size, and season. Mares larger than the average had gestation lengths that exceeded those of smaller females.

6. Home ranges influenced parameters associated with physical maturation. Foals from relatively better areas suckled longer, emigrated from natal bands earlier, reached puberty before and (for females) produced their own offspring at younger ages than individuals from regions with poorer resource bases. Regardless of home range, male foals suckled longer than female foals.

7. Age at weaning occurred generally around nine months, when mothers produced foals in the subsequent year. At this time, mothers faced the end of winter when food was least available and energy demands would be costly, since these mothers would also be in the last trimester of another pregnancy. For females that were barren the year after producing foals, weaning did not occur until their offspring were about sixteen months of age.

8. Reproductive status, sex, season, and home range influenced foraging budgets. Males generally fed less than females, while lactating mares fed longer than barren mares. In the winter, differences between these two categories of females were slight, probably because all individuals strived to offset body weight losses by feeding as often as possible.

Statistical Tests

1. Comparison between postpartum estrous before ($N=17$) and after ($N=75$) 1 April of each year.

Mann-Whitney U test: $z=3.04$; $p<0.002$.

2. Comparison of variation of time (days) of estrous periods after birth at different times of the year (see 1 above).
F-Max test: $F_{12,74}=3.93$; $p<0.001$.

3. Comparison of time expected until birth and that observed in two categories of females (six or more months pregnant and less than six months pregnant) when male takeovers occurred.
G test: $G=5.96$, $df=1$, $p<0.05$.

4. Comparison of accuracy of predicted birth dates among females in stable bands and those at different stages of pregnancy (see 3 above) whose bands were taken over by males.
G test: $G=.16$, $df=1$, NS.

5. Comparison among four categories of sites where parturition occurred in relation to that expected, based on estimated availability of sites.
G test: $G=26.52$, $df=3$, $p<0.001$.

6. Comparison between birth sites with and without rock cover, based on expected availability.
G test: $G=16.14$, $df=1$, $p<0.005$.

7. Comparison between male ($N=12$) and female ($N=14$) body weights for immobilized animals five years or older.
Student's t test: $t=.26$, $df=24$, NS.

8. Comparison between body weights of bachelors ($N=24$) and stallions ($N=30$) five years or older in late spring. Males in each year treated independently.
Student's t test: $t=1.48$, $df=52$, $0.10<p<0.20$.

9. Comparison between body condition of bachelors older ($N=5$) and younger ($N=12$) than fourteen years in late winter.
Student's t test: $t=2.87$, $df=15$, $p<0.02$.

10. Comparison between stallion or bachelor status in 7–14 yr age group ($N=39$) and other aged (5–6, 14++) individuals ($N=24$).
G test: $G=73.58$, $df=1$, $p<0.001$.

11. Correlation between body condition and (a) weight and (b) age in 54 females (five years or more).
Kendall rank correlation:
   (a) tau$=.63$, $df=52$, $z=6.73$, $p<0.001$.
   (b) tau$=.18$, $df=52$, $z=.57$, NS.

12. Comparison of winter and summer body condition in lactating and barren females (from 11).
G test: $G=217.04$, $df=2$, $p<0.001$.

13. Comparison between winter body condition in lactating and barren females (from 11).

G test: $G=129$, $df=1$, $p<0.001$.

14. Comparison of gestation length of male and female foals born between 1 April and 30 June each year.
Student's t test: $t=1.18$, $df=66$, NS.

15. Comparison of gestation length between females in stable and unstable bands whose body weights were above or below the average (data pooled for male and female offspring).
Analysis of variance:
   Stability: $F_{1,65}=7.97$, $p<0.01$.
   Size: $F_{1,65}=4.71$, $p<0.05$.
   Interaction: $F_{1,65}=7.06$, $p<0.03$.

16. Comparison of the effects of (a) home range and (b) sex on suckling rates (min/2 h) in one- to two-week-old foals.
Analysis of variance:
   (a) $F_{2,40}=20.90$, $p<0.001$.
   (b) $F_{1,41}=4.20$, $p<0.05$.

17. Comparison of suckling rates between the sexes at two-week intervals from birth to eight weeks.
Sign test: $X=0$, $N=9$, $p<0.002$.

18. Comparison of barren and lactating females that weaned offspring before and after one year of age.
G test: $G=22.74$, $df=1$, $N=40$, $p<0.001$.

19. Correlations between home-range quality and (a) male dispersal, (b) female dispersal, (c) female's first copulation, and (d) female's first offspring. (Differences in significance were not affected regardless of whether ties in the analyses were corrected or not; Siegel 1956.)
Spearman rank correlation coefficient:
   (a) $r_s=.63$, $df=18$, $T_s=3.45$, $p<0.01$.
   (b) $r_s=.60$, $df=17$, $T_s=3.09$, $p<0.01$.
   (c) $r_s=.77$, $df=13$, $T_s=4.66$, $p<0.001$.
   (d) $r_s=.67$, $df=10$, $T_s=2.86$, $p<0.02$.

20. Comparison between spring and fall foraging times in (a) stallions, (b) parous females, and (c) barren females.
Wilcoxin matched-pairs test:
   (a) $T=25$, $N=10$, NS.
   (b) $T=76$, $N=21$, NS.
   (c) $T=6$, $N=5$, NS.

21. Comparison between feeding times of parous and barren females for each season.
Mann-Whitney U test:
   Spring: $z=2.90$, $N=26$, $p<0.005$.

Summer: $U=9$, $n_1=4$, $n_2=17$, $p<0.05$.
Fall: $U=14$, $n_1=5$, $n_2=19$, $p<0.02$.
Winter: $U=12$, $n_1=4$, $n_2=17$, $0.05< p<0.10$.

22. Comparison between feeding times of stallions and parous females for each season.

Mann-Whitney U test:
Spring: $z=1.97$, $N=31$, $p>0.05$.
Summer: $U=17$, $n_1=9$, $n_2=17$, $p<0.002$.
Fall: $U=23$, $n_1=8$, $n_2=16$, $p<0.02$.
Winter: $U=29$, $n_1=10$, $n_2=20$, $p<0.002$.

7 Behavior and Social Organization

Darwin was the first to show us that the fierce battles and strange antics . . . under the exaltation of the sexual emotions are manifestations fraught with tremendous consequences to the race

W. P. Pycraft (1914)

7.1 INTRODUCTION

Males and females of the same species share many common properties, but reproductive interests and coincident behavior are rarely among them. The patterns of spacing and mating that result from interactions both between and among the sexes are generally referred to as a species' social organization (Eisenberg 1966, 1981). Such interactions form the topic of this chapter. Specifically, I concentrate on how the behavior of individuals molds the social organization of Granite horses, and I discuss adaptive and functional aspects of behavior.

Information in at least five areas of behavior and social organization is presented. The first area is patterns of spacing and association. These data provide a framework upon which later functional interpretations may be made. Second is descriptions of aggression and of situations in which aggression is used. The third point addresses behavioral changes as individuals grow older: When and why do males fight to obtain females? How much energy do males invest in harem defense or acquisition? Why do some individuals forsake their own reproductive interests to battle on behalf of nonrelated males? Fourth is female dominance hierarchies, a topic that has only recently received attention among studies of natural populations. Although dominance hierarchies are well known in domestic horses, I remain skeptical about their biological significance, at least in Granite horses. Fifth is conflict between the sexes, which is exemplified most strikingly by feticide—the conspecific killing of fetuses.

7.2 GROUPING PATTERNS OF MALES AND FEMALES

An obvious feature of horse societies is year-round bands—a grouping pattern found in all populations that have been studied for at least six months, as well as in two species of zebras (Klingel 1967; Joubert 1972), and even in a population of feral asses (Mc-Cort 1980). Only a single possible exception comes to mind: Hoffman (1983) speculated that horses in central Australia may fail to form such permanent associations. Where extreme xeric conditions prevail, it seems logical to expect that the band structure would break down because of presumed difficulties males would have in maintaining harems and still meeting the constant stresses associated with water demands. Yet even in Death Valley, perhaps the most arid climate in North America, feral horses occurred in small bands of only two to three adult individuals (personal observation in 1979). What are bands really, and how long do they persist?

Band Compositions and Associations

Most studies have found that bands consist of females, their young, and a single stallion (Feist and McCullough 1975; Keiper 1976; Berger 1977; Miller 1981). In the Granite Range, 88% of the bands that persisted longer than seven months contained one stallion, while the remainder had two or more stallions. Most other multi-male bands were short lived and lasted from several hours to several months. Sons rarely remained in bands longer than two to three years, although the extreme case lasted just over four years (see fig. 6.10). Miller (1981) found basically the same pattern in horses in the Red Desert of Wyoming.

Two of the more conspicuous and intriguing events in bands concerned the emigration of daughters and relationships among females. Daughters usually remained in bands until they reached puberty. Once attaining it they often urinated during their first estrus in a conspicuous spread-legged posture (see Klingel 1969b; Asa, Goldfoot, and Ginther 1979) and sometimes pranced with their tails raised in front of nonharem males. Resident stallions typically ignored these solicitations to nonharem males. About 81% (21 of 26) of such nubile females failed to return to their natal bands following their first consortships with males. Of the 5 that returned, all departed permanently within two years after puberty.

Female age was a factor that affected band compositions since young females often changed bands voluntarily. Twenty-six females, four years of age or less, changed bands voluntarily (simply by moving away) while only 7 (of 80 possible) older mares moved to new bands [1]. One three-year-old moved to four bands in four hours and to at least six bands over two days. Regardless of a female's age, I never observed stallions forcing females from their bands. Sometimes mares gradually strayed from their bands, and, despite persistent attempts by resident stallions to keep them, such mares were picked up by other males a few days later.

Mean harem sizes changed little annually throughout the study; the mean number of potentially breeding females (daughters excluded) per band varied from a minimum of 2.73 in 1980 to a maximum of 3.67 in 1983 ($\bar{X}=3.10\pm1.64[SD]$). The frequency distribution of harem sizes is shown in figure 7.1. Although older females showed greater stability relative to younger females, by the

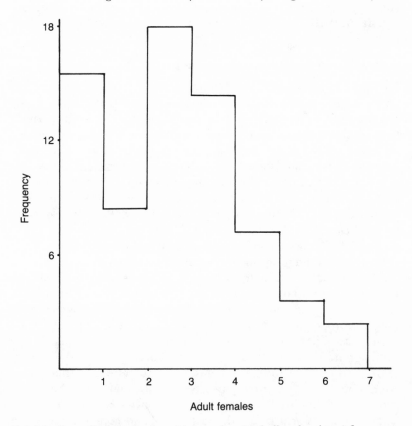

FIG. 7.1 Frequency distribution of harem sizes (excluding daughters) for groups that persisted longer than two months in the Granite Range. Each year was treated independently.

end of the study less than 50% of the mares that were four years or older when the study began remained with original band females. About 55% (42 of 76) of the mares that changed bands did so as a result of direct male appropriations, while the remainder did so primarily by wandering solitarily (or with their offspring) and subsequently being picked up by males from different bands.

Regardless of the events that mediated band changes, these data suggest that females do not remain together for life. Despite a wide margin of variation among individuals, less than half of the Granite females formed associations that lasted at least five years. By the time an animal reaches fifteen years of age, the chances are less than 1 in 8 that she will remain with females she has known that long. Unfortunately, data on associations or bonding in Common zebra females are not available to determine whether Klingel's (1967) idea that females may bond together for life is valid. In Mountain zebras, Penzhorn (1984) reported three mares that had remained together for ten and a half years, but not the proportion of females that had changed groups.

Bachelor Males

Males unable to obtain harems remained alone or formed bachelor groups. Based on 2,146 scan samples in 1981 and 1982, those aged from two to five years were alone only about 2% of the time, whereas males six to fourteen years old were alone 8% of the time; males fourteen years or more were alone the most, although the amount of time they spent solitary never exceeded 35%. These age-graded grouping responses of males also occurred in 1983 when differences among age categories were also significant [2]. Overall, the composition of bachelor groups was extremely flexible. Over the study period, groups varied in size from two to seventeen males; median group size in midspring of each year averaged just above four.

Bachelors regularly approached bands, but they were almost always thwarted by stallions in their efforts to obtain mates. During the peak of spring breeding, encounters between stallions and bachelors averaged almost one per hour/individual (0.92), although bands with centrally located home ranges were approached more often than others.

7.3   AGGRESSION AND COMBAT

Aggression in horses has attracted much interest, and it is now clear that motor patterns differ little if at all between domestic and feral horses (Houpt and Wolski 1980; Waring 1983). There are, however, at least two important differences in frequency of occurrence. In domestic horses, aggression and combat among males is less frequent and among females is more frequent than in feral populations (Houpt and Keiper 1982; Houpt, Law, and Martinisi 1978; Clutton-Brock, Greenwood, and Powell 1976). Reasons are numerous, but the most obvious, of course, are related to husbandry practices. Males are frequently isolated from other males, and invariably many (if not most) are castrated, while it is not unusual for females to be enclosed with other females in small paddocks or corrals.

Although aggression has been studied in feral populations (Feist and McCullough 1976; Berger 1977; Miller 1981), it is necessary to gain a better idea of how often and in what contexts it is used among Granite horses before making suggestions about its functional significance. Therefore, I offer some brief descriptions of social interactions and uses of various agonistic behaviors.

Interband Encounters

Almost all encounters among Granite bands were aggressive, regardless of the time of year. By this I simply mean that elements of threats were given by one or more males (less than 1% of the over 2,150 interband interactions included female-female involvement). Ordinarily, males pranced, arched their necks, or kicked or head tossed at their rivals. Fewer than 0.9% involved playful (see Fagen 1981) or amicable greetings. This does not imply that aggression was rampant; more than 98% of a stallion's annual time budget was spent in nonaggressive activities. As in zebras (Klingel 1975), bands of horses often graze adjacently without aggression or perceptible concern regarding others. The most impressive concentration of wild horses I observed was 210 animals in 1977. They grazed peacefully in adjacent bands southeast of Hart Mountain, Oregon, an area where fossils of the first grazing horses were once found (Downs 1961).

Description of Interactions

Typical encounters between males included stallions that left their harems unguarded to travel up to 400 m away to confront rivals. Males subsequently displayed (see below) to one another, interacted usually for a few brief moments, and then returned to their harems. The most striking characteristic of these interactions was the lack of clarity over the outcome. In 499 such cases between March and July 1982, a dominant (or "winner") could be identified

FIG. 7.2 Aggressive encounter between two males. Note arched neck in male on right and front-leg kick and retracted ears in other horse. Photo by Emory Kristof, © National Geographic Society.

in less than 3.5% of the interactions. Nevertheless, it would be inappropriate to conclude that aggression was lacking in the remaining interband encounters or that these were not serious events. During interband encounters stallion behavior often became stereotyped and rigid. Their necks became arched (fig. 7.2), heads were lowered into the shoulders of rivals, and males mutually sniffed each other's penises. The tightening of the neck musculature resulted in an enlarged or bulging appearance. At close range, vocalizations were audible (usually from about 400 m to 600 m). Kicking, bared teeth, biting, and chasing with ears retracted testified to the agonistic nature of such interactions. But only when an individual chased the other away was it clear that one was dominant at that time over the other. In 96.5% of the interactions among males I was unable to assign dominance status.

Why did males interact aggressively with other males? The establishment of dominance in itself would seem to be an inadequate reason since no immediate benefit is conferred upon males that dominate in social interactions. Horses are not territorial, and they defend neither grazing nor watering areas (Berger 1977; Miller and Denniston 1979). Access to water or food sources seems not to be the principle cause of male-male aggression.

Females were probably the single most cause of aggression

among males: during interactions when females were absent, aggression among males was less intense and less persistant than when mares were present; and males became more aggressive during interactions with conspecifics when one or both had harems (see below). While females may have been the underlying cause of male aggression, it is unclear why, at one time or another, 100% of the resident stallions left their females unguarded and ran to encounter other males. Since size differences in the sexes are imperceptible (at least to me), perhaps stallions viewed horses that grazed adjacently as potential mates and approached simply to obtain more visual information. In their initial greeting, males distinguished between the sexes by using both behavioral and olfactory cues. In fact over 75% of 499 male-male skirmishes averaged less than ninety seconds, perhaps because individuals assessed the sex, prowess, or identity of the other individual.

Not all interband encounters involved active aggression; some were subtle or passive. Bands could be supplanted, although irregularly, when others moved into the vicinity to graze. During droughts, bands whose stallions vary in behavioral characteristics have differential access to waterholes, an indication that interband dominance can be passive (Berger 1977; Miller and Denniston 1979). The relative abundance of water in the Granite Range may have precluded clearcut interband dominance hierarchies during drinking.

Combat and Use of Agonistic Behavior Patterns

Biting is one of the more generalized fighting techniques available to mammals. It is widespread in carnivores (Ewer 1973), primates (Symons 1978), and rodents (Banks and Popham 1975), and it occurs in horned ungulates among "weaponless" females (Barrette 1977; Leuthold 1977). Escalated aggression in native equids shows many similarities to that in feral horses; biting is the primary offensive tactic for each. Combative behaviors are used to deliver or thwart successful bites, most of which are achieved after an individual has lost or been knocked off balance (see fig. 7.3; Berger 1981). In onagers and zebras, rearing up enhances the probability of scoring successful bites but it also carries the greatest risks (Berger 1981).

Equids have developed a means of minimizing injury to the most vulnerable portions of their bodies, their legs. They drop on their knees to assure protection against bites (fig. 7.4). Animals with leg injuries are possible victims of predation (Schaller 1972; Kruuk

Fig. 7.3 Biting and rearing of two stallions on a precipitous ledge in the Grand Canyon. Note disinterest of the females.

1972). Although leg biting is not often observed in domestic horses, it occurs in wild ones (fig. 2.7), and biting at the legs is not uncommon in equid play (fig. 2.6). Equid defensive maneuvers may be somewhat analagous to morphological structures associated with defense (e.g., dermal shields) in that only male equids regularly drop on their knees. In male impalas (Jarman 1972), mountain goats (Geist 1967), and roe deer (Sokolov and Danilkin 1979), dermal shields occur; presumably they are the result of intrasexual selection. Contrary to popular belief and cinematic productions, wild equids (including horses) rarely rear up on their hind legs when they are not fighting or playing.

In contrast to fights between stallions, aggression within the band is limited to infrequent kicking and biting of a less serious nature. Both are relatively infrequent events (Miller 1981). Of course, variations occur in the use of the behavior patterns, and males and females occasionally bite and kick each other, but not with the intensity observed in interband encounters.

The frequency with which various behaviors were observed in interactions between Granite Range stallions are as follows: arched necks (80%), prancing (71%), rearing up (18%), sniffing genitals (16%), front-leg kicking or attempts (13%), body biting or attempts

(6%), and leg biting or attempts (1%). These results are in substantial accordance with Miller's (1981) data, although his samples included bachelors and mine do not.

7.4 Male Takeovers, Fighting, and Tenure

Male horses acquire or enlarge harems in three basic ways. First, they may appropriate females that wander. Such "acquisitions by

Fig. 7.4 Onagers employing offensive and defensive postures while fighting. Above, combatant tucking legs inward to avoid possible bite while using leverage (body weight) to force opponent's head downward; below, aggressor (left) dropping on forelegs and attempting to bite rival, while individual on right remains on legs and avoids possible injuries to them.

chance" accounted for 45% (34 of 76) of the reproductive-aged females secured. Over 75% of these were young females. Second, males obtain mates by deposing resident stallions through escalated aggression and fighting. Acquisitions by combat accounted for 48% of the females. A third possible way, through cooperation and alliances, resulted in only 6% of the acquisitions.

Should Males Fight to Acquire Mates?

Since males can obtain mates almost as often by chance as by deposing stallions, why should they risk injury by fighting rather than simply waiting for wandering females? One reason for fighting is that waiting may offer few and unpredictable rewards. Males cannot assess when (or how often) they will encounter wandering females, and females obtained in this fashion were almost always (94% of the time) by themselves. Moreover, such females were most often young and, hence, not likely to reproduce annually for several years (chap. 5). If a male's best interests are in immediate reproductive rewards, waiting for wandering females might not be the best option chosen.

Age is a factor that should govern behavioral options. Older males, with fewer reproductive opportunities remaining, might benefit more by fighting to obtain harems rather than by waiting for solitary females. Still, the prospects for securing female mates through fighting are remote since only about 1 out of every 690 bachelor-stallion encounters resulted in a harem turnover. Whether or not males should fight to obtain mates depends on the benefits and costs of fighting. What are these and how do they change with age?

As mentioned, the basic options available to bachelors are (1) to locate young females—about six females per year wandered singly, or (2) to depose resident stallions. (Another option—cooperation with resident stallions—is discussed separately in sec. 7.6.) Because fighting entails the greatest risks (Maynard Smith 1976), young males might profit more by adopting large home ranges (a low-risk option since horses do not defend areas), feeding on high-quality foods, wandering widely, and sharpening their combat skills through play or practice. For young males, later opportunities for reproduction are available. However, for old bachelors, with fewer reproductive options, the cost/benefit ratio changes. If old bachelors are relatively skilled combatants, the chances of injury while overthrowing a stallion may be well worth the risk since several females could be obtained at once. Nevertheless, old males in poor

condition with their concommitant low reproductive value would
have few options but to fight for females or go unmated. Perhaps
they might wander widely and feed on high-quality food for a yet
later attempt to secure mates. Middle-aged bachelors would be between young and old bachelors. Based on the above, the choice of
whether to fight for females should depend on one's physical condition, age, and combat skills, and on what tactics others in the
population adopt (Maynard Smith 1976; Dawkins 1976).

Which Males Fight for Mates?

Older bachelors were involved in a greater proportion of escalated
contests with harem-holding males than were younger bachelors
[3], although only bachelors that were six to eight years old actually

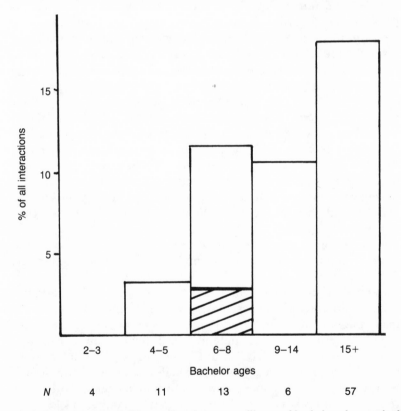

FIG. 7.5   Percentage of all interactions between stallions and bachelors that resulted
in escalated contests. Cross-hatching represents the proportion of interactions in
which bachelors won harems. Sample sizes refer to the frequency of escalated contests in 1981 and 1982.

won harems in combat (fig. 7.5). During these interactions bites and kicks were either attempted or successfully directed to a rival's head and legs. Escalated interactions with bachelors that were fifteen years or older occurred almost 20% of the time, whereas escalated aggression among younger bachelors happened in less than 12% of the events (fig. 7.5). As might be expected, variation among individuals was considerable. Some middle- or old-aged bachelors hardly fought while a few young ones did so frequently. Among young bachelors (two to five years) more time was committed to social play than aggressive interactions, while the converse applied to old males (see chap. 8). Although bachelors fifteen years or older were more likely to escalate encounters with stallions, the probability of winning them was not as great as it was for six- to eight-year-old bachelors (fig. 7.5). The foregoing suggests that aggression and older age may be related.

Is Aggression Related to Old Age?

The relationship between aggression and age is complicated by numerous variables. Both the conditions under which to fight and age could be important in mediating aggression. Resources such as females are valuable commodities since they influence reproductive success. Whether or not males are found regularly with females (e.g., their resource-holding potential; Parker 1974) can be used to predict which males will fight and the conditions under which they will do so. If aggression is related not only to age but to females or to a combination of these two factors, analysis of escalation tendencies among equal-aged males with and without females would reveal the extent to which possession of females mediates escalated aggression.

Comparison of the same individuals as bachelors and as stallions when fifteen years or older revealed the effects of harem possession on male behavior (fig. 7.6). Once males lost harems they were more desperate than harem holders to secure females. This was indicated by a 428% increase in escalated aggression by males recently deposed by other males [4]. Although harem holders would be expected to escalate only when challenged (and as indicated by their lower escalation frequency in fig. 7.6), nonharem holders escalated aggression more frequently. Perhaps old bachelors escalated encounters more often because of their relatively lower reproductive value. Other factors, such as poor body condition or risks associated with marginal resources, would also be expected to modify situations in which males might fight intensively.

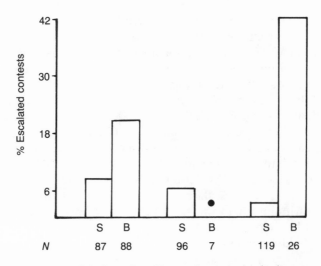

FIG. 7.6 Comparison of the intensity of intermale aggression in three more-than-fifteen-year-old males that lost and regained harems. (S) stallion; (B) same stallion that has become bachelor. Percentage calculated by number of escalated encounters divided by the total frequency of encounters (N) (1979–82). Data included for periods within two weeks of gaining or losing harems. Dot represents a male that was injured during the loss of his harem; he made no attempts to secure new mates.

In response to the question: Is aggression related to old age? the answer is only a qualified yes. Escalated aggression increased with old age in males, but it was also influenced strongly by resource-holding potential. Males that lacked harems were more likely to fight than were males that consorted regularly with females.

Loss of Harems by Old Stallions

Most males lost harems to rivals through aggressive contests. However, some old stallions, apparently with short attention spans, were not always near their females, nor did they always appear attentive toward their mates. Occasionally these old stallions were separated from their females by 50 m to 100 m or more. Old males were the only age cohort that slept as their females moved out of view. On one such occasion Moscha, a twenty-two-year-old, awoke only to search for at least five hours for his females. During this time he sniffed the ground, walked, ran, and covered an estimated 16 km. Twice he approached within 50 m of other bands before veering off in pursuit of the missing females. Moscha's harem was not picked up by other males since his home-range location was poor and few males used it regularly. His females had remained in a portion of the home range with which they were familiar.

In spite of these exceptional events, all harems appropriated by other males were won by direct combat. Three cases are briefly described to illustrate the dynamics and intensity of interactions.

The first involved Harry, a six-year-old bachelor that fought Moscha (at twenty-one years) for a little over three days. The battle was not continuous (e.g., each animal fed in between bouts of aggression), but by its termination Harry had traversed about 50 km and Moscha only a few less. Harry incessantly circled Moscha and sporadically engaged in direct combat. On at least eight occasions both dropped on their knees to avoid bites, although each appeared injured several times since they showed lameness. Harry apparently had more energy and pranced back and forth throughout entire chases, at times dashing into the harem. Moscha gave chase, but toward the end of the fight he seemed exhausted and pursued Harry for only a few meters, whereas earlier pursuits were up to 75 m to 125 m. At the close of the contest, Moscha stood with his head facing the ground, too tired to move very far, and Harry led the harem away.

The second fight was between Frank, a seven-year-old, and Ely, a 17-year-old male. Ely was usually a solitary bachelor, but in this instance he was with several females that had become separated from Frank's large harem only a few days before. Frank saw the small group 80 m away and galloped directly toward them. Without display Frank reared up, kicked Ely with a foreleg, and then kicked two more times with both rear legs simultaneously. As Ely fell to the ground, Frank herded the females away. Ely did not pursue them.

The final encounter included three bachelors—Billy (three years), Sanat (five years), and Ellmer (three years)—that have obtained a female, and Bart (a ten-year-old stallion and Billy's father). The bachelors were approached by Bart at a canter while his harem remained feeding about 170 m away. Bart failed to display and thereby gained a rapid advantage over Billy, who was bitten on his side. Both individuals fought furiously for about 170 seconds, most of which was spent attempting and avoiding leg bites. Bart succeeded in knocking Billy off balance, kicked him squarely in the jaw, and then chased him at full gallop for about 180 m. Billy departed.

Upon returning, Bart fought Ellmer, again without display, and managed to grab the young male's tail by his teeth. Ellmer, quite literally, was swung from side to side three times, although he never quite fell to the ground. As his tail was released, he kicked Bart in the face or jaw three times, in the chest once, and then galloped away for over 1 km although he was not chased.

Bart remained and shook his head at least four times and then walked 20 m away from the last bachelor (Sanat) and the female, both of whom had observed the interaction. After about 60 seconds, Bart

pranced toward Sanat who simply turned and ran away. Bart pursued
for about 250 m and then returned to the female whom he herded
toward his harem for the next hour. During this time he copulated with
her, although she was not in estrus (see sec. 7.8).

Bart was immobilized three days later: he had a superficial leg
wound and a broken canine, although it is uncertain that the tooth ab-
normality resulted from the recent battle.

Tenure

Generally young males were not successful at holding harems for
longer than a few months; three- to five-year-olds averaged less
than a week. Among older animals tenure was more varied. For 15
stallions, six years or older when the study began, that possessed
harems during the study, tenure averaged 3.16 ($\pm$1.98) years. This
figure is somewhat misleading because 5 stallions maintained
harems throughout the study. When the study terminated, these
males ranged in age from eleven to fifteen years. I considered the
effective minimum breeding age of males to be six years during the
first three years of the study since no younger animals sired foals.
During the final years, five was considered the minimum age at
which younger bachelors attained females, although they too were
unsuccessful at fathering offspring. Presumably, the minimum
breeding age in male horses from the Granite Range will decrease
because as the population grows (1) more males will be recruited,
(2) these males will increase the intensity of competition for female
mates, and (3) some males will be successful at securing females at
younger ages. In an analogous situation, LeBoeuf (1974) found
that, as an elephant seal population expanded, a greater proportion of young males bred.

7.5   Costs and Energetics of Mate Defense and Acquisition

While males may vary in their tenure, they also incur costs associated with harem acquisition or defense. Estimating what these
mating costs may be poses problems. Measurements of energy expenditures on reproduction are available for females in a variety of
taxa including lizards (Shine 1980), birds (Ricklefs 1974), and rodents (Randolph et al. 1977), but there are few uniformly agreed
upon areas on which to base such measurements for males. Some
of the difficulties encountered in estimating mating costs of males
may be overcome for horses since information on the energetics of
different activities is available for domestic horses (Hoyt and Taylor 1981; Hintz et al. 1971).

Males incur three principal costs associated with reproduction. The first cost is losses in feeding time through activities related to vigilance. Second is energy debits incurred through running, chasing, and fighting for females. Third is those associated with injury or death. The relationships of these variables to stallion reproduction are each considered below. Additional information on one or more of these activities in male mammals is available for baboons (Stacey 1986), red deer (Clutton-Brock, Guinness, and Albon 1982), marmots (Barash 1981), and bats (Morrison and Morrison 1980).

Vigilance and Feeding Times

The time spent by stallions in vigilance (ears forward, eyes fixed forward) varied considerably, and no relationships among stallion age, band size, or home-range quality were noticeable. Stallions from peripherally located bands (M, P, and B) spent the least time being vigilant—about 90 sec/hr—presumably because their core areas overlapped other bands to the least extent (fig. 4.2). Vigilance was not studied in bachelor males, and therefore it was not possible to determine what effect harem possession may have played in stallion vigilance. However, differences between lactating mares and stallions could be examined on a seasonal basis. Throughout the study, stallions were more vigilant than parous mares [5], but both groups were most vigilant in spring when stallions averaged 2.15 min/hr and lactating females 1.15 min/hr of vigilance. Only about 10% of the nonlactating females exceeded stallions or parous females in vigilance.

Studies of ungulates (Berger 1978; Lipetz and Bekoff 1982) suggest that antipredator behavior greatly modifies foraging time budgets (Berger, Daneke, Johnson, and Berwick, 1983). This did not appear to be the case with horses. The vigilance I detected in Granite Range horses was virtually inconsequential in relation to their feeding budgets (see fig. 6.11).

Energy Expenditure and Harem Size

Although time spent in vigilance detracted little from stallion feeding budgets, harems are not defended by mere vigilance. Energy must be spent in harem defense by displaying, fighting, or even by retreating from opponents. In addition to direct defensive costs resulting from threats by rivals, stallions also herd and chase their females—activities referred to here as harem maintenance (for example, fig. 7.7). A positive relationship between harem size and its defensive (and maintenance) costs might be expected in stallions

FIG. 7.7   Characteristic herding posture which stallions use to move or drive their harems.

since (1) more rival males might be attracted to large harems and thus require greater defensive efforts, or (2) there are more females to keep track of or herd away from rivals. What evidence is available concerning relationships between energy expended by males and the number of females with whom they associate?

To address this question, it is necessary to consider first how energy expenditures may be approximated. If the distance traveled per unit time (velocity) during interactions and the body masses are known, crude estimates of the energy needed to propel individuals can be derived because oxygen consumption (a measure of metabolic energy) and speed are related linearly (Taylor, Heglund, and Maloiy 1982). In horses digestible energy requirements ($DE_{\text{Mcal.day}-1}$) based on activity have been calculated according to:

$$DE_{\text{Mcal.day}-1} = 5.97 + .021(Wt_{kg}) + 5.036X - .48X^2,$$

where $X = kg-km \times 10^3$ (Anderson et al. 1983). Since data concerning these variables were known for Granite horses, DE above maintenance was calculated and then converted to joules.

Several problems are encountered in extrapolating from studies performed under controlled conditions to those in the field. The degree to which metabolic rates and muscular efficiencies vary among individuals, particularly those of different ages, is unknown. The incorporation of individual differences, in addition to differences in weather conditions and slopes traversed, is not practical. Also, only data on locomotor costs are known for domestic horses, yet there are obvious additional expenditures. For instance, the literature on exercise physiology in humans indicates that wrestling or boxing costs are also substantial (Mathews and Fox 1976). Therefore, I assumed male horses that pranced, displayed, reared, or kicked expanded their energy requirements above maintenance by 23.0×10^3 Kcal per kg (body weight) $\cdot$ hr^{-1} since cantering or jumping in domestic horses entails this expenditure (National Research Council 1978). Although accurate values of the energetics of harem defense cannot realistically be achieved, the adoption of the above rather crude method is of heuristic value and serves to highlight relative differences among individuals.

The estimates to be presented include data on males above the locomotor or exercise activities of females. For example, if all band members ran distance d but stallions also moved $d + y$, estimates would be based on the additional costs of moving y. Only data on intermale interactions, intraband herding of females (as illustrated in fig. 7.7), and the (attempted) acquisitions of females were included. Thus, the estimates are conservative since courtship, feeding, nocturnal behavior, and other events difficult to interpret energetically were omitted.

The relationship between energy costs of harem defense (and maintenance) and the number of mates was roughly linear (fig. 7.8) [6], a surprising find given the crude method of estimation. Stallions with larger harems expended more total energy in defense of their mates than those with smaller harems, but they expended less energy on each female.

The least energy was expended by older stallions. Nevertheless, such males did not escape the higher costs of greater defense since trade-offs were involved. Either they had to fight to demonstrate their prowess regularly or adopt home ranges that minimized chances of costly encounters that would expose them to injuries or waste energy. Usually such home ranges were those of the lowest quality. It appeared that older males opted for the latter as illustrated by the occupation of peripheral (and the relatively poor) home ranges of Q, P, and M.

The above data are also of interest because they indicate some of the costs of harem acquisition. Two bachelors, seventeen and three years in age, were followed for thirty days, during which time their energy outputs exceeded body maintenance by 54% and 87% respectively—values that exceeded 82% of the stallions (fig. 7.8). During this period these bachelors harassed stallions, fought, charged into harems, and attempted to secure wandering females. Still, neither bachelor was successful at holding harems longer than seven days, which means that such efforts were essentially wasted. It was evident that for these bachelors the energy cost of obtaining females was markedly greater than the cost of keeping them.

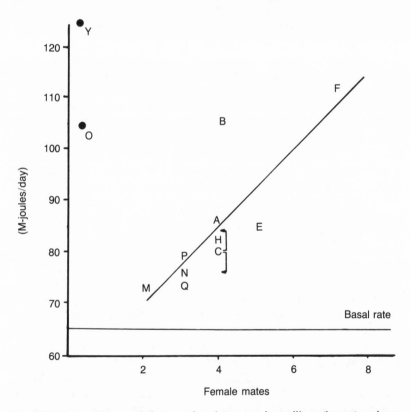

Fig. 7.8   Costs of harem defense and maintenance by stallions (letters) and two bachelors (dots; y= young, o= old) expressed in digestible energy requirements per daylight period. Basal rate is digestible energy without work (from National Research Council 1978) for mean weight of Granite stallions. Mean and individual values are indicated for each C stallion. Data for stallions were based on 70 days (March–June 1982), while for bachelors the data were for 30 days (during the same period).

The most active stallions expended about 48 M-joules/day over basal rate—a value that exceeded by almost 700% the energy spent on harem defense by the least active stallions. Seven of 11 stallions increased their daily *DE* requirements by 16% to 26%. If these horses' daily *DE* requirements, which were collected during a three-month period in 1982, are converted solely into what would be needed to cover a distance, the maximum and minimum distances that stallions would have traversed would be 212 km and 23 km, respectively.

Whether the increased energy that is spent on mates affects harem tenure or increases male mortality, as it does in some male insects (Partridge and Farquhar 1981) and has been postulated for other ungulates (Geist 1971), is now unclear. Stallions that expended the most energy in defense conceivably offset some costs since they fed in the highest quality home ranges. Such stallions may also derive physiological benefits from their repeated workouts since enlarged muscle masses and improved cardiopulmonary performances result from continued exercise (Åstrand and Rodahl 1970). Fighting skills might even have improved if they were practiced regularly (see Symons 1978). However, if any of these hypothesized benefits were gained, nutritional demands must be met, a topic for which little data exist. Clearly stallions with smaller harems fed in the worst areas, experienced the longest feeding times (sec. 6.7), and were older. If the animals that incurred the greatest energy costs were susceptible to heightened mortality, the trend was not obvious in the Granite data. Death probably results from a combination of factors that include energy debits, poor nutrition, catabolic androgens, and especially injuries (see below) and not just energy expenditures.

Injuries and Deaths

Ninety-six percent of the adult males in the population in any given year showed signs of bite-related wounds (fig. 7.9). Among those four years or older, one had well over fifty distinct scars on his body, 21% had open bloody sores, and 13% had leg injuries as suggested by lameness or bloody lacerations (fig. 7.10). Although lameness was never permanent in the Granite horses, in an ecosystem with large carnivores, animals with leg injuries are more susceptible to predators (Schaller 1972; Kruuk 1972). Horses with leg injuries rarely interacted, and one stallion remained lying on his side next to his foraging females for 3 ½, 5 ½, 5, and 4 hours on successive days after a leg wound.

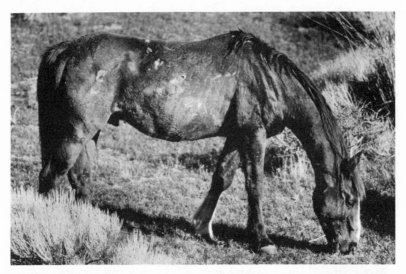

FIG. 7.9   Flesh and open wounds and scars of an old Granite Range bachelor. Photo by Emory Kristof, © National Geographic Society.

Although wounds must influence an animal's overall efficiency, neither their immediate nor long-term effects were very obvious. In addition to infections and subsequent diseases that can result from open wounds, foraging can be impeded by injuries sustained in combat. Dental anomalies (the suspected result of receiving kicks) can diminish feeding efficiency and the body condition of the afflicted animal. Both males and females with broken teeth were consistently in poor condition (sec. 6.5). Death through combat-induced wounds may be more common than once believed. In 1769 Gmelin reported observations of what he believed to be a tarpan stallion killing a less-able domestic stallion in a contest over a domestic female. Zeuner's (1963,313) translation is as follows:

> A wild stallion once saw a tame stallion with tame mares. He was interested only in these, but the tame stallion would not put up with it and they got into a violent fight. The tame stallion defended himself with his feet; the wild one, however, bit his adversary with his teeth and in spite of all resistance he succeeded in biting the tame one until he was dead, so that he could abduct his coveted mare.

More recently, a male horse on Assateague Island lost an ear in a fight but did not die, perhaps only because humans intervened (Keiper, personal communication). Kownacki (1980) reported one death resulting from a fight among free-ranging horses in Poland.

In the Granite Range two males (five and seven years old) died from fighting, and another disappeared after a highly escalated fight and was presumed to have died. In the confirmed deaths the forelegs of each animal became infected and festered for several months after the fights.

The social antecedents surrounding the death of a domestic five-year-old were unique and implicate (albeit anecdotally) the importance of developing fighting skills through practice. The male had lived on a nearby ranch whose other males were castrated. Mock fighting was reduced in the geldings, and the normal male was deprived of aggressive social interactions. In other species, reduced juvenile social play results in diminished behavioral repertoires as adults (Berger 1979a, 1980), and thus the domestic five-year-old must have been poor at exercising fighting skills. When he became a stallion of the ranch females, a Granite bachelor thoroughly outmatched him in combat. The domestic stallion died as a result of the body or foreleg wounds incurred in that battle. Because the number of males alive at the end of each year and the number that died as a result of combat-related injuries were known, the proportion of adult males (five years or older) that died due to fighting could be estimated. To be conservative, I omitted the (above) domestic male but included the three Granite males that perished. The sum of the total number of males alive at the

FIG. 7.10   Bite wound on the foreleg of a more-than-twenty-year-old male. Note exposed flesh, dried blood, swelling, and pus. The anterior portion of the leg had an equal-sized laceration.

end of each year of study was 98. Thus, about 3% of the males died as a result of fighting.

Among other mammals injury and death are not uncommon (Geist 1971, 1978b), although they are by no means frequent. Most red deer stags are probably injured in their lifetimes (Clutton-Brock, Guinness, and Albon 1982), 5% to 10% of musk-ox bulls die from fight wounds (Wilkinson and Shank 1977), and Dall sheep (Murie 1944), mule deer (Robinette, Hancock, and Jones 1977), nyalas (Anderson 1980), and other antelopes (Leuthold 1977) perish in fights. Walruses (Miller 1975), narwhals (Best 1981), and rodents (Rose and Gaines 1976; Sherman and Morton 1984) are regularly injured during aggressive encounters.

The above data on horses and the accounts of other species are indicative that male mating costs are high. Yet evidence that mating efforts reduce the lifespan of male mammals is equivocal. The most successful bull elephant seals are never seen again after the height of their breeding (LeBoeuf 1974); quite reasonably, they are believed to have died. However, comparable data on the lifespan of equal-aged animals that did not incur such efforts are lacking. In populations of zebras where the intensity of intermale aggression exceeds the average, predation on males is greater than expected. Nevertheless, it is unclear whether predated males are bachelors or stallions (Berger 1983a). The best information on male mating costs comes from red deer where an inverse, but not significant, relationship between male reproductive success and lifespan was found (Clutton-Brock, Guinness, and Albon 1982).

7.6 COOPERATION AND MATE PROTECTION

Observations of cooperation in mammals are not new. One of the first reported cases concerned horses on the Falkland Islands, where Charles Darwin reported two males aiding one another in a battle to steal females from a third male (Darwin [1871] 1888). Since then, behaviors performed on behalf of others have generated much interest because of their importance in understanding why individuals act in seemingly benevolent fashions. Most explanations of helping have been based on kin selection hypotheses, but examples of helping among nonkin are found in social carnivores (Rood 1974, 1978; Packer and Pusey 1982, 1983), higher primates (Packer 1977; Walters 1980), bats (McCracken 1984; Wilkinson 1984), an African antelope (Wirtz 1981, 1982), and possibly killer whales (Smith et al. 1981).

In Granite horses, individuals cooperate even though they are not related genetically to each other. To understand why this behavior occurs requires information on the kind and frequency of helping as well as on the identities of individuals that receive and give aid.

Associations among Males

On seventeen occasions during the study two or more males possessed harems together, situations that I referred to as alliances since males worked together to defend harems from rival males. However, most alliances were short lived. Only two (12%) exceeded seven months in duration. In thirteen cases where genealogies were known completely, alliances never consisted of brothers or half sibs. Most alliances were among young bachelors (two to five years) that obtained their first females, but the longer consortships were between individuals seventeen and eleven years old, lasting two and a half years, and between Carter (fourteen years) and Creagan (eleven years), lasting at least four years.

Alliances and Reciprocity

One of the most notable features of bands that contained two or more stallions was that one individual clearly dominated the other(s). Dominance was defined on the basis of dyadic encounters and resultant access to mates. Thus, dominant males spent more time closer to harem females, and when males remained in the group for long periods of time, they fathered more offspring. For example, in the two prolonged consortships, one dominant male fathered eighteen times more foals than the subordinate; in the other, the alpha individual accounted for thirteen foals and the subordinate none. Not only did such subordinate males remain with bands for varying periods of time, but during these periods they (1) risked injuries to prevent theft of females that they had little access to, and (2) aided alpha stallions in encounters with bachelors or rival stallions.

Three other points are important concerning alliances. First, dominant stallions initiated harem defense significantly less often than subordinates (fig. 7.11) [7]. In other words, subordinate males became involved in aggressive encounters with rival males more often than did dominant stallions. And, because subordinates were involved in relatively more encounters than dominant males (see "defensive initiations" of dominants and subordinates in fig. 7.11), subordinates actually ran the risk of fight injuries more frequently than did dominant stallions. Second, both individuals risked fight

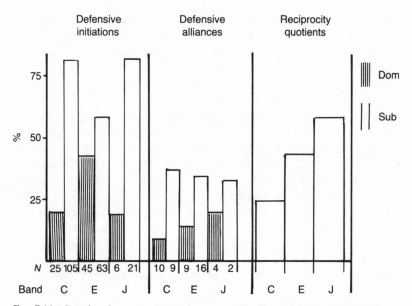

FIG. 7.11　Intraband cooperation and parameters of harem defense in three bands that persisted for 4 months (J), 2½ years (E), and more than 4 years (C). Percentage refers to encounters when one stallion initiated defense of the harem (defensive initiations) and a second stallion in the same band provided subsequent aid (defensive alliances) to his band mate. Percentage for defensive alliances is derived by dividing frequency of initiations by frequency of subsequent aid. Dom=dominant stallion; Sub=subordinate stallion; N=number of interband interactions. Calculation of reciprocity quotients in Appendix 7.

injuries to aid the other, a situation that I referred to as "defensive alliances" (fig. 7.11). At these times, one stallion initiated harem defense, *but* the other stallion later aided his partner in physical defense of their harem. During defensive alliances both males fought together against intruders on behalf of their common interests (e.g., their harem). Since stallions of multimale bands each initiated encounters and came to the aid of their alliance partners, they mutually helped each other.

The third point is that the distribution of favors was skewed toward dominant males (fig. 7.11). When one stallion defended the harem against rival males while the other stallion benefited by *not* having to fight or challenge the rivals, I considered the action to be a "favor." Despite reciprocity in the giving of favors between stallions of the same multimale bands, there was no equality in helping. Subordinate males aided dominants in defensive alliances significantly more often than dominants helped subordinates [8].

In figure 7.11, dominant males in three multimale bands can be seen to initiate both harem defense and defensive alliances relatively less often than subordinate stallions.

The extent to which stallions aided one another during harem defense varied among bands. Some multimale-band stallions directed more aid to alliance partners than those in other multimale bands. These interband differences in helping were quantified by calculating reciprocity quotients (RQs). This technique involved interband comparisons of the relative frequencies that dominants aided subordinates already involved in active harem defense with frequencies of aid given by subordinates when dominants were already involved in defense (Appendix 7). In simplified terms, this measure contrasts the degree to which dominants helped subordinates and vice versa. For example, in band C RQ=.25. This means that the dominant stallion (Creagan) garnered relatively more aid from the subordinate male (Carter) than that given in other bands where RQs were substantially greater (fig. 7.11).

The above information differs from the picture of reciprocity reported in other mammals. Unlike findings for lions (Bygott, Bertram, and Hanby 1979), alliances in horses did not confer greater reproductive advantages per male, nor did they result in longer periods of tenure. Stallions from bands experienced significantly greater tenure when they were from single-male bands than those from multimale bands [9]. Also, the chances that subordinates inherit breeding status, as observed in waterbuck (Wirtz 1981) or suggested for mongooses (Rood 1978), were slight in horses. In the single case in which it occurred, a subordinate male obtained half a harem only after the dominant and five other band members perished in a winter snowstorm (Berger 1983c). Thus, a dilemma encases the seemingly altruistic behavior of subordinate stallions. Why should subordinates remain with dominant stallions, fight on behalf of dominants, expend more energy, and risk injuries even though the probability of obtaining mates is low?

Costs and Benefits of Helping

To gain some idea of the reasons why individuals help, it is useful to examine costs and benefits to participants in alliances. These are summarized in table 7.1. Benefits conferred by dominance include access to mates, reduced energy expenditure, and a possible reduction of injuries since dominants defend harems less than subordinants. Observations to support these potential benefits have already been pointed out (above); they can be summarized as fol-

Table 7.1   Major Potential Costs and Benefits
to Dominant and Subordinate Stallions of Alliance Formation

Dominant	Subordinate
Benefits	
1. Energy losses and risks of injuries in interband encounters minimized since subordinates do most of the fighting	1. Sneak copulations
	2. Inherit harems
2. Access to mates	
Costs	
1. Injuries due to frequent assertions of dominance toward the partner	1. Energy losses and risks of injuries in interband encounters since they do most of the fighting
2. Sneak copulations by subordinates	2. Injuries due to intraband fights

lows: (1) dominant males left more offspring than subordinates, and (2) in band C the dominant male spent on the average about 7.1×10^6 joules/day less than the subordinate (fig. 7.8). Thus, the evidence is reasonable that dominant males benefit or, more appropriately, that they incur relatively fewer direct costs than subordinates.

The foregoing leaves unresolved why subordinates do not abandon multimale bands and go elsewhere in their attempts to achieve mating success. What benefits might be obtained by remaining in bands as subordinate stallions? The possible benefits appear meager but include sneak copulations when dominant stallions may be away from their females, copulations with wandering (e.g., nonharem) females, and perhaps increased access to high-quality foods. These benefits are not often realized. As indicated earlier, sneak copulations were rare. In only two cases did two subordinate stallions achieve copulations. One occurred only after the subordinate remained in a band after three years; the other was secured after two and a half years. In the latter case the subordinate was forced by the dominant to leave the band within two months after the copulation. Another potential benefit might be copulations with wandering females, but it seemed that subordinate males had no greater chance at successfully fertilizing such females than did bachelors or other stallions.

Do subordinates benefit by residing in high-quality home ranges? Probably not. Only one multimale band occupied a high-quality home range. In all other cases single male bands used high-quality ranges. The suggestion that males gain access to high-quality home ranges by being subordinate does not appear tenable.

Do subordinate stallions have greater mating opportunities than bachelors? A tentative answer is no, given that bachelors obtained females, whereas the only subordinate male to do so was after the dominant male (and half the harem) died in a high-altitude snow storm (Berger 1983c). Only 1 of 17 subordinates secured females through inheritance, while 9 of 33 bachelors sooner or later obtained females.

Overall, the lack of access to mates, the greater energy expenditures of subordinates (relative to dominant stallions), and the lack of access to better feeding sites suggest that few direct benefits are accrued by subordinate stallions. This explains why most alliances were short lived; 88% lasted less than seven months. By going elsewhere, subordinates had better chances to sire offspring than if they remained.

Old Age and Last Chances

Ages of subordinates have not yet been considered, and age seems to be the factor that best accounts for helping by subordinates. In the four longest consortships, subordinates were old males. The subordinate's tenure length, and his age and that of the dominant male at the end of tenure were as follows: 4 yrs (minimum)/14 and 11; 2½ yrs/17 and 11; 7 months/18 and 14—the dominant died; and 4 months/14 and 7. Although the data indicate that subordinate males were older in these cases, it was unclear whether older males were more tolerant of subordination and therefore joined single-male bands or whether prime-aged males tolerated older ones. In other words cause and effect could not be separated.

Observations of the responses of two dominant stallions to two subordinates that copulated provided few clues as to which tolerated which since the responses differed in each situation. In the first, a sneak copulation seems to have resulted in the subordinate's forced emigration about two months later, despite his tenure of two and a half years in the group. In the other instance, the subordinate went unmated with his harem's females for two years, after which several copulations occurred, without expulsion, with the dominant male's daughter. Following an additional year with the band, both the subordinate and the dominant male copulated with each of the two new females that were added to the band. Indeed there may be reproductive "payoffs" associated with long-tenure periods of subordination.

The evidence for cooperation among males can be summarized as follows: Most alliances occurred among young males; these terminated after relatively short periods of time, probably because access to female mates was poor. Among older males helping was not altruistic. Instead it was better explained by supposing that these males aided themselves by increasing their proximity to females. For old males, helping dominant stallions defend their harems may have been the easiest way to increase breeding opportunities, even if chances for actual mating were poor. Nevertheless, not all old males attempted to form alliances; some went unmated for the remainder of their lives while others eventually procured females.

Older individuals' attempts to increase their fitness by cooperating with group members may not be so unusual among social mammals, though the underlying causes probably differ. Malcolm and Marten (1982) reported that old males constituted 20% of the male helpers found in Serengeti wild dogs. Such individuals regurgitated food to pups and chased predators. In this case, kin selection best explained the behavior since old males shared genes in common with the pups.

7.7   FEMALES AND THEIR RELATIONSHIPS

Females are not often as overtly aggressive as males (Hrdy 1981), and they tend to adopt different behavioral tactics for reproduction. In many species females are social and form complex relationships with relatives and nonrelatives. It is surprising that only a few studies (Clutton-Brock, Guinness, and Albon 1982; Geist 1971; Hogg 1984; Rutberg 1984) have focused on ungulate females, since the effects of sociality on female reproduction or on their relationships have been considered in carnivores (Rood 1980), primates (Dunbar 1980; Rowell 1970, 1974), bats (McCracken and Bradbury 1981), and colonial rodents (Downhower and Armitage 1971; Murie and Michener 1984).

Female ungulates have continual nutritional demands (Geist 1971; Ralls 1976); their reproductive performance is dependent upon their ability to convert food into offspring or milk. The energy demands may be especially heavy in female equids, which might spend eleven months of each year pregnant, lactating through nine of them (sec. 6.6). Even under good nutritional conditions females have little reprieve from these incessant energy drains. For instance, consider a female that produced ten foals in her lifetime and, to be conservative, weaned each by eight months of age. Although most people might not intuitively consider horses as producers of large quantities of milk, a mare's lifetime milk production under the above conditions could vary from 8,231 kg to 18,454 kg (9 to 20 tons) of milk. (Calculations based on minimum and maximum values from data found in Linzell 1972; Pollock 1980; National Research Council 1978.)

Females must devote considerable effort to fulfilling their nutritional needs. In doing so, they strive to locate favorable environments and obtain high social ranks. In numerous species the attainment of high social status affects reproduction, but is this so among female feral horses?

How Important Are Dominance Hierarchies?

Classically, it has been thought that through aggressiveness individuals may achieve high rank and access to limited food resources (reviewed by Wittenberger 1981). This did not seem to be the case among Granite Range females. Mares were not often aggressive to those with whom they were familiar (e.g., band mates of either sex). Intraband variation in aggression was considerable, but even in early spring when food was most limited and new vegetative growth had not yet begun, few feeding displacements occurred. The most food-related supplantations observed in an hour was nine, but this was exceptional. On the average less than one individual per three hours of observation would be involved in food-related aggression during the most stressful season. At best, an aggressive individual may have gained direct access to a particular clump of grass or food morsel, although, indirectly, dominant individuals might have gained more due to avoidance by others.

Aggression among band females was detectable in two other broadly defined situations; these concerned water and infants. In winter when water sources froze or in summer when they sometimes slowed to a trickle, females (infrequently) congregated for access to water. When doing so, they inevitably kicked and pushed their bodies at one another. Most intraband aggression occurred, however, when individuals approached too close to a newborn foal. Aggression also was observed when weaned yearlings annoyed their mothers and attempted to suckle.

Females established dominance mostly by retracting their ears and moving simultaneously toward the intruder (about 92% of the cases; $N=1,342$). Bite attempts or biting (8%) or kicking (less than 0.01%) were not common. Female horses in the wild rarely kicked at other females, a situation radically different from farm animals (Waring 1983). In one instance dominance was achieved through tool use (Beck 1980) after a 400 kg mare supplanted a 540 kg band mate by raising and shaking a dead sage bush. The larger female probably moved simply because she was startled.

The importance of dominance, although controversial, has traditionally been viewed as enabling priority of access to limited resources (reviews in Wilson 1975; Wittenberger 1981). For example, in wild primate populations dominant individuals are less likely to die in years of food shortages than are subordinates (Dittus 1977, 1979). In food-provisioned primates dominance may (Silk et al. 1981) or may not (Gouzoules, Gouzoules, and Fedigan 1982; Wolfe 1984) bestow reproductive advantages, depending on countless variables—the most important of which concern density, food availability, and mates.

If dominance confers reproductive benefits upon female horses, some effects of dominance should be discernible. Over the study period no clear correlates between reproductive success and dominance emerged. This probably stemmed from the fluctuating ranks held by females at different periods of the year. Rarely were the same females consistently the dominant members of their bands. Dominance relationships changed regularly and most often over periods that spanned a few days to several weeks. Because feeding displacements were rare and dominance changed among individuals, it was difficult if not impossible to assign a "dominant female" status for intraband hierarchies. In fact, the only periods when females consistently dominated others in their bands were after the births of their foals; a similar situation may exist in Mountain zebras (Penzhorn 1984). Only one female in the entire Granite population retained alpha status in her band, and the number of foals she produced was no better nor worse than the three other females with whom she associated for four years.

In contrast to assertions of the importance of high rank in other populations (Houpt and Keiper 1982; Wells and von Goldschmidt-Rothschild 1979), dominance appeared inconsequential in Granite females. The argument that the influence of rank was obscured in this study because it was conducted over a period of food abundance (since the population was increasing) does not appear valid. Numerous bands used mediocre or poor foraging sites (sec. 4.9). Mares from these areas had (1) foals that suckled for relatively short periods of time (fig. 6.8), and (2) poor reproductive performances relative to females from better areas (fig. 4.7). In such bands increased aggression and accentuated hierarchies might be expected for limited resources, but there were no differences in rates of intraband displacements over food between bands in poor and other home ranges [10]. Studies of horses in the New Forest, where animals were food limited especially in the winter (Pollock 1980), also indicated that food shortages rarely resulted in increased antagonism among band members. In Granite Range horses intraband dominance seems to be of little biological importance and had no effect on female reproductive success.

Scramble Competition and Implications for Female Behavior

The idea that animals compete by "scrambling" to consume rather than by contesting for resources (Nicholson 1957) appears to be a more potent force in competition among female equids than does dominance alone. Scramble competition occurred among bands. It was best illustrated by the observation that females that occupied better home-range areas produced more offspring; those offspring then suckled longer and grew faster. The data suggest that female reproductive success was affected more by access to and use of resources than it was by intraband interactions.

Although scramble competition was passive and females rarely behaved aggressively toward band members, the notion that female behavior is unimportant in structuring horse societies seems unfounded. Mares exercised social options to minimize potential resource competition. They behaved aggressively toward *potential* band members such as mares newly procured by resident stallions. This was true of females that lived together for several years in harems larger than median. These mares were significantly more aggressive toward female intruders than were those that resided in small or newly formed bands [11], although both familiarity and harem size were interactive [12]. Females that joined existing harems were noticeably "uncomfortable." They were displaced, bitten, and chased by resident females, and their attempts to leave their new bands were almost always thwarted by stallions, which herded and at times bit them.

Why do females immigrate? Perhaps they can gain access to more favorable food environments by transferring to other groups. However, this option was exercised by only about 7% of the females (five years or older) each year. Moreover, emigration from a band with subsequent immigration to another could be subtle. Emigration involved gradually foraging progressively further from the group over a period of several weeks. Resident stallions regularly herded such female stragglers back to the harem and occasionally bit them. One such female had three distinct bite wounds and bled from above her hip.

Basically, females had two choices once they joined a new band. They could make the best of it by forming alliances (see below) and keeping aggressors away or they could bide their time for later opportunities to emigrate. The evidence suggests they did both.

Cooperation among Females

Females do not often show behaviors that benefit conspecifics except for mutual grooming when insects are bothersome (Tyler 1972; Wells and von Goldschmidt-Rothschild 1979). The most interesting aspects of female cooperation concern sexual harassment after male takeovers. In these instances, males interrupt female foraging, sniff ano-genital regions, occasionally stand with erect penises, and sometimes attempt to copulate with their new females (sec. 7.8). At these times nonharassed females jeopardized their own well-being by aiding their female band mates. The most dramatic case of cooperation involved two nonrelated mares (four and twenty-two years old) that had lived in the same band for three years. These females became separated from their original band and each other, but a few days later they re-met in a band that had a new stallion. For the next three days, during numerous forced copulation attempts toward both by this stallion, the females reciprocally aided each other (thirteen times and eighteen times respectively) by kicking and biting the stallion as he persistently and aggressively made ano-genital approaches. On other occasions nonrelated females helped one another in similar fashion but not as frequently as in the incident presented above. Although female cooperation occurred under conditions associated with male takeovers and happened less frequently at other times (e.g., coalitions against nonband females), female alliances were not common. On the average they were observed two or three times each year.

7.8 SEXUAL CONFLICT AND FETICIDE

The information presented so far indicates that males and females differ in the ways in which they achieve mating success. Males attempt to secure mates for as long as possible. Females breed throughout most of their lives and form complex associations with other within-band females, occasionally helping each other at times of duress. Although the reproductive interests of the sexes differ, direct aggression or conflict between the sexes is not very common. Yet, it is never more obvious than when males take over groups of females. In other taxa such as carnivores (Bertram 1975) or primates (Hrdy 1979), evidence now suggests that the postnatal killing of young and even induced abortions (Pereira 1983) are evolved traits, exerting strong selective pressures on adult male and female behavior (Packer and Pusey 1983). In ungulates it is therefore perplexing that either no species have developed similar tactics or that these behaviors have not been reported, especially since ungulates share common features in their social systems with the above groups (Eisenberg 1981; Hogg 1984) and ungulates have been extensively studied (Geist and Walther 1974; Wemmer 1986). In at least one ungulate, pronghorn, in utero siblings compete for maternal resources and not all are carried to gestation (O'Gara 1969).

Forced Copulations and Unfamiliar Females

When new stallions take over harems they almost always investigate the ano-genital regions of females and may engage in sexual behavior. Of thirty-eight cases where males encountered unfamiliar females, fourteen females (37%) were forced to copulate. Four females successfully blocked copulation attempts by kicking at, running from, and turning away from their pursuers. In cases where males were successful they chased, herded, and bit the females that ran. I judged copulations to be successful when males mounted, intromitted, and then ejaculated (as inferred by pelvic thrusts during copulations and flacid penises and listlessness in the males afterward). One stallion intermittently pursued and tried to bite a female for three hours, during which time she kicked at him at least fifty times (some of which were successful), traversed 5 km, and was copulated with five times. At no time was she courted (smelled, licked, nibbled, or whinnied to). Although females always protested assaults by kicking and running, they were not often able to avoid the sexual behavior of new males if their resident stallions were not present. The males most responsible for forced copulations in the Granite Range were never virgins, and they ranged in age from six to fifteen years.

The inescapable conclusion resulting from the encounters described above is that females were raped. Twelve were already pregnant when forced to copulate (see below), and their protests were unable to thwart the aggressive sexual assaults of males. Although the use of such vocabulary may be offensive when applied to nonhuman subjects (Gowaty 1982), the term *rape* is perhaps a more appropriate portrayal of the actions bestowed on these relatively defenseless mares. In nonhumans rape has been reported in insects (Thornhill 1980), fish (Farr 1980), birds (McKinney, Derrickson, and Mineau 1983), and mammals (Hrdy 1981).

Such behavior has also been noted previously in free-ranging equids. McCort (1980) reported that bachelor burros "gang rape" unreceptive females, and Tyler (1972) found male horses that attempted forced copulations with anestrous mares. She stated, "they drove mares for long periods and often singled out mares, which they drove relentlessly. They bit them and tried to mount them," but the extent to which males copulated successfully was not reported. On Assateague Island, Keiper (unpub.) also reported similar behavior, "[the stallion] repeatedly tried to copulate with the female, mounting her and staying up while she walked along for 30 feet or more. She tried to back-kick him and her actions prevented any successful copulation that I saw. However, the forced copulation attempts continued for more than an hour and until after dark."

The idea that mares ran from males to stimulate sexual interests is unlikely, at least in the Granite Range, for two reasons. First, males responded to nonharem females with sexual aggression whether or not they were in estrus. If females lifted their tails or allowed courtship they might be courted, but if they did not, males still chased and forced copulations upon them. Second, of 244 copulations between stallions and harem females, all involved one or more aspects of courtship (e.g., smelling, licking, nibbling, or whinnying) and at no time were they forced to copulate. (These data are based on nonhuman manipulations. In one case [see below] a forced copulation occurred after a female was immobilized.) If females stimulated male sexual appetites by running, there is no reason why escape tactics should be confined only to nonharem females. These courtship differences in male behavior toward familiar and nonfamiliar females were strikingly and significantly different [13].

One experimental line of evidence indicates that stallions will force copulation upon females with whom they are familiar. A female in her first trimester of pregnancy was immobilized and separated from band A with whom she had remained for four prior years. Upon encountering Bart (a ten-year-old stallion), she was chased for 3 km, bitten at least five times even though she kicked him at least ten times, and was forced to copulate at least twice. During the next day she left Bart's band and returned 5 km to A. As she approached A, a naso-naso greeting took place between her and Alvin, the stallion. I suspect they were quite familiar with each other because the prior four-year association had included courtship, copulation, and protection of their foals from predators (sec. 8.4). However, at this time (and the only time witnessed for a familiar female) copulation was forced; ten to twelve days later she was again courted by Alvin.

Although these observations are based on a single sample, they are consistent with other evidence that males force copulation upon females to advance their own reproductive interests. They also indicate that males may protect their own genetic investments by copulating with females that have been away from their protection. In the case involving Alvin and the immobilized A female, it was not possible for Alvin to observe the copulations between his former female and Bart, but Alvin nevertheless copulated with the mare by force upon her return to his harem.

Why are familiar females not forced to copulate? Probably the best answer is that these females are already in harems and are usually pregnant. When they are not, males can afford to wait until ovulation occurs since the chances are small that females will be fertilized by nonharem males. Thus, male reproductive interests can be maximized simply by holding onto females.

New Social Environments

To assess whether females in bands taken over by new males were more likely to not reproduce than were those in stable bands (i.e., those not experiencing stallion changes), the frequency of foals borne by females in the next reproductive season was compared in bands with new and resident stallions. Foal production by females in stable bands exceeded that in unstable ones by 40% (80% versus 40% respectively; fig. 7.12), but these results were influenced by female age. Hence, foal production was compared between females of equivalent age cohorts (four years or less and those older) in both stable and unstable bands. Regardless of age, mares from unstable bands had significantly lower reproductive success in the next parturition season than those from stable bands [14]. However, both age and band stability are correlated and affect reproductive performance. In addition to age, the data also indicate that band instability mediated decreased female fecundity.

Similar findings have been reported for Sable Island horses (Welsh 1975) and Mountain zebras (Penzhorn 1985). In this latter case, none of seventeen mares in groups taken over by new stallions produced young within twelve months of the takeovers, despite the population's mean foaling rate of 32%. Based on this foaling rate, five to six foals would have been expected in the absence of takeovers. Penzhorn (1985) felt that mares from the unstable bands may have aborted their young.

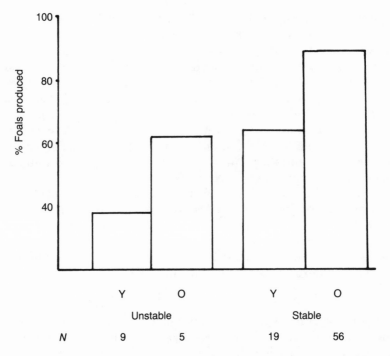

Fig. 7.12 Histogram of percentages of foals born to adult females in stable and unstable bands in the next reproductive period. (Y) young (2–4 yrs); (O) older.

Abortions and Male Reproductive Success

If males enhance their reproductive success by acquiring new females, they should increase their own genetic representation in the population, diminish that of others, or both. These predictions could be evaluated for Granite horses because paternity and pregnancy rates were established through observations of (1) copulation and birth dates, and (2) consortships with females during receptive and nonreceptive periods (Appendix 8).

Continuous observations of 14 pregnant females before, during, and after male takeovers offered insight into how males altered the genetic contributions of their competitors as well as of themselves. In 11 cases females were less than six months pregnant, and, following encounters with strange males, 9 of the fetuses died; also 9 of the females were forced to copulate, and 78% (7/9) of their fetuses died (table 7.2). In cases where females were not forced to copulate ($N=4$), 3 abortions still followed, presumably in response to harassment (by the resident females or stallion) or other stresses imposed by changing social environments. In 86% (12 of 14) of the above cases, females were reinseminated by the new male, although not all of his offspring lived (table 7.2). In 3 of these instances, females returned to estrus as suggested by stallion courtship and copulation on the eighth, fourteenth, and sixteenth (and again for the latter female on the eighteenth) day after the forced copulation, respectively. In another case, the female was courted on the tenth through the twelfth days past the forced copulation, an indication that she had resumed cycling.

Only one female more than six months pregnant was forced to copulate, and her fetus survived (table 7.2). Two other females also changed bands when more than six months pregnant, and the younger (three years old) aborted even though she was not forced to copulate. Months later she was courted by the new male and gave birth fourteen months after she entered that band. The other female (five years old) was not forced to copulate; she gave birth about one month after entering the new band (table 7.2). Numerous other females were involved in band changes after they were more than halfway through their pregnancies. Although it was not clear whether some females were forced to copulate because observations were discontinuous, females more than halfway through their pregnancies gave birth within five months of takeovers by males (see sec. 6.3). These data indicate that most fetuses under 180 days perish in utero after band changes whereas older fetuses survive events associated with changed social environments.

The data presented above show that 82% of the females procured by new males when less than six months pregnant aborted their fetuses; 82% were forced to copulate. The evidence is good that new males profited by (1) the diminution of genetic investments of rival males, and (2) reinsemination of females that aborted (despite the approximately 50% probability that their unborn offspring would survive that year; table 7.2).

Functional Considerations

The proximate mechanisms responsible for increased abortions in female horses that changed bands is not well known. In part, the increase stems from the possible effects of forced copulations and presumed physiological changes imposed by harassment or other social factors in new environments. It is likely that each of these generic sets of factors contribute, particularly because females that were less than six months pregnant and not forced to copulate still

TABLE 7.2 Status of Females during Male Takeovers and Subsequent Fate of Their Previous and New Fetuses

	Month of Pregnancy When Encountering New Male					
	6th Month or Less			More than 6th Month		
Fate of Fetuses of Deposed Stallions	Maternal Age (yr)	Forced Copulation	Fate of New Fetus	Maternal Age (yr)	Forced Copulation	Fate of New Fetus
Previous fetus died	4	+	Aborted near birth	3	—	Foal born 14 months later
	4	+	Died postnatally			
	5	+	Aborted near birth			
	7	+	Aborted near birth			
	8	+	Survived			
	10	+	Survived			
	10	$-^a$	Survived			
	11	$-^a$	Survived			
	20	+	Survived			
Previous fetus lived	5	$+^b$	Aborted near birth	2	+	Fetus survived
	11	$+^b$	Survived	4	$?^c$	Fetus survived
				5	—	Fetus survived
				7	$?^c$	Fetus survived
				10	$?^c$	Fetus survived
				13	$?^c$	Fetus survived

Notes: Previous fetuses are those from prior resident stallions whereas new fetuses are those resulting from impregnations by new stallions following takeovers.

[a] Not forced to copulate but female returned to estrus at least 6 weeks after takeover and was reinseminated by the new male.

[b] Unclear whether the fetus of the resident stallion survived because the forced copulation occurred 30 days after the first copulation, yet no subsequent estrous cycles were detected.

[c] Band changes occurred (one individual changing twice) but discontinuous observations precluded direct knowledge of forced copulation.

aborted, as did a female that was more than six months pregnant (table 7.2). Forced copulation could cause physical damage to the mother or fetus due to the penetration of the cervix during pregnancy, resulting in spontaneous abortion, or it might introduce disease vectors. Other stresses could also be involved. A myriad of causes underlie equid abortions (Roberts 1968; Mahaffey 1968; Laing 1979; van Niekerk and Morgenthal 1982; Studdert 1974). Prenatal stress is known to result in a greater incidence of abortion in mice (Herrenkohl 1979) and primates (see Pereira 1983; Dunbar 1980; Silk 1983), and there is no reason why it could not happen in horses.

Although it is clear that some males ultimately enhance their reproductive success, functional considerations must still rely upon which sex exerts greater control (Labov 1981). If females were incapable of preventing abortions, the advantage would lie exclusively with males (Schwagmeyer 1979), which seems to be the case at early stages of pregnancy. However, because some females failed to abort at later stages of pregnancy and others aborted despite the lack of copulation, consideration of multiple factors are certainly necessary in further study.

Origins

Three hypotheses concerning the origin of feticide in equids can be advanced. First, feticide is a product of domestication. There are no data bearing on this idea nor is there an easy way of determining whether this may be the case since ancestors of domestic horses cannot be studied. Second, feticide is a pathological behavior under abnormal population conditions. Since comparative studies of pregnancy and paternity rates are not available for unmanipulated wild populations or those at different densities, this alternative cannot be dismissed. However, it seems an unlikely one because individual males benefit (table 7.2) and the Granite population is not unusually dense for feral horses.

A third possibility is that feticide has evolutionary roots in related African and Asian forms. If this was the case, similarities in the social organization, forms of male aggression, and birth seasons between native equids and wild horses might be expected. Mountain zebras (Penzhorn 1975), Common zebras (Klingel 1969b), and Przewalski's horses (Mohr 1971; Groves 1974) all live in year-round bands; both zebra species breed throughout the year (although they have peaks as do Granite horses); and female reproductive tracts are similar among all species (King 1965; Smuts 1976b). Observations in zoological parks (National Zoological Park, Minnesota Zoological Park; unpub.) reveal forced copulatory attempts toward unfamiliar zebra and Przewalski's females. The possibility that feticide occurs in some native equids, particularly in Mountain zebras, gains support from Penzhorn's (1985) field data on reduced fecundity in mares after male takeovers.

Infanticide

No cases of infanticide occurred in the Granite Range, nor did any infants die or disappear with male takeovers as found in primates or carnivores (Hrdy 1979; Schaller 1972; Bertram 1975; Packer and Pusey 1983). However, stallions were aggressive to nonharem foals, and this behavior appeared related to infant sex. Such events were exceedingly rare. On three occasions, stallions attacked male infants less than three days old, and once three bachelors kicked a day-old male separated from his natal band. Two cases involved successful kicks to the foals' bodies and the other was an attempted body bite. In all cases, resident stallions fought on behalf of their foals, and when the bachelors attacked the day-old infant, both his mother and father provided aid. In contrast to male infants, females were not attacked although opportunities existed. A two-day-old solitary female was discovered by eight bachelors with whom she associated for twenty-three hours. Despite seventeen hours of observation, no infant-related aggression occurred.

It is remarkable that males can discriminate between infant sexes and may attack male foals. Although the Granite sample is small, Duncan (1982) reported that domestic stallions killed eight foals, all of them male, despite an equal abundance of both sexes. Duncan hypothesized that such behavior may remove potential nonrelated, same-sexed future competitors.

Attempted or successful infant killing by male equids may not be as restricted as once believed. Six possible cases of foal killing in the New Forest have been reported (Tyler 1972), and at least three cases of Mountain zebra stallions killing foals also exist (Penzhorn 1975). In captivity a male foal was killed by an unrelated Przewalski's stallion in 1983 (Ryder, San Diego Zoological Society, personal communication), and in India a captive kiang stallion attacked a foal (David 1966). Even a red deer calf was attacked and killed by feral ponies, although the sex of the horses involved were unknown (Clutton-Brock, Guinness, and Albon 1982).

Among antelopes, both attacks of infants and harassment of pregnant females occur. Addax bulls are known to butt newborns

(Manski 1978), and they also herd, court, butt, and force females in late stages of pregnancy to stand (Manski 1982). At least one case of a male wildebeest attempting to copulate with a pregnant female also exists (Watson 1969). However, it is not yet possible to distinguish in the above species between males acting to diminish contributions of rival males and those simply responding to cues that may simulate estrus in females, as suggested by Manski (1982).

Reproductive Consequences

Infanticide and induced abortions are phenomena with similar reproductive consequences for the sexes. Adult males benefit by reducing the genetic contributions of rivals relative to their own. On the other hand, adult females incur an immediate reproductive cost since their pre- or postnatal offspring perishes.

The disparity in frequency between infanticide and feticide in Granite Range horses appears puzzling for at least two reasons. First, in other populations (and equid species) infanticide has been reported while feticide has only been hinted at. This could be due either to real population differences or to lack of collection of long-term data on the appropriate variables (e.g., paternity, gestation periods, etc.).

Second, even though feticide occurs more often than infanticide, both events seem to have identical effects on male reproductive fitness. The apparent paradox is resolved by examining more closely the differing consequences of infanticide and feticide upon the rates at which male horses benefit. Unlike lions or primates in which the killing of neonates results in decreased interbirth intervals (Chapman and Hausfater 1979), most prime-aged female horses breed annually regardless of whether their infants live or die. Little would be gained by male horses killing foals since female interbirth intervals would not be decreased. Females generally experience a postpartum estrous or, if not pregnant one year, come into estrus during the following "breeding season," late March through June. Most unfamiliar mares encountered by males would already be impregnated by rivals. By causing the females to abort these fetuses, new males could increase their genetic contributions in the population more rapidly since intervals between births would decrease. Males that failed to employ behavior destructive to fetuses might be cuckolded into protecting the genetic investments of rival males. For although males might acquire females, they might wait over thirty-two months for their own young to be born if the females they obtained were one month pregnant at acquisition and failed to produce foals the next year. Even if the females produced foals annually it would still be twenty-one months instead of about eleven to twelve until the new stallions' first offspring were born. Hence, through inducing abortions and then reinseminating newly acquired females, males may improve their own fitness relative to others in the population.

7.9 SUMMARY

1. Horses were organized into year-round bands, 88% of which contained a single stallion. Mean band size changed little annually throughout the study. Because the population was increasing, the lack of change in band size suggests that older stallions did not consistently monopolize females.
2. Young mares changed bands more often than older (and previously bonded) mares. Direct male appropriations of mares accounted for about 55% of the changes, while mares that wandered away from bands accounted for the remainder.
3. Males were often aggressive to other males, but dominance was discernible in less than 5% of all interactions. Stallions regularly left their females unguarded to travel up to 1 km away to investigate other horses. The possibility that these other horses were females may have been the reason for such jaunts.
4. Almost half of the females acquired were won in combat. Old males were the most likely age cohort to escalate contests for females, but not all old males fought for females.
5. Among old males, those that had recently lost females were more likely to escalate aggression during encounters with stallions than were males that already had females. Old bachelors with their lowered reproductive value tended to be more aggressive than other males.
6. Males experienced costs associated with harem maintenance and the attempted acquisition of females. These included energy expenditures above basal values and injuries. The energy stallions invested in defense of their harems increased linearly with harem size. However, with larger harems relatively less energy was expended in defense of each female. Older stallions spent the least (total) energy in harem defense, while the energy outputs of a young and an old bachelor exceeded that of 82% of the stallions. More than 95% of the males in any given year were scarred from fights and an average of 3% of the males five years or older died from combat-related wounds.

7. About 12% of the bands consisted of two or more stallions, none of whom were closely related. In such multimale bands, one individual was dominant and maintained mating access to estrous females. Nevertheless, all stallions fought on behalf of other stallions in the band to protect their harems from nonband males. Such aid was reciprocated, but it was also skewed in favor of dominant stallions. They benefited to a greater extent than subordinates because (a) subordinate males initiated more encounters with intruding males, and (b) subordinate males came to the rescue of dominants more than the reverse. Old males formed alliances more often and for longer periods of time than other males, probably because such associations represented their last (or easiest) chances for mating.

8. Intraband dominance appeared to be of little biological importance to females. Within bands, dominance status changed often, and it was only after births that mothers were consistently dominant. Displacements over food were not common; they occurred no more frequently among females from home ranges of poor food quality than they did among females from other areas. Band access to high-quality food sites affected parameters associated with reproductive success (e.g., suckling times, ages that offspring attained puberty, foal production) more clearly than did any intraband relationship. It was through scramble competition among bands, rather than through individual dominance within bands, that parameters associated with female reproductive success were affected.

9. Conflict between the sexes was most evident after males encountered new females or when males took over harems. Males regularly forced copulations upon females, even when they were not receptive or pregnant. This occurred despite persistent attempts by females (and sometimes their band mates) to thwart male aggression by kicking and fleeing. Females that experienced such aggression suffered more prenatal losses than females that were protected by their resident stallions. Mares that aborted returned to estrous soon thereafter, and they were courted and then copulated with by their new stallions.

Statistical Tests

1. Comparison of frequency with which females four years or less and those five years or more were involved in transfers without male force (natal-band emigrations not included). Data cor-

rected for total numbers of individuals in populations available for transfer (1979–82).

G test: $G=15.90$, $df=1$, $N=33$, $p<0.001$.

2. Comparison of frequencies with which three categories of males (2–5 yrs, 6–14 yrs, 15+ yrs) were observed solitary, based on expected values of their occurrence in the population in 1983.

G test: $G=6.92$, $df=2$, $N=396$, $p<0.05$.

3. Comparison of observed and expected frequencies with which bachelors of four age groups (2–3 yrs, 4–5 yrs, 8–14 yrs, 15+ yrs) interacted with stallions. Individuals treated independently for each year (1981–82).

G test: $G=17.35$, $df=3$, $N=633$, $p<0.01$.

4. Comparison of frequency of escalated intermale contests versus total contests in three 15+-yr-old males (pooled) with and without harems

G test: $G=38.10$, $df=1$, $N=352$, $p<0.001$.

5. Comparison of the feeding times of stallions and parous females for each season.

Mann-Whitney U test:

Spring: $z=2.09$, $N=31$, $p<0.04$.

Summer: $U=41$, $n_1=9$, $n_2=17$, $0.05<p<0.10$.

Fall: $U=30$, $n_1=8$, $n_2=16$, $p<0.05$.

Winter: $U=23$, $n_1=8$, $n_2=20$, $p<0.002$.

6. Correlation between estimated digestible energy requirements and number of female mates (excluding daughters).

Pearson product-moment correlation coefficient: $r=.84$, $df=8$, $p<0.01$, $Y=7.71X + 54.21$.

7. Comparison between frequency of defensive initiations by dominants and subordinants and those expected at parity.

G test: $G=24.08$, $df=1$, $N=189$, $p<0.001$.

8. Comparison of frequencies in defensive alliances between dominant and subordinate stallions.

G test: $G=26.40$, $df=1$, $N=313$, $p<0.001$.

9. Comparison of harem tenure in 17 multimale versus 25 single-male bands.

Mann-Whitney U test: $z=2.51$, $N=42$, $p<0.01$.

10. Comparison between frequency of food displacements between bands in poor and better home ranges (controlled for differences in hours sampled).

G test: $G=.19$, $df=1$, $N=290$, NS.

11. Comparison of frequency of aggression directed toward new

band members by females that (*a*) were in larger versus smaller bands than the median, and (*b*) remained together for periods that exceeded or were shorter than median durations.

G test:

> (*a*) $G=7.56$, $df=1$, $N=49$, $p<0.01$.
> (*b*) $G=24.29$, $df=1$, $N=49$, $p<0.001$.

12. Comparison of interaction between band size and length of time females remained together (e.g., familiarity).

G test: $G=31.85$, $df=1$, $N=98$, $p<0.001$.

13. Comparison of frequency of courtship in familiar and unfamiliar females.

G test: $G=66.72$, $df=1$, $N=285$, $p<0.001$.

14. Comparison of the proportions of (*a*) young (2–4 yrs) and (*b*) older females that produced foals in stable and unstable bands

Arcsine transformation:

> (*a*) $z=3.08$, $N=57$, $p<0.002$.
> (*b*) $z=2.02$, $N=72$, $p<0.05$.

8 Parental Investment and Offspring Ecology

In the vast majority of species, the male's only contribution to the survival of his offspring is his sex cells. In these species female contribution clearly exceeds male and by a large ratio.

R. L. Trivers (1972)

8.1 INTRODUCTION

One of the problems that confronts mothers and fathers is the amount and timing of support to their offspring. Since each parent directly increases its inclusive fitness when its progeny produce young (Hamilton 1964), reproductive interests should converge in the area of offspring development. Nevertheless, in polygynous species and particularly in ungulates, females and males differ in the extent to which they invest in their young. Male ungulates do not often feed, carry, play with, or care for young, and only in pigs may young derive some gains—perhaps through warmth provided by adult males (Kleiman and Malcolm 1981).

Horses are one of few species of ungulates that live in bands year-round and in which opportunities arise for both males and females to invest in their progeny. In this chapter I explore two themes: parental investment and offspring development. I use the term *investment* to mean any contribution made by a parent that improves its offspring's chances to survive and to reproduce. Because survival in a genetic sense requires more than just parental care, I have also included information about the challenges that sons and daughters face when dispersing and relationships between dispersal and incest.

8.2 MATERNAL INVESTMENT
Birth Sex Ratio

Granite mares produced a slightly, but not significantly, greater number of male than female foals at birth (table 8.1). Birth sex

TABLE 8.1 Birth-Sex Ratios of Foals
in the Granite Range

	% Males	N
By Year		
1979	64	11
1980	61	18
1981	50	26
1982	53	30
1983	61	28
By Home Range		
Poor	64	14
Medium	56	54
High	56	45
By Age (yrs)		
2–4	68	28
5–17	54	80
18+	40	5

ratios did not vary systematically with maternal age, home-range quality, or year of birth. Only one mother produced five successive sons, and no mothers had daughters in every year of study.

In horses, as in other equids, a slightly but not significantly greater number of males are born (table 8.2), although overall differences are rarely statistically significant. Charles Darwin provided information on the births of 25,560 domestic foals and found sex ratios to be at parity (Darwin [1871] 1888). Whether sex ratios are immutably fixed at 50:50 (Fisher 1930; Maynard Smith 1978) or vary adaptively (Trivers and Willard 1973; Simpson and Simp-

TABLE 8.2 Birth Sex Ratios in Native and Feral Equid Populations

Species and Location	% Males	Source
Horses		
Grand Canyon, Arizona	1.20 (11)	Berger 1977 & unpublished
Assateague Island, Maryland	1.13 (199)	Keiper 1979
Pryor Mts., Montana	1.12 (35)	Feist & McCullough 1975
Jicarilla, New Mexico	1.33 (21)	Nelson 1980
Sable Island, Nova Scotia	0.99 (143)	Welsh 1975
New Forest, England	?1.0 (282)	Tyler 1972
Asses		
Ossabau Island, Georgia	0.44 (23)	McCort 1979
Mountain zebras		
Mountain Zebra National Park, South Africa	0.70 (46)	Penzhorn 1975
Plain's zebras		
Kruger Park, South Africa	1.12 (216)	Smuts 1976a

Note: Sample sizes in parentheses.

son 1982; Clutton-Brock, Guinness, and Albon 1984) are subjects of debate (Williams 1979; Clutton-Brock and Albon 1982b).

Differential Investment toward Sons

Maternal investment was greater in male than in female offspring. Sons were carried for longer periods, and they suckled more often than daughters (fig. 6.8; table 6.1); the literature on domestic horses indicates males are also heavier at birth (Hintz, Hintz, and van Vleck 1979). In Camargue horses, evidence suggests that males receive more milk than females (Duncan et al. 1984). Also, Pfeifer (1984) found that in another monomorphic species—scimitar-horned oryx—male infants were heavier than female ones and garnered more nourishment. Although it has been established that in sexually dimorphic species such as red deer (Clutton-Brock, Guinness, and Albon 1982) and elephant seals (Reiter, Stinson, and LeBoeuf 1978), preweaning investment in males was greater than in females, the above data suggest that such patterns are not restricted to sexually dimorphic ungulates.

Postweaning investment in horses is probably more similar to that in elephant seals where there are no sex differences (Reiter, Stinson, and LeBoeuf 1978) than to that in red deer or ground squirrels where grown female offspring may end up sharing resources with their mothers (Clutton-Brock, Guinness, and Albon 1982; Michener 1980). In horses, both daughters and sons emigrate from natal bands, as they do in other equids (Klingel, 1975). The differences between the dispersal ages of twenty-six females ($\bar{X}=2.01$ yrs) and twenty-nine males ($\bar{X}=2.20$ yrs) were not significant [1] (see sec. 8.5).

It seems there are few if any differences in postweaning investment by mares toward male or female offspring. The chances that daughters share maternal home ranges are small since female home ranges vary in size and are determined by the stallions with whom the females consort (chap. 4). This does not rule out the possibility that the home ranges of daughters will at some time overlap those of mothers, particularly because males move farther from natal ranges ($\bar{X}=3.3$ km) than females ($\bar{X}=.5$ km) [2]. However, if daughters benefit by using maternal home ranges, such effects may be derived incidentally. In native equids, data have yet to be collected on how or if maternal home ranges are adopted, data that are crucial to an assessment of the degree of postweaning investment in equids. In migratory equids, such as numerous populations of Plain's zebras, it appears that postweaning investment would be minimal.

A problem in the foregoing concerns how investment may be equalized between the sexes as predicted by theory (Fisher 1930; Clutton-Brock and Albon 1982b). Because male foals are born heavier and suckled more vigorously than female foals, investment could be equalized if males were weaned earlier. Information on twenty-nine males and twenty-six females suggests that weaning occurs at similar ages—0.78 yrs versus 0.77 yrs, respectively, as has also been found in Camargue horses (Duncan et al. 1984). Perhaps sons are more costly to produce than daughters. If so, mothers that produced sons in a given year should be more likely to be barren in the next year than mothers that produced daughters (Clutton-Brock and Albon 1982b). To examine this idea, the effects of band changes on female reproductive performances were removed by considering only females from stable bands. Seven of the ten mares that became barren the year after foaling had produced males in the previous year. Because the sample was small, the data are difficult to interpret. They are, however, in line with the suggestion that males are more costly to produce than females, although not significantly more [3].

8.3   LOST FOALS AND MISTAKEN IDENTITIES

Mothers rarely became separated by sight from their offspring during the first six months after birth. Mortality has resulted from separations in the Red Desert of Wyoming (Boyd 1979). On the few occasions in the Granite Range (about four per year) when mothers and young became separated it was most often because foals were sleeping as their bands gradually foraged farther away. During such situations mothers and young became excited, whinnied, stared, and ran back and forth. Little concern was perceptible in stallions or in other band members regardless of genealogical relationships to the mother and foal. Band members usually continued feeding except in cases when mothers left the band and ran (presumably to search); the other horses usually followed.

Confusion among mothers over foal identity was rare, but it did occur. On one occasion Mahari and Ceymang, both multiparous females from the same band, became aggresssive toward each other after four-day-old Ceylon became lost. Ceymang subsequently approached Mahat (Mahari's six-day-old foal), but was rebuffed by Mahari's biting. Although Ceymang whinnied and continued to retract her ears as she approached Mahat, Mahari successfully thwarted contact between the two. During the next twenty hours aggression diminished and Ceymang's vocalizations failed to entice Mahat from Mahari. During the time that elapsed Ceylon was discovered by eight bachelors more than a kilometer away. She followed them and attempted to suckle (from the males!) at least fifteen times. During the next day, when Ceymang's band fortuitously foraged nearby, Ceylon and Ceymang were reunited.

Only once did a foal suckle from a mare that was not its mother, and the bout lasted only five seconds. On another occasion a newborn foal wobbled toward the wrong mare; it was kicked twice and fell to the ground, and it later imprinted on its real mother.

In other species mistaken identities have also been noted (Riedman 1982), and occasionally young are cared for or suckled by foster mothers. A Soay sheep ewe that had lost her lamb adopted a young lamb that lived within her home range. The lamb suckled both its real and surrogate mother, and its growth rate exceeded that of its peers (Grubb 1974b). Although foals rarely tried to suckle (or "steal") milk from nonmothers, the practice occurs in other ungulates (Espmark 1971; Geist 1971; Berger 1979b; Douglas-Hamilton 1975), whereas in peccaries communal nursing is common (Byers and Bekoff 1981). Neither communal nursing nor thief suckling have been reported in equids (Klingel 1975; Moehlman 1974) although a case of adoption has been found in Mountain zebras (Lloyd and Harper 1980).

8.4 MALE INVESTMENT AND RECOGNITION OF SONS
Investment Patterns

By virtue of their home ranges, stallions indirectly provide food that will be available to their band mates and will later be converted into offspring. To this extent stallions contribute to their own reproductive interests, since resource availability influences maternal reproduction and the suckling and growth rates of foals (chap. 6). However, benefits obtained in this fashion by stallions could be derived incidentally. Certainly, the food stallions contribute to their offspring is not as direct as, for example, food provisioned by male carnivores (Kleiman and Malcolm 1981).

In horses there are two direct investments that males might make to enhance immediate offspring survival. First, progeny can be protected from mortality. This type of investment entails both defending unborn offspring from induced abortions (sec. 7.8) or young foals from predators. On only a few occasions did stallions (or even mares) respond to predators. One observation included a stallion that chased three coyotes approaching within 20 m of his three- and six-day-old foals as their mothers watched. In several other instances stallions aided their foals when the young were threatened by nonharem males. However, the death of a newborn also resulted after a stallion forced a primparous female to leave her foal and follow the band. Although the foal was the stallion's son, it had not stood. About an hour after the band departed, a coyote preyed on the foal (Berger and Rudman 1985).

A second way that stallions may invest in their offspring is by playing with their sons. Since play may enhance the development of motor patterns used in later life (Berger 1979a, 1980; Fagen 1981; Bekoff 1984), stallions might help their sons develop combat skills through play fighting. Play between stallions and their sons rarely occurred while sons remained in natal bands. It occurred most often after young males joined bachelor groups, and, upon attempting to appropriate females, they reencountered their fathers. By comparing how often play fighting occurred between stallions and intruding bachelors that were either sons or nonsons, it was possible to evaluate the extent to which stallions may have invested in their own offspring.

Of 346 interactions between stallions and bachelors whose genealogies were completely known, stallions initiated play fighting 34 times. Of these, some aspect of play fighting (e.g., neck fencing, rearing, nipping) occurred 20 times with sons and 14 times with nonsons. Since males that were not sons were more than 4.6 times as available, fathers played with sons more than 659% as much as they did with nonsons [4]. This information indicates that stallions subsequently recognize young males with whom they have previously associated and that they play with them more often. It does not suggest very strongly that through this additional exposure of sons to mock combat, fathers have contributed to their sons' later reproductive success. Still, the possibility that fathers invest in their sons by exposing them to additional aggressive play cannot be ruled out, especially because some evidence exists that more successful males interact more often (see sec. 8.3).

Based on the fragmentary information available on other species of ungulate fathers and sons, it is not obvious whether fathers act differentially toward sons, if indeed they are ever encountered later in life. For other mammals the evidence is also scant. In gibbons on the Mentawai Islands of Indonesia, fathers have accompanied sons on trips away from natal areas prior to permanent dispersal, but fathers also aggressively rebuffed the later attempts of sons to reenter these areas (Tilson 1981).

Factors in Recognition

Stallions chose to play with specific bachelors on the basis of their familiarity with individual animals and not necessarily on the basis of genetic affiliations. Opportunities arose for examining the differences in play fighting due to familiarity and genealogy because adult males encountered both sons and nonsons as intruding bachelors. Natural experiments were also created when new males took over harems; stallions associated with both sons and nonsons for varying lengths of time after takeovers but before the young emigrated. As a result, young males grew up with stallions that were not their true fathers. Such stallions later encountered these nonrelated but familiar males as well as their true sons (whom they rarely knew well) as intruders.

Two lines of evidence suggest that familiarity influenced play fighting between stallions and bachelors to a greater extent than genetic relationships. First, of twenty times that fathers played with their sons, nineteen of these occurred between sons that had lived in their fathers' bands for at least two years. Stallions played about 430% more with sons with whom they had associated for at least two years than with those they had not [5]. Second, play with unfamiliar sons (4.5% of the time) was in the same diminished proportion as it was with nonsons (5.0%) [6]. These differences in stallion play-partner preferences between familiar and unfamiliar bachelors indicate that length of associations and not genealogies influenced stallion play choices. Stallions chose individuals that they recognized.

It is important to point out that the effects of familiarity were not long lasting. Of the 346 interactions that occurred between bachelors and stallions, various combinations of relatedness and familiarity occurred between interactants, including combinations of familiar and unfamiliar bachelors that were related and unrelated to stallions and that had remained in natal bands for at least two years before dispersing. Bachelors that had been away from their natal bands for more than eighteen months and then encountered their natal-band stallions were treated by the stallions as if they were unfamiliar males [7]. Since neither familiar nor unfamiliar bachelors were played with preferentially once they had been away from their maternal bands for more than eighteen months [7], it appeared that stallions were no longer able to recognize (or remember) males from their bands. In numerous mammals, length of prior association is important in recognition (Porter, Wyrick, and Pankey 1978; Holmes and Sherman 1983).

8.5   DISPERSAL OF YOUNG HORSES
Proximate Factors Influencing Dispersal

More than 97% of the females and males between the ages of one and four years moved away from their mothers' bands. Females were incorporated into new bands by stallions or occasionally by bachelors, while young emigrating males were either ignored or chased by stallions and bachelors. Only a few characteristics associated with dispersers were clearly identifiable. In females, the attainment of puberty was the only factor that appeared to mediate dispersal. At first estrus, 81% (21 of 26) left their bands permanently. The other 5 females also left at puberty, but after short consortships with their first nonfamiliar males, these females returned to their original bands. Within an additional two years each of them left their original bands permanently.

Do social factors have a role in mediating dispersal from natal bands? For instance, it has been suggested that the number of intraband playmates influences the ages at which dispersal occurs in Plain's zebra males (Klingel 1972). If Klingel's "playmate hypothesis" is valid and is applied to wild horses, then young males with relatively few playmates should disperse from their natal bands earlier than males with more peers for interaction. To investigate this possibility the ages at which eighteen males moved away from their maternal bands were compared. I used males from the same home-range areas (either high or medium quality) and compared them to other males from the similarly ranked areas to remove influences that might have been due to food alone. Thus, males from bands that differed in the number of peers (the social environment) were compared among bands of similar home-range quality to see whether the number of equal-aged (potential) playmates affected dispersal ages. Individuals not more than two years apart in age were considered peers.

The number of peers did not influence male dispersal ages. Males with no same-sexed play partners departed no earlier or later than those in bands with more potential male interactants [8]. To judge whether young females might have affected this relationship, the analysis was expanded to include young females as peers in addition to young males. Still, there was no association between the number of juvenile conspecifics and emigration age

[9]. The "playmate" hypothesis could not satisfactorily account for the ages at which male horses left their natal bands.

Perhaps dispersal that was aggressively promoted (e.g., forced) by stallions was an important cause of the age at which young males left their natal bands. Stallion-directed aggression toward young males was infrequent. Only about 11% of the young dispersing males were bitten within a week of emigration or actively driven away from the band. However, in cases where stallions (true fathers) were deposed by new males, 40% (4 of 10) of the young males that remained with their mothers departed within two months of the takeovers. Only once was aggression by new stallions toward these male youngsters witnessed.

The evidence is not strong that dispersal in young males is related to either forced expulsions or lack of peers. But dispersal was related to one aspect of the social environment—prior exposure to bachelors. Seventy-six percent or more of the males that dispersed permanently from their bands had at least once in their past voluntarily departed and engaged in social interactions with bachelors. Most often young males permanently departed from natal bands as solitary individuals, although in two different years sets of full brothers (e.g., two brothers in each year) left together and never returned.

Undoubtedly, numerous proximate factors subsumed male emigration, and whether any single variable can by itself account for dispersal age seems unlikely. Dispersal occurred at some time after (presumed) puberty, and it was influenced by meetings with other bachelors. Forays into new environments may have been of importance also—a factor that has been implicated in at least one other harem-dwelling species, marmots (Downhower and Armitage 1981).

Fates of Females and Males

It is commonly argued that selection for dispersal has been strong and that the benefits of leaving must outweigh those of remaining (Bekoff 1977; Gaines and McClenaghan 1980; Moore and Ali 1984). Regardless of disperser sex, individuals that leave interact with strangers and enter unfamiliar social and occasionally unfamiliar physical environments. What is the nature of such interactions for females and males, and how may later reproduction be affected? In addressing these questions it is important to distinguish between dispersal from the natal band and from the natal area. I considered the latter to be movements out of Granite Basin on the low-altitude ranges and north of July Peak at high altitudes. In either of these areas individuals had to traverse unfamiliar terrain, descend (or move through) mountain passes, and cross, at best, poor potential grazing areas.

For emigrating females, first social interactions outside of natal bands included socio-sexual investigations by unfamiliar males and often harassment and aggression by females already residing in other bands. About 80% of the females that emigrated remained within eyesight of familiar terrain, but the others moved to new ranges. Two such dispersers remained nulliparous for over 3 years after dispersal, although the mean time for postdispersal foal production was 1.7 years. Because of stressful events associated with female emigration and the smaller size of such females relative to nontransferring females, it was not surprising that reproduction after emigration was poor.

Young dispersing males were also beset with new experiences when they visited bachelor bands or when they joined them permanently later on. Within the first hour of arriving, these young males were sniffed, nipped, bitten, or chased 1,240% more than the average bachelor already within such groups. About 45% (5 of 11) of the young males were mounted at these times. My first impression early in the study of a horse that joined a bachelor group was that it was a female; the horse was mounted unsuccessfully a total of six times by three different bachelors in less than thirty-five minutes. Only several hours later did I discover that "she" was a he.

In contrast, such behavior was not directed toward new males if they were at least three and a half years old, even if they were joining bachelors for the first time. It is unclear why young arrivals were the recipients of homosexual behavior more than resident bachelors [10]. In other ungulates homosexual behavior among males is not uncommon (Schaller 1967; Dubost and Feer 1981), and larger ones may mount smaller ones as a form of dominance (Geist 1971). I observed captive male onagers mount subordinates after defeating them in battle, but this behavior has not been observed in Granite horses and has only been reported for Mountain zebras (Penzhorn 1984). The meaning of homosexual mounting in bachelor groups of horses or other equids is not known.

Unlike emigrating females, which became incorporated into bands and were bred, dispersing males had poor prospects for immediate reproductive rewards; but this was also true for males that remained. The percentage of males that produced offspring within three years of leaving their natal bands was less than 5% compared to over 80% for females. As mentioned earlier, males emigrated greater distances than females, presumably because opportunities for acquiring females would be greater in new areas.

Do males that emigrate away from Granite Basin improve their opportunities for mating? Those that left the Basin were more successful at obtaining females than those that did not, but this was largely a result of the relative ease with which domestic females from a nearby ranch could be procured. Still, neither the existence of the ranch itself nor its females can explain satisfactorily why eleven bachelors moved at least 13 km north of the ranch (18 km north of Granite Basin) (see sec. 5.6). Perhaps these wide-ranging bachelors moved in search of better food or females. It was clear that in their movements, these bachelors encountered no competition from stallions over females since no bands occupied these regions to the north of Granite Basin. Overall, the mating prospects for males immediately after dispersal were never good. No males less than five years old sired offspring, although in the final year of study a three-year-old and two four-year-olds each acquired single females.

Sex differences in mortality the year after emigration from either natal bands or natal areas did not occur; survival was 100%. In native equids it is unknown whether either sex incurs greater costs following dispersal, and, if so, whether such effects are due to predation or other factors. One would suspect that males suffer greater mortality than females since equid sex ratios are biased in favor of live females at adulthood, despite parity at birth (Berger 1983a). In other ungulates, young dispersing males may die more often than dispersing females (Geist 1971; Ralls, Brownell, and Ballou 1980).

Functional Considerations

Dispersal is a mechanism through which individuals achieve outbreeding and locate potential mates or food (Howard 1960; Bekoff 1977). In mammals where the members of one sex may be related, the opposite sex tends to disperse (Greenwood 1980). For example, females in prides of Serengeti lions are related and males emigrate (Schaller 1972; Bertram 1975), whereas in wild dogs the situation is reversed (Frame and Frame 1976; Malcolm and Marten 1982). In horses, indeed, in all harem-dwelling equids, both sexes emigrate from natal conspecifics (sec. 8.2; Klingel 1972).

What selective pressures favor the dispersal of the young of both sexes? In horses, as is probably true of other harem-dwelling species, two principle forces seem to be operating—one on females and the other on males. For females, the most important selective agent is presumably the avoidance of mating between close relatives. If male tenure length (in horses or other harem-dwelling species) exceeded the time required for females to attain puberty and females did not disperse, then mating between fathers and daughters would result (see Moore and Ali 1984). Among Granite stallions tenure could last at least five years, well in excess of the time needed for females to attain puberty. Still, all (26) daughters emigrated and no father-daughter matings occurred within the band (but see below). Of 5 daughters that did not leave natal bands permanently when puberty was attained, each had copulated with wandering males outside the bands and not with their fathers. For young females, consanguineous matings were avoided by leaving natal bands, though it was not always clear that it was the behavior of young females rather than that of resident stallions that resulted in the lack of breeding.

Selective pressures favoring dispersal in young males apparently differ from those on young females. The argument that males leave natal bands to avoid consanguineous matings (e.g., with their mothers) is unlikely for at least three reasons. These can be viewed from the conflicting perspectives of sons and parents. First, although growing sons are probably physically capable of breeding, they have neither the prowess nor fighting skills needed to dominate stallions and achieve successful matings. Even if sons did not mate with their mothers, they conceivably could breed with other (nonrelated) adult females within the band. Yet, they do not; few mating opportunities exist because of the defensive behavior of stallions. The observation that young males leave suggests that either mating competition within natal bands is too intense or skills needed for acquiring mates can best be obtained elsewhere. These possibilities—leaving the band because of local mate competition and joining bachelor groups to develop skills—are not alternatives. Rather, they are complementary tactics used by young males to improve chances for later reproduction.

Second, there is no good evolutionary reason why stallions should tolerate mother-son matings. By copulating with such females themselves, stallion reproductive success relative to that of their sons would be greater. This is because, for stallions, the resultant offspring would not be inbred (stallions are not related to their mares), while for sons, the progeny resulting from mother-son crosses would, of course, be inbred. Since inbreeding between close relatives results in reduced juvenile survivorship, a stallion could improve his inclusive fitness more by precluding his sons from mating with their mothers and by mating with such females himself. Only once did I observe an attempted copulation between a son and his mother, and it was aggressively prevented by both the mother and the father.

Third, young males should leave because not only do stallions render chances for mating poor, but adult females do so as well by not permitting inexperienced males to copulate. Though evidence for female choice in equids (and in most mammals) is not very good, sexually receptive females may avoid copulations with relatively small males (Geist 1971). Perhaps mares, which are larger than their dispersing sons anyway, would avoid possible matings because of their dominance in interactions. The chances for sons to breed within a band are poor, and the chances are not enhanced by the relatively small size of these males. On different occasions, three- and four-year-old males temporarily acquired older mares with whom they could not breed successfully because of resistance from larger mares. It seems that mares would avoid, if possible, mating with males that failed to demonstrate competitive abilities. Young or small males that remained in bands would be likely to encounter resistance in their mating attempts by both the adult males and females.

To summarize, two major evolutionary factors appear responsible for the dispersal of either sex from natal bands. Prolonged male harem tenure (and inbreeding avoidance) is likely to be the principle force underlying the emigration of daughters. For sons, it may be that within-band mating competition from dominant males renders prospects for breeding so poor that sons are better off going elsewhere. Some support for the idea that these two different forces promote dispersal stems from observations on South American camelids (Franklin 1983), marmots (Downhower and Armitage 1981), hyraxes (Hoeck 1982), and hamadryas and olive baboons (Kummer 1968; but see Packer 1979). In these groups both sexes leave their natal areas, females live in groups defended by males, and it is unlikely that male replacement occurs annually. Hence, young females may leave to avoid the consequences of inbreeding and young males emigrate to reduce breeding competition (or suppression) from their fathers.

8.6 INCESTUOUS MATINGS

Although some information has been presented on matings between close relatives, a more detailed look is necessary to examine the causes and frequency of inbreeding. How often did brothers mate with sisters, sons with mothers, and fathers with daughters? Data were not available to address the first two possibilities since males rarely bred prior to six years of age. Information on father-daughter matings and inbreeding avoidance are available.

Of the twenty-six females that attained sexual maturity, copulations involving twenty-one were observed. Five of these females changed bands prior to puberty when they either accompanied their emigrating mothers or their bands were taken over by new stallions. The result was that several nonmature females grew up in bands with stallions that were not their fathers. These events permitted comparison of the influence of familiarity versus genealogy upon stallion copulatory behavior. I examined whether related (true fathers) or nonrelated (stepfathers) stallions mated with maturing females.

In none of the above cases did stallions of either category mate or even attempt to mate with females that matured within their bands. That stallions failed to discriminate between related versus unrelated familiar females in their breeding behavior suggests that mating with close kin may be avoided through familiarity, an idea proposed for human mating preferences almost a hundred years ago (Westermarck 1891). This point is further substantiated by the nineteen observations of stallions copulating with young, but unfamiliar, females. The idea that familiarity inhibits reproductive behavior is not new; it has been suggested as operative in numerous groups including quail (Bateson 1980), primates (Harcourt 1978; Pusey 1980), and humans (Shepher 1971).

At periods following initial dispersal from natal bands, consanguineous matings are more apt to occur since fathers might encounter daughters with whom they are no longer familiar. In two cases females that emigrated from natal bands at puberty were reincorporated into bands containing their real fathers at a minimum of nineteen months after the daughters first dispersed. In both instances the daughters were successfully mated by their fathers, and one inbred foal was born. There were no indications of individual recognition between fathers and daughters. In five other cases, young females emigrated from natal bands and then returned to them in less than twenty-four hours. Usually this transient behavior lasted one to three days. Copulations between these females and stallions from different bands (e.g., nonfathers) were observed in three of these cases. Since foals were later born to two of these females while they still remained in their original bands, the fathers might have erroneously been assumed to be the sires, had either the copulations or the young female consortships away from natal bands gone undetected.

The data, summarized in table 8.3, indicate that father-daughter matings are uncommon. Of copulating horses whose genealogies were known, only 3.1% were between fathers and daughters. Incest avoidance was strongest when fathers were familiar with their daughters.

One inexplicable case of apparent recognition occurred in a multimale band. In the single instance, where a dominant stallion's daughter failed to disperse at puberty, only the subordinate stallion copulated. What is perplexing is not that the dominant did not try to thwart mating efforts by the subordinate (since the female was the dominant's daughter's daughter), but whether or how the dominant assessed the female as a daughter. Since stallions probably cannot remember with whom they have copulated, two events are surprising. First, in contrast to the data presented so far, the subordinate mated with an individual with whom it was familiar although not related. Second, the dominant stallion did nothing to prevent the subordinate from mating with this particular female. The most parsimonious explanations that account for the avoidance of incestuous matings are based on inherited tendencies for young females to disperse and for breeding stallions to avoid copulating with familiar young females.

The applicability of the Granite data to other populations or species of equids is unclear. In sedentary populations it is likely that a small proportion of matings between closely related individuals

TABLE 8.3   Potential Incestuous Matings

Dyadic Category	# Possible	# Observed in Dyad
Stallion unfamiliar and unrelated to young female (encountered away from natal band)	21	21
Father familiar with daughter (daughter emigrated at puberty)	16	0
Father familiar with daughter (daughter did not emigrate at puberty)	5	0[a]
Stallion familiar with nondaughter that grew up in his band and emigrated at puberty	5	0
Father (once familiar with daughter that emigrated at puberty) reencounters her later	2	2[b]

[a]In 3 cases daughters were observed copulating with nonfamiliar males prior to returning to original bands. In the other 2 cases, no copulations were observed.

[b]Minimum period since last father-daughter contact was 19 months.

will occur due to chance alone. Knowledge of the frequency and biological significance of incest in native species of equids is fragmentary, especially for migratory populations. In small populations of captive ungulates, including Przewalski's horses (Bouman 1977) and zebras, numerous deleterious effects of consanguineous matings have been found; these include increased juvenile mortality, lowered offspring production, and decreased longevity (Ralls, Brugger, and Ballou 1979). Evidence for inbreeding depression in domestic horses is equivocal (Bouman and Bos 1979; Jones and Bogart 1971), although in other domestic species breeding between close relatives often results in decreased fecundity or survival (Lasley 1978).

8.7   BACHELORHOOD: FIGHTING SKILLS AND FEMALE ACQUISITIONS

While information on how parents invest in their progeny and how offspring may enhance breeding opportunities has been presented, I have not focused specifically on bachelor males. Bachelors are interesting since they present opportunities to examine ontogenetic pathways through which skills are developed and the possible importance of such skills in acquiring their first harems. It is generally believed that males that compete successfully for mates must attain a threshold body size (e.g., weight), level of fighting proficiency, or both (Appleby 1982; Gibson and Guinness 1980; Symons 1978). Observations of nine animals that eventually secured harems—four were known since birth and five were followed from one to three years before obtaining females—allowed an assessment of the importance of different factors to harem acquisition. What common patterns did these bachelors share?

Successful and Unsuccessful Males

Males were considered successful if they acquired and retained harems. In a strict sense, successful males should be defined as those that sire relatively more offspring over their lifetimes, but these data were unavailable for young males except over short periods. Based on the comparisons of the 9 males that were known as bachelors and that later acquired females (table 8.4), several tentative conclusions can be reached.

First, few immediate patterns uniformly apply to bachelors that obtained their initial females. The more obvious relationships were (a) bachelors five years or younger were likely to lose their first females (5 of 7; 71%), whereas those six years or older were not

TABLE 8.4 Characteristics of Bachelors When Obtaining Their First Females

Age at First Acquisition	Tenure as a Bachelor (yrs)	Body Weight (kg)	Rank of Body Weight in Bachelor Population (Percentile)	Females Secured		
				By Combat	Unknown	As They Wandered
2*	.5	307	low (10th)			X
3*	1.8	396	low (25th)			X
4*	1.8	396	high (68th)		?	
4	1.5	410	high (80th)			X
5*	.6	434	high (90th)		?	
5*	2.5	412	high (70th)	X		
5	3+	412	high (83d)	X		
6	3+	434	high (80th)	X		
6	2+	410	medium (50th)			X

Notes: Asterisks refer to males that subsequently lost females. Plus (+) designates minimum period as a bachelor. Rank of body weight in bachelor population is weight estimated in late spring of the year when females were obtained.

(none did); (*b*) no bachelors four years or younger won females by fighting, whereas those five years or more (3 of 4; 75%) did so by fighting; and (*c*) by their fewer numbers alone, older bachelors, when attaining their first harems, represented a smaller proportion of the single male population.

Second, 75% (3 of 4) of the relatively heaviest bachelors won females by fighting whereas all (3 of 3) of the lightest bachelors secured females by acquiring them as they wandered. Each of these latter males lost them subsequently in fights. Only a four-year-old male, whose estimated weight ranked within the heaviest 20% of the bachelors, did not lose his females in a fight. These data implicate the importance of weight (or size) in determining whether males should fight for or wait for females.

Third, tenure as a bachelor could not clearly be separated from other parameters because the sample was small and 3 of the 4 heaviest bachelors had also spent the longest times as single males (table 8.4). If a relatively high weight and relatively long tenure as a bachelor were important characteristics of males that held onto females, were fighting skills not essential to such males?

Fighting Skills

The array of behavioral traits associated with combat, including strength, endurance, and proficiency, is operationally defined as fighting skills (see Fagen 1981). If such characteristics aided males in obtaining or retaining females then (1) poor fighters should lose females or avoid fights, and (2) tenacious or skillful fighters should win encounters. Conversely, if skills were not involved, (1) and (2) should show no relationship with the outcome of dyadic interactions.

Do Poor Fighters Lose Females? When the influence of weight and age were removed only 32 interactions over females matched stallions of similar ages and weights. These interactions included three males with their first harems, all of whom varied in their fighting abilities. Of these, one male (Wyoming, six years old) lost 10 consecutive interactions within a thirty-six-hour period, and another male (Applegate, five years old) was neutral in 12 of his 13 interactions with equivalently ranked males. The third stallion (Jesse, six years old) was also neutral in his encounters with other males, but he was audacious and often initiated encounters whereas Wyoming and Applegate did so only infrequently. The responses of these new harem-holding males to the interactions just mentioned were as follows: Wyoming and his female shifted home ranges by 8 km after losing encounters, and Applegate and his two females also changed ranges to a peripheral range about 4 km away. Only Jesse failed to shift his home range. He fared better than the other two stallions during aggressive interactions with larger males, and Jesse's interaction history probably contributed to his ability to do well in contests. The percentages of the total number of encounters with all males in the population that were initiated by each of these three stallions during 1980 and 1981 were as follows: Jesse, 76% ($N=147$); Applegate, 31% ($N=19$); and Wyoming, 18% ($N=33$). Not only did Jesse apparently possess the best fighting skills, he initiated the greatest proportion of encounters and interacted at least 970% more often than the other stallions (data corrected for hours observed). It appeared that Jesse's relatively high interaction and initiation rates served to sharpen his fighting skills.

With regard to poorer fighters, both Applegate and Wyoming presumably avoided the loss of their females by modifying their home ranges and thereby diminishing the probability of aggressive interactions with other males. In these instances the effectiveness of fighting skills appeared to determine behavioral options concerning home-range locations. It was not possible in a strict sense to determine the effects that interactions with equal-ranked males may have had on these new harem holders since numerous other encounters occurred with unevenly matched rivals at irregular intervals. Consequently, there was no consistent way in which the effects of interactions themselves rather than fighting skills per se could be separated.

Do Tenacious Fighters Win Encounters? When age and weight asymmetries were removed, 37 interactions occurred among four-year-old males for females. One male clearly emerged victorious. He procured females and successfully defended them against not only equally ranked rivals but against larger four-to-six-year-olds on 26 additional occasions. A problem in interpreting these data is that skill is not necessarily related to tenacity or vice versa. A poor fighter might win due to persistence alone, whereas a skillful fighter might not have much endurance. Even though the effects of weight or age on outcomes can be removed, other variables may not be separated as easily. The extent to which skill alone accounted for winners in aggressive contests could not be determined.

Multiple Factors

The data presented above support the idea that multiple factors were involved in the acquisition and retention of females. With other factors equal, males that were good fighters should have done better than less-skilled fighters because they would not have to shift home ranges or face the potential loss of their harems through continued challenges by rivals. Although the small sample suggested that this was the case, other factors were not equal. Age and weight were also important as shown by (1) the greater success of larger and older males in obtaining harems for the first time through fighting, and (2) observations of smaller males that failed to fight for females and appropriated them by more fortuitous means (e.g., wandering). One additional factor needs to be mentioned—experience. Studies of aggression in ungulates (Appleby 1982; Gibson and Guinness 1980) and other mammals (Ginsberg and Allee 1942; see Geist 1978a) indicate that experience influences the outcome of encounters.

8.8   SUMMARY

1. The birth sex ratio favored males, but the difference was not significant. Maternal investment in sons was greater than that in daughters as indicated by (*a*) information in the literature that males are heavier at birth and that they have longer gestation lengths than females, and (*b*) field data that males suckle more than females. The idea that investment in the sexes is equalized at some later point in time could not be explained by sex differences in weaning ages, dispersal ages, postweaning support, or adoption of maternal home ranges. Male foals may be more costly to rear than female foals.
2. Stallions played with bachelor males that were their sons about 650% more often than they did with nonrelated bachelors. Familiarity rather than genealogy influenced stallions' choices for play partners. Individuals that grew up with stallions were the recipients of stallions' playful behavior after these individuals became bachelors. Recognition by stallions was short lived. Bachelors that had been away from natal bands for more than eighteen months were treated as if they were unfamiliar males, whether or not they were related to stallions.
3. Proximate variables that influenced the natal dispersal of young of both sexes were numerous. Most females left permanently

after they attained puberty. Males departed after they were driven out by stallions, after they interacted with bachelors, or after new males took over their natal bands.

4. Postdispersal reproduction was much greater in females than males. Within three years of leaving natal bands, over 80% of the females produced offspring while only 5% of the males did.

5. Male and female natal dispersal was explained by considering the effects of different selection pressures. The avoidance of inbreeding seemed to underlie female emigration, otherwise daughters would grow up in groups in which their fathers often had prolonged tenure. Sons probably left because their chances of mating were poor. This was due to the behavior of both adult males and females, each of which have good (evolutionary) reasons to avoid mating with young males from their bands.

6. Incest was rare. Only 3% of the copulations were between fathers and daughters, and these happened only after daughters were reincorporated into their fathers' bands. Copulations between fathers and daughters never occurred when daughters attained puberty nor when they were emigrating from their natal bands. Incest was avoided by the reluctance of stallions to mate with females that grew up within their bands and by the (seemingly) inherited tendency for these females to move away from familiar band mates.

7. Social and physical traits that characterized males likely to obtain and keep females were as follows: age (six-year-olds were more successful than younger bachelors), weight, and tenure as a bachelor. Fighting skills appeared important as well, and poor fighters abandoned their home ranges in favor of peripheral areas.

Statistical Tests

1. Comparison of ages at which males and females departed permanently from natal bands.
Student's t test: $t = .97$, $df = 53$, NS.

2. Comparison of dispersal distances in males and females one year after emigrating from their natal bands.
Mann-Whitney U test: $z = 2.83$, $N = 31$, $p < 0.005$.

3. Comparison of frequencies that barren females in stable bands produced sons versus daughters in the prior year.
Chi square test: $X^2 = 1.6$, $df = 1$, $N = 10$, NS.

4. Comparison of 346 interactions in stallions and bachelors when play ensued between individuals whose coefficients of re-

latedness were .5 or less. (Data corrected for availability, e.g., whether or not sons were present.)

G test: $G=23.09$, $df=1$, $p<0.001$.

5. Comparison of frequencies between stallions playing with their bachelor sons that had remained in natal bands for at least two years and playing with those that had emigrated earlier.

6. Comparison of the proportion of playful interactions between stallions with nonfamiliar sons and with nonfamiliar bachelors. Arcsine transformation: $z=.06$, $N=304$, NS.

7. Comparison of frequency of playful interactions between stallions and sons that were bachelors for at least eighteen months with (a) sons that were bachelors for less than eighteen months, and (b) unrelated males that were bachelors for at least eighteen months (only data for sons that remained in natal bands for two years were used).

G test:

(a) $G=6.82$, $df=1$, $N=50$, $p<0.01$.

(b) $G=.28$, $df=1$, $N=296$, NS.

8. Comparison of emigration ages of males above or below the median in bands with no other equal-aged males and with one or more equal-aged (or older) males. (Stallions not included as older males.)

G test: $G=.42$, $df=1$, $N=21$, NS.

9. Comparison of emigration ages of males above or below the median in bands with no other equal-aged horses and with one or more equal-aged (or older) horses. (Stallions and adult mares not included as above.)

G test: $G=.10$, $df=1$, $N=21$, NS.

10. Comparison between the frequency that newly arrived first-time bachelor males were mounted or herded by "veteran" bachelors with the normal frequency of similar behavior in the absence of new arrivals.

G test: $G=71.44$, $df=1$, $p<0.001$, $N=82$.

9 Reproductive Success and Natural Selection

No one supposes that all the individuals of the same species are cast in the same actual mold. These individual differences are of the highest importance for us, for they are often inherited. . . . and they thus afford materials for natural selection to act on.

Charles Darwin (1859)

9.1 INTRODUCTION

Artificially imposed selection has been responsible for numerous characteristics of domestic species (Bokonyi 1974; Darwin 1868; Zeuner 1963). Is there reason to suspect that, when domestic species become feral, natural selection operates to favor the more successful genotypes? In detecting whether selection is operative, a key variable is the period of time over which changes in gene frequencies might occur. Soay sheep on the island of St. Kilda provide a good example. These sheep have lived in a feral state for a minimum of a thousand years, and it is now believed that pelage thickness, horns, breeding seasonality, and other parameters of their biology have been altered by natural selection (Jewell, Milner, and Morton-Boyd 1974). Soay sheep are also interesting because they have a social system similar to that found in their wild progenitors (Geist 1971; Schaller 1977). It is not surprising that strong genetic links underlie the behavior of feral species and that found in their wild ancestors; yet, the influences of phylogeny versus those of other factors on the behavior of domestic species are still not well understood (Price 1984).

By definition, natural selection is identified by differences in gene survival. In long-lived species like horses, the demonstration of natural selection is difficult because it relies on the detection of changes in gene frequencies over successive generations. It is, however, possible to infer differential gene survival by examining whether a disproportionate number of progeny survive and if the magnitude of such variation is likely to be equilibrated within individuals' lifetimes. This chapter considers several of the relationships between natural selection and behavior in feral horses: (1) evidence that reproductive success varies among individuals of each sex and that such variation results in lifetime disparities; (2) whether feral species can be studied within an evolutionary framework; and (3) problems in understanding how well individuals are adjusted to their environments.

9.2   VARIATION AMONG MALES
Rationale and Assumptions

Male horses would be expected to vary in the number of progeny they sire relative to females because not all males maintain equal access to females. But how much variation exists? A major problem in determining the extent of such variation is selecting the time period over which assessments should be made. Measures reflecting only short periods of individuals' lives (e.g., weeks, months, single breeding seasons) can bias the data since individuals that are successful over a given period may be either more or less successful (or equivalent) at other periods in their lives. Ideally, reproductive contributions over a lifetime are the best measures, but only three studies of mammals—elephant seals (LeBouef 1974; Reiter, Pankin, and LeBoeuf 1981), prairie dogs (Hoogland and Foltz 1982), and red deer (Clutton-Brock 1986)—have ever generated those data. However, when a sufficient time period has passed, i.e., a period in which consistent interindividual differences occur *and* in which it is unlikely that these differences in breeding performances will ever be equalized (e.g., Gibson and Guinness 1980), then a "buffered" solution to the problem exists.

Information on male breeding performance in Granite horses is available for five consecutive years. In four of these, 88% of the paternity assignments were according to the procedure outlined in Appendix 8. Briefly, this method was based on direct observations: males were assigned paternal status when they were observed copulating and when subsequent birthdates during the next year fell within 2 *SD* (about 96.5%) of mean gestation lengths for offspring of each sex. The advantages of this method are that it does not rely solely on observed copulations for assessments of paternity, and it can be evaluated with information about whether or not mares gave birth (and, if so, when). These options would not have existed had only observations of sexual behavior been made (see Appendix 8). The remaining 12% of the paternity determinations had to be derived from indirect measures since copulations were not observed. These assignments were made by estimating periods of female receptivity (again by backdating birth dates by standard gestation lengths) and then by summing the proportions of the time that each male consorted with designated females.

The claim can always be made that paternity assignments were inaccurate because copulations by a few males could have gone undetected. This possibility clearly exists. But the overall influence of missed (or "sneak") copulations should be small and should not bias the data toward any particular category of males. The open terrain, long hours of observation from dawn to dusk, and systematic sampling of females resulted in information on 244 copulations. Also, both bachelors and stallions were included in the sampling, neither of which differed in their availability for observations. This does not mean that some matings went undetected, it merely provides an explanation for how data were collected. Sneak copulations should not have been any less observable (to the research team or myself) than regular copulations. Unless the identities of males copulating during the night differed from those copulating during the day, the methods used should have given a representative cross section of male mating.

In 1984, the year that followed the end of the study, it was not possible to assign paternity values because foals had not yet been born. In other words, gestation lengths could not be followed to completion, although twenty-four copulations with different females were recorded in 1983. To adjust for this problem, probabilities that pregnant females would bear foals were predicted from prior records of their home-range use, reproductive histories, and ages. These probability values of paternity were then assigned to males for 1983. To judge the accuracy of this method, I selected 1982 data and then applied the same criteria in the absence of information on 1983 births. The estimated 1982 paternity assignments and actual assignments of these same males based on 1983 birth-season records were then compared. Of 31 births predicted, 29 occurred. Also, a female that was assumed not to be pregnant produced a foal. Hence, two males were incorrectly credited with siring foals that were never born, and another male that was not observed copulating in 1982 would not have been given paternal status had the 1983 foal data not been available. Moreover, a total of 0.9 foals were attributed to four males that actually produced none, and two males were not given credit when, together, they deserved 1.0 foals. When the absolute differences between actual and expected paternity values are added, 4.9 mispredictions were made; the error factor was 4.9 of 29 or 16.9%. Thus, by the above method, 83.1% of the paternity assignments for twenty-seven adult males were predicted accurately if no other mistakes went undetected. These data can be treated as a chi square analysis with 26 degrees of freedom. The relatively low value, 14.52 ($p<0.95$), indicates that the values predicted from 1982 copulation data did not differ significantly from the actual paternity assignments that included the 1983 births. The foregoing suggests that the magnitude of error resulting from reliance on 1983 paternity assigments should be slight. These data have been included unless noted otherwise.

Number of Offspring Sired

Males only five years of age or older were considered, since younger males were not likely to sire offspring, even though a few managed copulations or held females for short lengths of time (sec. 7.4). Among males, the number of progeny fathered varied considerably (fig. 9.1). Two males, nine years and fourteen years old when the study ended, represented only 7% of the total males, but they fathered 20 and 16 foals, respectively—29% of the total number of foals. Sixty percent of the males five years or older accounted for a mere 8.3% of the neonates.

What factors might have contributed to these differences in reproductive success? Clearly, the variation among some males was not due to lifetime differences because the data did not span the lifetimes of most animals. Was it likely that the variation in reproductive success resulted from age differences in males? In other words, might all males be expected to breed equally? If so, could the observed variation then be a consequence of adult individuals in the population having dissimilar ages (see Rowell 1974)? These ideas (Gibson and Guinness 1980) would not be supported if individuals within the same age class differed in the number of offspring they fathered.

Male reproductive performance varied with age [1], and stallions that fathered the highest number of offspring in any given year were in the seven-to-ten-year cohort, followed by the eleven-to-thirteen-year-olds (fig. 9.2). However, large interindividual differences also existed (fig. 9.2). To control for age-related differences, six males between the ages of seven to eleven years were compared over three years during their breeding peaks. This measure was chosen because (1) it covers a period when differences

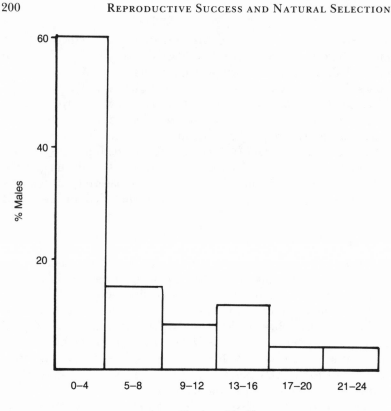

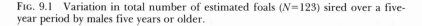

FIG. 9.1 Variation in total number of estimated foals ($N=123$) sired over a five-year period by males five years or older.

among males might be expected to be small since all males at these ages should be near their prime, and (2) it avoids potential disparities that could have arisen from comparing individuals from older age cohorts where differences in cumulative breeding performances might have already occurred but may have gone undetected since individuals were past their prime. Among these six males the most successful male left behind 12 foals, while the least successful sired none; intermediate values were 1, 4.9, 9, and 10 foals. The differences in reproductive success among these animals were great [2].

In addition to these observations, individuals within both younger and older age groups also differed in their reproductive success. Four individuals, aged nine, seven, five, and four years, died without reproducing, while a five-year-old (that also perished) fathered only 1 foal. Among older animals, a fifteen-year-old (that died) left behind no progeny, and a seventeen-year-old sired only 0.5 foals. But some males that were even older were more successful. A nineteen-year-old fathered 7.4 foals over the study duration, one male that was more than twenty-two years old was responsible for 2.4 foals. Despite inaccuracies that might have arisen due to aging techniques when applied to older horses, it is clear that such errors could not account for strong interindividual differences in reproductive success within most cohorts and that for some individuals (e.g., those that died) it is impossible to equilibrate differences.

9.3 CAUSES OF MALE VARIATION

Even though male reproductive success varied to some extent with age, age alone could not account for the large differences that persisted among individuals. Were other factors involved?

Weight

Only males weighing an estimated minimum of 386 kg sired offspring. Since animals below this weight were almost always (with

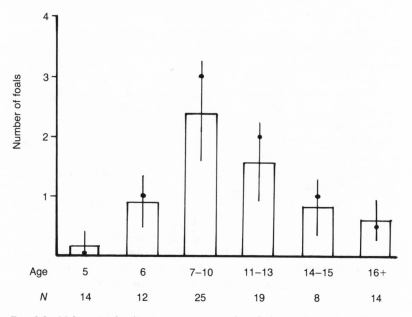

FIG. 9.2 Male reproductive success per year in relation to age over a five-year period. Means, standard deviations (extending lines), and medians (dots) indicated.

one exception) younger than five years, either light weight or inexperience might explain their lack in achieving breeding status. Up to a point, heavier stallions gained in reproductive advantage, as seen in section 8.7 where for nine males, relatively heavier individuals were more successful at retaining their first harems. Weight therefore may offer relatively better chances for reproduction early in a male's life. But, weight in itself was insufficient to assure successful reproduction. An average of 43% per year of the males that failed to breed were heavier than breeding males (table 9.1).

TABLE 9.1   Relationships between Breeding Status and Estimated Body Weight of Males in June

	$\bar{X}$ Wt (kg) of Breeding Males	% of Males Exceeding $\bar{X}$ Wt That Were 4 Yrs or More and Failed to Sire Offspring
1980	443 (10)	50
1981	450 (10)	40
1982	435 (12)	33
1983	425 (13)	58
1984[a]	432 (14)	33

[a]Based on copulations and subsequent probabilities of births (see sec. 9.2).

Weight may not be as important a factor in achieving successful reproduction in equids as it is in other species. Although weight (or size) may confer dominance advantages to participants in equid combat, it is primarily through imbalancing rivals and then relying on quickness and speed that one delivers successful bites, especially if opponents are nearly even in size (Berger 1981). In species such as bison, musk-ox, bighorn sheep, and red deer, advantages over conspecifics are gained by pushing, shoving, or dislodging opponents—forces generated by body mass (Geist 1966, 1971, 1978b; Clutton-Brock, Guinness, and Albon 1982). Among bison, for instance, only 20% of the nonbreeding mature males in a single rutting season exceeded the mean weight of copulating bulls (Lott 1979). Despite Lott's sample of males ($N=5$), the results are in accordance with the idea that weight in bison was important in achieving successful reproduction. If a consistently greater proportion of nonreproducing males exceeded mean breeding weights, it would indicate that in such species weight is less important than in species where the ratio of heavy nonbreeders to lighter breeders was less. In other words, weight can be inferred to be important, other factors being equal, only when lighter individuals are precluded from breeding. The consistently greater proportion of non-reproducing horses relative to mean breeding weight (table 9.1) when compared with bison suggests that weight may be more important in achieving dominance in bison than it is in horses.

Lott (1979) argued that neither weight nor age were closely associated with copulatory success in the bison he studied. The apparent discrepancy may be resolved by supposing that weight advantages in bison accrue when individual differences are large; when they are small, fighting skills or some combination of other factors will be of primary importance. It should not be surprising therefore that in monomorphic species, weight differences among individuals will most often be small and dominance will be achieved by relying on tactics that are independent of weight. Fighting is one such tactic.

Fighting

Differences in fighting abilities in horses should be expected to underlie discrepancies in reproduction among males. This is because (1) combat is important in obtaining and retaining harems (chap. 7), and (2) virtually all ontogenetic aspects of male social behavior (e.g., ages at independence, play fighting, challenging stallions, use of fighting tactics, etc.), which are geared toward achieving success in a combative role, vary among individuals (sec. 8.7).

Indeed, variation in individual reproductive success was associated with at least two aspects of individuals' "interaction" histories over a four-year period. These aspects were fighting and practice performances; the latter I judged to be the period of time spent in repeated nonescalated aggressive encounters with males. Practice activities included mock fighting and those cases of aggressive greetings when dominance was unclear but fighting did not ensue.

Twelve stallions were involved in a total of 124 fights and 2,618 practice sessions with other males (both stallions and bachelors). Positive correlations existed between stallions that left the most offspring and (1) the proportion of fights they won, and (2) the amount of time they practiced per week [3]. Although each of these variables was related to the other [4], some form of prior experience or practice was necessary to achieve high breeding status. Three males (aged six, six, and seven years old) that had participated only sparingly in fights and "hard" practice sessions as young bachelors failed to become successful breeders by the time the study terminated.

The foregoing illustrates that differences existed among fighting abilities; they were related in part to social ontogenies. It does not address the causes of these developmental differences. Evidence presented earlier suggested that such variation arose because of individual differences in males (sec. 8.7) and because males of different ages adopted various fighting techniques (sec. 7.4).

Home-Range Locations

Males varied in their relative reproductive success not only because of differences in fighting abilities and weights but also because of differences in their home-range locations. Males that used high-quality home ranges were responsible for more foals than those that used inferior sites. When the confounding effects of band changes and shifts to new home ranges are removed from foal production calculations, seventy-eight foals were born from 1980 through 1983. Males that used high-quality home ranges were responsible for more foals than those that used inferior sites. Those from the former areas accounted for 50% ($N = 39$) of the offspring, even though high-quality ranges comprised less than 20% of the available areas. As with other factors, use of the best feeding areas was also related to age. Only prime-aged males accounted for foals from high-quality areas whereas males from all other age cohorts bred in intermediate or low-quality regions [5]. In these two latter cases the greatest proportion of breeding males were either young or old; they were not of prime age. Nevertheless, at least 30% of the males within a given cohort (4–6, 7–13, and 14+ yrs) in any year could be found not using home ranges of the same quality. Thus, although age effects persisted during the time that stallions occupied the best home ranges, individual differences persisted as well.

Reproductive Lifespan

Breeding lifespans can extend until at least twenty-two years, as shown by Moscha siring two foals that were born in 1983. Not all males attain that venerable age, but if they do, most will not possess harems. Of 7 males that were fourteen years or older, only one consistently held a harem (he was the youngest of the 7), 2 never obtained any females, 2 held but lost harems, and 2 wandered solitarily throughout most of the study, although they occasionally picked up (but lost) females. Whether these males had harems when they were prime aged is unknown, but clearly successful reproduction was not limited to younger males. Nevertheless, younger males accounted for a greater proportion of the breeding (fig. 9.2).

By definition, reproductive lifespan affects how long an individual breeds but not how many offspring are left behind. For instance, individual horses that died early in life or reproduced for only a few years could conceivably still produce an equal or greater number of foals than those that reproduced longer if the former were more successful in their few reproductive years. The evidence (sec. 9.2) showed that reproductive parity did not occur due to strong interindividual differences during prime ages. Reproductive disparities were probably accentuated further as individuals grew older since some old animals were successful while others were not.

Few data on these topics exist for other free-ranging equids. A few male Burchell's zebras manage to hold onto harems and breed up to nineteen years of age (Smuts 1976c), while Mountain zebra stallions may remain active breeders in the wild until at least fifteen years (Penzhorn 1979) or to twenty-three years in captivity (Canyon Colorado Equid Sanctuary, unpub.). In the only study of feral burros in which breeding ages were reported, McCort (1980) found that the oldest male, a thirteen-year-old, still sired foals.

Incidental Opportunities

Horses that were in the right place at the right time experienced opportunities to reproduce. During the study, at least fourteen bachelor males encountered wandering mares and were successful in keeping them for a minimum of twelve hours. For instance, in spring 1982 a four-year-old bachelor, Frampton, spent more than 90% of his time 3 km south of a Granite Basin waterhole which he visited only to drink. In that year, band E relied on water and food located about 6 km to 8 km north and below Granite Basin. In late May, E forayed into Granite Basin when one of its females, Elna, became separated because her newborn foal could not keep pace with the band. Elna remained with her newborn and they later visited one of the Basin's springs to drink. As she approached Frampton happened to be there. The fortuitous timing led subsequently to Frampton's eighteen-hour association with Elna. Although Frampton attempted to copulate by force he was unsuccessful, and Elna returned to band E.

This example illustrates that incidental acquisitions occur. Some acquisitions are shaped, in part, by the wide-ranging behavior of bachelor males. Bachelors have larger home ranges than would be predicted on the basis of food alone (table 4.1), move greater diurnal and nocturnal distances than other categories of horses (table 4.2), and enlarge emigration distances when population density (and mating competition) increases (sec. 5.6), all of which suggests that bachelors design their movements to better their opportunities for meeting females. Still, such chance encounters may not be easy for males to come by. Some females wandered for up to four days before being discovered by bachelors, and on at least three occasions groups of two and three mares went undetected for three days. Additionally, during fourteen instances when wandering females were acquired by males, at least forty-nine bachelors missed chances simply because they were in the wrong place at the wrong time.

9.4   Variation among Females
Rationale and Assumptions

It was less difficult to evaluate reproductive success in females than in males because relationships between juveniles and mothers could be identified more easily. Young animals suckle from their mothers for the better part of a year, and they usually follow their mothers until emigrating from their natal bands. By determining whether mares observed in the first year of study were accompanied by yearlings, reproductive status could be inferred in the prior year. This method is biased since it does not account for females that may have foaled earlier in the year and then lost their progeny, but since postnatal survival of foals up to six months of age was 92%, the error involved would be small.

In determining reproductive success during the final year of study I estimated the probability that copulations occurring in that year would lead to foals in the subsequent year. As mentioned (sec. 9.2), this estimate was based on actual female reproductive histories up to that point. Thus, the information to be presented on reproductive performances in some females could span up to seven years (1978 through 1984), six of which were based on actual observations of mothers and young. Females were credited with producing an offspring successfully if their foals lived to six months, except for 1984 when 100% survival was assumed.

Number of Offspring Produced

A female that maximized her reproductive output in any given year would only produce a single foal, since twinning in horses is exceedingly infrequent (see chap. 6) and no twins have been reported in field studies of feral horses. Because not all females in a population bear young every year, variation among individuals would be expected if such differences were not equalized over a female's lifetime.

Among Granite females, the greatest potential disparity between the most and least successful individuals could have been 7 foals (over a seven-year period), but this difference never occurred. For females that were sexually mature when the study began and whose reproductive performances were known over a six-year period (1978–83), the least successful individuals produced 2 young while the most successful produced 6. Variation among females over this period was evident. Forty-six percent of the mares produced 2 or fewer foals while only 10% produced 6 foals (fig. 9.3).

Like males, the differences in offspring production by females could be explained partly because specific age cohorts varied in their fecundity. As pointed out in chapter 5, a strong age-depen-

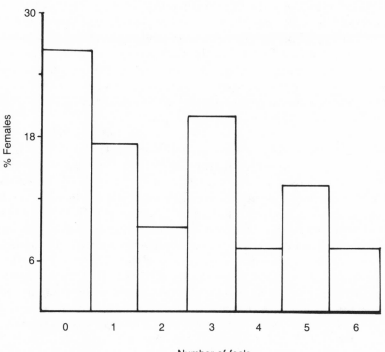

FIG. 9.3 Variation in total number of foals ($N = 127$) produced over a six-year period. Females were included in the sample the year after they attained puberty.

dent relationship emerges (fig. 5.2) when foal production per year
is compared among different age groups [6]. Both the youngest
(2–4 yr old) and oldest (18+ yr old) mares were the least likely to
foal annually and were the most variable in reproductive output.
With their influences removed, no differences occurred in offspring production for the groups ranging from five to seventeen
years [7].

By comparing individuals within age classes over the same specified time period of their lives it was possible to detect the extent
that individual differences (rather than those among age classes)
contributed to the observed variation. Within the youngest age cohort, females capable of giving birth on their second birthday were
compared for each year until they were four yrs old. The most
successful mares produced 3 foals while the least successful produced none. Additionally, two young but mature females died, one
of whom was accompanied by her foal which also succumbed.
These females could not possibly have equalized the disparities that
had accrued in reproductive perfomances between them and more
successful females. For the two-to-four-year-olds as a group, differences in foal production among individuals were significant [8].
A small sample of females in the eighteen-year-or-older category
precluded a similar analysis. Thus, for these older females it was
not possible to know whether individual differences in addition to
age-graded ones were responsible for the variability found in this
group.

Females in the five-to-seventeen-year-old category showed the
least variation in reproductive performances. However, the possibility remains that individuals within this age cohort still differed
in their propensity to produce offspring. Therefore, I compared
the maximum reproductive performances of individuals for each
year over a five-year period; their ages were at least five years when
the study began and never went above seventeen years when the
study ended. This measure is conservative since it probably under-
estimates differences among females over their five-year peak performances rather than accentuating differences, as might be the
case if less than maximal periods were selected for comparison.
Over this period the greatest number of offspring produced was 5
while the fewest was 3. Over 83% of the females gave birth to at
least 4 foals. Of the 3 mares that produced 3 foals each, all died
during the study. Also, 2 five-year-old females, 1 six-year-old, and
1 twelve-year-old died early in the study. Two of them had offspring at the time of their deaths, but, because their prior re-

productive histories were unknown, they were excluded from the sample. Although the magnitude of differences among females that ceased foal production (due to death) and those that continued to reproduce would be great, there was remarkably little difference among individuals over the five-yr period [9]. Unlike other age categories, females aged anywhere between five to seventeen years were likely to be equally successful at producing foals.

The above data on females of various age cohorts indicate that the greatest variation in reproductive performances among individuals occurred between two and four years of life. After this age, individual differences were slight and not significant. Only age at death accounted for marked differences in foal production. However it would be incorrect to assume that, because females between five to seventeen years varied little in their foal output, subtle differences could not affect their reproductive success relative to others. Mothering abilities (e.g., milk production, weaning, etc.), offspring quality, and growth might have important consequences for a mare's lifetime reproductive success (sec. 9.6).

9.5 CAUSES OF FEMALE VARIATION

As described above, female age had important effects on reproductive performances. Up until five years of age individual differences were substantial, but for females five years or older there was only a small amount of variation in foal production [9]. What factors caused such differences early in life and in what ways were their effects mollified as animals grew older?

Home Range of Birth

Because nutrition early in life influences later growth and physical condition (Sadleir 1969), infants born and residing in relatively better home-range areas should have improved chances of producing foals once they attain breeding age over those who do not live in such areas. This would be expected because such animals not only suckle for longer periods of time (fig. 6.8) but also subsist on better food resources once they have been weaned. Thus, it is not surprising that a significantly greater proportion of foals from high-quality home ranges were more successful at bearing young a year after they attained puberty than were those born in inferior areas [10]. These data agree well with information available on domestic horses (see Belonje and Van Niekerk 1975; Mitchell and Allen 1975), which suggests that early breeding performance is related to nutrition.

TABLE 9.2   Ecological and Social Correlates of Foal Production
for Two- and Three-Year-Old Sexually Mature Females

	Home Range Born in (A)	Home Range Lived in While Pregnant (B)	Band Stability (C)	(B) and (C)
Home-Range Quality				
High	75% (8)	63% (16)	—	—
Medium to poor	21% (14)	31% (26)	—	—
Band Stability				
Stable	—	—	57% (30)	—
Unstable	—	—	8% (12)	—
High-Quality Home Range				
Stable	—	—	—	91% (11)
Unstable	—	—	—	20% (5)
Medium-to-Poor Quality Home Range				
Stable	—	—	—	37% (19)
Unstable	—	—	—	0% (7)

Notes: Foal production = number of foals produced/total number possible × 100.
Sample sizes in parentheses.

Home-Range Residency While Pregnant

Young females that lived in high-quality home ranges during their pregnancies produced relatively more foals than those from poorer areas (table 9.2) [11]. For a female, the chances for improving her reproductive success early in life would seem to be best if (1) she was born in a relatively good home-range area, and/or (2) she resided in a relatively good area during pregnancy. Perhaps one of these variables was more important to successful reproduction than the other, but the relative influence of each is not known. All foals that were born in high-quality ranges, except for one, later resided in such areas when pregnant.

Band Stability

While ecological factors had clear effects on female reproductive rates, social ones did as well. Band stability had marked consequences on a young female's reproduction, as can be shown by contrasting foaling rates in females that remained in stable bands with those that changed social environments (table 9.2). In stable bands, 57% (17 of 30) of the young mares produced foals while only 8% (1 of 12) of the two- and three-year-olds from unstable bands were successful [12].

To what extent did home-range occupation and band stability

affect reproduction? Females were separated into those from high-quality areas and those from medium-to-poor-quality areas. Several points can be made about the ways that these factors affected foal production (summarized in table 9.2). Within high-quality ranges, the proportion of females that foaled from stable bands exceeded the proportion from unstable ones (91% versus 20%) [13]. Females from medium-to-poor-quality areas fared better if they were from stable bands—37% versus 0% for those in unstable ones [13]. These data indicate that each factor (home range and band stability) altered an individual's immediate reproductive performance.

The evidence accumulated so far with regard to early breeding performances of females (e.g., before they reach four years of age) can be summarized as follows: Both ecological and social factors altered reproductive rates. Foals that were born into high-quality home ranges or that resided within them *and* remained in stable bands had better reproductive records than those that did not. This was because environmental sources of infant growth were tied to home range. Mothers converted food obtained within their home ranges into milk for their neonates (and the offspring of mothers from better home ranges experienced longer suckling times, at least during the first two months of life [sec. 6.6]). Ultimately, the growth of young animals was determined by a combination of factors that included benefits derived from the mother and from food within the home range itself. Probably the most important social factor that modified reproduction was band stability. Individuals that did not change bands or were not in bands taken over by new males were not harassed by males or females. Perhaps these individuals also benefited because, by not changing bands or home ranges, they were already familiar with foraging, watering, and sheltering sites.

Body Size/Weight Relationships

Unlike young females, those aged from five to seventeen years showed a small amount of variation in their fecundity. These older individuals were larger in body size than the younger females, a factor that apparently ameliorated the effects of extreme environmental conditions and offered a greater capacity for stored reserves. Since size was associated positively with physical condition (fig. 6.5), possibly because smaller mothers had fewer body reserves (sec. 6.6), small females might be expected to experience poorer reproductive success than larger ones. Examining this hy-

pothesis required a comparison of females within similar age cohorts, of similar home-range qualities, and of similar band
stabilities. Females that were above or below the median for estimated population weight (430 kg) within the five-to-seventeen-
year-old cohort and from stable bands were compared only when
they used the same home-range areas. No significant differences
were found in breeding rates between these two categories of
mares, even though comparisons were made within both high- and
medium-to-poor-quality areas.

It would seem peculiar that size differences did not affect foal
production, particularly in light of earlier evidence (fig. 6.5) that
larger females emerged from winter in better body condition than
smaller animals. Might these apparently contradictory findings
about body size and condition and reproduction arise from lack of
consideration of the hypothesis that size is disadvantageous only
among the relatively smallest females? The data suggest that this is
the case.

The relatively smallest females in the population were those
whose weights were estimated as below 410 kg, and they comprised
less than 30% of the five-to-seventeen-year-old mares from stable
bands. Based on comparisons of females from above and below 410
kg and according to the quality of their home-range areas, the following results emerged. Foal production was 94% ($N=16$) for
females that exceeded 410 kg from high-quality home-range areas;
80% ($N=10$) for smaller females from the same ranges; 93%
($N=29$) for mares heavier than 410 kg from medium-to-poor-quality areas; and 67% ($N=9$) for females less than 410 kg from medium-to-poor-quality areas. Resource-base location had little
influence on reproductive performance in big females as shown by
parity (94% versus 93%) in foal production. Likewise, on high-
quality ranges large body size (versus small body size; 94% and
80%, respectively) did not confer a significant advantage [14]. Regardless of size, females that fed in high-quality home ranges were
able to acquire the reserves needed for successful reproduction.

The selection of high-quality areas for comparison obscures a
possible relationship between female size and breeding success because the availability of relatively good resources can overcome the
depressive effects of small size. Evidence that size/weight relationships play a role in successful reproduction might be more apparent for females living in medium-to-poor-quality areas. Indeed,
foal production in females above and below 410 kg from medium-
to-poor areas was significantly depressed from 93% to 67%, respec-

tively [15]. These data on prime-aged adult females suggest that a point is reached when larger individuals use body reserves that could be lacking in smaller conspecifics, reserves that cannot be accumulated by females foraging in home ranges of relatively poor quality. Hence, small size/low weight is relatively more disadvantageous for reproduction in females from poorer resource areas than it is to mares from better regions.

In most mammals size/weight relationships are correlated with age until at least puberty (and perhaps after). Studies of ungulates (Grubb 1974a; Sinclair 1977; Reimers 1983) have revealed that once full body weight is attained by females, they are more fecund than their lighter (and younger) conspecifics. It has not proved easy to separate the effects of weight/size versus age on reproductive performances, especially when females become adults; without knowledge of individual differences in these parameters and without knowledge of coincident reproductive histories, interindividual comparisons cannot be set up to look at the effects of specific variables. For example, growth in both size and weight in East African warthogs continues after puberty, which is reached at about one year of age. Growth proceeds until at leave five years, and female fecundity increases concomitantly (Boshe 1981). It is unclear which factor—age or size/weight (or both acting together)—may be responsible for increased numbers of offspring in older, heavier females. In contrast, among red deer hinds size/weight was not directly correlated with reproduction after a given age (Clutton-Brock, Guinness, and Albon 1982). Instead, body condition was implicated as a good predictive factor of later reproduction. However, unlike red deer, size or, more appropriately, weight was an important factor underlying successful reproduction in mares that occupied less than the best home ranges. These data on horses reaffirm Ralls's (1976) suggestion that bigger mothers are more likely to be better or more fecund mothers.

These somewhat conflicting findings concerning size may have resulted from different analyses used in the various studies. Initially, prime-aged feral mares above and below the median weight were compared, and when no differences in reproductive performances were found, the focus centered on even smaller individuals (e.g., those less than an estimated 410 kg). In doing so, the effects of lighter weight were exacerbated, although they still indicated that small size was a reproductive handicap when resources were less than optimal. Seal (unpub. data) also found that smaller mares were less likely to reproduce. Of the feral horses he sampled from

Idaho, two-to-three-year-olds and four-year-olds that were not pregnant weighed on the average 46 and 38 kg less than their pregnant and equal-aged conspecifics. Here, additional weight was associated with greater pregnancy rates. In one other mammal—humans—size (or weight) may offer reproductive rewards: "Women who are genetically short, whose growth has not been stunted, are on the whole less efficient at reproduction than women who are genetically tall" (Thomson 1959, as quoted in Ralls 1976). Recent studies of human females have found that individuals who were small at birth experienced "problem pregnancies," including giving birth to lighter babies and babies with respiratory problems (Hackman et al. 1983). Clearly, maternal size and weight are important factors that mediate reproductive success.

Anomalous Situations and Possible Trade-offs

Several females occasionally acted in ways that are difficult to reconcile with the idea that individuals behave to maximize their reproductive success. Band P, for example, which had migrated to the same high-altitude summer ranges for several years, lost two adult females and a juvenile when these individuals became separated on different sides of a ridgetop. Unlike other times, when separated individuals whinnied to their band mates, these females ran downslope. In about one hour they descended almost 500 m and traversed about 8 km. That summer they remained at a low altitude, wandering without a stallion for over one month. In the next year, neither of the adult females produced foals.

Some females remained in poor home ranges without emigrating. As indicated earlier, females residing in such regions were less likely to produce offspring, and the offspring they did produce suckled for shorter periods of time and attained puberty at a later age than offspring belonging to mothers from better areas.

In asking why these females did not switch home-range locations by changing bands, it might be argued that the costs (harassment, possible forced copulation, nonfamiliar mates, and uncertain food or watering locations) outweighed the benefits of emigrating. That females remaining in stable bands were more likely to produce offspring than those leaving them suggests that a major reproductive advantage may be gained by remaining in a group. Females in stable bands derive benefits because they are not often harassed, they occasionally gain support from familiar mates during times of duress (sec. 7.7), and they know feeding and watering sites due to a high degree of home-range fidelity (sec. 4.4). Nevertheless, the crucial test lies in determining whether the long-term benefits of remaining in a band outweigh the short-term negative effects of changing bands. This would entail comparisons of inclusive fitness in females from each category.

An additional trade-off in reproduction worthy of mention is the allocation of energy either to reproduction or growth in young females. On a short-term basis young mares that produced offspring gained a reproductive advantage over those of similar ages that failed to reproduce. Other factors equal, the age at which the first offspring is born influences potential lifetime fecundity (Cole 1954; Stearns 1976). But there are costs associated with reproduction (Clutton-Brock, Guinness, and Albon, 1983) that may be more acute in animals of small body size, perhaps because young females that reproduce at small sizes sacrifice opportunities for future reproduction when they would be larger (and, hence would have additional reserves). An important question here is: Do young females that reproduce when small ever make up the difference in size that might have been achieved had they not reproduced at an early age (or small size)? To my knowledge, no data answer this question for mammals. In Granite horses, females that reproduced at two or three years of age were smaller in size by an average of about 45 kg than those that did not reproduce until older (the small sample precluded statistical testing). It could be that over an individual's lifetime the advantage gained by early reproduction could be negated in an environment with restricted resources if the possibility for attaining larger size is sacrificed.

Harem Size

The combined effects of age, body size, home-range condition, and band stability coupled with the relatively few foals born in respective categories prevented analysis of whether harem size affected foal production. It has been suggested that in habitats where resources vary in quality, individuals distribute themselves such that the potential to maximize reproductive success is even—the result being that, although local densities vary among habitats, reproduction among individuals is broadly equivalent based on resources. "Ideal free distributions," as the phenomena is called (Fretwell and Lucas 1970), has been studied in insects (Whitham 1978, 1979) and birds (Brown and Balda 1977) but not in mammals (see chap. 10). Perhaps this is due to the complex web of variables already mentioned, coupled with problems inherent in measuring the quality of resources. However, an inverse relationship between harem size and female reproductive success was found in marmots (Down-hower and Armitage 1971). In this case, the contribution of various interrelated variables, including food resources, was unknown. But there is no reason why harem size per se, in horses, marmots, or other species, could not be an important density-dependent factor in mediating reproduction.

9.6   BEHAVIORAL AND ECOLOGICAL STRATEGIES OF MARES AND STALLIONS

Males and females differed in the ways in which they achieved their mating success. Stallions, compared to mares, were successful for relatively short periods in their lives. While some mares began reproduction at two years and others had the capability to foal until twenty-two years of age, most stallions fortunate enough to breed did not begin until five or six years. Some males never bred at all. Of those that did breed, average harem tenure was less than four years. In what ways might males and females improve their reproductive performances relative to others in the population, and how might these change with age?.

Convergence in Neonatal Tactics

Regardless of sex, infant survival is dependent upon immunity from diseases and obtaining sufficient nutrients and energy reserves. As infants, both males and females receive maternal nourishment through milk. Although the two sexes may differ in their relative success at garnering maternal resources, they each (presumably) obtain as much milk as they are able to. Since growth (Foxcroft 1980) and later reproduction (Clutton-Brock, Guinness, and Albon 1982) depend, at least in part, on early nutrition, both males and females should make the best use of all resources available. This would mean not only acquiring milk, but developing food preferences and putting on as much weight as possible early in life. In short, males and females may reflect common behaviors at an early age because they share interests, such as weight gain, which are important to each in terms of later reproductive success. However, once they attain puberty the ways in which they may go about achieving reproductive success differ.

Adult Females

Daughters obviously cannot choose the areas into which they are born. However, once they achieve puberty, females can modify their reproductive fates to some extent. Whether to leave or remain in natal bands, the age at which to depart, how long to stay in other bands, and where to feed are options exercised by females. Costs and benefits are associated with all of these choices (see above). Although ecological variables, especially home-range resources, had profound influences on reproductive performances, social factors like band stability also had major effects on later reproduction. Additional behavioral associations (e.g., bonding, cooperation, grooming partners, and even intraband dominance) may have had important effects, but they could not be detected with the data at hand.

Overall, most females in the population encountered little difficulty breeding. Although competition among individuals occurred, it was achieved primarily through the effects of home-range differences and scramble competition, not through aggression or active exclusion of females from feeding sites. For any female the best route to maximize reproductive success over her lifetime would be to attain a large body size, remain in a stable band, and feed in a high-quality home range. The road toward maximizing individual fitness is filled with complex, interwoven behavioral trade-offs.

Adult Males

Compared to females, competition among males was greater as indicated by higher rates of aggression, fighting-related injuries, and deaths, *and* greater variation in reproductive success. Some characteristics of successful males (see table 9.3) included large body sizes

TABLE 9.3 Ecological and Behavioral Factors Influencing Reproductive Success in Each Sex

---

Reproductive lifespan: Of greater duration in females than males.

Body size/weight: Important to females when resources are limited. Of possible significance for achieving dominance in females (but undetected in this study). For males, important up to a point in gaining and keeping harems.

Fighting abilities: Of minimal value to females but of importance to males.

Skill development: Of minimal value to females but important to males.

Home range: Of central importance for both sexes. Male and female reproductive success (i.e., offspring production) is affected by many home-range characteristics.

Alliance formation: Of undetermined value for each sex.

Band stability: Important for females and males since offspring production is affected by band stability.

Age-dependent behavioral changes: Detected in young females that are more inclined to change bands voluntarily than in older females. Highly detectable in males that change fighting and defense tactics as they age.

(at least during life as a bachelor), sound fighting abilities, numerous social interactions as bachelors in which fighting skills were used, occupation of good home ranges, and the effective defense of harems. Some interrelated factors were (1) energetics of harem defense and harem size (sec. 7.5), (2) age and home-range location (sec. 9.3), and (3) age and fighting style (sec. 7.4).

It would be easy to claim that behavioral tactics adopted by males during two phases of their lives were crucial for maximizing their reproductive success. As bachelors they should develop fighting skills and feed in high-quality areas. As stallions they should fight when necessary and obtain as many females as defendable without sacrificing later fecundity. The problem with this scenario is that not one set of behavioral strategies may be the best, and the success of the tactics employed is contingent on what others in the population are doing (Maynard Smith 1976).

9.7   LIFETIME REPRODUCTIVE SUCCESS: ESTIMATIONS AND SPECULATIONS

Dilemmas, Rationale, and Assumptions

Measuring lifetime reproductive success is conditional upon counting the number of offspring that survive to sexual maturity (Arnold 1983). It is still unclear which characteristics most closely approximate lifetime mating success. Should the parameters be the total number of offspring produced over an animal's life, only those offspring that live to a certain age, or only those offspring that reproduce (see Arnold 1983; Clutton-Brock 1986; Howard 1979; Maynard Smith 1958)? For my purposes I chose the number of offspring that survived to six months, but this does not alleviate the problem that few individuals were followed throughout their entire reproductive careers.

For males, a five-year period appeared sufficient to reflect lifetime reproductive differences among individuals because the extent of individual variation was so great that the likelihood that any difference would be equalized was small (sec. 9.2), a result consistent with findings in red deer (Gibson and Guinness 1980). For females, the differences were not great among individuals. I therefore estimated how long females might live and then calculated their corresponding offspring production. For each sex, the available data (figs. 9.2, 5.2) on mean reproductive success per individual per year were added to arrive at values that might simulate the number of offspring each sex might contribute over its reproductive career. Still, without knowing how long many individuals lived and because lifespan varies under different conditions (Caughley 1977), it was not possible to arrive at a single representative value for males or females.

A female's lifetime production is essentially a product of her longevity. A mare that lived to ten years of age would on the average leave behind 5.88 foals, while one that lived to fifteen years would produce 10 foals. Even a female that reproduced better than the average mare and that also lived to fifteen years would produce only 13 foals, assuming that she began foaling at two years and did so every year until death. In contrast, an average male that lived to fifteen years would produce 16.2 foals. At the extremely proliferous end, the most successful stallion in the Granite Range sired over 20 foals by the time he was nine years. It is clear that the potential number of progeny that successful males and females can leave behind differs, with males showing a considerably greater number and more variability than females.

An apparent anomaly in these data is that sex differences occurred in the average number of offspring produced by adults of each sex. If birth sex ratios are at parity (which they were in the Granite Range), then average male and female reproductive success must be equal (Fisher 1930). That they were not merely reflects more females than males living in the population when estimations of reproductive success were made.

Variance among Males and Females

Although the above comparisons might be interesting, two factors need to be considered: (1) on the average males live slightly shorter lives and are more variable in their reproductive performances than females; and (2) it is through the differences in variance in reproductive success between the sexes that selection operates. It is also the effects of this variance on particular traits that are important for models of sexual selection (Arnold 1983; Wade and Arnold 1980; Clutton-Brock 1986). I used two measures to provide an idea of the variation that occurs between the sexes. The first is a relative comparison between "average individuals," while the second takes into account the variability inherent among individuals within each sex.

Mean age of death was 7.86±2.06 yrs for females and 7.23±6.06 yrs for males. Males were more variable in their lifespans, and their median for longevity was less than for females (4.5 yrs versus 6 yrs, respectively). At mean age of death, an average female would be more than twice as successful as an average male (3.91 versus 1.60

foals left behind respectively; calculated from age-specific fecundity, figs. 9.2, 5.2). Though these measures fail to take variability into account, they indicate that in an average life females are likely to experience greater reproductive success than average males, principally because females breed both earlier than males and throughout their lives. After the mean age of death, some males are far more successful in leaving behind offspring than are equal-aged females.

How much greater was the variation in lifetime reproduction in males relative to females? These data are still unavailable for horses or, for that matter, for all other mammals except black-tailed prairie dogs, red deer, and elephant seals. To offer rudimentary comparisons I calculated "variance relative to mean success separately for both sexes" (Clutton-Brock 1986). The resulting values (see table 9.4) indicate the intensity of selection (see Arnold 1983).

Three sets of conditions were chosen in which to calculate variation in reproductive success between the sexes. These allowed comparison of the variability in sex differences in reproductive success that resulted from different assumptions about breeding performances and lifespans. For each comparison prime-aged males (seven to eleven years old) and females (five to seventeen years old) were used so that the effects age had upon reproduction were not confounded.

Measure A included all prime-aged males and females as well as individuals whose lifetime reproductive success was known. This measure is probably the best of the three since it incorporates all potential breeders. While it may be biased to some extent by the inclusion of animals that died young, it is a conservative measure. This is because it compares individuals at the peak of their poten-

TABLE 9.4   Measures Used to Estimate Variation
in Maximal Reproductive Success (Mean/Variance^2)
between the Sexes

Measure		Males	Females
A	Variation in success	2.45	0.54
	N	14	23
B	Variation in success	0.47	0.08
	N	6	18
C	Variation in success	0.11	0.08
	N	4	18

Note: Prime-aged individuals were used during their three best years. N is the sample size.

tial breeding performances—a time when the differences in reproductive success among individuals were the least extreme (sec. 9.3). Thus, measure A offered a picture of reproductive variation among prime-aged individuals regardless of whether or not they mated, and it also included individuals whose lifetime reproductive contributions were known. Under these conditions, reproductive variation was the greatest in each sex.

Measure B excluded individuals that died early in life or that failed to breed. This measure reduced the variation in reproductive success within each sex. Nevertheless, it is questionable whether the exclusion of these nonbreeders is biologically realistic since selection acts on variation in genetic contribution to subsequent generations.

Measure C compared only individuals that were in their prime, breeding, and alive when the study ended. This method also decreased the variance in reproductive success, but it is more restrictive than previous measures because the number of males included was reduced.

Three important points emerge from these comparisons: (1) regardless of method, males vary in reproductive success to a greater extent than females; (2) average reproductive success during the prime age is greater for males than females; (3) depending upon the method selected, the differences in comparative values between the sexes can be large, but the methods probably do little to alter the direction of differences.

Quandaries concerning Sexual Selection in Ungulates

In polygynous species, it is widely supposed that males vary to a greater extent in their reproductive success than females (Ralls 1976; LeBoeuf 1974; Trivers 1972). In red deer, where actual measurements of lifetime differences in offspring production are available, variation in males ranges from 0 to 24 calves and in females from 0 to 13 calves (Clutton-Brock, Guinness, and Albon 1982). As would be predicted, mean values for hinds and stags were not appreciably different, but males varied to a much greater extent than females, a finding that also applies to Granite horses.

Unlike red deer, which are a polygynous and sexually dimorphic species, horses are monomorphic despite being polygynous. This is difficult to reconcile with the theoretical prediction that variation in male reproductive success leads to selection favoring secondary sexual characteristics and often larger body size in males (Alexander et al. 1979). Clutton-Brock (1986) has pointed out, however, that it is not just the variance that is important: "Monomorphism in size is likely to be found where body size has a similar effect on the breeding success of both sexes whether or not variation in breeding success differs between the sexes." Variance establishes only the upper limits for the intensity of sexual selection. Its actual intensity is determined by its relationship to the trait, which in this case was body size.

Horses fit this hypothesis reasonably well. Body size had important effects on the breeding performances of each sex (sec. 9.3, 9.5). For males, breeding success was related in part to weight and fighting skills, while in females, those larger than a given size improved their reproductive performances. The data also indicated that heavier males did not necessarily have greater breeding opportunities than lighter males. Weight may not be as crucial to male breeding success in a monomorphic species as it is in a dimorphic species (sec. 9.3). Although the effects of body weight on breeding success in male and female horses may not be exactly equivalent, they may not be too dissimilar. Thus, data for at least one monomorphic species—horses—fit Clutton-Brock's prediction reasonably well.

Other ideas have been put forth to account for ungulate monomorphism, including (1) a "territorial defense" hypothesis where members of both sexes participate in resource defense (Geist 1978a, 1978b), and (2) an "intersexual grouping" hypothesis where dimorphism in weapons and body size is reduced in gregarious species when both sexes live together. Geist (1978a, 79) reasoned that "where individuals maximize security by grouping, it is clearly a disadvantage to possess weapons that inflict severe pain and trigger retaliation in kind." While these suggestions are interesting, they are not directly applicable to harem-dwelling equids (see Kiltie 1985). Neither sex is territorial, nor does evidence exist that this has ever been the case, and weapons in themselves may have little to do with factors that select for group living. The evolutionary mechanisms that resulted in monomorphism are more parsimoniously explained by considering effects of body size on fitness.

Still, problems exist. The failure to distinguish among taxa of ungulates when making interspecific comparisons is misleading and obscures important phylogenetic differences. For instance, the presence or absence of particular traits such as sexual dimorphism or the lack of conspicuous secondary sexual characteristics (horns, antlers, tusks, etc.) may be accounted for simply by examining phylogenetic patterns of inheritance. Among the Perissodactyla (equids as well as tapirs and rhinos), monomorphism is the rule as is also the case for some nonperissodactyls such as Old and New World camelids. The available evidence points toward polygyny in these species (Eisenberg 1981). These species also share a morphological feature in that none are true ruminants. Camels are tylopods and possess a three-chambered stomach, while the perissodactyls are all cecal fermentors. It is not obvious why monomorphism and the lack of conspicuous weapons have characterized such groups and whether there may be some subtle link with digestive physiology or foraging limitations (see Janis 1982; Kiltie 1985).

Despite recent improvements in unraveling evolutionary processes at the interface of behavior and morphology, we may not always be able to uncover the selective forces that shaped the origins of features in different taxonomic groups. As information accumulates on monomorphic species that are polygynous, it will be interesting to see the possible influences that body size has on breeding success within each sex. Species such as oryx, a monomorphic ruminant, may play a valuable role in our understanding of some of the effects that phylogeny and sexual selection have had on the evolution of sexual dimorphism in ungulates.

9.8   ADAPTATION AND SELECTION IN A FERAL SPECIES

While the preceding sections have presented data on reproductive success and based interpretations of behavioral phenomena on evolutionary theory, it is essential to know whether natural selection operates on feral species. If it does not, then reliance on evolutionary arguments is clearly an inappropriate paradigm on which to base explanations of behavior. How does one decide when natural selection is operating on a population of large free-ranging mammals that cannot be handled? And if natural selection is operating, how well adapted are feral horses to their environments? Answers to these questions are important for improving our understanding of processes at the confluence of ecology, evolution, and behavior, especially in feral species.

On Native and Feral Species

Earlier in this chapter it was demonstrated that differences in reproductive success were (1) greater among males than females, (2) likely to result in lifetime variation among males, and (3) attributed mostly to nonrandom factors. If a disproportionate representation of genes accumulates over time in Mendelian populations, no fundamental difference occurs in the way that natural selection operates on feral and native species. This does not mean, of course, that properties of species that are maintained over time are equivalent in both kinds of species nor that such species are equally adapted. George Williams, in his classic book *Adaptation and Natural Selection* (1966, 261), stated that adaptations can not be ascertained solely by observation and that to conclude that some characteristics confer benefits, "one should never imply that an effect is a function unless he can show that it is produced by design and not by happenstance."

In many studies the assumption is made that animals are adapted to their environment, but seldom is it clear what is meant by *adapted*. For instance, would it be safe to conclude that a population was well adapted because its individuals reproduced and their progeny survived to do the same? Conversely, if a population declined, would it follow that the individuals were not adapted? Or should the length of time that a population survives determine how well it is adapted? The study of adaptation is quite complex. It poses numerous interpretations and in its present form suffers from a lack of clear terminology. At the very least, the level of adaptation (individuals or species) and proximate and ultimate factors must be disentangled and clarified before understanding just how well adapted populations might be (Gould and Lewontin 1979). For my purposes adaptations refer to differences in characteristics that contribute to an individual's fitness (Williams 1966; Clutton-Brock and Harvey 1979).

Concerning feral horses, the degree to which behavioral and morphological characters affect an individual's immediate survival can be considered within the context of selection pressures: Has selection been intense on certain biological factors? How might such factors be modified during the periods in which animals have been feral? I focus on four aspects of horse biology: pelage color, parturition characteristics, habitat use, and antipredatory behavior.

Coat Color Patterns

In the American West, wild horses occur in many color morphs—duns, bays, pintos, palaminos, sorrels, chestnuts, and more. In these populations as well as those on some islands where populations may have been feral for at least two hundred years (Keiper 1976; Rubenstein 1981; Welsh 1975), coloration is not uniform. If differently colored animals were selected against, populations should converge on a single color, as has been observed in the majority of nondomesticated mammals (Hamilton 1973).

The failure of feral horses to become uniformly colored suggests weak selection pressures on pelage color. Presumably this stems from the absence of predation or other factors that selectively remove variable properties (Endler 1977). Over a century ago, a similar conclusion was reached: "these several facts show that [feral] horses do not soon revert to any uniform color" (Darwin 1868, 62). It is possible, although unlikely, that horses may return to a uniform color (such as is observed in Przewalski's horses), but not enough time has elapsed to produce the changes.

Parturition-Related Characteristics

As selection has modified numerous birth parameters, including seasonality, time of day, and site preferences, in ungulates (Estes 1976; Lent 1974; Leuthold 1977), would it not also be operating on these features in feral horses? The evidence is strong that past selection pressures have molded these characteristics in horses. Of these, the least labile trait in Granite horses was the timing of births—they almost invariably occurred at night (sec. 6.3)—a pattern also evident in domestic horses (Rossdale and Short 1967) and presumed to be operating in zebras.

The other two characters are more variable, implying either (1) that genetic components to birth seasonality or microhabitat preferences are not as rigorously fixed within the genome as circadian timings of birth, or (2) that differential gene survival has not yet been intense enough to mold these factors. These are not necessarily mutually exclusive alternatives. Selection against foals born outside the major breeding season has been acute, despite foaling peaks in the Granite and other populations. In both native and domestic ungulates from temperate climates, selection has honed breeding seasons of birth to more narrow periods (Jewell, Milner, and Morton-Boyd 1974; Guinness, Gibson, and Clutton-Brock 1978).

Two hypotheses might explain the persistence of nonseasonal births in some temperate populations of feral horses. First, the time needed for selection to work against individuals giving birth outside of parturition peaks has been inadequate. Implicit in this idea is that breeding seasons should be restricted annually. For instance, on St. Kilda Island where perhaps 125 generations of Soay sheep have lived (assuming one generation is broadly equivalent to eight years), most births are limited to a 6-to-7-week period (Jewell and

Grubb 1974). Selection may have operated long enough to favor those individuals lambing at that time.

The second hypothesis—that mares giving birth outside of breeding peaks may not be at a disadvantage—does not necessarily mean that selection is inoperative or that it has had inadequate time to act. That numerous ungulates, including zebras (Klingel 1969a, 1969b) and bighorn sheep (Lenarz 1979; Bunnell 1982), have variable and prolonged birth periods cannot be taken as evidence that selection has been weak. Perhaps individuals vary in their temporal ability to give birth under different conditions. The above hypotheses are not mutual alternatives because, as evolution proceeds, different tactics can be favored during various climatic regimes and at different population densities.

The third birth characteristic on which selection may have acted—birth site preference—did not seem to be strongly favored, since mothers were inconsistent in the microhabitats in which they gave birth. Unlike feral or domestic goats (Licklichter 1984; O'Brien 1983) and some native ungulates (Lent 1974; Geist 1971) that show rather strong birth site preferences, horses demonstrated only minor preferences (sec. 5.4). Without knowledge of whether native horses ever preferred certain sites for births, it is not possible to determine how (or whether) domestication has modified this behavior in feral horses.

Problems in Interpreting Habitat Use

Numerous native and domesticated ungulates have been introduced into new environments in many areas of the world where they survive in a wild state. Examples include water buffalo, banteng, camels, goats, horses, and asses in Australia (Baker and Manwell 1981; McKnight 1976), red deer, moose, pigs, and chamois in New Zealand (Whitaker and Rudge 1976; Caughley 1971), aoudad, tahr, gemsbok, ibex, asses, horses, and pigs in North America (Decker 1978), and sheep and Chinese water deer in Great Britain. The list is far from complete. Although such species survive and reproduce in areas where they did not evolve, it is improbable that enough time has passed for selection to modify species-specific characteristics to new surroundings. Some of the new environments may well approximate original habitats of some species, and in these cases individuals may then exploit such areas, much in the same manner as they did in original environments.

For domestic species such as horses for which few good data are available on habitat use in ancestral species, it is difficult to know whether contemporary patterns of land use represent past or new (or combinations thereof) methods of resource exploitation. Consequently, evaluating how efficiently horses use their environments remains conjectural. Some insight may be gained by comparing habitat use in horses with native Granite Range ungulates.

Food and shelter are two of the more salient environmental characteristics that affect an individual's reproductive success. Because native Granite Range species (pronghorn, bighorn, mule deer) migrate altitudinally at different seasons to exploit resources, there is no reason why horses should not do the same. As pointed out earlier (chap. 4), horses also migrate in elevation. However, horses die at high altitudes due to unpredictably heavy snowstorms (Berger 1983c)—a situation probably different from that of other ungulates that evolved in mountainous areas. In this respect domestic ungulates may not be as able to cope with inclement conditions, or at least they may more frequently fail to avoid such conditions.

Antipredatory Behavior

The basic suite of characteristics associated with zebra predator avoidance—vigilance, grouping, male defense of harems, and flight—also appears in horses. Some of these characteristics may not be as strong as might have been expected had predator pressures been constant throughout the duration of domestication. In other words, a relaxation in predation during domestication might have resulted in reduced selection for wariness. For instance, if Granite horses are compared to average bighorn sheep (in groups of six to ten individuals), which spend roughly 20% of each foraging bout in nonfeeding activities (Berger 1978), or sympatric pronghorn (in groups of four to eight), which average about 23% vigilance (Berger, unpub. data), or klipspringers (in family groups), which average 32% vigilance (Tilson 1980), horses were unwary. When average vigilance in Granite horses during the spring (sexes combined) is contrasted with mean values of the above three species, the latter are (in order) 740%, 850%, and 1,185% more vigilant than horses.

Granite horses might be less vigilant because (1) they are a large-bodied species whose only predators are man and mountain lions (since predation has been slight, perhaps the only reason to be wary is to focus on conspecifics), and (2) the comparison with non-domesticated ungulates is misleading at best since the latter are small bodied and exposed to predation (whereas horses are not).

Table 9.5   Presumed Influences of Past Pressures of Natural Selection, Domestication, and Feral Conditions on Characteristics of Horses

	Presumed Past Selection	Presumed Effect of Domestication	Predicted Direction of Selection
Coat color pattern	strong	modified	relaxed
Timing of birth	strong	negligible	?
Season of birth	strong	modified	strong
Site of birth	?	?	relaxed
Food exploitation	strong	negligible	strong
Shelter seeking	strong	modified	strong
Vigilance	strong	modified	relaxed
Antipredator grouping	strong	negligible	?
Flight	strong	negligible	strong
Individual competitive abilities	strong	negligible	strong

Selection Pressures

Given an ecological niche for a species to exploit, an introduced population can become established in numerous ways. The simplest is for its individuals to feed successfully, avoid predators, and reproduce. A species may already be preadapted if its previous existence was in a similar environment or if the propensity to exploit a wide array of conditions had existed within its gene pool. A species may also experience chance favorable mutations that allow it to survive, although adequate time has probably not elapsed for this to occur in domesticated animals that have become feral. In horses, the extent to which various characteristics have been modified by natural and artificial selection and how they might be influenced by selection under feral conditions are summarized in table 9.5. Each of the variables designated was presumably under strong selection when Przewalski's horses lived in the Palearctic. In contrast, pressures on coat color, timing of birth, and antipredatory behavior may become even further relaxed in feral horses in the future, assuming predation to be the major selective force (see table 9.5). Since a genetic component for foaling at night and for grouping when startled appears entrenched with equid genomes, future selection pressures will probably have little influence on these factors.

9.9   Summary

1. Reproductive success was calculated in males and females by attributing the number of offspring born to respective parents. Among males, the number of foals sired varied considerably. Seven percent of the males fathered 29% of the foals. Male re-

productive performances varied with age, but age alone could not account for the wide margins of variation.

2. Reproductive success in males was affected by at least four other factors. Body weight and fighting abilities were important, although weight seemed to be of lesser importance. Stallions that won the greatest proportion of their fights and those that practiced the most left the most offspring. The other two factors were home-range locations and reproductive lifespans.

3. Among females, foal production varied little between the ages of five to seventeen years. Younger or older mares reproduced more poorly. The greatest variation in reproductive performances occurred among two-to-four-year-olds.

4. At least three factors influenced female reproductive success. First, females born in relatively better quality home ranges produced proportionately more foals as they grew older than did females from other areas. This was because environmental sources of infant nutrition (e.g., milk, food) were tied to home ranges. Second was band stability. Mares that did not change bands or were not in bands associated with male takeovers did not experience harassment by new individuals. They also produced more offspring than females from unstable bands. Third was body weight. Heavier mares had a buffer against environmental harshness. In medium-to-poor-quality home ranges, larger mares were more successful foal producers than smaller ones. This may have been because bigger individuals rely on body reserves unavailable to their smaller conspecifics.

5. That natural selection operates on feral horses was inferred through differences in reproductive success among individuals. It was unlikely that the magnitude of reproductive variation would be equalized over individual lifetimes.

6. Lifetime reproductive success was estimated by employing various assumptions about longevity and factors that influenced mating success. Reproductive success is a product of longevity in mares, while for males it is more contingent upon successful reproduction during a relatively few prime years. Variation in reproductive success among males was greater than it was in females, regardless of the methods used in its calculation.

7. Monomorphism occurs in horses despite variation in male mating success relative to female mating success. This could be because size confers little reproductive advantage to males, a hypothesis that gained some support. In monomorphic species weight may not affect male reproductive success to the extent

that it does in sexually dimorphic species. However, the lack of distinction among taxonomic groups often obscures important phylogenetic differences. Tactics that work in some groups may not work in others. Understanding factors that cause individual differences in reproductive success may say little about the evolutionary origins of interspecific differences in weaponry or sexual dimorphism.

8. Selection pressures on feral horses are difficult to compare with those that may have existed on Przewalski's horses, primarily because the latter can no longer be studied under natural conditions. Coat color patterns and timings of birth presumably came under strong selection in Przewalksi's horses, whereas they may now be relaxed in feral horses.

Statistical Tests

1. Comparison between male reproductive success and age per year for a five-year period.
   Analysis of variance: $F_{5,91}=24.92$, $p<0.001$ (data normalized by square root transformation).

2. Comparison of number of foals sired by six prime-aged (7–11 yrs) males during their three most productive years.
   Kruskall-Wallis analysis of variance: $H=16.17$, $df=5$, $p<0.001$.

3. Correlation between reproductive success of stallions in single male bands and (a) percentage of fights they won as stallions, and (b) relative amount of time spent interacting with males per week (of observation time).
   Kendall rank correlation coefficients:
   (a) tau=.48, $N=12$, $z=2.19$, $p<0.03$.
   (b) tau=.55, $N=12$, $z=2.33$, $p<0.02$.

4. Correlation between percentage of fights won by stallions in single male bands and practice time (time spent interacting with all males (as in 3).
   Partial rank order correlation: tau=.67, $N=12$, $z=2.81$, $p<0.005$.

5. Comparison of the frequency that young-, medium-, and old-aged males used feeding areas of low, medium, and high quality. (Each male was assigned a frequency of 1 for overall use of a given area per year.)
   G test: $G=14.62$, $df=4$, $N=57$, $p<0.01$.

6. Comparison between female reproductive success and age per year for a six-year period.

Analysis of variance: $F_{9,172} = 13.57$, $p < 0.001$ (data normalized by square root transformation).

7. Comparison among female reproductive success per year in relation to age for mares between five and seventeen years old. Analysis of variance: $F_{5,101} = .69$, NS (data normalized by square root transformation).

8. Comparison of differences in foaling frequencies/yr among sexually mature females from their second through fourth year of life. Analysis of variance: $F_{21,65} = 6.23$, $p < 0.001$.

9. Comparison of foaling frequencies/yr among prime-aged females during five of their most productive years. Analysis of variance: $F_{17,89} = .052$, NS.

10. Comparison of the proportion of foals produced that survived to six months of age between females from high- and medium-to-poor-quality home-range areas (comparisons were made a standard gestation length after females attained puberty). Arcsine transformation: $z = 2.45$, $N = 22$, $p < 0.01$.

11. Comparison of the proportion of foals produced that survived to six months of age between females that spent their pregnancies in high- and medium-to-poor-quality home-range areas. Arcsine transformation: $z = 2.22$, $N = 42$, $p < 0.03$.

12. Comparison of the proportion of foals produced that survived to six months of age between young females (2–3 yrs) from stable and unstable bands. Arcsine transformation: $z = 2.86$, $N = 42$, $p < 0.005$.

13. Comparison of the proportion of foals produced that survived to six months of age in young females (see 12) from (a) high-quality home ranges in stable and unstable bands, and (b) medium-to-poor-quality home ranges in stable and unstable bands. Arcsine transformation:
    (a) $z = 2.84$; $N = 16$, $p < 0.005$.
    (b) $z = 1.88$; $N = 26$, $p < 0.06$.

14. Comparison between foal production in five- to seventeen-year-old females, from good resource areas, that weighed more and less than 410 kg. Arcsine transformation: $z = 1.09$, $N = 26$, NS.

15. Comparison between foal production in five- to seventeen-year-old females, from medium-to-poor-quality resource areas, that weighed more and less than 410 kg. Arcsine transformation: $z = 2.06$, $N = 38$, $p < 0.04$.

10 Ecology and Social Regulation of Population Size

The struggle for existence . . . rarely takes the form of actual combat. Ordinarily it is simply competition for resources in limited supply.

E. Mayr (1982)

10.1 INTRODUCTION

Behavior both brings individuals together and separates them. It is involved in spacing, migrations, aggression, and mating. Behavior also affects pregnancy rates (sec. 6.3), and it is through male-male competition that adult sex ratios are modified (sec. 5.5). But is it valid to conclude that behavior regulates populations?

This chapter explores ways that social and ecological factors interact to depress population sizes. Specifically, I discuss some of the problems inherent in evaluating the role of behavioral factors in population dynamics and the interplay between resources and animal distributions. I conclude that behavioral factors depress the rate at which a population grows but that by themselves they do little to control total population size.

10.2 RESOURCES AND REGULATION BY BEHAVIOR

As indicated in chapter 1, regulation refers to a feedback system in which density-dependent factors stabilize a population (Krebs and Perrins 1978; Sinclair and Norton-Griffiths 1982). Although extrinsic factors tend to regulate populations (Andrewartha and Birch 1954; Davis and Christian 1976), my primary emphasis will be on intrinsic factors.

Do social factors limit population growth, and can they modify the level a population would reach in the absence of behavioral influences? Two hypothetical examples, one from an expanding and the other from a declining population, will help illustrate the difficulties involved in answering these questions. First, a growing population reaches the point at which its resources can support no more individuals. It then matters little whether behavior, topography, predation, or other factors caused an absence of growth because (by definition) the resources rather than other factors limited the population. In this situation social factors will undoubtedly influence which individuals leave behind offspring, but these factors will not influence the total population size. Second, a population exceeds its environmental carrying capacity and then diminishes. If the decline is mediated by a lack of resources, then behavioral factors are irrelevant to the decrease. Behavioral factors can be important for limiting total population size only when they themselves suppress populations to levels that are not compensated for by other factors.

Demonstrating that social factors alter population size has proved difficult because resources, behavior, weather variation, predation, disease, and other variables must be controlled so that their relative influences can be separated (Krebs and Perrins 1978; Watson 1977). At least two, not necessarily discrete approaches have been used to examine how behavioral interactions might alter population sizes. These have been developed in part from earlier work by Brown (1969, 1975), Chitty (1967), and Krebs et al. (1973). The first is a listing of criteria based on Watson and Moss (1970); the second is the "ideal free distribution" model of Fretwell and Lucas (1970).

10.3 CRITERIA NEEDED TO DEMONSTRATE SOCIAL EFFECTS

Is there evidence that social factors limit population size in horses? Watson and Moss (1970) argued that substantiation of social effects on upper limits of population size relied on the demonstration that (1) a proportion of the adult population does not breed, (2) these nonbreeders are capable of reproduction, especially in the absence of breeders, (3) breeding animals are not completely usurping some resource (if they were, then the resource would be limiting), and (4) mortality due to behavior is compensated for by other factors (e.g., "if other mortality factors in the environment increase their effects on a population, behaviorally induced mortality will decrease" [Tamarin 1983, 701]). These four conditions are discussed below with regard to the Granite population.

First Two Criteria

Some Granite males failed to breed. These males affect the overall population density, but they have little influence on pregnancy rates since females do not go unmated. The important points concern whether there are nonbreeding females, and whether the reproductive efficiency of some females is lowered to the point that depressive effects on the total population size are greater than might have occurred otherwise. (*Lowered efficiency* refers to the suite of characteristics associated with suboptimal reproductive success, such as lowered fecundity or the production of slow-growing young that reach sexual maturity at a relatively later age in life.) If this occurs, then a case may be made that such females are ultimately diminishing the size the population could achieve had they been reproducing faster. Because the reproductive contributions of these young females are important to overall population size, a demonstration of their reduction will satisfy the first two criteria if lowered reproductive efficiency was socially induced.

Females that aborted as a consequence of male takeovers either failed to reproduce later that year or experienced a reproduction delay that was longer than would have occurred in the absence of abortion. Interbirth intervals were increased in these females due to the direct effects of aggressive social behavior (sec. 7.8). A conservative estimate of the reduction in potential population size would be five foals (based on the sum of delays that occurred in birth intervals plus the number of fetuses that should have survived but failed to). The estimate is conservative because none of the individuals were assumed to have produced offspring of their own—a condition that would most likely be untrue if females were born and went on to produce their own young later in their lives. Nevertheless, this estimate amounts to a 4.4% reduction in foal population size (1980–83) that was attributable to males or, more appropriately, resulted from the effects of male-male competition.

Other effects might also have arisen from competition among individuals, but they did not clearly stem from social behavior. For instance, aggression by resident females toward new ones could have reduced fecundity in immigrant females, although other factors also affected female reproduction (sec. 9.5). Another social effect was the relegation of some females to poorer quality home ranges simply because their stallions were not prime aged and often avoided more dominant males (sec. 8.7). Thus, age-specific changes in male behavior are possible confounding factors that need to be considered in evaluating causes for density regulation. An equally effective (and more probable) argument for the use of medium-to-poor-quality feeding areas is that high-quality ranges were in short supply. Hence, resources, and not behavior per se, could have had important effects on female distribution. If this scenario is correct, then resource limitations rather than social ones explain lowered fecundity.

With regard to the Watson/Moss criteria, I conclude that females capable of breeding were restricted from doing so solely because of the effects of social behavior in only a few instances. These were the mares that aborted due to male behavior, but the effects of such behavior resulted in a lower population size.

Last Two Criteria

The argument that breeders are not usurping resources that would be available for nonbreeders is invalid for the most part. Since more successful females inhabited better home-range areas (chap. 9), there is no need to rely on socially induced mechanisms when the use of poor food resources can explain relatively lower reproductive performances. It is only for the mares that failed to reproduce due to social factors alone that a resource hypothesis can be excluded.

With regard to mortality, the sample was too small to know whether behavioral factors were compensatory. Hence, I concluded that only a small reduction in population size was attributable solely to social influences. These were the mortalities that resulted from male-male competition and the depressive effects on infant recruitment (e.g., feticide). The array of possible effects are summarized in table 10.1. As can be seen, at the present stage of

TABLE 10.1 Social Behavior and Its Relationship to Resources and Population Size in Granite Horses

Behavior	Relationship to Resources	Social Effect on Reproduction	Effect on Population Size
Takeover-related abortion	none detected (e.g., no density-dependent effects)	slight depressive effect	slight
Use of home-range sites	dependent on population density	possible suppressive influences on growth rates mediated through restricted access to food	slight
Male-male combat	none detected	slight, possibly mediated through injuries	slight
Male hierarchies	none detected	none	none
Female hierarchies	none detected	depressive but confounded by many factors	unclear

population growth in the Granite Range, behavior has played a role in depressing the total number of individuals, but its influence has been small.

Comparisons with Other Species

Does behavior limit population size in other mammals? The evidence until 1970 (summarized by Watson and Moss 1970) indicated that, although behavior modified spacing and rendered some individuals nonbreeders, factors other than behavior were involved in mediating population size. Tamarin (1983) found no new cases of behavioral regulation, but provided insight into how behavior and habitat variables interact to affect cyclic rodents. Recent experimental manipulations of adult sex ratios in vole populations further support the notion that resources rather than behavior per se regulate population density (Boonstra and Rodd 1983).

The most likely ways that behavior in itself would modify population sizes would be through the removal of individuals that would otherwise survive to breed. When conspecific-induced deaths occur in rodents, carnivores, primates, and pinnipeds, infants (and adults) die most often as a result of aggression by males. If the number of individuals removed by behaviorally induced mortality is not compensated for by other factors and these individuals do not usurp resources that would otherwise be available to conspecifics, then the population is depressed by that number. When the removed individuals are females, the population is potentially reduced by their reproductive value.

Though the above situation is theoretically possible, its practical demonstration remains elusive. Even with appropriate field measures and long-term data, the reduction due to behavior alone would probably not be very large. For Granite horses a conservative estimate of the reduction in foal population due to social factors alone was 4.4%. Given the observed parity in sex ratio at birth, 2.2% would represent the percentage of females that went unborn from 1980 to 1983. Because natural mortality of foals was low (only 8%, sec. 5.4), the relative proportion of socially induced infant mortality was large (over 50%). Still, compared to the total number of foals born, deaths induced by social factors were uncommon. For other wild populations a few rough estimates can be found where depressive effects of social factors were not resource related. Sherman (1981) found that twenty-six young Belding's ground squirrels died as a result of infanticide (8% of the juveniles born) over a four-year period. The twenty-six deaths represented 29% of the juvenile deaths prior to weaning. In African lions, Bertram (1975) found that only about 14% of the cubs born attained subadulthood, while Schaller (1972) found that 21% of the cub mortality was due to conspecific aggression (another 28% was due to starvation). With increasingly sophisticated data from long-term studies it may soon be possible to determine the extent to which some social factors affect total population size.

On the other hand, due to the destruction of today's natural environment many populations no longer live at densities that approximate those in which they evolved or lived until recently. Emigration into neighboring populations is often precluded by recent habitat destruction. Because density affects behavior, one needs an idea of the range of natural densities for a species if conclusions drawn about social influences on population sizes are to be valid. Already it may be too late to learn what happens under what has been termed "completely natural or wild conditions." For example, in Namibia's Etosha Park animal densities may become artifically high and then crash. Predation and disease can limit wildebeest and perhaps other species due to "the fencing . . . which precludes migration, the development of alkaline gravel pits for road building, and the construction of artificial water points" (Berry 1981, 241). The problems reported in Etosha are not unique. Further attention needs to be directed toward the effects that densities mediated by human interference may have upon behavior and social organization. In experimental populations of captive deer and rodents it has been well substantiated that, although food may be abundant, fecundity is limited when densities become abnormally high (Ozoga, Verme, and Bienz 1982; Southwick 1955; Christian and Davis 1964; see also Albon et al. 1983).

While populations may not be regulated by behavior, behavior plays an important role in individual survival. Mammalian examples are numerous and include (1) infant, juvenile, and subadult primates which suffer greater mortality than adults during food shortages due to low social status (Dittus 1979, 1981), and (2) female marmots which die or reproduce poorly when excluded from winter hibernacula (Anderson, Armitage, and Hoffman 1976). In these cases, as with Granite horses, resources ultimately controlled population sizes, but properties of individuals determined who survived or reproduced.

10.4   DENSITY, RESOURCES, AND REPRODUCTION

The most intriguing work on the ecological significance of behavior has resulted from experimental field studies of birds (Brown 1969; Watson and Miller 1971; Krebs and Perrins 1978). In numerous cases, breeding density is regulated through use of exclusive areas. And although variations on this theme are recurrent, models of "ideal free distributions" (Fretwell and Lucas 1970; Fretwell 1972) provide yet another way of distinguishing between ecological and social factors that affect breeding densities.

The Model: Ideal Free Distributions

Consider an environment supporting fewer individuals than it can carry. An animal can forage freely in any direction and is able to select the best foraging sites. With the addition of more individuals, not all of the best sites remain; individuals are either forced into subpar areas or they remain in the better areas but at relatively higher densities. Thus, under ideal free conditions the model predicts that over time density will be adjusted according to habitat quality so that net fitness per individual is similar. Alternatively, if "despotic conditions" prevail, individuals that are more dominant use the best resources and subordinates are forced to rely on relatively poorer resource parcels. In this case, reproductive rewards per individual are not equilibrated and despots reap the greatest gains (Fretwell and Lucas 1970; Fretwell 1972). In short, under ideal free conditions behavioral factors are not mediating movements and individuals attain the same relative fitnesses; under despotic conditions, higher rewards are achieved by those monopolizing better quality areas. Are these differing scenarios in accord with observations of Granite horses?

Horse Distributions: Ideal or Despotic?

To examine the model's predictions three essential ingredients are needed. First is habitat quality, which allows for comparisons of relative effects of varying resource bases. Second is densities during different years, which provides ways of evaluating spacing in relation to resources. Third is reproductive success per individual per year—the crucial item since it offers glimpses at rewards achieved under different ecological conditions. Although measures for each of these variables are available in varying degrees of resolution for horses, important issues remained unresolved. In which sex should reproductive success be measured? If in males, should only breeding individuals or all males be included? What breeding densities should be incorporated—only Granite Basin densities or those for areas that include Granite Basin Emigrés? And should breeding densities include both males and females or should they be sex specific? Depending on the answers chosen, different findings with regard to the model will emerge.

In addressing these problems, both sexes were included in density calculations since there is no evidence that male and female horses consume different foods. Density of the entire population rather than of individuals within the Basin was used since the measure incorporates effects that emigration has upon spacing. If only Granite Basin densities had been used, measures would be restricted to performances in a specific area. They would not take into account the potential for broad scale effects reflected at the level of the entire population. And only females were used to examine reproductive success since females are influenced more by resources per se than are males (chap. 9).

To examine the model, we must first know how horses use space when additional horses enter the population. Despite the insularity of most of the Granite Range, a corridor below and to the north of Granite Basin is sometimes used by horses to gain access to other available habitats (sect. 5.6). If a positive relationship existed between population size and population density it could mean that (1) all available habitat was used, (2) horses had not yet discovered areas toward which to emigrate, or (3) no impetus to emigrate existed. Conversely, an absence of such a relationship over time indicates that density is relatively constant and suggests that density would depend on population size since individuals would become more scattered as the population grows (fig. 10.1). My early suspicions that animals moved into or through the corridor as a result of density-dependent effects were confirmed by the lack of positive or negative relationship between density and population size (fig. 10.1). It therefore seemed that Granite animals expanded their range in later years due to the effects of increasing intraspecific competition which stemmed from a rapidly enlarging population.

The spreading out of the population suggests both that individuals were competing for resources and that they were using space in ways that might minimize competition. But were reproductive rewards then equalized at different densities as would be predicted by ideal free distributions? Earlier it was shown that home-range quality affected female reproductive success. By contrasting reproductive success (foals/adult mare) with density in

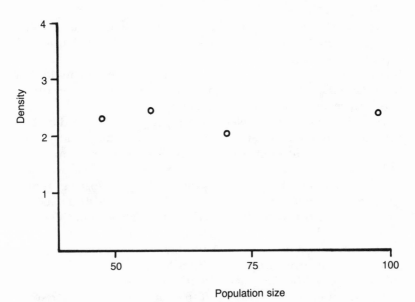

FIG. 10.1 Granite Range population size (yearlings and older) and density (individuals/km^2 of 90% frequency-use areas) during winter.

areas that varied in quality over a multiple-year period, the possibility that horses were despotically or ideally distributed could be investigated. Density calculations were based on animals one or more years of age per square kilometer of 90% frequency-use areas (see chap. 4).

Four important points emerged from the comparisons. First, individuals from richer resource areas reproduced better than those from poorer regions. Second, the lack of parity in reproductive success between females from good- and medium-to-poor-quality ranges (fig. 10.2) indicates that substantial costs were incurred by inhabitants of lower quality ranges, despite the lower densities there. Third, a density-dependent reduction in foal production (per female) occurred in good home ranges. Yet mares from these areas were still more successful breeders than those from poorer quality ranges, even though densities at the former were higher (fig. 10.2). As a result the reproductive rewards at higher densities, which declined with increasing density, would not have been obtained by moving to less populated, but lower quality, areas. Fourth, within lower quality ranges the relative parity of reproductive success over a multiple-year period (see fig. 10.2) suggests that individuals may be more apt to space themselves more widely to avoid competition for food resources when resources are less than the best.

Thus, the findings with regard to the model can be summarized as follows: Horses behaved as despots since some individuals were forced into lower quality areas where they tolerated smaller net rewards. In higher quality areas the stakes were greater and individuals experienced both higher densities and density-dependent reductions in reproductive success. In lower quality areas individuals were more apt to distribute themselves more evenly because the differences in rewards were not as great. In other words, where resources were not as restricted nor as hotly contested, individuals were more likely to arrange themselves in accordance with predictions of ideal free distributions. Hence, both despotic and ideal free conditions prevailed in Granite horses.

Little mention is made of factors in other populations that determine distributional patterns in relation to density, and views are often contradictory about the varying roles of dispersal and philopatry. Darwin (1845, 219) wondered why horses that had been

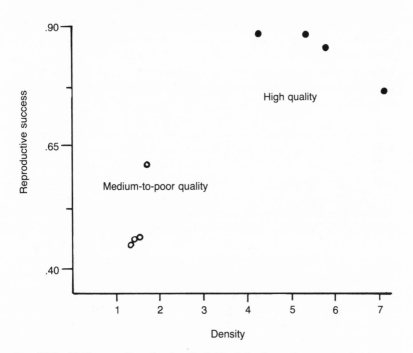

FIG. 10.2 Habitat quality, density (individuals/km²), and reproductive success (foals per adult female) in the following year in Granite Range horses.

feral for at least sixty years on the Falkland Islands failed to spread to the other half of the island, "though asserting this to be the case, [gauchos] were unable to account for it excepting for the strong attachment which horses have to any locality to which they are accustomed." Darwin considered the island "not to appear fully stocked. . . . [And] that part of the island is not more tempting than the rest." Still, in North America feral horses moved across the Central Plains from Mexico to Canada (Wyman 1945), and in South America from Buenos Aires in 1537 to the Straits of Magellan by 1580 (Darwin 1845). In each of these regions the possibility that native Americans were involved in the geographic expansion of ranges cannot be omitted.

Large Mammals and Ecological Models

Some complications arise when placing long-lived mammals into ecological frameworks designed for testing on less complex animals. Ideal species in which to study spacing in relation to habitat selection would be small bodied, short lived, occur in large numbers, and produce progeny that could be easily counted. Recent elegant work on gall-forming aphids is testimony to advantages gained by working with not-so-glamorous species (Whitham 1978, 1979, 1980).

Although the data at hand showed that horses acted both as despots and ideal distributors, some subtle biases exist. For instance, since generally old or young stallions occupy subpar home ranges (chap. 9), lower female reproduction in these areas might simply be explained as a product of male social competition and have little to do with female ecology. This leaves unexplained why some females do not abandon poor areas to seek better feeding sites. Some do, but for other females such behavior has not yet proved to be a strongly distinguishing feature in their biology (see sec. 9.5).

Large mammals are not the ideal organisms for studying some ecological models, but trade-offs must sometimes be made. Large diurnal and social mammals provide reasonably good opportunities to observe interactions between ecology and behavior and to extend hypotheses that were generated for smaller organisms to larger ones. In species such as horses, elephant seals, and red deer, opportunities to measure reproductive success with relatively direct methods are far better than in more secretive mammals. Perhaps most importantly, working with mammals also offers a chance to examine factors that might influence mammals in themselves but be unimportant for other taxonomic groups.

Comparisons with Other Ungulates

Behavioral influences on ungulate breeding densities have been observed most commonly when territoriality plays a prominent role in social organization and when resources are in short supply. There are two basic ways in which exclusive-use areas might modify density. In species like impala (Jarman and Jarman 1973), waterbuck (Wirtz 1981), and pronghorn (Kitchen 1974), males defend territories against other males but females wander through these areas without being the focus of aggression. In such cases the argument that males limit population density by precluding larger potential congregations of individuals per unit area seems to hold, but other factors must be considered. For example, why do some territories have few females (Owen-Smith 1977), what effects do varying resources have on the intensity of male competition (Clutton-Brock, Guinness, and Albon 1982), and how might changes in male competition affect breeding densities?

Exclusive-use areas could alter density in a second way if both sexes participate in defense. Monogamous species such as dik-diks and duikers might be expected to exhibit this behavior, and field observations suggest that both sexes may help in territorial defense (Dunbar and Dunbar 1980). Moreover, studies of species such as elephant shrews, whose social organization resembles that of forest-dwelling ungulates (Rathbun 1979), have shown that replacement of residents by immigrants occurs when either sex dies or disappears. This certainly is not prima facie evidence that behavioral factors limit breeding densities, but it is clear that social factors influence spacing, as has been reported in studies of territorial birds (i.e., Brown 1969; Watson and Miller 1971; Stacey 1979; Wittenberger 1981; Krebs 1970).

10.5   WILD HORSES, PHYLOGENY, AND GENERALIZATIONS

At the outset of the book I asked (1) what can be learned about a species that evolved over millions of years, but that had recently been domesticated and then exposed to wild conditions? and (2) What can be learned about social mechanisms that affect population levels? I have presented new data and summarized previous information about wild horses. In doing so, I have kept in mind that wild horses are really feral horses that were derived from domestic horses. Their ancestors were native horses that evolved under pressures of natural selection, just as other wild mammals did. The horses I observed exhibited many similarities in behavior and

reproductive biology to native equids, and, because I could uncover no evidence to indicate otherwise, I relied on paradigms of
evolutionary biology to help construct functional interpretations.

Evidence from Granite horses implies that individuals are still
under pressures to maximize their genetic representation in future
generations. It would be surprising if other feral species were not
also under pressures of natural selection. However, whether feral
species exist under the same selective regimes that their progenitors faced is uncertain. In some, if not many instances, selective
pressures would be similar, especially where environmental conditions are similar. However, in today's world of ecological disasters,
such conditions must be the exception rather than the rule. Despite
the generally undisturbed conditions and protection offered by the
insularity of the Granite Range, horses did not evolve in insular
mountains. According to the best evidence available, they were
large, grazing, savanna- and steppe-dwelling ungulates. Thus, it
seems reasonable to ask whether the conclusions drawn about the
Granite population offer insight into the biology of other horses or
equids.

Answers will depend upon which parameters are examined. Migration schedules of Granite horses offer few clues about the movements of barrier island ponies. On the other hand, most free-
ranging horses in North America live in the American West in habitats not too dissimilar to those found in the Granite Range. Factors
that influence reproductive success also would probably not be very
different, but without detailed comparative studies of other equids
answers cannot be known.

With regard to interactions between behavior and populations,
the Granite data provided information about resources, spacing,
and levels of intraspecific competition. The rapidly growing population had reached a point where resources slowed its rate of increase. The increased population resulted in (1) declining
recruitment rates (fig. 5.9; fig. 10.2), (2) increased density in better-
quality home ranges (fig. 10.2), (3) greater male emigration distances (fig. 5.10), and (4) an overall enlargement of habitat used
(see fig. 10.1).

The idea that the population was regulated primarily by social
behavior was rejected since few direct social limitations of population size were found. Patterns of home-range use and emigration
were explained by relying on resource-related arguments. Interband dominance and the immediate exclusion of individuals from
food or mates was rarely applicable without consideration of the

effects of both resource availability and animal ages. Only the relatively few mortalities that resulted from male-male combat or terminated pregnancies due to male takeovers may validly be regarded as socially induced limitations. Social effects were seen to modify population density but not to impose a ceiling on population growth. The conclusion that resources and not behavior place upper limits on populations is not new. As Darwin said (1859, 55), "The amount of food for each species of course gives the extreme limit to which it can increase."

10.6   SUMMARY

1. Criteria needed to demonstrate that social behavior regulates populations are presented. Females that were likely to breed but did not as a direct result of male-male competition reduced the total population size by the number of offspring that should have been born. This amounted to only a 4.4% reduction in the number of foals born over the study period. In addition to this socially imposed mortality, a few adult deaths resulted from combat. Overall, limitations on population size due solely to social effects were few.

2. Information on resource, rather than behavioral restrictions offered better clues to how horse populations may be regulated. Arguments based on resource-related competition could explain distributional patterns, use of feeding sites, changes in annual population densities, and recruitment rates in different areas.

3. Biological and ecological features of feral horses are suitable for comparative analyses with native species. They are also compatible with evolutionary interpretations.

11 Horses and Conservation in the Great Basin Desert

One of the penalties of an ecological education is that one lives alone in a world of wounds . . . , an ecologist must either harden his shell and make believe that the consequences of science are none of his business, or he must be the doctor who sees the marks of death in a community that believes itself well and does not want to be told otherwise.

Aldo Leopold (1949)

11.1 INTRODUCTION

In the United States, feral horses and burros have been the subjects of innumerable controversies, some of which include congressional acts and mandates. Basically, two viewpoints are expressed: conserve them or get rid of them. Of course, the actual situation is not nearly so simple (Wagner 1983). Numerous biological and practical problems must be resolved before effective conservation plans can be implemented. The most fundamental biological question concerns how horses affect their environments, a question for which there are few solid data (National Research Council 1982). Even if such information was available, other problems persist. Opponents might argue for the horses' removal because they are not native wildlife or because they eat the same grasses that cattle feed upon. Proponents might ask why horses but not other introduced species are singled out as potential pests. The logic is suspect in either case since many species have been introduced by man, but some are controlled and some are not. Even native species (e.g., coyotes or sagebrush) rightfully or wrongly often fall under management regimes. Is there any reason why horses should be different and go unmanaged? Although management of ecosystems may be needed, the purpose of the management must be defined. Is it to protect native species, to provide economic rewards, to maintain the aesthetics of the area, or for an infinite number of other reasons? These issues embrace philosophical as well as scientific realms, especially where the constituents of ecosystems are concerned. Ques-

246

tions like How many horses might the land support? or How might the negative effects of horses on their environments be mitigated? could be addressed if sufficient data were available.

My aim here is to discuss the conservation of exotic ungulates. The emphasis is on the Great Basin although I bring in examples of feral species from other environments. I examine the various ways that horses may damage their habitats, and I ask how horses interact with other ungulates. Specifically, I compare the potential effects of horses upon native ungulates through considerations of biomass, food, habitat, and interspecific social interactions. Finally, different conservation options and management dilemmas are presented.

11.2   PRIOR CONSERVATION EFFORTS

No systematic protection of habitat has been implemented in the Great Basin. Perhaps this is due in part to the sparse human population—the density is lower than in any other comparably sized area of the lower United States. Within an area that covers about 380,000 km², the estimated 1980 density was 0.25 persons per km². Although land has been set aside for national parks or monuments in other western states, to "conserve the scenery and the natural and historical objects and the wildlife therein, and to provide for the enjoyment of the same and by such means as will leave them unimpaired for the enjoyment of future generations" [16 (U.S. Congress 1–18(f) 1964], there are no Great Basin national parks. In Nevada alone where 24,601,304 hectares are federally owned (87% of the total area), 99.57% of these are for military, energy, or multiple use (e.g., mining, livestock, timber, etc.) (U.S. Dept. of the Interior, Public Land Statistics 1982). Of the National Park Service land that exists to the north and east of Death Valley, only a 640 acre parcel, Lehman Caves National Monument, could be considered within the Great Basin proper. Thus, an infinitesimal fraction (0.00001) of federally owned land has been established to meet the objectives cited above. At this time, none of the land is restricted solely for the preservation of native fauna or flora.

Numerous aesthetic and economic reasons exist for why such lands deserve absolute protection (Brokaw 1978; Houston 1971; Soulé and Wilcox 1980). An often overlooked, but essential scientific justification is that the effects of human use, whether through mining, military activities, or even introduced herbivores, cannot be rigorously assessed without comparisons to events in sufficiently large natural areas. If progress is ever to be made in mitigating

effects on ecosystems or simply in understanding natural processes, areas representing pristine conditions must be established
and protected. Unfortunately, the chief stewards of federal lands
lack ecological backgrounds or the insight needed for rendering
scientifically sound decisions that preserve large chunks of habitat
in the Great Basin.

The lack of appropriate planning and interagency orchestration
of conservation measures has resulted in a rapidly changing Great
Basin environment. Overgrazing by cattle has been rampant (Vale
1975b), valuable wetlands have been lost (Menke 1983), Lake Winnemucca has been turned into a waterless playa, and nesting colonies of California gulls and white pelicans are jeopardized by sink-
ing water levels and the concomitant emergence of land bridges at
Mono and Pyramid lakes. Still, no new federally controlled natural
areas have been established.

11.3   ECOLOGICAL SEGREGATION OF UNGULATES

To understand how exotics (primarily feral horses and cattle) may
have influenced native Great Basin ungulates, information is
needed on both past and extant distributional patterns. In the absence of human interference, modifications of these animal distributions or changes in population sizes might be due to the
influence of one species upon another.

Prior to settlement of the Great Basin in the 1800s the predomi-
nant ungulate fauna consisted of bighorns and pronghorns
(Grayson 1982). Elk were sparsely distributed in a few northeastern
mountain ranges (Hall 1946), and scattered bison herds probably
occurred on all but the western and southern fringes of the Great
Basin (Butler 1978; Merriam 1925). It is unlikely that mule deer
were common during the early periods of exploration since they
were not frequently noted in the journals of such early explorers as
Jedediah Smith, John Frémont, and Pete Ogden (Papez 1976).
Large-bodied grass feeders such as the endemic horses and other
Pleistocene relics had been extinct for at least 15,000 years
(Grayson 1982). Thus, the Great Basin ungulate fauna consist of
but a few medium-sized species.

Biomass of Ungulate Species

The comparisons that follow reflect total estimated biomass at the
end of 1980, and they refer to "crude" rather than "ecological"
measures (Eisenberg and Seidensticker 1976). Several data sources
were combined (e.g., U.S. Dept. of Interior, Bureau of Land Man-

agement 1982b), and only geographical but not ecological distributions were specified. The analysis covered about 30 million public hectares—all of Nevada and those portions of Utah west of the Wasatch cordillera. In looking at these estimates it is important to remember that (1) no controlled experimental manipulations have been performed on any of the species, (2) population sizes have rarely, if at all, been sampled systematically, and (3) long-term information on population trends is lacking.

In 1980, population sizes for native ungulates were 5,900 pronghorn, 4,500 bighorn, and 80,000 mule deer. Populations of domestic herbivores included 269,284 sheep and goats and 310,434 cattle. There were 31,660 feral horses. Sheep, goats, and cattle were grouped as livestock since, theoretically, all were owned and permits had been issued for grazing privileges. However, I have no doubt the figures on livestock are conservative since many of my colleagues and I routinely encountered numbers well in excess of the figures established by permits. Feral horses were considered separately because they were neither native wildlife nor privately owned.

These figures on population size alone do not offer a realistic view of the intensity with which these species use their environments. First, the species differ in weight, size, and digestive strategies (horses are cecal fermentors; Janis 1976; sec. 2.4); hence, their food requirements differ. Second, they vary in their preferred food (see below). Third, livestock use public lands for only a portion of the year, whereas native and feral species use these areas year-round. To some extent these differences can be taken into account by comparing ungulate biomass over the same period. However, the topic of preferred food resources poses different problems; these will be dealt with separately.

Collectively, native ungulates numbered about 90,000 individuals, but their biomass represented a mere fraction of the total—5.05% (fig. 11.1). For every kg of native ungulate, there were 18.78 kg of exotics (horses and livestock combined). If the contribution of native ungulates to total biomass is considered separately, mule deer constituted 4.46%, while the species most prevalent prior to European settlement—bighorn and pronghorn—accounted for 0.24% and 0.35% respectively. These latter species, presumed to constitute the bulk of the biomass 150 years ago, comprise only 0.59% of the total biomass today. Feral horses contributed 17.80% of the total while livestock comprised 77.15% (fig. 11.1).

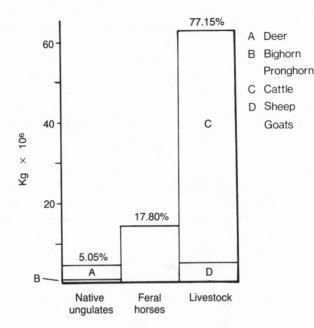

Fig. 11.1   Biomass and different categories of ungulates on public lands in the Great Basin Desert of Nevada and Utah in 1980 (standardized for twelve months of use). (A) deer; (B) bighorn and pronghorn; (C) cattle; (D) sheep and goats. Mean weights of males and females taken from Great Basin pronghorn (Smith and Beale 1980), bighorn (McQuivey 1978), and mule deer (Papez 1976). Sex ratios of .67 males per 1.0 female are assumed. Domestic sheep and goats were 45.4 kg; cattle and horses were 454 kg. Population estimates derived from U.S. Dept. of Interior (1982b), and Utah Division of Wildlife, Nevada Division of Wildlife, and Bureau of Land Management (unpub.).

Resource Partitioning in Native Species

Given the differing biomasses of horses, native ungulates, and exotics, does it follow that resource competition occurs among species? The question is not easily answered because of its imprecision. If *resource competition* simply implies that different species use a common feature (e.g., food, water, air, etc.), then it occurs often. However, *competition* is usually reserved for cases in which resources are limiting and the actions of one species directly depresses the growth rate of another. Among ungulates, resource competition has proved remarkably difficult to demonstrate because of problems in controlling for interrelated variables.

There has been little evidence of interspecific resource competition in native Great Basin ungulates. But competition would not be expected since bighorn sheep and pronghorn differ in habitat and diet preferences. Native sheep are primarily grazers, exploiting graminoids in the vicinity of rocky precipitous terrain (Welles and Welles 1961; Wehausen 1980). Although bighorns also feed on some shrubs and forbs and occasionally move into open areas, their biology is inexorably tied to trade-offs between foraging sites and terrain needed for predator avoidance (Geist 1971; Wehausen 1983). Sheep that have strayed too far from escape cover have even been roped by cowboys on horseback, an indication of their lack of fleetness (McQuivey 1978). In contrast, Great Basin pronghorn inhabit "steppe" environments where browse species rather than grasses make up the bulk of their diets (Smith and Beale 1980) and rapid flight is used to avoid predators. As a consequence of different feeding and antipredator behavior, resource overlap between bighorns and pronghorns has been minimal.

Unlike these native and climax-adapted species, mule deer are rather recent invaders of the Great Basin—at least in terms of their overall contribution to native ungulate biomass—where they have successfully exploited seral communities (Longhurst, Leopold, and Dasmann 1952; Wagner 1978). Deer habitats vary, but thickly wooded and shrubby ecotones are important components. Forbs and shrubs are browsed throughout the year except during a short period in spring when grasses are consumed (Hanley and Hanley 1982; Papez 1976).

This admittedly simplified summary of resource profiles in native Great Basin ungulates suggests that potential conflicts over food are avoided primarily through habitat segregation and different food preferences, as has been noted in a Montana grassland ecosystem (McCullough 1980). Potential competition may arise between deer and pronghorn in a few areas of the Great Basin where ranges and diets overlap seasonally (Hanley and Hanley 1982; Vavra and Sneva 1978).

Introduced Ungulates: Facilitators or Competitors?

Facilitation is the idea that the use of the environment by some species increases the availability of resources for different species (Vesey-Fitzgerald 1960). It has been offered and reevaluated (Sinclair and Norton-Griffiths 1982) as a hypothesis to explain feeding relationships in several migrant ungulates in East African savannas. Documentation of facilitation among native North American ungulates is lacking, although it has long been suspected that bison once enhanced feeding conditions for pronghorn on the American plains through heavy grazing and trampling (Wagner 1978; Mack and Thompson 1982).

Because herbivores such as sheep, goats, horses, and cattle (hereafter called exotics unless designated otherwise) that were introduced into the Great Basin have modified their environments, they have been viewed either as facilitators for (Neal 1982) or competitors of (McQuivey 1978; Papez 1976) native ungulates. Perhaps exotics serve as both, depending upon ecological conditions (Heady and Bartolome 1977; Mackie 1976; Reiner and Urness 1982) or management options (Wagner 1978).

Three hypotheses can be used to explain the degree to which these ecological processes have operated in the past (fig. 11.2). However, they do not apply equally to all species due to the mitigating influences of historical (man-related) factors (see below). For simplicity three groups of large herbivores are presented—presettlement ungulates (pronghorn and bighorn), an invading native ungulate (mule deer), and exotics.

Hypothesis 1 postulates that *exotics exert no effect on resident species*. If this hypothesis was so, both species of native ungulates should remain unaffected after the introduction of exotics. Clearly such has not been the case. Unlike the hypothetical situation depicted in A of figure 11.2, mule deer populations have not remained constant and presettlement ungulates have declined (Wagner 1978).

Hypothesis 2 is that *exotics compete with native ungulates* (fig. 11.2, B). Data indicative of declines in either presettlement species or mule deer would suggest interspecific competition, if other factors did not cause reductions in population sizes. The decline in presettlement ungulates is an unlikely result of the introduction of exotics because bighorns preferentially occupy habitats that horses and cattle do not (Wehausen 1983), and pronghorn diets differ from those of exotic grazers (Olsen and Hansen 1977; Meeker 1979). However, in a strict sense the hypothesis cannot be evaluated for pronghorn and bighorn. Other factors obscure any possible relationships concerning these ungulates. Their declines also correlate with increasing human exploitation and with the introduction of domestic sheep about eighty to a hundred years ago (McQuivey 1978; Yoakum 1978; Wehausen 1983). Also, bighorn sheep habitat preferences in the past may not have been as restricted to precipitous areas, as evidenced by earlier use of rolling terrain in Death Valley (C. Douglas, personal communication).

With regard to mule deer the hypothesis is incorrect because their numbers have actually increased rather than decreased, as portrayed in the hypothetical situation shown in B of figure 11.2. Hence, hypothesis 2 does little to explain what has really happened to Great Basin ungulates.

Hypothesis 3 is that *exotics facilitate at least one species of native ungulate* (fig. 11.2 C). The available evidence supports this idea. By removing grasses, horses and cattle promote growth of shrubs and forbs, both of which are consumed by deer. These successional

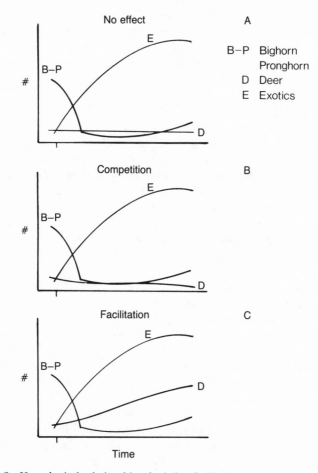

Fig. 11.2 Hypothetical relationships depicting facilitation or competition between exotic ungulates and mule deer. (B-P) bighorn and pronghorn; (D) deer; (E) exotics. In all cases, presettlement species (pronghorn and bighorn) decline due to historical factors.

changes have contributed to increases in mule deer populations, changes that have occurred only after the Great Basin was settled by man (Heady and Bartolome 1977; Longhurst, Leopold, and Dasmann 1952; Neal 1982; Urness 1976). Even though deer abundance has delinced in recent years for numerous reasons (Longhurst et al. 1976), wildlife managers have traditionally relied on successional vegetation—induced by disturbances—to maintain deer herds. It appears that exotics have facilitated mule deer population growth. Nevertheless, proper control of exotics has been stressed if interspecific competition is not desired (Wagner 1978). For example, in Death Valley where bighorn sheep and feral burros overlap in food and water use, burros have increased at the expense of bighorns (Dunn and Douglas 1982; Ginnett and Douglas 1982).

Interspecific Social Interactions and Dominance

Associations among Great Basin ungulates are not common due to differing population sizes and habitat preferences. Even when associations occur, interspecific aggression is rarely observed. Usually animals feed peacefully in close proximity. If, however, dominance in interspecific interactions occurs, individuals of larger species are likely to gain in advantage (Fisler 1977). Observations of interactions among sympatric bighorns, pronghorns, mule deer, and feral horses, mainly in eastern Oregon and in northern Nevada from 1976 to 1983, offer a glimpse of the resulting dominance relationships.

A total of 30 interspecific social interactions (ISI) were observed (table 11.1). An ISI is defined as one in which an individual or group retreats by running away from another individual or group of a different species. Horses, the largest species, were involved in 21 interactions; 12 were with mule deer, with horses dominating in 92% of these. In fact, in virtually all cases, native species were subordinate to exotics (table 11.1), that is, horses supplanted deer 11 times, bighorns 2 times, and pronghorn 6 times. Burros were observed infrequently, which is also reflected by the few ISI that involved them. However, I included in the table 2 ISI witnessed with burros. One was with feral horses in Death Valley in 1979, the other with mule deer in the Grand Canyon in 1974.

Most interactions involved simple displacements where individuals singly or in groups approached from 250 m to within 1 m before retreats took place. Combat was never observed, but on 3 occasions horses head tossed at rivals (once at pronghorn and twice

TABLE 11.1 Interspecific Dominance Relationships among Native and Feral Ungulates

| Subordinate | Dominant | | | | | | | | | | Summary of Total Displacements |
| | Horses | | Burros | | Deer | | Bighorn | | Pronghorn | | |
	S	G	S	G	S	G	S	G	S	G	
Horses — S	—		2	①	2	⑪ 5	1	②	2	⑥ 3	by horses — 20
Horses — G			2	1		2	1			1	by opponents — 1
Burros — S			—		①	1					by burros — 1
Burros — G											by opponents — 1
Deer — S	①				—		③	3	①	1	by deer — 5
Deer — G		1					2*				by opponents — 14
Bighorn — S					②	2*	—		①	1	by bighorn — 3
Bighorn — G											by opponents — 6
Pronghorn — S							①	1	—		by pronghorn — 1
Pronghorn — G											by opponents — 8

Notes: Numbers refer to frequency of displacements and designate whether initiators or recipients were solitary (S) or in groups (G) of two or more individuals. Total number of interactions between species is encircled. Dominance is recorded horizontally; supplantations are displayed vertically. Species are arranged from largest to smallest. Hunter and Kinghorn 1950 also reported a group of antlerless mule deer being supplanted by bighorn sheep (not included in this table).

at deer), and on 1 occasion each, horses chased pronghorns and mule deer. Other observations included (1) two male pronghorn that chased a group of twelve bighorns (ewes, young rams, and juveniles) about 300 m, after which a bighorn ewe and male pronghorn threatened each other with horns; and (2) a bighorn ram with a three-fourths horn curl that displayed his horns to a pronghorn buck that had made no obvious response. In this latter case both fed, and the pronghorn gradually moved away while feeding.

No native ungulate species was clearly dominant over any other (table 11.1). In all ISI ($N=8$) only groups (and never solitary animals) ever displaced groups of another species. ISI between single individuals were not observed except in the aforementioned case that involved a bighorn and pronghorn. In other areas, where population densities of various species are greater, interactions may be more frequent. For example, on the National Bison Range, an enclosed area of about 19,000 acres in Montana, McCullough (1980, 72) found that solitary male pronghorns were aggressive to mule deer while maintaining territories, but "mule deer were observed to be dominants in aggressive encounters with pronghorn males during this non-territorial period."

It is difficult to evaluate whether interspecific interactions or dominance play an important role in partitioning niches among species. Instantaneous advantages seem to be accrued by individuals of species that are larger in size. But whether these interactions result in niche segregation among pronghorns, bighorns, mule deer, and wild horses remains to be seen.

11.4   Horses, Other Feral Ungulates, and Their Environmental Effects

In the preceding section I indicated that (1) few data had been accumulated to substantiate resource competition between native Great Basin ungulates and feral horses; (2) when exotics are managed properly, differing habitat and diet preferences among these and native species permit coexistence; and (3) evidence supported the facilitation hypothesis—that habitat disturbance created primarily by exotics allowed mule deer to prosper (fig. 11.2, C). Because the foregoing indicates that mule deer have benefited indirectly from vegetation change or other disturbances and few negative effects of horses have been verified, one might ask whether the control or removal of horses is desirable or biologically justifiable.

The question is not easily answered since *desire* evokes personal opinions and biological justifications tend to vary with one's training. Consider the conflicting interests of a rancher and a wildlife photographer, both of whom share concerns for environmental planning. Cattle might be equitable components of ecosystems for the rancher, whereas the photographer might prefer an environment with only native ungulates, or perhaps wild horses, or even cattle. The differences can be large depending upon one's preferences. That management policies have often been controversial testifies to the disagreement that occurs even among professionals (Houston 1982; Jewell, Holt, and Hart 1981). If a single view of locally abundant populations emerges, it is that a system's equilibrium should not be compromised. However, just what constitutes this balance may never be agreed upon (Caughley 1981), even within national park management (Houston 1971; Sinclair 1981).

Rather than readdress this issue, particularly as it pertains to Great Basin horses, I will mention some of the adverse effects that feral and exotic mammals have had upon their environments. This is not to say that benefits do not result from feral and exotic animals; many products of health and economic importance are derived from domesticated animals that use public lands. However, there may be costs as well. In evaluating these costs, interactions between exotics and their environments are considered in three examples: negative effects on oceanic islands, Australian deserts, and American deserts.

Feral Mammals on Oceanic Islands

Introduced feral mammals occur on islands in the Atlantic, Pacific, and Indian oceans. The most complete and presumably most damaging array of species is located on the Galápagos where feral cattle, sheep, goats, pigs, burros, horses, dogs, cats, and house mice occur (Hoeck 1984). One or more of these species also are found on numerous other oceanic islands, including the Channel Islands (Coblentz 1978), St. Kilda (Jewell, Milner, and Morton-Boyd 1974), Aldabra (Gould and Swingland 1980), New Zealand (Whitaker and Rudge 1976), and Hawaii (Van Riper and Van Riper 1982).

Because many plants and animals of true oceanic islands evolved in the absence of predator pressures (whether from large herbivores, which prey on plants, or carnivores), they lack defenses against many invading species. The results of such introductions have proved catastrophic. By being fed upon and trampled, native vegetation has been impaired, alien species have flourished, and soils have been eroded. On several islands of the Galápagos archi-pelago, replacement of native bush and tussock grasslands has oc-curred, forest highlands have changed to pampas grasslands, cactus stands have been decimated, and reptile and bird eggs are frequently destroyed (Hoeck 1984). Unless efforts to control the spread of exotics succeed in these areas, many more highly spe-cialized and endemic species will become extinct—a fate corrobo-rated all too often (Coblentz 1978; see also Soulé and Wilcox 1980).

Exotics in Australian Deserts

The predominate feral ungulates in Australia are water buffalo, horses, asses, camels, goats, and pigs (McKnight 1976; see also Baker and Manlove 1981). These species, in addition to cattle and sheep, have had marked influences on Australian ecosystems. In desert and woodland areas trampling, soil erosion, and disclimax vegetation have also modified the distribution of native species. Among the unique marsupials of Australia, species such as desert bandicoots, pig-footed bandicoots, spectacled hare wallabies, and nail-tailed wallabies have been eliminated from most of their for-mer ranges because they "had their homesites eaten out from over them. Such dispossession would have exposed them to increased risks of predation" (Newsome 1975, 417) from dingos and possibly feral dogs and cats. Not only has the physical destruction of micro-habitats diminished native species' abundance but so has in-terspecific competition for food. Burrowing rat-kangaroos and rabbit-eared bandicoots, which initially benefited after increased disturbance, have become extirpated from most of their native ranges (Newsome 1975).

However, not all native marsupials in Australian deserts have declined as a result of exotics. As in the Great Basin, livestock have apparently facilitated some species. Two large macropods—red kangaroos and especially euros—have proliferated as a result of massive disturbances wrought by sheep and cattle and by the drill-ing of new water sources. Still, Newsome's (1975, 419) ecological warning is cause for somberness:

> The response curve of the red kangaroo to continued uncontrolled grazing of its ancestral habitats by introduced ruminants is one of initial increase, lasting perhaps 30–50 years or more, followed by decrease and even rarity, just as for its smaller relatives. Thus, the general rule of seral degradation and instability induced in the flora by the introduced ruminant stock can be extended to the large and medium-sized mar-supial fauna.

Exotics in American Deserts

Over one hundred years ago John Wesley Powell was aware of potential grazing limitations in the American West: "Though the grasses of the pasturage lands of the West are nutritious, they are not abundant" (1879). Some of the modifications that have occurred since then include loss of native species, declining water tables, salinization of topsoil and water, and unnaturally rapid erosion. Collectively these symptons are designated "desertification"— a problem in many arid ecosystems of the world and one still plaguing the Sonoran, Great Basin, Mojave, and Chihuahuan deserts of the United States (Sheridan 1981). A subset of symptoms associated with desertification involves interactions between exotics and native species. Because few hard data exist concerning this topic for horses and burros, their influences must be surmised from what is known about livestock-environment relationships (e.g., Menke 1983; National Research Council 1980).

Generally, changes in plant communities are related to grazing pressures, with greater habitat use resulting in more rapid transitions (Ellison 1960). Native ungulates (Houston 1982), rodents and lagomorphs (Rice and Westoby 1978), and insects (Hewitt 1977) all occasionally shift ecosystems away from their dynamic equilibria. But the changes to which I refer (below) are those suspected of modifying ecosystems beyond what are "normally" imposed by native species.

Disclaimers have been offered often to explain why livestock grazing on a controlled basis is not detrimental (Holecheck 1981). Yet the fact remains that, historically, western ecosystems were overgrazed (Wagner 1978; Brotherson and Brotherson 1978) and heavily overstocked ranges suffer losses in plant productivity or potential (Lacey and van Poollen 1981). In areas such as the Challis region of Idaho or the Rio Puerco Basin of New Mexico, not only have exotics caused disclimax communities but extreme soil erosion has followed (Sheridan 1981). Similar sequences of habitat degradation have been noted throughout xeric areas, including the Grand Canyon where feral burros trampled vegetation for about seventy-five years (U.S. Dept. of Interior, National Park Service 1980). Even though abiotic factors precipitate erosion, overgrazing accentuates the process (Reynolds and Packer 1962; see also U.S. Dept. of Interior, National Park Service 1980).

By modifying plant/soil interactions, exotics also cause changes in animal communities. For instance, in the Grand Canyon both the average absolute density of small mammals and species diversity were higher in study plots not grazed by feral burros than in grazed areas (Carothers, Stitt, and Johnson 1976). Cattle grazing is also known to decrease avian breeding faunas (Kantrud 1981), but such relationships may vary with ecosystems and prior disturbance (Ryder 1980). The above examples highlight the logical finding that unregulated or poorly managed populations of exotics cause profound, long-term, and adverse effects on their new environments.

11.5   Great Basin: Confounding Issues and Conservation Dilemmas
Preserves and Questions about Ecosystem Dynamics

In the preceding two sections I suggested that Great Basin horses probably had few direct negative effects on extant, native ungulates but that, if populations remain unmanaged, ecosystem damage may result or may have already occurred in some areas. Two fundamental issues were not addressed: (1) whether ecosystems inhabited by horses demonstrated enough resiliency to recover; and (2) whether dynamic equilibria could be established such that ecosystems did not collapse. Unfortunately, ideas about how ecosystems function in the face of ungulate eruptions will remain only hypotheses until such events are followed to their conclusion (Sinclair 1981). In the case of Great Basin horses it may never be possible to collect biological data concerning ecosystem dynamics because appropriate control areas—areas that have been without feral horses, cattle, or other exotics—have never been established.

A Great Basin National Park was proposed in 1966, but it did not receive serious consideration. Given the present economic and political climate, chances for its creation appear remote, as are opportunities to preserve faunal, floral, and geological resources. Unless areas are set aside, scientific enquiry about natural ecosystems will soon be less than meaningful in the Great Basin due to the eternal loss of baseline or control data which are mandatory for ecological comparisons. Although humans probably have had some impact on most ecosystems, it is refreshing to believe in the premise that "a somewhat unnatural baseline is probably better than no baseline at all" (Jenkins and Bedford 1973). In the long term, the creation of a park would help us learn how exotic ungulates have influenced their environments, but it would do little toward remedying immediate problems or controversies about horses.

Grasses and Large Grazers

Horses evolved in association with graminoids since at least the late Oligocene or early Miocene, and today both native (e.g., Przewalski's) and feral horses feed primarily upon grasses (see sec. 4.3). Even though feral horses receive much attention and condemnation for problems in the Great Basin, cattle inhabit the same environment and also feed chiefly upon grasses. However, cattle and other exotics comprise nearly 80% of the annual biomass of Great Basin ungulates (fig. 11.1). Concern about ecological impacts such as the removal of grasses might more profitably be analyzed in terms of the disproportionate influence of cattle rather than horses. This is not to say that I favor the removal of all cattle or all horses, or that cattle and horses should be treated equally, only that management decisions should be constructed on the basis of biological as well as economic parameters.

11.6   CONCLUDING REMARKS

The scientific management of ecosystems has been attempted in parks as different as Serengeti and Yellowstone, and that management has only been successful in varying degrees (Sinclair and Norton-Griffiths 1979; Houston 1982). In the Great Basin progress toward a uniform theme of ecosystem conservation or scientific management has been stifled. As parks and preserves are established to protect treasures or certain ecosystems, would a logical tenent then be that unprotected areas should fall to the onslaught of exotics or other detrimental interests? Of course not. And, although the situation is not typical of all parts of the Great Basin, neither is it too far from reality. Some public lands in the Great Basin are treasures worthy of strong safeguards, not of frivolous, post hoc management.

Decisions about the future of horses and their environments have confronted wildlife and range administrators and politicians for at least a dozen years (National Research Council 1982; Wagner 1983). Ultimately, political factions will again deal with these issues. A primary goal in future policy decisions should be to design management practices that will enhance knowledge about interactions between exotics and their environments. Without decisive action and protection, the tragic consequences of neglect, which are already too visible, will only magnify problems and needless controversy.

All too often historical wisdom and intuition is unheard or ignored. Almost 150 years ago Darwin recognized the chaos caused by exotics: "We may infer . . . what havoc the introduction of any new beast of prey must cause in a country before the instincts of the indigenous inhabitants have become adapted to the stranger's craft of power" (Darwin 1845). Elton (1957) pointed out that native species suffer from invading species regardless of whether the aliens are rodents, weeds, or microorganisms.

Unless we are satisfied with artificial ecosystems—those environments created by us and allowed to be dominated by a preponderance of exotics—rather than those shaped by natural forces, introduced species should be controlled. Management by crisis is an unhealthy substitute for planning before crisis. It would be sad indeed, both for aesthetic and scientific reasons, for all Great Basin horses to be culled. But it would be insidious if areas of the Great Basin were not preserved.

Today, wild horses and the Great Basin are entwined in controversy, but I am reminded of times past when a different perspective echoed from the writings of prominent men. In 1911 the distinguished naturalist John Muir wrote, "[It is] a country of wonderful contrasts, hot deserts bounded by snow-laden mountains, cinders and ashes scattered on glacier-polished pavement,—frost and fire working together in the making of beauty" (pp. 307–8). In that same year, cowboy Rufus Steele reported, "the horses wander down into the valleys, making inroads upon planted ground, but the mountains, the very peaks, are their refuge and home" (p. 758). While no doubt each man traveled the Great Basin and knew it intimately, the problems concerning land use 75 years ago were not as acute as they are today. Indeed all denizens on our planet once had homes, not just the horses Steele referred to. But without careful planning and wise management, horses, native species, and people will soon be without fresh air, clean water, and room to run.

11.7   CONSERVATION RECOMMENDATIONS

While I was in the final stages of completing this book, the U.S. Congress passed legislation that designated "wilderness" areas in Idaho, California, Arizona, and other states. Despite this hint of emerging consciousness in the stewards of federal lands, none of the acreage was in the Great Basin—though over one million acres in central and eastern Nevada and even more in northwestern Nevada had been formally recommended for similar status. The shining peaks, the vast fragant valleys engulfed by sage, and the bleached dry lake beds had been ignored once again, ostensibly as the sink between the Rockies and the Sierras—"the place where no one lives" or, perhaps, cares.

Worse yet, conservation options are few. The relentless asssaults continue. Geothermal sites, wetlands, and minerals are still being exploited. Pronghorn, mule deer, and eagles are regularly poached. Once a local sheriff extolled to me the virtues and, indeed, the pleasure of killing coyotes with sophisticated automatic weapons. Specially designed racing vehicles shatter the silence, scream across sensitive deserts, and sear landscapes in pursuit of world speed records.

Though my despair is shared by many colleagues, the network of red tape to undo these injustices is formidable. My hope lies in keeping a reasonably intact Great Basin Desert and some wild horses. Below, I offer a plan for action.

1. A national park should be established immediately. Because the Great Basin is not a homogeneous environment, the park should encompass different units that preserve unique features of mountains, valleys, deserts, and fauna, floral, and aquatic resources. Whenever possible, such lands should be buffered on all sides by other federal lands. Grazing by exotics should not be permitted within the park.

The founding of such an area would offer the public a chance to view portions of this unique desert and mountainous region without the ravages of modern society, protect areas from off-road vehicles, mining, trampling, grazing, etc., and provide chances to learn more about how ecosystems function without exotics or other non-natural influences.

2. At least three wild horse preserves should be created—relatively small areas, ranging from 20,000 to 40,000 acres in size— that could support up to about two hundred horses each. To minimize costs, refuge boundaries could consist of natural barriers such as canyons, playas, or lakes. Undoubtedly, some fencing would be required as has been done in the Pryor Mountains near the Montana-Wyoming border. The refuges should be located in different habitats and should vary in the degree to which horses are managed. Thus, some populations will be heavily cropped, others marginally, while some perhaps not at all. Different practices would then produce long-term experimental information about factors that influence populations and the effects of horses upon their environments. Horse preserves should be managed for the benefit of horses and native species. Cattle should not be allowed in these areas.

3. Establish information centers at each of the preserves. Whether museums or vistor centers, these could be analogous to those set up at national parks and would provide facts about historical, biological, and controversial aspects of wild horses. Additionally, some wild horses could be maintained in large enclosures for viewing by the public. Without a strong committment to interpretative programs in education, many sectors of the lay public will continue to display attitudes based more on myth than fact.

4. Allow existing horse populations in unfenced and undefined regions to persist in only a few areas. These could be scattered throughout several states and consist of large remote tracts of land (e.g., entire mountain chains, valleys, etc.) where five hundred to fifteen hundred animals might occur. These populations would represent a "business-as-usual" policy where horse grazing, cattle grazing, and other forms of land practice under federal multiple-use edicts would continue. However, routine control programs should be employed every few years to maintain an area near its carrying capacity and to prevent environmental damage.

The continuance of some completely free-roaming, non-restricted horses is crucial for two reasons. First, it minimizes chances for local extinctions, which might be more apt to occur in the confines of relatively small reserves. Second, it counteracts possible complaints that all horses have been placed in reserves with formal boundaries that prevent dispersal or wide-ranging movements, destroying the wild quality that many people enjoy.

Horse populations should be removed from all regions not designated as preserves or from those few areas of large, remote tracts where they will roam freely. Despite an absence of horses, additional cattle should not be immediately placed in areas where horses are removed. Instead, vigorous and sound rehabilitation programs need to be instituted to assure improvements in range quality and plant productivity.

5. Increase (or develop) a permanent scientific staff that will make use of experiments (both artificial and natural) to further knowledge about wild horses and their problems. These individuals should be located in field offices rather than in Washington, D.C.

6. During periods before plans for action are implemented, some government "wild horse specialists" should be trained to understand ecological principles. They should examine existing horse populations with respect to body sizes, metabolism, density, food needs, and spatial requirements. They should then intensively

monitor a few populations within their areas of jurisdiction. The areas should vary in environmental parameters (vegetation types, food availability, density, etc.) so that some of the crude effects that different variables have upon horse demography may be detected.

The potential benefits of resource conservation must be articulated if successful protection (in this case, of both wild horses and the Great Basin) is ever to come about. Based on the above recommendations, the public would benefit by the availability of a Great Basin park, the existence of wild horses in several areas without the possibility of their removal, the creation of employment opportunities in association with the construction, operation, and administration of the horse preserves and a national park, and the aid that increased tourism would bring to local economies.

No plan staves off all of the critics. Given the diverse opinions about wild horses, mine, no doubt, will not be the exception. Progress in conservation can arise only by compromise. While this may be a sad caveat for environmentalists, victories are far too few and defeats all too many to delay concessions any longer. My plan is a compromise. But without swift and decisive action, the Great Basin ecosystem continues to be stripped. Soon it will be too late—and all of us will have lost.

11.8   SUMMARY

1. There has been no systematic protection of land in the Great Basin Desert, and only about 0.00001% of the federal domain is under the jurisdiction of the National Park Service. Lack of appropriate planning and interagency implementation of conservation measures have resulted in a rapidly deteriorating environment.
2. Native ungulates comprise less than 5% of the total ungulate biomass. Livestock accounts for about 77%, while feral horses make up the rest. Little evidence for interspecific resource competition between exotics (horses and livestock) and native species (bighorn sheep, pronghorn, and mule deer) exists. Moderate levels of resource use by exotics have presumably enhanced deer populations in the Great Basin.
3. During interspecific social interactions, horses dominate deer, bighorns, and pronghorns. However, interactions are infrequent, and there is no evidence that behavioral events mediate niche segregation among these species.
4. Feral and exotic mammals such as goats, pigs, sheep, horses,

burros, dogs, cats, and mice have caused many adverse biological effects on islands. These include altering plant communities,
destroying vertebrate life, and facilitating erosion. In Australian
and American deserts, similar effects are also found.

5. The need exists to know how ecosystems work in the absence of
management. Only after this knowledge is obtained can management practices proceed wisely. A goal in future policy decisions should be to design management practices that will
enhance knowledge about ecosystem dynamics. A plan to establish wild horse preserves and a Great Basin National Park is outlined. Such areas would resolve some land-use problems and, in
the long run, help to educate and benefit segments of the public.

Appendixes

APPENDIX 1   Common and Scientific Names of Extant Mammals and Birds Mentioned in the Text

MAMMALS
Order Marsupialia

Red kangaroo	*Macropus rufus*
Burrowing rat-kangaroo	*Bettongia lesueur*
Euro	*Macropus robustus*
Pig-footed bandicoot	*Chaeropus ecaudatus*
Rabbit-eared bandicoot	*Macrotis lagotis*
Nail-tailed wallaby	*Onychogalea spp.*
Spectacled hare wallaby	*Lagorchestes conspicillatus*

Order Insectivora

Elephant shrew	*Elephantulus rufescens*
Shrew	*Sorex* spp.

Order Primata

Kloss's gibbon	*Hylobates klossi*
Hamadryas baboon	*Papio hamadryas*
Olive baboon	*Papio anubis*
Chimpanzee	*Pan troglodytes*
Common langur	*Presbytis entellis*

Order Lagomorpha

Pika	*Ochotona princeps*
Rabbit	*Sylvilagus* spp.

Order Rodentia

Ground squirrel	*Spermophilus* spp.
Belding's ground squirrel	*Spermophilus beldingi*
Chipmunk	*Eutamias* spp.
Yellow-bellied marmot	*Marmota flaviventris*
Jumping mouse	*Zapus hudsonius*

Black-tailed prairie dog	*Cynomys ludovicianus*
House mouse	*Mus musculus*
Wood rat	*Neotoma* spp.
North American porcupine	*Erethizon dorsatum*

Order Chiroptera

Spear-nosed bat	*Phyllostomus hastatus*

Order Carnivora

Wolf	*Canis lupus*
Coyote	*Canis latrans*
Dingo	*Canis familiaris*
Domestic dog	*Canis familiaris*
Black-backed jackal	*Canis mesomelas*
African wild dog	*Lycaon pictus*
Gray fox	*Urocyon cinereoargenteus*
Kit fox	*Vulpes macrotis*
Black bear	*Ursus americana*
Grizzly bear	*Ursus arctos*
Racoon	*Procyon lotor*
Ringtail	*Bassariscus astutus*
Weasel	*Musetla* spp.
American badger	*Taxidea taxus*
Striped skunk	*Mephitis mephitis*
Dwarf mongoose	*Helogale parvula*
Spotted hyena	*Crocuta crocuta*
Lion	*Panthera leo*
Mountain lion (puma)	*Felis concolor*
Bobcat	*Felis rufus*
Domestic cat	*Felis domesticus*

Order Hyracoidea

Tree hyrax	*Heterohyrax brucei*
Rock hyrax	*Procavia johnstoni*

Order Proboscidea

African elephant	*Loxodonta africana*

Order Perissodactyla

Tapir	*Tapirus* spp.
White rhino	*Ceratotherium simum*
Black rhino	*Diceros bicornis*
Horse	*Equus caballus*
Ass	*Equus asinus*
Przewalski's horse	*Equus przewalskii*
Common (Plain's) zebra	*Equus burchelli*

Mountain zebra	*Equus zebra*
Grevy's zebra	*Equus grevyi*
Asiatic half-ass	*Equus hemionus*

Order Artiodactyla

Pig	*Sus scrofa*
Warthog	*Phacochoerus aethiopicus*
Giraffe	*Giraffa camelopardalis*
Caribou	*Rangifer tarandus*
Reindeer	*Rangifer tarandus*
Red deer	*Cervus elaphus*
Elk	*Cervus canadensis*
Moose	*Alces alces*
Mule deer	*Odocoileus hemionus*
Roe deer	*Capreolus capreolus*
Chinese water deer	*Hydropotes inermis*
Wildebeest	*Connochaetes taurinus*
Hartebeest	*Alcelaphus buselaphus*
Nyala	*Tragelaphus angasi*
Impala	*Aepyceros melampus*
Addax	*Addax nasomaculatus*
Waterbuck	*Kobus defassa*
Duiker	*Cephalophus* spp.
Dik-dik	*Madoqua kirki*
Klipspringer	*Oreotragus oreotragus*
Gemsbok	*Oryx gazella*
Asian water buffalo	*Bubalus bubalis*
Banteng	*Bos banteng*
Cattle	*Bos taurus*
African buffalo	*Syncerus caffer*
Bison	*Bison bison*
Yak	*Bos grunniens*
Nilgiri tahr	*Hemitragus hylocrius*
Ibex	*Capra ibex*
Domestic goat	*Capra hircus*
Chamois	*Rupicapra rupicapra*
Musk-ox	*Ovibus moschatus*
Rocky Mountain goat	*Oreamnos americanus*
Saiga	*Saiga tatarica*
Bighorn sheep	*Ovis canadensis*
Dall's sheep	*Ovis dalli*
Soay sheep	*Ovis aries*
Llama	*Lama lama*
Guanaco	*Lama guanicoe*
Camel	*Camelus* spp.
Pronghorn	*Antilocapra americana*

Order Pinnipedia

Narwhal	*Monodon monoceros*
Killer whale	*Orcinus orca*
Elephant seal	*Mirounga angustirostris*
Walrus (Pacific)	*Odobenus rosmarus*

Birds

White pelican	*Pelecanus erythrorhynchos*
Bewick's swan	*Cygnus columbianus*
Turkey vulture	*Cathartes aura*
Bald eagle	*Haliaeetus leucocephalus*
Sage grouse	*Centrocercus urophasianus*
Gambel's quail	*Lophortyx gambelii*
California gull	*Larus californicus*
Black-billed magpie	*Pica pica*
Common raven	*Corvus corax*
Loggerhead shrike	*Lanius ludovicianus*
House (English) sparrow	*Passer domesticus*
Western meadowlark	*Sturnella neglecta*
Red-winged blackbird	*Agelaius phoeniceus*
Sage sparrow	*Amphispiza belli*

APPENDIX 2 Common and Scientific Names of Some Frequent Plant Species in the Granite Range

Grass and Grasslike Plants

Crested wheatgrass	*Agropyron cristatum*
Bluebunch wheatgrass	*A. spicatum*
Spike bent grass	*Agrostis exarata*
Big brome	*Bromus marginatus*
Cheatgrass or downy brome	*B. tectorum*
Clustered fieldsedge	*Carex praegracillis*
Great Basin wild rye	*Elymus cinereus*
Idaho fescue	*Festuca idahoensis*
Galeta	*Hilaria jamesii*
Rush	*Juncus* spp.
Wood rush	*Luzula* spp.
Sandberg's bluegrass or little bluegrass	*Poa sandbergii*
Nevada bluegrass	*P. nevadaensis*
Needle-and-thread grass	*Stipa commata*
Thurber's needlegrass	*S. thurberiana*

Forbs

Yarrow	*Achillea millaefolium*
Nodding onion	*Allium cernuum*
Pussytoes	*Antennaria* spp.
Loco weed	*Astragalus* spp.
Balsamroot	*Balsamorhiza sagittata*
Paintbrush	*Castilleja* spp.
Elk thistle	*Cirsium* spp.
Tansy mustard	*Descurainia richardsonii*
Nodding buckwheat	*Eriogonum cernuum*
False forget-me-not	*Eritrichium nanum*
Sweetscented bedstraw	*Galium trifolium*
Geranium	*Geranium* spp.
Sweetvetch	*Hedysarum* spp.
Alpine lilly	*Lloydia serotina*
Desert parsley	*Lomatium macrocarpum*
Lupine	*Lupinus* spp.
Microsteris	*Microsteris gracilis*
Small-flowered forget-me-not	*Myosotis laxa*
Lousewart	*Pedicularis* spp.
Brown's peony	*Paeoni brownii*
Phlox	*Phlox austromontana*
Russian thistle	*Salsoli kali*
Dandelion	*Taraxacum* spp.
Clover	*Trifolium repens*
Mullein	*Verbascum thapsus*

Violet   *Viola* spp.
Death camas   *Zigadenus venenosus*

Shrubs

Rubber rabbitbush   *Chrysothamnus nauseosus*

In estimating the ages of animals whose birth dates were unknown, I followed standard tooth-wear guidelines for domestic horses (e.g., American Association Equine Practitioners 1971). These give reasonable estimates of age up to about fifteen years.

I also compared the ages of 8 known-aged domesticated range animals and 1 known-aged Granite horse with the above established patterns. Three of the horses consumed the same basic foods as Granite horses since they ranged freely on a ranch adjacent to the Granite Range. The other 5 horses had consumed both Great Basin fodder and food provided by their owners. The differences in wear patterns between the domestic Great Basin animals and those established by the American Association of Equine Practitioners for other domestic horses seemed slight. Until about twelve years of age, the known-aged individuals appeared one to two years older than they actually were. Since Galvayne's groove had not emerged on the lateral upper incisors (see American Association of Equine Practitioners 1971) prior to its expected development at eleven to twelve years, it seemed to be a reasonable diagnotistic character for older animals. Still, after the appearance of Galvayne's groove the animals' ages become notoriously more difficult to predict. To minimize this problem, I categorized older animals as follows: very old (exceeding 20+ yrs), when Galvayne's groove traversed or covered the lower half or disappeared from the lateral incisors in conjunction with other analyses of occlusal surfaces (see American Association of Equine Practitioners 1971); and old (14 to 19 yrs), according to the length of the groove and the above other factors. Younger animals were aged according to incisor surface wear and molar eruption patterns. Although these data have limitations they should be accurate within a year or two except at upper ages, when errors might be greater but of less biological significance. More important, however, my age comparisons reflect relative differences among individuals of the Granite Range population

The analyses of home ranges were designed to display variation in vegetation characteristics. The method I chose required not only knowledge of the distribution, relative abundance, and food value of Granite Range plants but also some way of describing the relative importance of various areas for foraging horses.

As indicated in chapter 4, 153 line-intercept transects (Canfield 1941) were positioned systematically throughout the study site. The frequency with which shrubs, forbs, grasses, and waste (inorganic substances, dead vegetation, or feces) were encountered at each meter along each transect was noted. Composition and utilization of the herbaceous layer was then determined by locating 1,090 m² quadrats along line-intercept transects. Within each quadrat percentage of ground cover was estimated visually and percentage of use by mean volume consumed from all species in each plot. Species cover values were calculated by (1) averaging coverage for each species for each plot, (2) assigning resultant values to cover classes (Daubenmire 1959), and (3) multiplying cover class values by the frequency of that species along the transect.

Because the nutritional values of foods were unknown, species foraging values were estimated. These were based on average ranks (-1 to 7, e.g., poisonous species, no value, very poor, etc., to excellent) of species from the literature. For example, statements concerning the forage value of clustered fieldsedge were found in Dayton et al. (1937), Judd (1962), Mueggler and Stewart

(1980), and Sampson (1917). Based on their respective discussions I ranked this species good (rank = 5), excellent (7), fair to good (3 and 5, respectively) and fair (3); mean rank equaled 4.6. Species with mean values of 5 or greater were often based on at least five references, and none received less than three independent ratings. References consulted were U.S. Dept. of Agriculture, Forest Service (1914), Craighead, Craighead, and Davis (1963), Dayton (1960), Dayton et al. (1937), Hermann (1966), Judd (1962), Laycock (1967), Mueggler and Stewart (1980), Nawa (1978), and Sampson (1917). When temporal differences were reported in the literature, seasons were given separate ratings. This system provided a relative scaling of nutritional values of species, but it failed to account for geographical variation. Nevertheless, species of extreme value differences are easily separated, and there is general uniformity concerning the relative food value of most species to grazing herbivores.

By incorporating the above measures a foraging quality index (FQI) was calculated for each of the 34 microhabitats (in sec. 4.3) defined by discriminant function analyses. These calculations were based on the following:

$$FQI = \sum_{y=0}^{\infty} \sum_{x=0}^{\infty} \frac{(\bar{x}_v)(\bar{x}_f \bar{x}_c)}{Ny},$$

where x is each species encountered along a transect, $\bar{x}_v$ is a species foraging value, $\bar{x}_f$ is its frequency, $\bar{x}_c$ is its cover class, and y is each transect within a cover type.

FQI values ranged from maximums of 180.0 in shrublands (mean=118.3) to 174.8 in meadows (mean=145.5), to 144.1 in grasslands (mean=108.5), to 44.8 in juniper forests (mean=37.8), and to 8.6 in rabbitbrush patches (mean=3.1). Riparian and waste areas were not surveyed. In evaluating home-range use by bands, FQI values of microhabitats rather than FQI means of cover types were used since variation in FQIs among microhabitats within cover types was considerable.

Though the methods I relied on were based on simple transects, they generated data that compared relative values of areas used both heavily and infrequently by horses. The vegetation data went unanalyzed intentionally until after the study's completion. I performed the fieldwork in the absence of verifiable information on quality differences among areas so that I might not bias my impressions of behavioral or ecological perfomances of individuals. Indexes of home-range quality were made independent of (and prior to the availability of) information on reproductive performances. In other words, I purposefully avoided an omnipresent tautology—that home ranges were better because they led to greater reproductive success. In fact, only after data were analyzed did I discover which home ranges were really the best, the intermediate, and the worst.

APPENDIX 5   Food Profiles of Granite Horses

Low-Altitude Ranges			
Species	% Freq.	% Cover	% Use
Agropyron spicatum cristatum	24.3	3.2	54.4
Bromus tectorum	89.9	12.0	27.3
Carex praegracillis	17.5	1.3	6.3
Elymus cinereus	14.9	5.5	45.0
Festuca idahoensis	18.1	1.6	53.4
Juncus spp.	3.1	0.5	16.4
Luzula spp.	1.0	0.1	0.0
Poa secunda nevadaensis	32.5	2.9	56.4
Stipa spp.	6.4	0.5	43.6
Achillea millefolium	1.0	0.1	0.0
Allium cernuum	1.8	0.05	0.0
Antennaria spp.	1.2	0.2	17.6
Astragalus spp.	5.2	0.2	0.0
Balsamorihza sagitata	3.7	0.3	0.02
Cirsium spp.	0.8	0.1	0.0
Descurainia richardsonii	1.1	0.1	0.0
Eriogonum cernuum	0.3	0.02	0.0
Geranium spp.	0.2	0.01	0.0
Lloydia serotina	0.3	0.01	0.0
Lomatium macrocarpum	11.5	0.6	0.02
Lupinus spp.	4.5	0.4	0.0
Microsteris gracilis	36.5	0.9	0.0
Salsola kali	24.7	3.5	0.0
Taraxacum spp.	8.5	0.5	4.4
Trifolium repens	0.3	0.03	0.0
Verbascum thapsus	0.7	0.05	0.0
Viola spp.	0.2	0.01	0.0
Zigadenus venenosus	0.2	0.01	0.0

High-Altitude Ranges			
Species	% Freq.	% Cover	% Use
Agropyron spicatum cristatum	35.6	7.0	3.72
Agrostis exarata	3.6	43.6	0.05
Bromus marginata	1.1	17.2	0.0
B. tectorum	0.6	2.8	0.0
Carex praegracillis	20.0	7.5	3.61
Elymus cinereus	41.0	23.7	3.45
Festuca idahoensis	0.7	3.8	21.35
Hillaria jamesii	4.9	2.0	9.39
Juncus spp.	12.1	8.0	0.19
Luzula spp.	1.2	4.7	0.10
Poa secunda nevadaensis	43.3	6.4	14.24
Stipa spp.	3.6	3.3	12.98
Achillea millifolium	0.2	2.5	0.0
Antennaria spp.	4.5	3.0	0.0
Astragalus spp.	1.4	2.7	0.0
Castilleja spp.	1.6	2.7	0.0

APPENDIX 5   (Continued)

	High-Altitude Ranges		
Species	% Freq.	% Cover	% Use
Cirsium spp.	0.9	1.5	0.0
Descurainia richardsonii	0.2	2.5	0.0
Erithrichium nanum	1.3	11.5	0.0
Galium triflorum	0.7	1.2	0.0
Hedysarum spp.	2.9	3.0	0.12
Lomatium macrocarpum	1.5	1.1	0.0
Lupinus spp.	39.3	3.2	0.94
Myosotis laxa	5.1	2.1	0.0
Pedicularis spp.	1.8	3.8	0.0
Phlox spp.	0.3	2.5	0.0
Salsola kali	0.6	1.8	0.0
Taraxacum spp.	11.3	1.8	5.70
Viola spp.	0.2	2.5	0.0
Zigadenus venenosus	2.5	1.4	8.0

Only data meeting the following three conditions were used to estimate gestation periods. First, copulations with ejaculations were observed. Since multiple copulations are normal during an estrous cycle, I assumed that the median one observed impregnated the female. Periods of receptivity in females are short (four to six days; Hafez 1980; Waring 1983) with ovulation occurring within the last thirty-six hours (Ginther 1979). Errors in conception dates by a day or two affect the overall results minimally. Second, pregnancies were determined. Females were considered pregnant in conjunction with the above when no further sexual behavior or estrous cycles were observed for six weeks. This measure is conservative. It may actually underestimate the frequency of embryonic deaths since diestrous in horses ranges from fourteen to seventeen days (Ginther, Whitmore, and Squires 1972; Waring 1983; Nishikawa and Hafez 1974). The reliability of this method depends on the subsequent detection of estrous cycles if conception failed during the first cycle. Based on the above conditions I estimated that conception occurred in 79.5% of the first estrous cycles. Of 78 copulations from which foals were later born, 62 occurred during the first cycle and 16 during the second estrous period. Third, birth dates were known due to observations of foals on their first day of life. Since exact copulation and birth dates were available, gestation periods were calculated. However, since season of birth affects fetal development (Howell and Rollins 1951), gestation lengths prior to and after 1 April were separated. Means and standard deviations were 339.1 (± 9.1) days ($N=12$) and 346.8 (± 8.3) days ($N=66$), respectively—significantly different for such time periods. These values correspond well with those reported on variability in domestic horses (Ropiha et al. 1969; Rollins and Howell 1951; Nishikawa 1959).

To avoid confusing the effects of cooperative harem defense with cooperative attempts to acquire mates, data resulting from attempts to steal females by one or both stallions (in a multimale band) were excluded from the following calculations. For each band a reciprocity quotient (RQ) was calculated to quantify the relationship between aid gained by dominant and by subordinate stallions in harem defense. Consider, for instance, two stallions of equal dominance status living in the same band. Equality in reciprocity would be predicted if one horse initiated defensive encounters and aided the other with the same relative frequency that the other performed such behaviors.

The RQ is calculated by

$$RQ = \frac{a/b}{c/d},$$

where a=frequency that dominant males aided subordinates already involved in defense; b=frequency that subordinate males initiated defensive interactions and received no aid; c=frequency that subordinate males aided dominants already involved in defense; and d=frequency that dominant males initiated defensive interactions and received no aid. The RQ generates values that allow direct comparisons of the within-band (multimale) relationships of stallions to those of other multimale bands under conditions when dominant stallions reap gains. Thus, $b < a$ and $c > d$ must occur. Under these specified conditions RQ ranges from 0 to 1.0, where 1.0 indicates parity in reciprocal defense and lower values suggest that defensive benefits are skewed in favor of dominant individuals.

The use of RQs proved useful for the Granite data since in all multimale bands subordinate stallions were involved in defense more than dominant males. However, because of the restricted conditions of the index, its use may not be as valuable when more complex relationships between dominants and subordinates occur.

A challenging area of evolutionary biology is the measurement of an individual's reproductive contribution. Recent work on red deer (Clutton-Brock, Guinnes, and Albon 1982) has shown that short-term study of reproductive success can lead to erroneous conclusions because (1) males might die after a few years of successful reproduction and thereby leave relatively few offspring, (2) differences in reproduction could be age dependent, or (3) fertilizations might correlate poorly with reproductive success (Gibson and Guinness 1980). Only with the acquisition of data on individual ages, paternity, and reproductive lifespans (or their probabilities) can some of these difficulties be overcome.

Assessment of Paternity in Horses

I relied primarily on observations of copulations and detections of birth dates to measure paternity. When males copulated and respective females bore young within predicted periods, an offspring was assigned to respective stallions. In 98% of 244 copulations with estrus females, only a single male mated. On the few occasions when more than one male copulated, each was assigned equal representations of that foal since I did not know who the real father was.

Over the period during which matings were documented, 88% of the foals could be attributed to stallions. In cases where foals were born but copulations went undetected, gestation lengths were backdated to estimate estrus dates. Resident stallions were assumed the fathers if females were in such bands at predicted estrus, unless the females were their daughters. Since stallions rarely copulate with daughters (sec. 8.6), I could not determine who the real fathers were. Only two such cases occurred and paternity estimations were not made.

Evaluation of Alternative Assumptions and Methods

Because the above method uses direct observations to determine male reproductive success, it avoided many of the pitfalls inherent in other assessments. Paternity exclusion analyses were not employable due to logistical problems. Such analyses have been done for two populations of horses that roamed freely within 335 and 500 hectare enclosures. These provide comparisons of the reliability of direct behavioral observations of copulations with genetic evidence of paternity. In the first determination, biochemical data were consistent with observations of mating behavior in Camargue horses (Duncan et al. 1984). In the second, Japanese Misaki stallions sired most of the offspring within their respective harems, but such males were not always the true fathers (Kaseda, Nozawa, and Mogi 1982). However, it is difficult to generalize from the results of this study because detailed behavioral observations on copulatory success were not available and because mating competition among males was reduced since the bachelors consisted of fifteen geldings (Kaseda 1981).

Without direct knowledge of dates of copulations and births or genetic evidence, estimations of male reproductive success are problematic. Some alternative and intuitively appealing procedures often necessitate unfounded assumptions. Below, I briefly contrast how estimations of male reproductive success might differ based on two scenarios, each comparing measurements that result from direct observations of copulations and births and those from assumptions of indirect approaches.

Scenario 1 is predicated on the common idea that observed copulations result in offspring. This does not appear unreasonable, especially since in most mammals it is not possible to observe when births occur. In the absence of information on female age and home-range ecology, the magnitude of error in estimating male reproductive success might be great if this assumption was employed. For example, if stallions were scored foals for each copulation observed with different females, reproductive success of individual males in the Granite population would have been overestimated by 48% since not all females that were copulated with gave birth.

Scenario 2 is confined to those species found in harems at some point during the breeding season. Males are often assigned values of reproductive success in relation to the number of females in a given group per unit of time. Had I applied such criteria on 15 June of each year (although any consistent date would suffice), I would have expected forty more foals in the population than there actually were. The overall error would have been 37% in paternity assignments.

These examples illustrate the poor agreement that resulted from assumptions concerning male reproductive success in a very visible mammal. However, with additional information about female reproductive success the accuracy of reproductive assignments to males improved. It will become increasingly necessary to examine assumptions prior to accepting broad generalizations about male reproductive success or methods of calculating it.

References

Albon, S. D.; Mitchell, B.; and Staines, B. W.. 1983. Fertility and body weight in female red deer: A density-dependent relationship. *J. Anim. Ecol.* 52:969–80.

Alexander, R. D.; Hoogland, J. L.; Howard, R. D.; Noonan, K. M.; and Sherman, P. W. 1979. Sexual dimorphism and breeding systems in pinnipeds, ungulates, primates, and humans. In *Evolutionary biology and social behavior: An anthropological perspective,* ed N. A. Chagnon and W. Irons, pp. 402–35. N. Scituate, Mass.: Duxbury Press.

Allen, G. M. 1940. Order Perissodactyla: Odd-toed ungulates. In *The mammals of China and Mongolia: Natural history of central Asia,* vol. 11, part 2, ed. W. Granger, pp. 1279–81. New York: American Museum of Natural History.

Altmann, J. 1974. Observational study of behavior: Sampling methods. *Behaviour* 49:227–67.

———. 1980. *Baboon mothers and infants.* Cambridge: Harvard University Press.

Amaral, A. 1977. *Mustang: Life and legends of Nevada's wild horses.* Reno: University of Nevada Press.

American Association of Equine Practitioners. 1971. *Official guide for determining the age of the horse.* Golden, Colo.

Anderson, C. E.; Potter, G. D.; Kreider, J. L.; and Courtney, C. C. 1983. Digestible energy requirements for working horses. *J. Anim. Sci.* 56:91–95.

Anderson, D. C.; Armitage, K. B.; and Hoffman, R. S. 1976. Socioecology of marmots: Female reproductive strategies. *Ecology* 57:552–60.

Anderson, J. L. 1979. Reproductive seasonality of the nyala, *Tragelaphus angasi:* The interaction of light, vegetation phenology, feeding style, and reproductive physiology. *Mamm. Rev.* 9:33–46.

———. 1980. The social organisation and aspects of behaviour of the nyala *Tragelaphus angasi* Gray, 1849. *Z. Sauget.* 45:90–123.

Andrewartha, H. G., and Birch, L. C. 1954. *The distribution and abundance of animals.* Chicago: University of Chicago Press.

Andrews, R. C. 1933. The Mongolian wild ass. *Nat. Hist.* 33:3–16.

Antonius, O. 1937. On the geographical distribution in former times and today of the recent Equidae. *Proc. Zool. Soc. Lond.* 107:557–64.

Appleby, M. C. 1982. The consequences and causes of high social rank in red deer stags. *Behaviour* 80:259–73.

Arnold, G. W., and Birrell, H. A. 1977. Food intake and grazing behaviour of sheep varying in body condition. *Anim. Prod.* 24:343–53.

Arnold, G. W., and Dudsinski, M. L. 1978. *Ethology of free-ranging domestic animals.* Amsterdam: Elsevier.

Arnold, S. J. 1983. Sexual selection: The interface of theory and empiricism. In *Mate choice,* ed. P. Bateson, pp. 67–108. Cambridge: Cambridge University Press.

Asa, C. S.; Goldfoot, D. A.; and Ginther, O. J. 1979. Sociosexual behavior and the ovulatory cycle of ponies (*Equus caballus*) observed in harem groups. *Hormones and Behavior* 13:49–65.

Ashman, D. 1976. Mountain lion investigations. Nevada Divison of Wildlife, Reno. Typescript.

Åstrand, P. D., and Rodahl, K. 1970. *Textbook of work physiology.* New York: McGraw-Hill.

Autenrieth, R. E., and Fichter, E. 1975. On the behavior and socialization of pronghorn fawns. *Wildl. Monog.* 42:1–96.

Awan, A. K. 1967. *Length of gestation.* Lahore: Maternity and Child Welfare Assoc.

Axelrod, D. I. 1958. Evolution of the Madro-Tertiary geo-flora. *Bot. Rev.* 24:433–509.

———. 1976. History of the coniferous forests: California and Nevada. *Univ. Calif. Publ. Bot.* 70:1–62.

Azara, Don F. de. 1838. *The natural history of the quadrupeds of Paraguay and the river La Plata.* Vol. 1. Edinburgh: Adam and Charles Black.

Baker, C. M. A., and Manlove, C. 1981. Fiercely feral: On the survival of domesticates without care from man. *Z. Tierzuchtg.* 98:241–57.

Banks, E. M., and Popham, R. 1975. Intraspecific agonistic behavior of captive brown lemmings, *Lemmus trimucronatus. J. Mammal.* 56:514–16.

Bannikov, A. G. 1967. *Biology of the saiga.* Jerusalem: Israel Program for Scientific Translations.

Barash, D. P. 1981. Mate guarding and gallivanting by male hoary marmots (*Marmota caligata*). *Beh. Ecol. Sociobiol.* 9:187–93.

Barclay, H. B. 1980. *The role of the horse in man's culture.* Canada: J. A. Allen.

Barrett, M. W. 1982. Distribution, behavior, and mortality of pronghorns during a severe winter in Alberta, *J. Wildl. Mgmt.* 46:991–1002.

Barrette, C. 1977. Fighting behavior of muntjac and the evolution of antlers. *Evolution* 31:169–76.

Baskett, J. 1980. *The horse in art.* Boston: New York Graphic Society.

Bateson, P. P. G. 1980. Optimal outbreeding and the development of sexual preferences in Japanese quail. *Z. Tierpsychol.* 53:231–44.

Beale, D. M., and Smith, A. D. 1970. Forage use, water consumption, and productivity of pronghorn antelope in western Utah. *J. Wildl. Mgmt.* 34:570–82.

———. 1973. Mortality of pronghorn antelope fawns in western Utah. *J. Wildl. Mgmt.* 37:343–52.

Beck, B. 1980. *Animal tool behavior.* New York: Garland Press.

Bekoff, M. 1977. Mammalian dispersal and the ontogeny of individual behavioral phenotypes. *Amer. Nat.* 111:715–32.

———. 1984. Social play behavior. *Bioscience* 34: 228–33.

Bekoff, M.; Wieland, C.; and Lavender, W. A. 1982. Space out: Graphic programs to study and to simulate space use and movement patterns. *Beh. Res. Meth. Instr.* 14:34–36.

Bell, R. H. V. 1970. The use of the herb layer by grazing ungulates in the Serengeti. In *Animal populations in relation to their food resources,* ed. A. Watson, pp. 111–23. Oxford: Blackwell.

———. 1971. A grazing ecosystem in the Serengeti. *Sci. Amer.* 224:86–93.

Belonje, P. C., and van Niekerk, C. H. 1975. A review of the influence of nutrition upon the oestrous cycle and early pregnancy in the mare. *J. Repro. Fert.,* suppl., 23:167–69.

Belovsky, G. E. 1981. Optimal activity times and habitat choice of moose. *Oecologia* 48:22–30.

Berger, J. 1977. Organizational systems and dominance in feral horses in the Grand Canyon. *Behav. Ecol. Sociobiol.* 2:131–46.

———. 1978. Group size, foraging, and anti-predator ploys: An analysis of bighorn sheep decisions. *Behav. Ecol. Sociobiol.* 4:91–100.

———. 1979a. Social ontogeny and behavioral diversity: Consequences for bighorn sheep inhabiting desert and mountain environments. *J. Zool. Lond.* 188:251–66.

———. 1979b. Weaning conflict in desert and mountain bighorn sheep: An ecological interpretation. *Z. Tierpsychol.* 50:188–200.

———. 1979c. Weaning, social environments, and the ontogeny of spatial associations in bighorn sheep. *Biol. Beh.* 4:363–72.

———. 1980. The ecology, structure, and functions of social play in bighorn sheep. *J. Zool. Lond.* 192:531–42.

———. 1981. The role of risks in mammalian combat: Zebra and onager fights. *Z. Tierpsychol.* 56:297–304.

———. 1982. Female breeding age and lamb survival in desert bighorn sheep. *Mammalia* 46:183–90.

———. 1983a. Predation, sex ratios, and male competition in equids (Mammalia: Perissodactyla). *J. Zool. Lond.* 201:205–16.

——— 1983b. Induced abortion and social factors in wild horses. *Nature* 303:59–61.

———. 1983c. Ecology and catastrophic mortality in wild horses: Implications for sociality in fossil assemblages. *Science* 220:1403–4.

Berger, J.; Daneke, D.; Johnson, J.; and Berwick, S. H. 1983. Pronghorn foraging economy and predator avoidance in a desert ecosystem: Implications for the conservation of large mammalian herbivores. *Biol. Cons.* 25:193–208.

Berger, J.; Koch, M.; Cunningham, C.; and Dodson, N. 1983. Chemical restraint of wild horses: Effects on reproduction and social structure. *J. Wildl. Dis.* 19:265–68.

Berger, J., and Rudman, R. 1985. Predation and interactions between coyotes and feral horse foals. *J. Mammal.*, 66:401–2.

Berry, H. H. 1981. Abnormal levels of disease and predation as limiting factors for wildebeest in the Etosha National Park. *Madoqua* 12:242–53.

Bertram, B. C. R. 1975. Social factors influencing reproduction in wild lions. *J. Zool. Lond.* 177:463–82.

Best, R. C. 1981. The tusk of the narwhal (*Monodon monoceros L.*): Interpretation of its function (Mammalia: Cetacea). *Can. J. Zool.* 59:2386–93.

Billings, W. D. 1950. Vegetation and plant growth as affected by chemically altered rocks in the western Great Basin. *Ecology* 31:62–74.

Blaxter, K. L. 1961. Lactation and the growth of the young. In *Milk: The mammary gland and its secretion*, ed. S. K. Kon and A. T. Cowie, pp. 305–61. New York: Academic Press.

Bokonyi, S. 1974. *The Przevalsky horse*. London: Souvenir Press.

Boonstra, R., and Rodd, F. H. 1983. Regulation of breeding density in *Microtics pennsylvanicus. J. Anim. Ecol.* 52:757–80.

Boshe, J. I. 1981. Reproductive ecology of the warthog *Phacochoerus aethiopicus* and its significance for management in the eastern Selous Game Reserve, Tanzania. *Biol. Cons.* 20:37–44.

Botkin, D. B.; Mellino, J. M.; and Wu, L. S. Y. 1981. How ecosystem processes are linked to large mammal population dynamics. In *Dynamics of large mammal populations*, ed. C. W. Fowler and T. D. Smith, pp. 373–88. New York: John Wiley & Sons.

Bouman, J. G. 1977. The future of Przewalski horses *Equus przewalski* in captivity. *Int. Zoo Yrbk.* 17:62–68.

Bouman, J. G., and Bos, H. 1979. Two symptoms of inbreeding depression in Przewalski horses living in captivity. In *Genetics and hereditary diseases of the Przewalski horse*, pp. 111–16. Rotterdam: Foundation for Preservation and Protection Przewalski Horse.

Bouman, J. G., Bouman, I., and Grueneveld, A. 1982. *Breeding Przewalski horses in captivity for release into the wild*. Rotterdam: Foundation for Preservation and Protection Przewalski Horse.

Bowen, W. D. 1982. Home range and spatial organization of coyotes in Jasper National Park, Alberta. *J. Wildl. Mgmt.* 46:201–16.

Boyd, L. 1979. The mare-foal demography of feral horses in Wyoming's Red Desert. In *Symposium on the ecology and behavior of wild and feral equids*, ed. R. H. Denniston, pp. 185–204. Laramie: University of Wyoming.

Brokaw, H. P., ed. 1978. *Wildlife and America*. Council on Environmental quality. Washington, D.C.: Government Printing Office.

Brotherson, J. D., and Brotherson, W. T. 1978. Grazing impacts on the sagebrush communities of central Utah. *Great Basin Nat.* 41:335–40.

Brown, J. H. 1971. Mammals on mountaintops: Non-equilibrium insular biogeography. *Amer. Nat.* 105:467–78.

———. 1978. The theory of insular biogeography and the distribution of boreal birds and mammals. *Great Basin Nat. Mem.* 2:209–28.

Brown, J. L. 1969. Territorial behavior and population regulation in birds. *Wilson Bull.* 81:293–329.

———. 1975. *The evolution of behavior.* New York: Norton.

Brown, J. L., and Balda, R. P. 1977. The relationship of habitat quality to group size in Hall's babbler, *Pomatostomus halli. Condor* 79:312–20.

Bunnell, F. L. 1982. The lambing period of mountain sheep: Synthesis, hypotheses, and tests. *Can. J. Zool.* 60:1–14.

Burt, W. H. 1943. Territoriality and home range concepts as applied to mammals. *J. Mammal.* 24:346–52.

Butler, B. R. 1978. Bison hunting in the desert west before 1800: The paleo-ecological potential and the archaeological reality. *Plain's Anthrop. Mem.* 14:106–12.

Butterworth, M. H., and Blore, T. W. D. 1969. The lactation of Persian Blackhead ewes and their growth of lambs. *J. Agr. Sci.* 73:133–37.

Byers, J. A., and Bekoff, M. 1981. Social, spacing, and cooperative behavior of the collared peccary, *Tayassu tajacu. J. Mammal.* 62:767–85.

Bygott, J. D.; Bertram, B. C.; and Hanby, J. P. 1979. Male lions in large coalitions gain reproductive advantages. *Nature* 282:839–41.

Campitelli, S.; Carenzi, C.; and Verga, M. 1982. Factors which influence parturition in the mare and development in the foal. *Appl. Anim. Ethol.* 9:7–14.

Canfield, R. 1941. Application of line interception method in sampling range vegetation. *J. For.* 39:388–94.

Caraco, T. 1979. Time budgeting and group size: A test of a theory. *Ecology* 60:618–27.

Carothers, S. W.; Stitt, M. E.; and Johnson, R. R. 1976. Feral asses on public lands: An analysis of biotic impact, legal considerations, and management alternatives. *Trans. No. Amer. Wild. Conf.* 41:396–406.

Caughley, G. C. 1971. The season of births for northern-hemisphere ungulates in New Zealand. *Mammalia* 35:204–19.

———. 1977. *Analysis of vertebrate populations.* London: Wiley and Sons.

———. 1981. Overpopulation. In *Problems in management of locally abundant wild mammals,* ed. P. A. Jewell, S. Holt, and D. Hart, pp. 7–20. New York: Academic Press.

Caughley, G. C., and Krebs, C. J. 1983. Are big mammals simply little mammals writ large? *Oecologia* 59:7–17.

Chapman, M., and Hausfater, G. 1979. The reproductive consequences of infanticide in langurs: A mathematical model. *Beh. Ecol. Sociobiol.* 5:227–40.

Chitty, D. 1967. The natural selection of self-regulatory behaviour in animal populations. *Proc. Ecol. Soc. Australia* 2:51–78.

Christian, J. J., and Davis, D. E. 1964. Endocrines, behavior, and population. *Science* 146:1550–60.

Churcher, C. S., and Richardson, M. L. 1978. Equidae. In *Evolution of African mammals,* ed. V. J. Maglio and A. B. S. Cooke, pp. 379–422. Cambridge: Harvard University Press.

Clarke, W. H. 1886. *Horses' teeth: . . . The teeth of many other land and marine animals both, living and extinct.* 3d ed. rev. New York: Turf, Field, and Farm.

Clutton-Brock, J. 1981. *Domesticated animals, from early times.* London: British Museum of Natural History.

Clutton-Brock, T. H. 1977. Some aspects of intraspecific variation in feeding and ranging behaviour in primates. In *Primate ecology: Studies of feeding and ranging behaviour in lemurs, monkeys and apes,* ed. T. H. Clutton-Brock, pp. 539–56. London: Academic Press.

———. 1986 (in press). Sexual selection in the Cervidae. In *Biology and management of the Cervidae,* ed. C. M. Wemmer. Washington, D.C.: Smithsonian Institution Press.

Clutton-Brock, T. H., and Albon, S. D. 1982a. Winter mortality in red deer (*Cervus elaphus*). *J. Zool. Lond.* 198:515–19.

———. 1982b. Parental investment in male and female offspring in mammals. In *Current problems in sociobiology,* ed. King's College Sociobiology Group, pp. 223–47. Cambridge: Cambridge University Press.

Clutton-Brock, T. H.; Albon, S. D.; and Harvey, P. H. 1980. Antlers, body size, and breeding group size in the Cervidae. *Nature* 285:565–67.

Clutton-Brock, T. H.; Greenwood, P. J.; and Powell, R. P. 1976. Ranks and relationships in Highland ponies and Highland cows. *Z. Tierpsychol.* 41:202–16.

Clutton-Brock, T. H.; Guinness, R. E.; and Albon, S. D. 1982. *Red deer: Behavior and ecology of two sexes.* Chicago: University of Chicago Press.

———. 1983. The costs of reproduction to red deer hinds. *J. Anim. Ecol.* 52:367–83.

———. 1984. Maternal dominance, breeding success, and birth sex ratios in red deer. *Nature* 308:358–60.

Clutton-Brock, T. H., and Harvey, P. H. 1977. Primate ecology and social organization. *J. Zool. Lond.* 183:1–39.

———. 1979. Comparison and adaptation. *Proc. Roy. Soc. Lond.* 205:547–65.

Clutton-Brock, T. H.; Iason, G. R.; Albon, S. D.; and Guinness, F. E. 1982. Effects of lactation on feeding behaviour and habitat use in wild red deer hinds. *J. Zool. Lond.* 198:227–36.

Coblentz, B. E. 1978. The effects of feral goats (*Capra hircus*) on island ecosystems. *Biol. Cons.* 13:279–86.

Cole, L. C. 1954. The population consequences of life history phenomena. *Quart. Rev. Biol.* 29:103–37.

Conley, W. 1979. The potential for increase in horse and ass populations: A theoretical analysis. In *Symposium on the ecology and behavior of wild and feral equids,* ed. R. H. Denniston, pp. 221–34. Laramie: University of Wyoming.

Conover, W. J. 1971. *Practical non-parametric statistics.* New York: John Wiley and Sons.

Cottam, W. P., and Evans, F. R. 1945. A comparative study of the vegetation of grazed and ungrazed canyons of the Wasatch Range, Utah. *Ecology* 26:171–81.

Craighead, J. J.; Craighead, F. C.; and Davis, R. J. 1963. *A field guide to the Rocky Mountain wildlflowers.* Boston: Houghton Mifflin.

Critchfield, W. B., and Allenbaugh, G. L. 1969. Geographic distribution of *Pinaceae* in and near northern Nevada. *Madrono* 19:12–26.

Cronquist, A.; Holmgren, A. H.; Holmgren, N. H.; and Reveal, J. L. 1972. *Intermountain flora.* Vol. 1. New York: Hafner Pub. Co.

Cumming, D. H. M. 1975. *A field study of the ecology and behaviour of warthog.* Museum Memoirs, no. 7. Salisbury: National Museum of Rhodesia.

Darling, F. F. 1937. *A herd of red deer.* London: Oxford University Press.

Darwin, Charles. 1845. *Journal of researches.* New York: P. F. Collier and Son.

———. 1859. *The origin of species by means of natural selection.* London: Murray.

———. 1868. *The variation of animals and plants under domestication.* New York: D. Appleton and Co.

———. [1871] 1888. *The descent of man and selection in relation to sex.* Reprint. London: Murray.

Daubenmire, R. 1959. A canopy-coverage method of vegetation analysis. *Northwest Sci.* 33:43–66.

David, R. 1966. Breeding the Indian wild ass, *Equus hemionus khur,* at Ahmedad Zoo. *Int. Zoo Yrbk.* 6:197–98.

Davis, D. E., and Christian, J. J. 1976. Population regulation in mammals. *Soviet J. Ecol.* 7:9–20.

Dawkins, R. 1976. *The selfish gene.* Oxford: Oxford University Press.

———. 1982. Vehicles and replicators. In *Current problems in sociobiology,* ed. King's College Sociobiology Group, pp. 45–64. Cambridge: Cambridge University Press.

Dawson, W. M.; Phillips, R. W.; and Speelman, S. R. 1945. Growth of horses under western range conditions. *J. Anim. Sci.* 4:47–54.

Dayton, W. A. 1960. Notes on western range forbs: Equietaceae through Fumariaceae. U.S. Dept. of Agriculture. Handbook no. 161. Washington, D.C.: Government Printing Office.

Dayton, W. A., et al. (13 coauthors). 1937. *Range plant handbook.* U.S. Dept. of Agriculture, Forest Service. Washington, D.C.: Government Printing Office.

Decker, E. 1978. Exotics. In *Big game of North America: Ecology and management,* ed. J. L. Schmidt and D. L. Gilbert, pp. 249–56. Harrisburg, Pa.: Stackpole Books.

Demment, M. W., and Van Soest, P. J. 1985. A nutritional explanation for body-size patterns of ruminant and nonruminant herbivores. *Amer. Nat.* 125:641–72.

Dittus, W. P. J. 1977. The social regulation of population density and age-sex distribution in the toque monkey. *Behaviour* 63:281–322.

———. 1979. The evolution of behaviours regulating densisty and age-specific sex ratios in a primate population. *Behaviour* 69:265–302.

———. 1981. The social regulation of primate populations: A synthesis. In *The macaques,* ed. D. G. Lindburg, pp. 263–86. New York: Van Nostrand Reinhold Co.

Dobie, F. J. 1952. *The mustangs.* Boston: Little, Brown, and Co.

Douglas-Hamilton, I., and Douglas-Hamilton, O. 1975. *Among the elephants.* London: William Collins and Co.

Downhower, J. F., and Armitage, K. B. 1971. The yellow-bellied marmot and the evolution of polygamy. *Amer. Nat.* 105:355–70.

———. 1981. Dispersal of yearling yellow-bellied marmots (*Marmota flaviventris*). *Anim. Beh.* 29:1064–69.

Downs, T. 1956. The Mascall fauna from the Miocene of Oregon. *Univ. Calif. Publ. Geol. Sci.* 31:119–354.

———. 1961. A study of variation and evolution in the Miocene *Merychippus. L. A. Co. Mus. Contrib. Sci.* 45:1–74.

Dubost, G., and Feer, F. 1981. The behavior of the male *Antilope cervicapra* L.: Its development to age and social rank. *Behaviour* 76:62–127.

Duncan, P. 1980. Time-budgets of Camargue horses, 2: Time-budgets of adult horses and weaned sub-adults. *Behaviour* 72:26–49.

———. 1982. Foal killing by stallions. *Appl Anim. Ethol.* 8:567–70.

Duncan, P.; Feh, C.; Gleize, J. C.; Malkas, P.; and Scott, A. M. 1984. Reduction of inbreeding in a herd of natural horses. *Anim. Beh.* 32:520–27.

Duncan, P., Harvey, P. H., and Wells, S. M. 1984. On lactation and associated behavior in a natural herd of horses. *Anim. Beh.* 32:255–63.

Duncan, P., and Vigne, N. 1979. The effect of group size in horses on the rates of attack by blood-sucking flies. *Anim. Beh.* 27:623–25.

Dunbar, R. I. M. 1980. Determinants and evolutionary consequences of dominance among female gelada baboons. *Beh. Ecol. Sociobiol.* 7:263–65.

Dunbar, R. I. M., and Dunbar, E. P. 1980. The pairbond in klipspringer. *Anim. Beh.* 28:219–29.

Dunn, W. C., and Douglas, C. L. 1982. Interactions between desert bighorn sheep and feral burros at spring areas in Death Valley. *Des. Bighorn Counc. Trans.* 26:87–96.

Durrant, S. D. 1952. Mammals of Utah. *Univ. Kansas Publ. Mus. Nat. Hist.* 6:1–549.

Dyrmundsson, O. R. 1973. Puberty and early reproductive performance in sheep, 1: Ewe lambs. *Anim. Breed Abstr.* 41:273–89.

Eberhardt, L. L.; Majorowicz, A. K.; and Wilcox, J. A. 1982. Apparent rates of increase for two feral horse herds. *J. Wildl. Mgmt.* 46:367–74.

Ebling, F. J., and Stoddart, D. M. 1978. *Population control by social behaviour.* London: Institute of Biology.

Edwards, R. Y. 1956. Snow depths and ungulate abundance in the mountains of western Canada. *J. Wildl. Mgmt.* 20:159–68.

Egoscue, H. 1975. Population dynamics of the kit fox in western Utah. *So. Calif. Acad. Sci. Bull.* 74:122–27.

Eisenberg, J. F. 1966. The social organizations of mammals. *Handb. Zool., Band 8, Lieferung* 39, 10:1–92.

———. 1981. *The mammalian radiations: An analysis of trends in evolution, adaptation, and behavior.* Chicago: University of Chicago Press.

Eisenberg, J. F., and Seidensticker, J. 1976. Ungulates in southern Asia: A consideration of biomass estimates for selected habitats. *Biol. Cons.* 10:293–308.

Ellison, L. 1960. Influence of grazing on plant succession on rangelands. *Bot. Rev.* 26:1–78.

Elton, C. S. 1957. *The ecology of invasions.* London: Methuen.

Emlen, S. T., and Oring, L. W. 1977. Ecology, sexual selection, and the evolution of mating systems. *Science* 197:215–23.

Endler, J. A. 1978. A predator's view of animal color patterns. *Evol. Biol.* 11:319–54.

Espmark, Y. 1971. Mother-young relationship and ontogeny of behaviour in reindeer (*Rangifer tarandus L.*). *Z. Tierpsychol.* 29:42–81.

Espmark, Y., and Langvatn, R. 1979. Lying down as a means of reducing fly harassment in red deer (*Cervus elaphus*). *Beh. Ecol. Sociobiol.* 5:51–54.

Estes, R. D. 1969. Territorial behavior of the wildebeest (*Connochaetes taurinus* Burchell, 1823). *Z. Tierpsychol.* 26:284–370.

———. 1976. The significance of breeding synchrony in the wildebeest. *E. Afr. Wildl. J.* 14:135–52.

Ewer, R. F. 1973. *The carnivores.* Ithaca: Cornell University Press.

Ewers, J. C. 1955 [1980]. *The horse in Blackfoot Indian culture.* Reprint. Washington, D.C.: Smithsonian Institution Press.

Fagen, R. 1981. *Animal play behavior.* New York: Oxford University Press.

Farr, J. A. 1980. The effects of sexual experience and female receptivity on courtship-rape decisions in male guppies, *Poecilia reticulata* (Pisces: Poeciladae). *Anim. Beh.* 28:1195–201.

Feist, J. D., and McCullough, D. R. 1975. Reproduction in feral horses. *J. Repro. Fert.*, suppl., 23:13–18.

———. 1976. Behavior patterns and communication in feral horses. *Z. Tierpsychol.* 41:337–73.

Fisher, R. F. 1930. *The genetical theory of natural selection.* Oxford: Clarendon Press.

Fisler, G. F. 1965. Adaptations and speciation in harvest mice of the marshes of San Francisco Bay. *Univ. Calif. Publ. Zool.* 77:1–108.

———. 1977. Interspecific hierarchy at an artificial food source. *Anim. Beh.* 25:240–44.

Foose, T. J., and Foose, E. 1983. Demographic and genetic status and management. In *Biology and management of an extinct species,* ed. B. B. Beck and C. M. Wemmer, pp. 133–86. Park Ridge, N.J.: Noyes Publications.

Ford, B., and Keiper, R. R. 1979. *The island ponies: An environmental study of their life on Assateague.* New York: William Morrow and Co.

Foster, J., and Coe, M. 1968. The biomass of game animals in Nairobi National Park, 1960–1966. *J. Zool. Lond.* 155:413–25.

Fowler, C. W., and Smith, T. D. 1981. *Dynamics of large mammal populations.* New York: John Wiley and Sons.

Foxcroft, G. R. 1980. Growth and breeding performance in animals and birds. In *Growth in animals,* ed. T. L. J. Lawrence, pp. 229–47. London: Butterworths.

Frame, L. H., and Frame, G. W. 1976. Female African wild dogs emigrate. *Nature* 263:227–29.

Franklin, W. L. 1983. Contrasting socioecologies of South America's wild camelids: The vicuna and guanaco. In *Advances in the study of mammalian behavior,* ed. J. F. Eisenberg and D. G. Kleiman, pp. 573–629. Special publication no. 7. Lawrence, Kans. American Society of Mammalogists.

Frémont, J. C. 1844. Personal journals. In *The expeditions of John Charles Frémont, vol. 1: Travels from 1838 to 1844,* ed. D. Jackson and M. L. Spence. Urbana: University of Illinois Press.

Fretwell, S. D. 1972. *Populations in a seasonal environment.* Princeton: Princeton University Press.

Fretwell, S. D., and Lucas, H. L. 1970. On territorial behaviour and other factors influencing habitat distribution in birds. *Acta Biotheoretica* 19:16–36.

Fritts, S. J. 1982. Wolf depredation on livestock in Minnesota. *U.S. Fish and Wildl. Serv. Res. Pub.* 145:1–11.

Gaines, M. S., and McClenaghan, L. R., Jr. 1980. Dispersal in small mammals. *Ann. Rev. Ecol. Syst.* 11:163–96.

Galton, F. 1871. Gregariousness in cattle and men. *Macmillan's Magazine, Lond.* 23:353. In *Sociobiology.* See Wilson 1975.

Gates, S. 1979. A study of home ranges of free-ranging Exmoor ponies. *Mamm. Rev.* 9:3–18.

Gazin, C. L. 1932. A Miocene mammalian fauna from southeastern Oregon. *Carnegie Inst. Contrib. Paleon.* 418:39–87.

———. 1936. A study of the fossil horse remains from the upper Pliocene of Idaho. *Proc. U.S. Nat. Mus.* 83:281–320.

Geddes, P., and Thompson, J. A. 1911. *Evolution.* New York: Henry Holt and Co.

Geist, V. 1966. The evolution of horn-like organs. *Behaviour* 27:175–214.

———. 1967. On fighting injuries and dermal shields of mountain goats. *J. Wildl. Mgmt.* 31:192–94.

———. 1971. *Mountain sheep* Chicago: University of Chicago Press.

———. 1974. On fighting strategies in animal combat. *Nature* 250:354.

———. 1978a. *Life strategies, human evolution, environmental design: Toward a biological theory of health.* New York: Springer-Verlag.

———. 1978b. On weapons, combat, and ecology. In *Aggression, dominance, and individual spacing,* ed. L. Krames, P. Plimer, and T. Alloway, pp. 1–30. New York: Plenum Press.

Geist, V., and Walther, F. 1974. *The behaviour of ungulates and its relation to management.* New series 24. Morges, Switzerland: IUCN Pub.

General studbook of South Africa. 1981. Johannesburg: Jockey Club.

Gibson, R. M., and Guinness, F. E. 1980. Differential reproductive success in red deer stags. *J. Anim. Ecol.* 49:199–208.

Gingerich, P. D. 1981. Variation, sexual dimorphism, and social structure in the early Eocene horse *Hyracotherium* (Mammalia, Perrissodactyla). *Paleobiology* 7:443–55.

Ginnett, T. F., and Douglas, C. L. 1982. Food habits of feral burros and desert bighorn sheep in Death Valley National Monument. *Des. Bighorn Counc. Trans.* 26:81–87.

Ginsberg, V., and Allee, W. C. 1942. Some effects of conditioning on social dominance and subordination in inbred strains of mice. *Phys. Zool.* 15:485–506.

Ginther, O. J. 1979. *Reproductive biology of the mare.* Ann Arbor: McNaughton and Gunn, Inc.

Ginther, O. J.; Whitmore, H. L.; and Squires, E. L. 1972. Characteristics of estrus, diestrus, and ovulation in mares and the effects of season and nursing. *Amer. J. Vet. Res.* 33:1935–39.

Golden, H. 1982. Bobcat populations and environmental relationships in northwestern Nevada. Master's thesis, University of Nevada, Reno.

Goodall, J. 1977. Infant killing and cannibalism in free-living chimpanzees. *Folia Primatol.* 28:259–82.

Gould, M. S., and Swingland, I. R. 1980. The tortoise and the goat: Interactions on Aldabra Island. *Biol. Cons.* 17:267–79.

Gould, S. J., and Lewontin, R. C. 1979. The spandrels of San Marco and the Panglossian paradigm: A critique of the adaptationist programme. *Proc. Roy. Soc. Lond.,* series B, 205:581–98.

Gouzoules, H.; Gouzoules, S.; and Fedigan, L. 1982. Behavioural dominance and reproductive success in female Japanese monkeys (*Macaca fuscata*). *Anim. Beh.* 30:1138–50.

Gowaty, P. A. 1982. Sexual terms in sociobiology: Emotionally evocative and paradoxically jargon. *Anim. Beh.* 30:630–31.

Grayson, D. K. 1977. Pleistocene avifaunas and the overkill hypothesis. *Science* 198:691–93.

———. 1982. Toward a history of Great Basin mammals during the past 15,000 years. In *Man and environment in the Great Basin,* ed. D. B. Madsen and J. F. O'Connell, pp. 82–101. Washington, D.C.: Society American Archaeologists.

Green, N. F., and Green, H. D. 1977. The wild horse population of Stone

Cabin Valley, Nevada: A preliminary report. *Proc. Nat. Wild Horse Forum* 1:59–65.

Greenwood, P. J. 1980. Mating systems, philopatry, and dispersal in birds and mammals. *Anim. Beh.* 28:1140–62.

Groves, C. P. 1974. *Horses, asses, and zebras in the wild.* Hollywood, Fla.: Curtis Books.

Groves, C. P., and Mazak, V. 1967. On some taxonomic problems of Asiatic wild asses, with the description of a new subspecies (Perissodactyla; Equidae). *Z. Sauget.* 32:3211–55.

Groves, C. P., and Willoughby, D. P. 1981. Studies on the taxonomy and phylogeny of the genus *Equus,* 1: Subgeneric classification of the recent species. *Mammalia* 45:321–54.

Grubb, P. 1974a. Population dynamics of Soay sheep. In *Island survivors: The ecology of the Soay sheep of St. Kilda,* ed. P. A. Jewell, C. Milner, and J. Morton-Boyd, pp. 242–72. London: Athlone Press.

———. 1974b. Social organization of the Soay sheep and the behaviour of ewes and lambs. In *Island survivors: The ecology of the Soay sheep of St. Kilda,* ed. P. A. Jewell, C. Milner, and J. Morton-Boyd, pp. 131–59. London: Athlone Press.

———. 1981. *Equus burchelli. Mamm. Sp.* 157:1–9.

Grubb, P., and Jewell, P. A. 1974. Movement, daily activity, and home range of Soay sheep. In *Island survivors: The ecology of the Soay sheep of St. Kilda,* ed. P. A. Jewell, C. Milner, and J. Morton-Boyd, pp. 160–94. London: Athlone Press.

Guinness, F. E.; Gibson, R. M.; and Clutton-Brock, T. M. 1978. Calving times in red deer (*Cervus elaphus*) on Rhum. *J. Zool. Lond.* 185:105–14.

Gunn, R. G. 1972. Growth and lifetime production of Scottish Blackface hill ewes in relation to the level of feeding during rearing. *Anim. Prod.* 14:343–49.

———. 1977. The effect of two nutritional environments from 6 weeks pre partum to 12 months of age on lifetime performance and reproductive potential of Scottish Blackface ewes in two adult environments. *Anim. Prod.* 25:155–64.

Gwynne, M. D.; and Bell, R. H. V. 1968. Selection of vegetation components by grazing ungulates in the Serengeti National Park. *Nature* 220:390–93.

Hackman, E.; Emanuel, I; van Belle, G.; and Daling, J. 1983. Maternal birth weight and subsequent pregnancy outcome. *J. Amer. Med. Assoc.* 250:2016–20.

Hafez, E. S. E. 1980. Horses. In *Reproduction in farm animals,* ed. E. S. E. Hafez, pp. 387–408. Philadelphia: Lea and Febinger.

Haines, F. 1938. The northward spread of horses among the Plain's Indians. *Amer. Anthrop.* 3:424–37.

Hall, E. R. 1946. *Mammals of Nevada.* Berkeley: University of California Press.

Hamilton, J. B.; Hamilton, R. S.; and Mestler, G. E. 1969. Duration of life and causes of death in domestic cats: Influence of sex, gonadectomy, and inbreeding. *J. Gerontol.* 24:427–37.

Hamilton, J. B., and Mestler, G. E. 1969. Mortality and survival: Comparison of eunuchs with intact men and women in a mentally retarded population. *J. Gerontol.* 24:395–411.

Hamilton, W. D. 1964. The genetical evolution of social behaviour. *J. Theor. Biol.* 7:1–52.

―――. 1971. Geometry for the selfish herd. *J. Theor. Biol.* 31:295–311.

―――. 1979. Wingless and fighting males in fig wasps and in other insects. In *Sexual selection and reproductive competition in insects,* ed. M. S. Blum and N. A. Blum, pp. 167–220. New York: Academic Press.

Hamilton, W. J., III. 1973. *Life's color code.* New York: McGraw-Hill.

Hamilton, W. J., III.; Buskirk, R.; and Buskirk, W. H. 1977. Intersexual dominance and differential mortality of gemsbok, *Oryx gazella,* at Namib Desert waterholes. *Madoqua* 10:5–19.

Hanks, J. 1981. Characterization of population condition. In *Dynamics of large mammal populations,* ed. C. W. Fowler and T. D. Smith, pp. 47–74. New York: John Wiley and Sons.

Hanley, T. A., and Hanley, K. A. 1982. Food resource partitioning by sympatric ungulates on Great Basin rangeland. *J. Range Mgmt.* 35:152–58.

Hansen, R. M., and Clark, R. C. 1977. Foods of elk and other ungulates at low elevations in northwestern Colorado. *J. Wildl. Mgmt.* 41:76–80.

Harcourt, A. H. 1978. Strategies of emigration and transfer by primates with particular reference to gorillas. *Z. Tierpsychol.* 48:401–20.

Hartthorn, A. M., and Young, E. 1974. A relationship between acid-base balance and capture myopathy in zebra (*Equus burchelli*) and an apparent therapy. *Vet. Rec.* 95:337–42.

―――. 1976. Pulmonary hypertension in relation to acidaemia after maximum forced exercise in zebra and wildebeest. *J. So. African Vet. Assoc.* 47:187–89.

Harvey, P. H.; Kavanah, M. J.; and Clutton-Brock, T. H. 1978. Sexual dimorphism in primate teeth. *J. Zool.* 186:475–86.

Heady, H. F., and Bartolome, J. 1977. *The Vale rangeland rehabilitation program: The desert repaired in southeastern Oregon.* USDA For. Serv. Resource Bull. PNW-70. Washington, D.C.: Government Printing Office.

Hebert, D. M. 1973. Altitudinal migration as a factor in the nutrition of bighorn sheep. Ph.D. diss., University of British Columbia.

Helle, T., and Aspi, J. 1984. Do sandy patches help reindeer against insects. *Rep. Kevo Subarctic Res. Sta.* 19:57–62.

Helle, T., and Tarvainen, L. 1984. Effects of insect harassment on weight gain and survival in reindeer calves. *Rangifer* 4:24–27.

Hermann, F. J. 1966. Notes on western range forbs: Cruciferae through Compositae. U.S. Dept. of Agriculture Handbook no. 293. Washington, D.C.: Government Printing Office.

Herrenkohl, L. R. 1979. Prenatal stress reduces fertility and fecundity in female offspring. *Science* 206:1097–99.

Hewitt, G. B. 1977. *Review of forage losses caused by rangeland grasshoppers.* USDA Misc. Pub. no. 1348. Washington, D.C.: Government Printing Office.

Hillman, J. C., and Hillman, A. K. K. 1977. Mortality of wildlife in Nairobi National Park during the drought of 1973–1974. *E. Afr. Wildl. J.* 15:1–18.

Hintz, H. F. 1977. Problems associated with feeding. In *The horse,* ed. J. W. Evans, A. Borton, H. F. Hintz, and L. D. van Vleck, pp. 330–47. San Francisco: W. H. Freeman and Co.

Hintz, H. F.; Hintz, R. L.; and van Vleck. 1979. Growth rate of thoroughbreds. Effects of age of dam, year, and month of birth, and sex of foal. *J. Anim. Sci.* 48:480–87.

Hintz, H. F.; Roberts, S. J.; Sabin, S. W.; and Schryver, H. F. 1971. Energy requirements of light horses for various activities. *J. Anim. Sci.* 32:100–102.

Hoeck, H. N. 1982. Population dynamics, dispersal, and genetic isolation in two species of hyrax (*Heterohyrax brucei* and *Procavia johnstoni*) on habitat islands in the Serengeti. *Z. Tierpsychol.* 59:177–210.

———. 1984. Introduced fauna and conservation policy. In *Key environments: Galapagos Volume,* ed. J. E. Treherne, pp. 233–45. Oxford: Pergamon Press.

Hoefs, M., and Cowan, I. M. 1979. Ecological investigation of a population of Dall sheep (*Ovis dalli dalli Nelson*). *Syesis,* suppl., 1:1–81.

Hoffman, R. 1983. Social organization of several feral horse and feral ass populations in central Australia. *Z. Sauget.* 48:124–26.

Hogg, J. T. 1984. Mating behavior in Rock Mountain bighorn sheep: Male and female strategies in reproduction. Ph.D. diss, University of Montana.

Holecheck, J. L. 1981. Livestock grazing impact on public lands: A viewpoint. *J. Range Mgmt.* 34:251–54.

Holmes, W. G., and Sherman, P. W. 1983. Kin recognition in animals. *Amer. Scientist* 71:46–54.

Hoogland, J. L., and Foltz, D. W. 1982. Variance in male and female reproductive success in a harem-polygynous mammal, the black-tailed prairie dog (Sciuridae: *Cynomys ludovicianus*). *Beh. Ecol. Sociobiol.* 11:155–63.

Hopwood, A. T. 1936. The former distribution of caballine and zebrine horses in Europe and Asia. *Proc. Zool. Soc. Lond.* 109:897–912.

Houghton, J. G.; Sakamoto, C. M.; and Gifford, R. O. 1975. Nevada's weather and climate. *Nev. Bur. Mines Geol. Spec. Publ.* 2:1–78.

Houpt, K. A., and Keiper, R. R. 1982. The position of the stallion in the equine dominance hierarchy of feral and domestic ponies. *J. Anim. Sci.* 54:945–50.

Houpt, K. A.; Law, K.; and Martinisi, V. 1978. Dominance hierarchies in domestic horses. *Appl. Anim. Ethol.* 4:273–83.

Houpt, K. A., and Wolski, T. R. 1980. Stability of equine hierarchies and the prevention of dominance related aggression. *Equine Vet. J.* 12:18–24.

———. 1982. *Domestic animal behavior for veterinarians and animal scientists.* Ames: Iowa State University Press.

Houston, D. B. 1971. Ecosystems of national parks. *Science.* 192:648–51.

———. 1982. *The northern Yellowstone elk: Ecology and management.* New York: Macmillan Publishing.

Howard, R. D. 1979. Estimating reproductive success in natural populations. *Amer. Nat.* 114:221–31.

Howard, W. E. 1960. Innate and environmental dispersal of individual vertebrates. *Amer. Midl. Nat.* 63:152–61.

Howell, C. E., and Rollins, W. C. 1951. Environmental sources of variation in the gestation length of the horse. *J. Anim. Sci.* 10:788–96.

Hoyt, D. F., and Taylor, C. R. 1981. Gait and the energetics of locomotion in horses. *Nature* 292:239–40.

Hrdy, S. B. 1977. *The langurs of Abu: Female and male strategies of reproduction.* Cambridge: Harvard University Press.

———. 1979. Infanticide among animals: A review, classification, and examination of the implications for the reproductive strategies of females. *Ethol. Sociobiol.* 1:13–40.

———. 1981. *The woman that never evolved.* Cambridge: Harvard University Press.

Hubbard, R. E., ahd Hansen, R. M. 1976. Diets of wild horses, cattle, and mule deer in the Piceance Basin, Colorado. *J. Range Mgmt.* 29:389–92.

Huey, R., and Slatkin, M. 1976. Costs and benefits of lizard thermoregulation. *Quart. Rev. Biol.* 51:363–84.

Hughes, R. D.; Duncan, P.; and Dawson, J. 1981. Interactions between Camargue horses and horseflies (Diptera: Tabanidae). *Bull. Ent. Res.* 71:227–42.

Hunter, G. N., and Kinghorn, R. G. 1950. Mountain sheep drive mule deer from food. *J. Mammal.* 31:193

Hutchinson, G. E. 1957. Concluding remarks. *Cold Springs Harbor Symp. Quant. Biol.* 22:415–27.

IUCN–Survival Service Commission. 1982. Guidelines for the development of a captive management and re-introduction plan for *Equus przewalski.* Minnesota Zoological Gardens, Apple Valley. Typescript.

Janis, C. 1976. The evolutionary strategy of the Equidae and the origins of rumen and cecal digestion. *Evolution* 30:757–74.

———. 1982. Evolution of horns in ungulates: Ecology and paleoecology. *Biol. Rev.* 57:261–318.

Jarman, P. J. 1972. The development of a dermal shield in impala. *J. Zool. Lond.* 166:349–56.

———. 1974. The social organization of antelope in relation to their ecology. *Behaviour* 48:215–67.

Jarman, P. J., and Jarman, M. V. 1973. Social behaviour, population structure, and reproduction in impala. *E. Afr. Wildl. J.* 11:329–38.

Jenkins, R. E., and Bedford, W. B. 1973. The use of natural areas to establish environmental baselines. *Biol. Cons.* 5:168–74.

Jewell, P. A., and Grubb, P. 1974. The breeding cycle, the onset of oestrus and conception in Soay sheep. In *Island survivors*, ed. P. A. Jewell, C. Milner, and J. Morton-Boyd, pp. 224–42. London: Athlone Press.

Jewell, P. A.; Holt, S; and Hart, D., eds. 1981. *Problems in management of locally abundant wild mammals.* New York: Academic Press.

Jewell, P. A.; Milner, C.; and Morton-Boyd, J., eds. 1974. *Island survivors: The ecology of the Soay sheep of St. Kilda.* London: Athlone Press.

Jones, W. E., and Bogart, R. 1971. *Genetics of the horse.* Ann Arbor: Edwards Brothers.

Joubert, E. 1972. The social organization and associated behaviour in the Hartmann zebra *Equus zebra hartmannae. Madoqua,* series 1, 6:17–56.

———. 1974a. Composition and limiting factors of a Khomas Hochland population of Hartmann zebra, *Equus zebra hartmannae. Madoqua* 8:49–53.

———. 1974b. Notes on the reproduction in Hartmann zebra, *Equus zebra hartmannae,* in South West Africa. *Madoqua* 8:31–35.

Judd, B. I. 1962. Principle forage plants of southwestern ranges. Rocky Mountain Forest Range Experiment Station, no. 69. Ft. Collins: Colorado State University.

Kantrud, H. A. 1981. Grazing intensity effects on the breeding avifauna of North Dakota native grasslands. *Can. Field Nat.* 95:404–17.

Kaseda, Y. 1981. The structure of the groups of Misaki horses in Toi Cape. *Jpn. J. Zootech. Sci.* 52:227–35.

———. 1983a. Seasonal changes in time spent grazing and resting of Misaki horses. *Jpn. J. Zootech. Sci.* 54:464–69.

———. 1983b. Seasonal variations in heart rate and body temperature of Misaki horses. *Proc. 5th World Conf. Anim. Prod., Tokyo* 2:765–67.

Kaseda, Y., Nozawa, K. and Mogi, K. 1982. Sire-foal relationships between harem stallions and foals in Misaki horses. *Jpn. J. Zootech. Sci.* 53:822–30.

Keast, A. 1965. Interrelationships of two zebra species in an overlap zone. *J. Mammal.* 46:53–66.

Keiper, R. R. 1976. Social organization of feral ponies. *Proc. Pa. Acad. Sci.* 50:89–90.

———. 1979. Population dynamics of feral ponies. In *Symposium on the ecology and behavior of wild and feral equids,* ed. R. H. Denniston, pp. 175–84. Laramie: University of Wyoming.

Keiper, R. R., and Berger, J. 1982. Refuge-seeking and pest avoidance by feral horses in desert and island environments. *Appl. Anim. Ethol.* 9:111–20.

Keiper, R. R., and Houpt, K. 1984. Reproduction in feral horses: An eight-year study. *Amer. J. Vet. Res.* 45:991–95.

Keiper, R. R., and Keenan, M. A. 1980. Nocturnal activity patterns of feral ponies. *J. Mammal.* 66:116–18.

Keiper, R. R.; Moss, M. B.; and Zervanos, S. M. 1980. Daily and seasonal patterns of feral ponies on Assateague Island. *Conf. Sci. Res. in Nat. Parks* 8:369–81.

Kelsall, J. P. 1968. *The caribou.* Ottawa: Queen's Printers.

Kiltie, R. A. 1982. Intraspecific variation in the mammalian gestation period. *J. Mammal.* 63:646–52.

―――. 1985. Evolution and function of horns and hornlike organs in female ungulates. *Biol. J. Linnean Soc.* 24:299–320.

King, J. M. 1965. A field guide to the reproduction of the Grant's zebra and Grevy's zebra. *E. Afr. Wildl. J.* 3:99–117.

Kingdon, J. 1979. *East African mammals, vol. 3 (B): Large mammals.* London: Academic Press.

Kirkpatrick, J. F., and Turner, Jr., J. W. 1983. Seasonal ovarian function in feral mares. *J. Equine Vet. Sci.* 3:43–48.

Kitchen, D. W. 1974. Social behavior and ecology of the pronghorn. *Wildl. Monog.* 38:1–96.

Klecka, W. R. 1975. Discriminant analysis. In *Statistical package for the social sciences,* ed. C. H. Nie et al., pp. 434–67. New York: McGraw-Hill.

Kleiman, D. G. 1977. Monogamy in mammals. *Quart. Rev. Biol.* 52:39–69.

Kleiman, D. G., and Malcolm, J. R. 1981. The evolution of male parental investment in mammals. In *Parental care in mammals,* ed. D. J. Gubernick and P. H. Klopfer, pp. 347–87. New York: Plenum Press.

Klein, D. R. 1962. Rumen contents analysis as an index to range quality. *Trans. No. Amer. Wildl. Conf.,* 27:150–64.

―――. 1968. The introduction, increase, and crash of reindeer on St. Mathew Island. *J. Wildl. Mgmt.* 32:350–67.

Klimov, V. V., and Orlov, V. N. 1982. Present state and problems of conservation of *Equus przewalski. Soviet J. Zool.* 61:1862–69.

Klingel, H. 1967. Soziale organisation und verhalten freilbender steppenzebras (*Equus quagga*). *Z. Tierpsychol.* 24:580–624.

―――. 1968. Soziale organisation und verhaltensweisen von Hartmann– und Bergzebras (*Equus zebra hartmannae* und *E. z. zebra*). *Z. Tierpsychol.* 25:76–88.

―――. 1969a. The social organisation and population ecology of the Plain's zebra (*Equus quagga*). *Zool. Afr.* 4:249–63.

―――. 1969b. Social organization and reproduction in the Plain's zebra, *Equus burchelli boehmi:* Behavioral and ecological factors. *J. Repro. Fert.,* suppl., 6:339–45.

―――. 1972. Social behaviour of African Equidae. *Zool. Afr.* 7:175–85.

―――. 1975. Social organization and reproduction in equids. *J. Repro. Fert.,* suppl., 23:7–11.

―――. 1977. Observations on social organization and behaviour of African and Asiatic wild asses (*Equus africanus* and *E. hemionus*). *Z. Tierpsychol.* 44:323–31.

Kownacki, M. 1980. The primitive horses of Poland. *Wildlife* 22:38–41.

Krebs, C. J.; Gaines, M. S.; Keller, B. L.; Myers, J. H.; and Tamarin, R. H. 1973. Population cycles in small rodents. *Science* 179:35–41.

Krebs, J. R. 1970. Regulation of numbers in the Great Tit (Aves: Passeriformes). *J. Zool., London.* 162:317–33.

Krebs, J. R., and Davies, N. B. 1982. *An introduction to behavioural ecology.* Sunderland, Mass.: Sinauer Assoc.

Krebs, J. R., and Perrins, C. 1978. Behaviour and population regulation in the Great tit (*Parus major*). In *Population control by social behaviour,* ed. F. J. Ebling and D. M. Stoddart, pp. 23–47. London: Symposium Institute Biology

Kruuk, H. 1972. *The spotted hyena: A Study of predation and social behavior.* Chicago: University of Chicago Press.

Kummer, H. 1968. *Social organization of hamadryas baboons.* Chicago: University of Chicago Press.

Kurten, B. 1968. *Pleistocene mammals of Europe.* London: Weidenfeld and Nicolson.

Labov, J. B. 1981. Pregnancy blocking in rodents: Adaptive advantages for females. *Amer. Nat.* 118:361–71.

Lacey, J. R., and van Poollen, H. W. 1981. Comparison of herbage production on moderately grazed and ungrazed Western ranges. *J. Range Mgmt.* 34:210–12.

Laing, J. A. 1979. Normal fertility and incidence of infertility. In *Fertility and infertility in domestic animals,* 3d ed., ed. J. A. Laing, pp. 1–4. London: Bailliere Tindall.

Lasley, J. F. 1978. *Genetics of livestock improvement.* Englewood Cliffs, N.J.: Prentice-Hall.

Laws, R. M., and Parker, I. S. C. 1968. Recent studies on elephant populations in East Africa. *Symp. Zool. Soc. Lond.* 21:319–59.

Laws, R. M.; Parker, I. S. C.; and Johnstone, R. C. B. 1975. *Elephants and their habitats.* London: Oxford University Press.

Laycock, W. A. 1967. How heavy grazing and protection affect sagebrush-grass ranges. *J. Range Mgmt.* 20:206–13.

Leader-Williams, N. 1980. Population dynamics and mortality of reindeer introduced into South Georgia. *J. Wildl. Mgmt.* 44:640–57.

LeBoeuf, B. J. 1974. Male-male competition and reproductive success in elephant seals. *Amer. Zool.* 14:167–95.

Lenarz, M. S. 1979. Social structure and reproductive strategy in desert bighorn sheep (*Ovis canadensis mexicana*). *J. Mammal.* 60:671–78.

Lent, P. C. 1974. Mother-infant relationships in ungulates. In *The behaviour of ungulates and its relation to management,* ed. V. Geist and F. Walther, pp. 14–55. Morges, Switzerland: IUCN.

Leopold, A. 1949. *A sand county almanac.* New York: Oxford University Press.

Leutenegger, W., and Kelley, J. T. 1977. Relationship of sexual dimorphism in canine size and body size to social, behavioural, and ecological correlates in anthropoid primates. *Primates* 18:117–36.

Leuthold, W. 1977. *African ungulates: A comparative review of their ethology and behavioral ecology.* Berlin: Springer-Verlag.

Licklichter, R. E. 1984. Hiding behavior in domestic goat kids. *Appl. Anim. Ethol.* 12:245–51.

Linzell, J. L. 1972. Milk yield, energy loss in milk, and mammary gland weight in different species. *Dairy Sci. Abstr.* 34:351–60.

Lipetz, V. E., and Bekoff, M. 1982. Group size and vigilance in pronghorns. *Z. Tierpsycol.* 58:203–16.

Lloyd, P. H., and Harper, D. A. 1980. A case of adoption and rejection of foals in Cape Mountain zebra, *Equus zebra zebra. So. Afr. J. Wildl. Res.* 10:61–62.

Longhurst, W. A.; Garton, E. O.; Heady, H. F.; and Connolly, G. E. 1976. The California deer decline and possibilities for restoration. *Cal-Neva Wild. Trans.* 1976:74–103.

Longhurst, W. A.; Leopold, A. S.; and Dasmann, R. F. 1952. A survey of California deer herds, their ranges, and management problems. *Calif. Dept. Fish Game Bull.* 6:1–136.

Lott, D. F. 1979. Dominance relations and breeding rate in mature male bison. *Z. Tierpsychol.* 49:418–32.

MacArthur, R. H., and Wilson, E. O. 1967. *The theory of island biogeography.* Princeton: Princeton University Press.

McCort, W. D. 1979. The feral asses (*Equus asinus*) of Ossabau Island, Georgia: Mating system and the effect of vasectomies as a population control procedure. In *Symposium on the ecology and behavior of wild and feral equids,* ed. R. H. Denniston, pp. 71–83. Laramie: University of Wyoming.

———. 1980. The behavior and social organization of feral asses (*Equus asinus*) on Ossabaw Island, Georgia. Ph.D. diss., Pennsylvania State, University Park.

McCracken, G. F. 1984. Communal nursing in Mexican free-tailed bat maternity colonies. *Science* 223:1090–91.

McCracken, G. F., and Bradbury, J. W. 1981. Social organization and kinship in the polygynous bat *Phyllostomus hastatus. Beh. Ecol. Sociobiol.* 8:11–34.

McCullough, D. R. 1964. Relationship of weather to migratory movements of black-tailed deer. *Ecology* 45:249–64.

———. 1969. The tule elk: Its history, behavior, and ecology. *Univ. Calif. Publ. Zool.* 88:1–191.

———. 1979. *The George River deer herd: Population ecology of a K-selected species.* Ann Arbor: University of Michigan Press.

McCullough, Y. B. 1980. Niche separation of seven North American ungulates on the National Bison Range, Montana. PhD diss., University of Michigan, Ann Arbor.

Mack, R. N., and Thompson, J. N. 1982. Evolution in steppe with few large, hooved mammals. *Amer. Nat.* 119:757–73.

Mackie, R. J. 1976. Interspecific competition between mule deer, other big game animals, and livestock. In *Mule deer decline in the West: a symposium,* pp. 49–54. Logan: Utah State University.

McKinney, F.; Derrickson, S. R.; and Mineau, P. 1983. Forced copulation in waterfowl. *Behaviour* 86:250–94.

McKnight, T. 1959. The feral horse in Anglo-America. *Geog. Rev.* 49:506–25.

————. 1976. Friendly vermin: A survey of feral livestock in Australia. *Univ. Calif. Publ. Geography* 21:1–104.

McNab, B. K. 1963. Bioenergetics and the determination of home range size. *Amer. Nat.* 97:133–40.

McQuivey, R. P. 1978. The desert bighorn sheep of Nevada. Nevada Dept. of Fish and Game, Reno. *Biol. Bull.* 6:1–81.

Mahaffey, L. W. 1968. Abortion in mares, *Vet Rec.* 84:681–89.

Malcolm, J. R., and Marten, K. 1982. Natural selection and the communal rearing of pups in African wild dogs (*Lycaon pictus*). *Beh. Ecol. Sociobiol.* 10:1–13.

Malcolm, J. R., and van Lawick, H. 1975. Notes on wild dogs (*Lycaon predation*) hunting zebras. *Mammalia* 39:231–40.

Malthus, T. R. 1798. *An essay on the principle of population.* Reprint. New York: Macmillan Press.

Manski, D. A. 1978. Reproductive behavior of addax antelope. M.S. thesis, Texas A & M University.

————. 1982. Herding of and sexual advances toward females in late stages of pregnancy in addax antelope, *Addax nasomaculatus. Zool. Garten. N. E., Jena* 52:106–12.

Martin, L. D., and Neuner, A. M. 1978. The end of the Pleistocene in North America. *Trans. Neb. Acad. Sci.* 6:117–26.

Martin, P. S. 1967. Prehistoric overkill. In *Pleistocene extinctions: The search for a cause,* ed. P. S. Martin and H. E. Wright, Jr., pp. 75–120. New Haven: Yale University Press.

Martin, P. S., and Guilday, J. E. 1967. A bestiary for Pleistocene biologists. In *Pleistocene extinctions: The search for a cause,* ed. P. S. Martin and H. E. Wright, Jr., pp. 1–62. New Haven: Yale University Press.

Martin, P. S., and Wright, H. E., Jr. 1967. *Pleistocene extinctions: The search for a cause.* New Haven: Yale University Press.

Mathews, D. K., and Fox, E. L. 1976. *The physiological basis of physical education and athletics.* Philadelphia: W. B. Saunders Co.

Maynard Smith, J. 1958. *The theory of evolution.* Harmondsworth, England: Penguin.

————. 1976. Evolution and the theory of games. *Amer. Scientist* 64:41–45.

————. 1978. *The evolution of sex.* Cambridge: Cambridge University Press.

Maynard Smith, J., and Price, G. R. 1973. The logic of animal conflict. *Nature* 246:15–18.

Mayr, E. 1982. *The growth of biological thought*. Cambridge: Harvard University Press.

Meeker, J. O. 1979. Interactions between pronghorn antelope and feral horses in northwestern Nevada. Master's thesis, University of Nevada, Reno.

Menke, J. W., ed. 1983. *Proceedings of the workshop on livestock and wildlife-fisheries relationship in the Great Basin*. Agricultural Sciences Publications, no. 3301. Berkeley: University of California.

Mentis, M. T. 1970. Estimates of natural biomasses of large herbivores in the Umfoloze Game Reserve area. *Mammalia* 34:363–93.

Merriam, C. H. 1925. The buffalo in northeastern California. *J. Mammal.* 7:211–14.

Merrick, P. E. 1979. A study of the Truman Meadows and White Mountain wild horse populations of California and Nevada. U.S. Forest Service, Bishop, Calif. Typescript.

Messier, F., and Crête, M. 1984. Body condition and population regulation by food resources in moose. *Oecologia* 65:44–50.

———. 1985. Moose-wolf dynamics and the natural regulation of moose populations. *Oecologia* 65:503–12.

Michener, G. R. 1979. Spatial relationships and social organization of adult Richardson's ground squirrels. *Can. J. Zool.* 57:125–39.

———. 1980. Differential reproduction among female Richardson's ground squirrels and its relation to sex ratio. *Beh. Ecol. Sociobiol.* 7:173–78.

Mifflin, M. D., and Wheat, M. W. 1979. Pluvial lakes and estimated pluvial climates of Nevada. *Nev. Bur. Mines Geol. Bull.* 94:1–57.

Milagres, J. C.; Dillard, E. U.; and Robison, O. W. 1979. Influences of age and early growth on reproductive performance of yearling Hereford heifers. *J. Anim. Sci.* 48:1089–95.

Miller, E. H. 1975. Walrus ethology, 1: The social use of tusks and applications of multidimensional scaling. *Can. J. Zool.* 53:590–613.

Miller, R. 1981. Male aggression, dominance, and breeding behavior in Red Desert feral horses. *Z. Tierpsychol.* 57:340–51.

Miller, R., and Denniston, R. H., II. 1979. Interband dominance in feral horses. *Z. Tierpsychol.* 51:41–47.

Milner, J., and Hewitt, D. 1969. Weight of horses: Improved estimates based on girth and length. *Can. Vet. J.* 10:314–16.

Mitchell, B., and Brown, D. 1974. The effects of age and body size on fertility in female red deer (*Cervus elaphus*. L.). *Int. Cong. Game Biol.* 11:89–98.

Mitchell, B.; McCowan, D.; and Nicholson, I. A. 1976. Annual cycles of body weight and condition in Scottish red deer, *Cervus elaphus*. *J. Zool Lond.* 180:107–27.

Mitchell, B. L.; Skenton, J. B.; and Uys, J. C. M. 1965. Predation on large mammals in the Kafue National Park, Zambia. *Zool. Afr.* 1:297–318.

Mitchell, D., and Allen, W. R. 1975. Observations on reproductive performance in the yearling mare. *J. Repro. Fert.* 23:531–36.

Moberg, R. 1975. The occurrence of early embryonic death in the mare in relation to natural service and artificial insemination with fresh or deep-frozen semen. *J. Reprod. Fert.*, suppl., 23:537–39.

Moehlman, P. 1974. Behavior and ecology of feral asses (*Equus asinus*). Ph.D. diss., University of Wisconsin, Madison.

Moen, A. N. 1973. *Wildlife ecology.* San Francisco: W.H. Freeman and Co.

———. 1978. Seasonal changes in heart rates, activity metabolism, and forage intake of white-tailed deer. *J. Wildl. Mgmt.* 42:715–38.

Mohr, E. 1971. *The Asiatic wild horse.* London: Allen and Co.

Moismann, J. E., and Martin, P. S. 1975. Simulating overkill by paleo-Indians. *Amer Scientist* 63:304–13.

Monfort, A., and Monfort, N. 1978. Structure and repartition des populations de zèbres (*Equus burchelli*) du Parc de l'Akagera (Rwanda). *Mammalia* 42:315–22.

Moore, J., and Ali, R. 1984. Are dispersal and inbreeding avoidance related? *Anim. Beh.* 32:94–112.

Mooser, O., and Dalquest, W. W. 1975. Pleistocene mammals from Aquascalientes, Central Mexico. *J. Mammal.* 56:781–820.

Morris, W. 1981. *The American college dictionary of the English language.* Boston: Houghton Mifflin.

Morrison, D. W., and Morrison, S. H. 1980. Economics of harem maintenance by a neotropical bat. *Ecology* 62:864–65.

Moss, R.; Watson, A.; and Parr, R. 1975. Maternal nutrition and breeding success in red grouse (*Lagopus lagopus scoticus*). *J. Anim. Ecol.* 44:233–44.

Mueggler, W. F., and Stewart, W. L. 1980. Grassland and shrub habitat types of western Montana: App. no. 4, palatability ratings. U.S. Dept. of Agriculture Forest Service General Technical Report. INT-66.

Muir, J. 1878. *Steep trails.* Ed. W. P. Bade. New York: Houghton Mifflin.

———. 1911. *My summer in the Sierra.* New York: Houghton Mifflin.

Munro, J. 1962. A study of the milk yield of three strains of Scottish Blackface ewes in two environments. *Anim. Prod.* 4:203–13.

Murie, A. 1944. *The wolves of Mount McKinley.* U.S. National Park Service Series, no. 5. Washington, D.C.: Government Printing Office.

Murie, J. O., and Michener, G. R. 1984. *The biology of ground-dwelling scivrids.* Lincoln: University of Nebraska Press.

Murray, M. G. 1982. The rut of impala: Aspects of seasonal mating under tropical conditions. *Z. Tierpsychol.* 59: 319–37.

National Research Council. 1978. *Nutrient requirements of horses.* Washington, D.C.: National Academy of Sciences.

———. 1980. *Wild and free-roaming horses and burros: Current knowledge and recommended research, phase 1: Final report.* Washington, D.C.: National Academy Press.

———. 1982. *Wild and free-roaming horses and burros: Final report.* Washington, D.C.: National Academy Press.

Nawa, R. 1978. Foods of wild horses, deer, and cattle in the Granite Range,

Nevada. Bureau of Land Management, Elko district, Nevada. Typescript.

Neal, D. L. 1982. Improvement of Great Basin deer winter range with livestock grazing. *In Wildlife-livestock relationships symposium,* ed. J. M. Peek and P. D. Dalke, pp. 61–73. Proc. 10, University of Idaho Experiment Station.

Nelson, K. J. 1980. Sterilization of dominant males will not limit feral horse populations. USDA Forest Service Research Paper RM-226.

Newsome, A. E. 1965. The distribution of red kangaroos, *Megaleia rufa* (Desmarest), about sources of food and water in central Australia. *Austr. J. Zool.* 13:289–99.

————. 1975. An ecological comparison of the two arid zone kangaroos of Australia, and their anomalous prosperity since the introduction of ruminant stock to their environment. *Quart Rev. Biol.* 50:389–424.

Nichols, M. W. 1939. The Spanish horse of the Pampas. *Amer. Anthrop.* 41:119–29.

Nicholson, A. J. 1957. The self-adjustment of populations to change. *Cold Springs Harbor Symp. Quant. Biol.* 22:153–73.

Nishikawa, Y. 1959. *Studies on reproduction in horses.* (English translation). Tokyo: Japan Racing Assoc.

Nishikawa, Y., and Hafez, E. S. E. 1974. Horses. In *Reproduction in farm animals,* ed. E. S. E. Hafez, pp. 288–300. Philadelphia: Lea and Febinger.

Norment, C., and Douglas, C. C. 1977. Ecological studies of feral burros in Death Valley. University of Nevada Cooperative National Park Research Studies Unit Contribution 17.

O'Brien, P. H. 1983. Feral goat parturition and lying out sites: Spatial, physical, and meteorological characteristics. *Appl. Anim. Ethol.* 10:325–39.

Oftedal, O. T; Hintz, H. F.; and Schryver, H. F. 1983. Lactation in the horse: Milk composition and intake by foals. *J. Nutr.* 113:2196–206.

O'Gara, B. W. 1969. Unique aspects of reproduction in the female pronghorn (*Antilocapra americana* Ord). *Amer. J. Anat.* 125:217–32.

Olsen, F. W., and Hansen, R. M. 1977. Food relations of wild free-roaming horses to livestock and big game, Red Desert, Wyoming. *J. Range Mgmt.* 30:17–20.

Oosenberg, S. M., and Theberge J. B. 1980. Altitudinal movements and summer habitat preferences of woodland caribou in the Kluane Ranges, Yukon Territory. *Arctic* 33:59–72.

Orwell, G. 1946. *Animal farm.* New York: Harcourt, Brace, and Co.

Osborne, H. F. 1918. Equidae of the Oligocene, Miocene, and Pliocene of America. *Mem. Amer. Mus. Nat. Hist.,* new series, 2:1–330.

Owen-Smith, N. 1977. On territoriality in ungulates and an evolutionary model. *Quart Rev. Biol.* 52:1–38.

Ozoga, J. J.; Verme, L. J.; and Bienz, C. S. 1982. Parturition behavior and territoriality in white-tailed deer: Impact on neonatal mortality. *J. Wildl. Mgmt.* 46:1–11.

Packer, C. 1977. Reciprocal altruism in *Papio anubis*. *Nature* 265:441–43.

———. 1979. Inter-troop transfer and inbreeding avoidance in *Papio anubis*. *Anim. Beh.* 27:1–36.

Packer, C., and Pusey, A. E. 1982. Cooperation and competition within coalitions of male lions: Kin selection or game theory? *Nature* 296:740–42.

———. 1983. Adaptions of female lions to infanticide by incoming males. *Amer. Nat.* 121:91–113.

Papez, N. J. 1976. The Ruby Butte deer herd. Nevada Department Fish Game, Reno. *Biol. Bull.* 5:1–61.

Parker, G. A. 1974. Assessment strategy and the evolution of fighting behavior. *J. Theor. Biol.* 47:223–43.

Partridge, L., and Farquhar, M. 1981. Sexual activity reduces lifespan in male fruitflies. *Nature* 294:580–82.

Penzhorn, B. L. 1975. Behavior and population ecology of the Cape Mountain zebra, *Equus zebra zebra* L., 1758, in the Mountain Zebra National Park. Ph.D. diss., University of Pretoria.

———. 1979. Social organization of the Cape Mountain zebra, *Equus zebra zebra*, in the Mountain Zebra National Park. *Koedoe* 22:115–56.

———. 1982. Habitat selection by Cape Mountain zebras in the Mountain Zebra National Park. *So. Afr. J. Wildl. Res.* 12:48–54.

———. 1984. A long-term study of social organization and behaviour of Cape Mountain zebras *Equus zebra zebra*. *Z. Tierpsychol.* 64:97–146.

———. 1985. Reproductive characteristics of a free-ranging population of Cape Mountain zebra (*Equus zebra zebra*). *J. Repro. Fert.* 73:51–57.

Pereira, M. E. 1983. Abortion following the immigration of an adult male baboon (*Papio cynocephalus*). *Amer. J. Primatol.* 4:93–98.

Pfeifer, S. 1984. Effects of calf sex, cow parity, and cow age on suckling behavior of captive *Oryx dammah* calves. Typescript.

Pienaar, U. de V. 1969. Predator-prey relationships among the larger animals of Kruger National Park. *Koedoe* 112:108–76.

Pollock, J. I. 1980. *Behavioural ecology and body condition changes in New Forest ponies*. Horsham, Great Britain: RSPCA Scientific Publications.

Porter, R. H.; Wyrick, M.; and Pankey, J. 1978. Sibling recognition in spiny mice (*Acomys cabirinus*). *Beh. Ecol. Sociobiol.* 3:61–68.

Powell, J. W. 1879. *Report on the lands of the arid region of the United States*. Washington, D.C.: Government Printing Office.

Price, E. O. 1984. Behavioral aspects of animal domestication. *Quart. Rev. Biol.* 59:1–32.

Pusey, A. E. 1980. Inbreeding avoidance in chimpanzees. *Anim. Beh.* 28:543–52.

Pycraft, W. P. 1914. *The courtship of animals*. London: Hutchinson and Co.

Racey, P. A. 1973. Environmental factors affecting the length of gestation in heterothermic bats. *J. Repro. Fert.* 19:175–89.

Ralls, K. 1976. Mammals in which females are larger than males. *Quart. Rev. Biol.* 51:245–76.

Ralls, K.; Brownell, R. L., Jr.; and Ballou, J. 1980. Differential mortality by sex and age in mammals with specific reference to the sperm whale. *Rep. Int. Whal. Comm., Spec. Is.* 2:223–43.

Ralls, K.; Brugger, K.; and Ballou, J. 1979. Inbreeding and juvenile mortality in small populations of ungulates. *Science* 206:1101–3.

Randolph, P. A.; Randolph, J. C.; Mattingly, K.; and Foster, M. M. 1977. Energy costs of reproduction in the cotton rat, *Sigmodon hispidus. Ecology* 58:31–45.

Rathbun, G. B. 1979. The social structure and ecology of elephant-shrews. *Beihefte zur Z. Tierpsychol.* 20:1–77. Berlin: Verlag Paul Parey.

Reimers, E. 1983. Growth rate and body size differences in *Rangifer:* A study of causes and effects. *Rangifer* 3:3–15.

Reiner, R. J., and Urness, P. J. 1982. Effects of grazing horses managed as manipulators of big game winter range. *J. Range Mgmt.* 35:567–71.

Reiter, J.; Panken, K. J.; and LeBouef, B. J. 1981. Female competition and reproductive success in northern elephant seals. *Anim. Beh.* 29:670–87.

Reiter, J. R.; Stinson, N. L.; and LeBouef, B. J. 1978. Northern elephant seal development: The transition from weaning to nutritional independence. *Beh. Ecol. Sociobiol.* 3:337–67.

Retterer, T. E. 1977. *The Granite unit wildlife habitat plan: Final report.* Project W-48-7. Reno: Nevada Division of Wildlife.

Reynolds, H. G., and Packer, P. E. 1962. Effects of trampling on soil and vegetation. In *Range research methods,* pp. 116–22. USDA Miscellaneous Publication no. 940. Washington, D.C.: Government Printing Office.

Rice, B. and Westoby, H. 1978. Vegetation responses of some Great Basin shrub communities protected against jackrabbits or domestic stock. *J. Range Mgmt.* 31:28–34.

Ricklefs, R. E. 1974. Energetics of reproduction in birds. In *Avian energetics,* ed. R. A. Paynter, pp. 152–292. Cambridge: Nuttal Ornithology Club.

Riedman, M. L. 1982. The evolution of alloparental care and adoption in mammals. *Quart. Rev. Biol.* 57:405–35.

Riedman, M. L., and LeBoeuf, B. J. 1982. Mother-pup separation and adoption in Northern elephant seals. *Beh. Ecol. Sociobiol.* 11:203–15.

Riedman, M. L., and Ortiz, C. L. 1979. Changes in milk composition during lactation in the Northern elephant seal. *Physiol. Zool.* 52:240–49.

Robbins, C. T., and Moen, A. N. 1975. Milk consumption and weight gain of white-tailed deer. *J. Wildl. Mgmt.* 39:355–60.

Robbins, C. T., and Robbins, B. L. 1979. Fetal and neonatal growth patterns and maternal reproductive effort in ungulates and subungulates. *Amer. Nat.* 114:101–16.

Roberts, S. J. 1968. Equine abortion. In *Abortion diseases of livestock,* ed. L. C. Faulkner, pp. 158–79. Springfield, Ill.: C. C. Thomas.

Robertson, J. H., and Kennedy, P. B. 1954. Half-century changes on northern Nevada ranges. *J. Range Mgmt.* 7:117–21.

Robinette, L. W.; Gashwiler, J. S.; and Morris, O. W. 1959. Food habits of the cougar in Utah and Nevada. *J. Wildl. Mgmt.* 23:261–73.

Robinette, L. W.; Hancock, N. V.; and Jones, D. A. 1977. *The Oak Creek mule deer herd in Utah.* Publication no. 77–15; 1–148. Salt Lake: Utah State Division Wildlife Resources.

Rognmo, A., Markussen, K. A., Jacobsen, E., and Blix, A. S. 1982. Effects of high and low level nutrition of pregnant reindeer (*Rangifer tarandus tarandus*) on calf birth weight, growth, and mortality. *Third Int'l Theriological Cong.*, Helsinki, 1982. Abstr. 300.

Roe, F. G. 1955. *The Indian and the horse.* Norman: University of Oklahoma Press.

Rollins, W. C., and Howell, C. E. 1951. Genetic sources of variation of the horse. *J. Anim. Sci.* 10:797–806.

Romer, A. S. 1966. *Vertebrate paleontology.* 3d ed. Chicago: University of Chicago Press.

Rood, J. P. 1974. Banded mongoose males guard young. *Nature* 248:176.

———. 1978. Dwarf mongoose helpers at the den. *Z. Tierpsychol.* 48:277–88.

———. 1980. Mating relationships and breeding suppression in the dwarf mongoose. *Anim. Beh.* 28:143–50.

Roosevelt, T. 1885. *Hunting trips of a ranchman: Sketches of sport on the northern cattle plains.* New York: G. P. Putnam and Sons.

Ropiha, R. T.; Matthews, R. G; Butterfield, R. M.; Moss, F. P.; and McFadden, W. J. 1969. The duration of pregnancy in Thoroughbred mares. *Vet. Rec.* 84:552–55.

Rose, R. K., and Gaines, M. S. 1976. Levels of aggression in fluctuating populations of the prairie vole, *Microtis ochrogaster*, in eastern Kansas. *J. Mammal.* 57:43–57.

Rossdale, P. D. 1975. *The horse.* London: J. A. Allen and Co.

———. 1976. A clinician's view of prematurity and dysmaturity in Thoroughbred foals. *Proc. Roy. Soc. Med.* 69:27–28.

Rossdale, P. D., and Short, R. V. 1967. The time of foaling of Thoroughbred mares. *J. Repro. Fert.* 13:341–43.

Rowell, T. E. 1970. Baboon menstrual cycles affected by social environment. *J. Repro. Fert.* 21:133–41.

———. 1974. The concept of social dominance. *Beh. Biol.* 11:131–54.

Rubenstein, D. I. 1981. Behavioural ecology of island feral horses. *Equine Vet. J.* 13:27–34.

Rudnai, J. 1974. The pattern of lion predation in Nairobi National Park. *E. Afr. Wildl. J.* 12:213–25.

Rutberg, A. T. 1984. Competition and reproduction in American bison cows. Ph.D. diss., University of Washington.

Ryden, H. 1970. *America's last wild horses.* New York: Ballantine Books.

Ryder, O. A. 1978. Chromosomal polymorphism in *Equus hemionus. Cytogenet. Cell Genet.* 21:177–83.

Ryder, O. A.; Epel, N. C.; and Benirshke, K. 1978. Chromosome banding studies of the Equidae. *Cytogenet. Cell Genet.* 20:323–50.

Ryder, O. A., and Wedemeyer, E. A. 1982. A cooperative breeding programme for the Mongolian wild horse, *Equus przewalskii* in the United States. *Biol. Cons.* 22:259–71.

Ryder, R. A. 1980. Effects of grazing on bird habitats. In *Management of western forests and grasslands for nongame birds*, pp. 51–66. General Technical Report Int. no. 86. Ogden: USDA Forest Service.

Sadleir, R. M. F. S. 1969. *The ecology of reproduction in wild and domestic mammals.* London: Methuen.

Sakamoto, C. M., and Gifford, R. O. 1970. Spring and fall low-temperature and growing season probabilities in Nevada. Publication no. 26. Agriculture Experiment Station. University of Nevada, Reno, and U.S. Department of Commerce.

Salter, R. E., and Hudson, R. J. 1982. Social organization of feral horses in western Canada. *Appl. Anim. Ethol.* 8:207–23.

Sampson, A. W. 1917. Important range plants: Their life history and forage value. Department of Agriculture, no. 545. Washington, D.C.: Government Printing Office.

Schaller, G. B. 1967. *The deer and the tiger.* Chicago: University of Chicago Press.

———. 1972. *The Serengeti lion.* Chicago: University of Chicago Press.

———. 1977. *Mountain monarchs.* Chicago: University of Chicago Press.

———. 1980. *Stones of silence.* New York: Viking Press.

Schwagmeyer, P. L. 1979. The Bruce effect: An evaluation of male/female advantages. *Amer. Nat.* 114:932–38.

Seal, U.S., and Plotka, E. D. 1983. Age-specific pregnancy rates in feral horses. *J. Wildl. Mgmt.* 47:422–29.

Seegmiller, R. F. 1977. Ecological relationships of feral burros and desert bighorn sheep, western Arizona. Master's thesis, Arizona State University.

Seton, E. T. 1909. *Life histories of northern animals: An account of the mammals of Manitoba.* Vol. 1. New York: Scribner's.

Shank, C. C. 1982. Age-sex differences in the diets of wintering Rocky Mountain bighorn sheep. *Ecology* 63:627–33.

Shaw. H. G. 1981. Comparison of mountain lion predation on cattle in two study areas in Arizona. In *Wildlife-livestock relationships*, ed. J. M. Peek and P. D. Dalke, pp. 306–18. Moscow: University of Idaho Experiment Station.

Shepher, J. 1971. Mate selection among second generation kibbutz adolescents and adults: Incest avoidance and negative imprinting. *Arch. Sex. Beh.* 1:293–307.

Sheridan, D. 1981. *Desertification of the United States.* Council on Environmental Quality. Washington, D.C.: Government Printing Office.

Sherman, P. W. 1981. Reproductive competition and infanticide in Belding's ground squirrels and other animals. In *Natural selection and social behavior: Recent research and new theory*, ed. R. D. Alexander and D. W. Tinkle, pp. 311–31. New York: Chiron Press.

Sherman, P. W. and Morton, M. L. 1984. Demography of Belding's ground squirrels. *Ecology* 65:1617–28.

Shine, R. 1980. "Costs" of reproduction in reptiles. *Oecologia* 46:92–100.

Short, R. E., and Bellows, R. A. 1971. Relationships among weight gains, age at puberty, and reproductive performance in heifers. *J. Anim. Sci.* 32:127–31.

Shotwell, J. A. 1961. Late Tertiary biogeography of horses in the northern Great Basin. *J. Paleon.* 35:203–17.

Siegel, S. 1956. *Non-parametric statistics for the behavioral sciences.* New York: McGraw-Hill.

Silk, J. B. 1983. Local resource competition and facultative adjustment of sex ratios in relation to competitive abilities. *Amer. Nat.* 121:56–66.

Silk, J. B.; Clark-Wheatley, C. B.; Rodman, P. S.; and Samuels, A. 1981. Differential reproductive success and facultative adjustment of sex ratios among female bonnet macaques (*Macaca radiata*). *Anim. Beh.* 29:1106–20.

Simpson, G. G. 1951. *Horses.* New York: Oxford University Press.

Simpson, M. J. A., and Simpson, A. E. 1982. Birth sex ratios and social rank in rhesus monkeys. *Nature* 300:440–41.

Sinclair, A. R. E. 1977. *The African buffalo.* Chicago: University of Chicago Press.

————. 1979. Dynamics of the Serengeti ecosystem. In *Serengeti: dynamics of an ecosystem,* ed. A. R. E. Sinclair and M. Norton-Griffiths, pp. 1–30. Chicago: University of Chicago Press.

————. 1981. Environmental carrying capacity and the evidence for overabundance. In *Problems in management of locally abundant wild mammals,* ed. P. A. Jewell, S. Holt, and D. Hart, pp. 247–57. New York: Academic Press.

Sinclair, A. R. E., and Duncan, P. 1972. Indices of condition in tropical ruminants. *E. Afr. Wildl. J.* 10:143–49.

Sinclair, A. R. E., and Norton-Griffiths, M., eds. 1979. *Serengeti: Dynamics of an ecosystem.* Chicago: Universty of Chicago Press.

————. 1982. Does competition or facilitation regulate migrant ungulate populations in the Serengeti? A test of hypotheses. *Oecologia* 53:364–69.

Sinclair, W. J. 1905. New or imperfectly known rodents and ungulates from the John Day Series. *Univ. Calif. Publ. Geol.* 4:125–43.

Skogland, T. 1983. The effects of density dependent resource limitation on size of wild reindeer. *Oecologia* 60:156–68.

Smith, A. D., and Beale, D. M. 1980. *Pronghorn antelope in Utah: Some research and observations.* Publication no. 80-13. Salt Lake City: Utah Div. Wildlife Resources.

Smith, C. H. 1841. *Horses: The naturalist's library.* Vol. 12. Edinburgh: W. H. Lizars.

Smith, T. G.; Siniff, D. B.; Reichle, R.; and Stone, S. 1981. Coordinated behavior of killer whales, *Orcinus orca,* hunting a crabeater seal, *Lobodon carcinophagus. Can. J. Zool.* 59:1185–89.

Smuts, G. L. 1975a. Pre- and postnatal growth phenomena of Burchell's zebras. *Koedoe* 18:69–102.

———. 1975b. Home range sizes for Burchell's zebra *Equus burchelli antiquorum* from the Kruger National Park. *Koedoe* 18:139–46.

———. 1976a. Population characteristics of Burchell's zebra (*Equus burchelli antiquorum,* H. Smith, 1841) in the Kruger National Park. *So. Afr. J. Wildl. Res.* 6:99–112.

———. 1976b. Reproduction in the zebra mare, *Equus burchelli antiquorum* from the Kruger National Park. *Koedoe* 19:89–132.

———. 1976c. Reproduction in the zebra stallion (*Equus burchelli antiquorum*) from the Kruger National Park. *Zool. Afr.* 11:207–20.

Snedecor, G. W. 1956. *Statistical methods.* 5th ed. Ames: Iowa State College Press.

Sokal, R. R., and Rohlf, F. J. 1969. *Biometry.* San Francisco: W. H. Freeman and Co.

Sokolov, V. E., and Danilkin, A. A. 1979. A skin shield in Siberian roe males (*Capreolus capreolus pygargus* Pall.). *Mammalia* 43:391–97.

Solomatin, A. O. 1973. *Kulan.* Moscow: Akademiya Nauk SSSR.

Soulé, M. E., and Wilcox, B. A., eds. 1980. *Conservation biology: An evolutionary-ecological perspective.* Sunderland Mass.: Sinauer Assoc.

Southwick, C. H. 1955. The population dynamics of confined house mice supplied with unlimited food. *Ecology* 36:212–25.

Speelman, S. R.; Dawson, W. M.; and Phillips, R. W. 1943. Some aspects of fertility in horses raised under western range conditions. *J. Anim. Sci.* 3:233–41.

Spinage, C. A. 1973. The role of photoperiodism in the seasonal breeding of tropical African ungulates. *Mamm. Rev.* 3:71–84.

Srivastava, M. S., and Carter, E. M. 1983. *An introduction to applied multivariate statistics.* New York: North-Holland.

Stacey, P. B. 1979. Habitat saturation and communal breeding in the acorn woodpecker. *Anim. Beh.* 27:1153–66.

———. 1986. Comparative foraging ecology of three different-sized groups of yellow baboons (*Papio cynocephalus*). Beh. Ecol. Sociobiol. In press.

Staines, B. W. 1976. The use of natural shelter by red deer (*Cervus elaphus*) in relation to weather in north-east Scotland. *J. Zool. Lond.* 180:1–8.

———. 1977. Factors affecting the seasonal distribution of red deer (*Cervus elaphus*) at Glen Dye, N.E. Scotland. *Ann. Appl. Biol.* 87:495–512.

Staines, B. W., and Crisp, J. M. 1978. Observations on food quality in Scottish red deer (*Cervus elaphus*) as determined by chemical analysis of rumen contents. *J. Zool. Lond.* 185:253–59.

Stearns, S. C. 1976. Life-history tactics: A review of ideas. *Quart. Rev. Biol.* 51:3–47.

Steele, R. 1909–10. Trapping wild horses in Nevada. *McClure's Magazine* 34:198–209.

———. 1911. Mustangs, busters, and outlaws of the Nevada wild horse country. *American Magazine* 72:756–65.

Stirton, R. A. 1940. Phylogeny of North American Equidae. *Univ. Calif. Publ. Geol. Sci.* 25:165–98.

Studdert, M. J. 1974. Comparative aspects of equine herpesviruses. *Cornell Vet.* 64:94–122.

Symons, D. 1978. *Play and aggression: A study of Rhesus monkeys.* New York: Columbia University Press.

Tamarin, R. H. 1983. Animal population regulation through behavioral interactions. In *Advances in the study of mammalian behavior,* ed. J. F. Eisenberg and D. G. Kleiman, pp. 698–720. Special publications no. 7. Lawrence, Kans.: American Society of Mammalogists.

Tashiro, H., and Schwardt, H. H. 1953. Biological studies of horseflies in New York. *J. Econ. Entomol.* 46:813–22.

Taylor, C. R.; Heglund, N. C.; and Maloiy, G. M. 1982. Energetics and mechanics of terrestial locomotion, 1: Metabolic energy consumption as a function of speed and body size in birds and mammals. *J. Exp. Biol.* 97:1–21.

Thomas, H. S. 1979. *The wild horse controversy.* South Brunswick, N.J.: A. S. Barnes.

Thompson, R. S., and Mead, J. I. 1982. Late Quaternary environments and biogeography in the Great Basin. *Quat. Res.* 17:39–55.

Thomson, A. M. 1959. Maternal stature and reproductive efficiency. *Eugen. Rev.* 51:157–62.

Thomson, W., and Thomson, A. M. 1953. Effect of diet on the milk yield of the ewe and growth of her lamb. *Brit. J. Nutrit.* 7:263–74.

Thornhill, R. 1980. Rape in *Panorpa scorpion* flies and a general rape hypothesis. *Anim. Beh.* 28:52–59.

Thornhill, R., and Alcock, J. 1983. *The evolution of insect mating systems.* Cambridge: Harvard University Press.

Tilson, R. 1980. Klipspringer (*Oreotragus oreotragus*) social structure and predator avoidance in a desert canyon. *Madoqua* 11:303–14.

———. 1981. Family formation strategies of Kloss's gibbons. *Folia Primatol.* 35:259–87.

Tilson, R. 1980. Klipspringer (*Oreotragus oreotragus*) social structure and predator avoidance in a desert canyon. *Madoqua* 11:303–14.

Trivers, R. L. 1972. Parental investment and sexual selection. In *Sexual selection and the descent of man, 1871–1971,* ed. B. G. Campbell, pp. 136–79. Chicago: Aldine.

Trivers, R. L., and Willard, D. E. 1973. Natural selection of parental ability to vary the sex ratio of offspring. *Science* 179:90–92.

Tsevegmid, D., and Dashdorj, A. 1974. Wild horses and other endangered wildlife in Mongolia. *Oryx* 12:361–77.

Tueller, P. T. 1973. Secondary succession, disclimax, and range condition standards in desert shrub vegetation. In *Arid Shrublands Proc.*, 3d workshop, pp. 57–65. Reno, Nev.

———. 1975. The natural vegetation of Nevada. *Mentzelia* 1:3–6, 23–26.

Tyler, S. J. 1972. The behaviour and social organisation of the New Forest ponies. *Anim. Beh. Monog.* 5:85–196.

U.S. Department of Agriculture. Forest Service. 1914. *National forest range plants, part 1: Grasses.* Office of Grazing Studies. Washington, D.C.: Government Printing Office.

U.S. Department of Interior. Bureau of Land Management. 1982a. *Wild horse and burro report.* Washington, D.C.: Government Printing Office.

———. 1982b. *Public land statistics.* Washington, D.C.: Government Printing Office.

———. National Park Service. 1980. *Feral burro management and ecosystem restoration plan and final environmental statement.* Grand Canyon National Park. Washington, D.C.: Government Printing Office.

Urness, P. J. 1976. Mule deer habitat changes resulting from livestock practices. In *Mule deer decline in the West: A symposium,* pp. 21–35. Logan: Utah State University.

Vale, T. R. 1975a. Presettlement vegetation in the sagebrush-grass area of the intermountain West. *J. Range Mgmt.* 28:32–36.

———. 1975b. Report by Bureau of Land Management on range conditions and grazing in Nevada. *Biol. Cons.* 8:257–60.

Van Couvering, J. A. H. 1980. Community evolution in East Africa during the late Cenozoic. In *Fossils in the making,* ed. A. Behrensmeyer and A. P. Hill, pp. 272–98. Chicago: University of Chicago Press.

Van Niekerk, C. H., and Morgenthal, J. C. 1982. Fetal loss and the effect of stress on plasma progestagen levels in pregnant Thoroughbred mares. *J. Repro. Fert.*, suppl., 32:453–57.

Van Riper, S. G., and Van Riper, C., III. 1982. *A field guide to the mammals in Hawaii.* Honolulu: Oriental Publishing Co.

Van Soest, P. J. 1980. The limitation of ruminants. In *Proceedings of Cornell nutrition conference for feed manufacturers,* pp. 78–90. Ithaca, N.Y.

Vavra, M., and Sneva, F. 1978. Seasonal diets of five ungulates grazing the cold desert biome. In *Proc. First Int. Range. Cong.,* pp. 435–37.

Vernon, A. 1939. *The history and romance of the horse.* Boston: Waverly House.

Vesey-Fitzgerald, D. F. 1960. Grazing succession amongst East African game animals. *J. Mammal.* 41:161–70.

Vorhies, M. 1969. *Taphonomy and population dynamics of an early Pliocene vertebrate fauna, Knox Co., Nebraska.* Contributions Geological Special Papers no. 1. Laramie: University of Wyoming Press.

Wade, M. J. 1979. Sexual selection and variance in reproductive success. *Amer. Nat.* 114:742–46.

Wade, M. J., and Arnold, S. J. 1980. The intensity of sexual selection in relation to male sexual behaviour, female choice, and sperm precedence. *Anim. Beh.* 28:446–61.

Wagner, F. H. 1978. Livestock grazing and the livestock industry. In *Wild-life and America*, ed. H. P. Brokaw, pp. 121–45. Washington, D.C.: Council on Environmental Quality.

―――. 1983. Status of wild horse and burro management on public rangelands. *Trans. No. Amer. Wildl. Conf.* 48:116–33.

Wallace, R. E. 1946. A Miocene mammalian fauna from Beatty Buttes, Oregon. *Carnegie Inst. Contrib. Paleon.* 551:115–34.

Walters, J. 1980. Interventions and the development of dominance relationships in female baboons. *Folia Primatol.* 34:61–89.

Waring, G. H. 1983. *Horse behavior: The behavioral traits and adaptations of domestic and wild horses, including ponies.* Park Ridge, N.J.: Noyes Publications.

Waser, P. M., and Wiley, R. H. 1979. Mechanisms and evolution of spacing in animals. *Hand. Beh. Neurobiol.* 3:159–223.

Watson, A., ed. 1970. *Animal populations in relation to their food resources.* Oxford: Blackwell Scientific Publications.

―――. 1977. Population limitation and the adaptive value of territorial behaviour in Scottish red grouse, *Lagopus lagopus scoticus.* In *Evolutionary ecology*, ed. B. Stonehouse and C. M. Perrins, pp. 19–26. London: Macmillan.

Watson, A., and Miller, G. R. 1971. Territory size and aggression in fluctuating red grouse populations. *J. Anim. Ecol.* 40:367–83.

Watson, A., and Moss, R. 1970. Dominance, spacing behaviour, and aggression in relation to population limitation in vertebrates. In *Animal populations in relation to their food resources*, ed. A. Watson, pp. 167–220. Oxford: Blackwell Scientific Publications.

Watson, A.; Moss, R.; and Parr, R. 1984. Effects of food enrichment on numbers and spacing behaviour of red grouse. *J. Anim. Ecol.* 53. In press.

Webb, J. L., and Welles, R. W. 1924. Horse-flies: Biologies and relation to western agriculture. U.S. Department of Agriculture. Department bulletin no. 1218, pp. 1–36. Washington, D.C.: Government Printing Office.

Webb, S. D. 1977. A history of savanna vertebrates in the New World. Part 1: North America. *Ann. Rev. Ecol. Syst.* 8:355–80.

Wehausen, J. D. 1980. Sierra Nevada bighorn sheep: History and population biology. Ph.D. diss., University of Michigan.

―――. 1983. *White Mountain bighorn sheep: An analysis of current knowledge and management alternatives.* Bishop, Calif.: Administrative Report, Inyo National Forest, contribution no. 53-9JC9-0-32.

Welles, R. E., and Welles, F. B. 1961. *The bighorn of Death Valley.* Fauna Series, no. 6. Washington, D.C.: Government Publishing Office.

Wells, P. V. 1979. An equable glaciopluvial in the West: Pleniglacial evidence of increased precipitation on a gradient from the Great Basin to the Sonoran and Chihuahuan deserts. *Quat. Res.* 12:311–25.

―――. 1983. Paleobiography of montane islands in the Great Basin since the last Glaciopluvial. *Ecol. Monog.* 53:341–82.

Wells, S. M., and von Goldschmidt-Rothschild, B. 1979. Social behaviour and relationships in a herd of Camargue horses. *Z. Tierpsychol.* 49:363–80.

Welsh, D. A. 1975. Population, behavioural, and grazing ecology of the horses of Sable Island, Nova Scotia. Ph.D. diss., Dalhousie University.

Wemmer, C. M. 1986. *Biology and management of the Cervidae.* Washington, D.C.: Smithsonian Institution Press. In press.

Westermarck, E. A. 1891. *The history of human marriage.* London: Macmillan.

Wexler, M. 1982. Facing up to our fears about sharks. *Nat. Wildl.* 20:4–11.

Wheeler, S. S. 1979. *The Black Rock Desert.* Caldwell: Caxton Printers.

Whitham, T. G. 1978. Habitat selection by *Pemphigus* aphids in response to resource limitation and competition. *Ecology* 59:1164–76.

———. 1979. Territorial behaviour of *Pemphigus* gall aphids. *Nature, Lond.* 279:324–25.

———. 1980. The theory of habitat selection examined and extended using *Pemphigus* aphids. *Amer. Nat.* 115:449–66.

Whitaker, A. H., and Rudge, M. R. 1976. *The value of feral farm mammals in New Zealand.* Wellington, Australia: Information Series no. 1, Department Lands Survey.

Wilkinson, G. S. 1984. Reciprocal food sharing in the vampire bat. *Nature* 308:181–84.

Wilkinson, P. F., and Shank, C. C. 1977. Rutting-fight mortality among musk oxen on Banks Island, Northwest Territories, Canada. *Anim. Beh.* 24:756–58.

Williams, G. C. 1966. *Adaptation and natural selection: A critique of some current evolutionary thought.* Princeton: Princeton University Press.

———. 1979. The question of adaptive sex ratio in outcrossed vertebrates. *Proc. Royal Soc. Lond.* 205:567–80.

Willoughby, D. P. 1974. *The empire of Equus.* South Brunswick, N.J.: A. S. Barnes.

Wilson, E. O. 1975. *Sociobiology: The new synthesis.* Cambridge: Belknap Press of Harvard Universty Press.

Wilson, E. O., and Bossert, W. H. 1971. *A primer of population biology.* Sunderland, Mass.: Sinauer Assoc.

Wiltbank, J. N.; Kasson, C. W.; and Ingalls, J. E. 1969. Puberty in crossbred and straightbred beef heifers on two levels of feed. *J. Anim. Sci.* 29:602–5.

Wirtz, P. 1981. Territorial defence and territory take-over by satellite males in the waterbuck *Kobus ellipsiprymnus* (Bovidae). *Beh. Ecol. Sociobiol.* 8:161–62.

———. 1982. Territory holders, satellite males, and bachelor males in a high density population of waterbuck (*Kobus ellipsiprymnus*) and their associations with conspecifics. *Z. Tierpsychol.* 58:277–300.

Wittenberger, J. F. 1981. *Animal social behavior.* Boston: Duxbury Press.

Wolfe, L. D. 1984. Female rank and reproductive success among Arashiyama B Japanese macaques (*Macaca fuscata*). *Int. J. Primat.* 5:133–43.

Wolfe, M. L. 1980. Feral horse demography: A preliminary report. *J. Range Manage.* 33:354–60.

Wolfe, M. L. 1982. Alternative population limitation strategies for feral horses. In *Wildlife-livestock relationships symp.*, ed. J. M. Peek and P. D. Dalke, pp. 394–408. Proc. 10, University of Idaho Experiment Station.

Woodburne, M. O. 1982. A reappraisal of the systematics, biogeography, and evolution of fossil horses. *Paleobiology* 8:315–27.

Woodbury, R. 1981. In Colorado: Chasing the mustangs. *Time*, Nov. 16:19.

Woodward, S. L. 1979. The social system of feral asses (*Equus asinus*). *Z. Tierpsychol.* 49:304–16.

Wrangham, R. W. 1980. An ecological model of female-bonded primate groups. *Behaviour* 75:262–300.

Wyman, W. D. 1945. *The wild horses of the West.* Caldwell, Idaho: Caxton Printers.

Yoakum, J. D. 1978. Pronghorn. In *Big game of North America: Ecology and management*, ed. J. L. Schmidt and D. L. Gilbert, pp. 103–22. Harrisburg, Pa.: Stackpole Books.

Young, J. A., and Evans, R. A. 1973. Downey Brome: Intruder in the plant succession of big sagebrush communities in the Great Basin. *J. Range Mgmt.* 26:410–15.

Young, J. A.; Evans, R. A.; and Major, J. 1977. Sagebrush steppe. In *Terrestrial vegetation of California*, ed. M. G. Barbour and J. Major, pp. 763–96. New York: John Wiley and Sons.

Young, J. A.; Evans, R. A.; and Tueller, P. T. 1976. Great Basin plant communities: Pristine and grazed. In *Holocene environmental change in the Great Basin*, ed. R. Elston, pp. 187–215. Nevada Archaeological Survey Research Paper No. 6. Reno, Nev.

Young, S. P. 1946. *The puma: Mysterious American cat.* New York: Dover Publications.

Zervanos, S. M., and Keiper, R. R. 1979. Seasonal home ranges and activity patterns of feral Assateague Island ponies. In *Symposium on the ecology and behavior of wild and feral equids*, ed. R. H. Denniston, pp. 3–14. Laramie: University of Wyoming.

Zeuner, F. E. 1963. *A history of domesticated animals.* London: Hutchinson.

Zicardi, F. 1970. The African wild ass: Part 2. *Afr. Wild Life* 24:202–8.

Zimen, E. 1980. *The wolf: A species in danger.* New York: Delacourte Press.

Zimmerman, G. D. 1974. Cooperative nursing behavior observed in *Spermophilus tridecemlineatus* (Mitchilk). *J. Mammal.* 55:680–81.

Zirkle, C. 1941. Natural selection before the "Origin of species." *Proc. Amer. Phil. Soc.* 84:71–123.

Index